The British Economy, 1870–1939

*Other books by Derek H. Aldcroft*

BRITISH RAILWAYS IN TRANSITION: THE ECONOMIC PROBLEMS OF BRITAIN'S RAILWAYS SINCE 1914

BUILDING IN THE BRITISH ECONOMY BETWEEN THE WARS (*with Harry W. Richardson*)

THE DEVELOPMENT OF BRITISH INDUSTRY AND FOREIGN COMPETITION, 1875–1914

BRITISH TRANSPORT: AN ECONOMIC SURVEY FROM THE SEVENTEENTH CENTURY TO THE TWENTIETH (*with H. J. Dyos*)

*Other books by Harry W. Richardson*

ECONOMIC RECOVERY IN BRITAIN, 1932–39

BUILDING IN THE BRITISH ECONOMY BETWEEN THE WARS (*with Derek H. Aldcroft*)

REGIONAL ECONOMICS: LOCATION THEORY, URBAN STRUCTURE AND REGIONAL CHANGE

ELEMENTS OF REGIONAL ECONOMICS

# The British Economy 1870-1939

DEREK H. ALDCROFT
*Senior Lecturer in Economic History, University of Leicester*

HARRY W. RICHARDSON
*Director, Centre for Research in the Social Sciences, University of Kent at Canterbury*

MACMILLAN

*First published 1969 by*
MACMILLAN AND CO LTD
*Little Essex Street London* WC2
*and also at Bombay Calcutta and Madras*
*Macmillan South Africa (Publishers) Pty Ltd Johannesburg*
*The Macmillan Company of Australia Pty Ltd Melbourne*
*The Macmillan Company of Canada Ltd Toronto*
*Gill and Macmillan Ltd Dublin*

*Printed in Great Britain by*
RICHARD CLAY (THE CHAUCER PRESS) LTD
*Bungay, Suffolk*

# Contents

SECTION D
Bibliographical Survey 305

# Preface

THIS book does not claim to present a comprehensive survey of every aspect of the British economy over the period 1870 to 1939. To have done this would have required us to produce another text of the traditional type. We felt, however, that it was time to depart from the conventional approach and that what the student needed was an introductory volume to some of the central themes and problems of the period, together with a guide to the rapidly growing volume of literature on the subject. Thus in Section A we have attempted to provide a general view of the economy by examining some important aspects which are often inadequately treated in the standard texts. Section B consists of a reprint of some of the authors' earlier work. Though these essays cover somewhat controversial issues they do supplement the analysis in Section A. It is hoped that the nature of the approach in both these sections will stimulate the student into further inquiry and for this reason we have included a lengthy survey of the literature and a guide to the main statistical sources. The bibliographical section is not intended to be exhaustive but we feel sure that the reader will find it helpful in pursuing his studies.

We should like to thank the editors and publishers of the following journals for permission to reprint the articles contained in Section B: *The Scottish Journal of Political Economy*, XII (1965) for 1; *La Scuola in Azione*, V (1967) for 2; *Economic History Review*, XVII (1964) for 3; *Business History*, VIII (1966) for 4; *Oxford Economic Papers*, XVII (1965) for 5; *The Scottish Journal of Political Economy*, XIII (1966) for 6; *Economic History Review*, XV (1962) for 7; *Oxford Economic Papers*, XIII (1961) for 8. Articles 1, 5, 7 and 8 were written by Harry W. Richardson and articles 2, 3, 4 and 6 were written by Derek H. Aldcroft. These articles, written over the past eight years, are reprinted virtually unchanged. Some of the statistics quoted have been superseded, though the broad magnitudes of change remain unaltered. If the articles were being written afresh today, a few of the arguments might be modified or expanded. Finally, unlike the remainder of this book these articles express the individual views of their author, not a joint view, and some differences of opinion and minor inconsistencies may be found.

D. H. A.
H. W. R.

*October 1968*

# SECTION A

# I The Growth of the Economy

DESPITE the ever-increasing amount of economic literature on the period between 1870 and 1939 it is difficult for the student to obtain an overall picture of the growth and development of the British economy during these years. A major problem is that the standard texts tend to cover the ground sector by sector so that it is possible to find out much about particular segments of the economy, such as agriculture, transport and trade, without gaining a real knowledge of exactly what happened at the aggregate level. This section therefore presents an overview of the growth of the economy based on the latest data, and examines some of the chief sources of economic change.

## DIMENSIONS

There are two main ways of assessing an economy's performance. It can be judged by its past performance by relating one period to another; or alternatively it can be compared with the achievements of other countries, preferably with those economies at a similar stage of development. Both approaches will be adopted here, though because of the difficulties involved in making international comparisons the second method will be treated less extensively.

Seven main time series have been used to compile the compound growth rates for various periods and these are presented in Table 1. The results must be treated with caution, since none of the series is perfect in all respects. The most obvious feature is the fairly low rates of long-term growth. Except for income in the 1880s and exports in the 1900s growth rates of most indices rarely exceeded 3 per cent per annum for any length of time. Taking the period as a whole (1870–1938) income and production rose by about 2 per cent per annum. Owing to the rise in population real income per head grew somewhat less rapidly, while exports failed to maintain a 1 per cent rate largely because of the severe check to trade in the inter-war years. These rates were somewhat lower

TABLE I

Average Annual Rates of Growth of Selected Economic Indices of the U.K.

| | *Net national income* | *Real income per head* | *Output per man-hour* | *Industrial production (including building)* | *Industrial productivity* | *Exports* | *Consumers' expenditure per capita* |
|---|---|---|---|---|---|---|---|
| | (1) | (2) | (3) | (4) | (5) | (6) | (7) |
| 1860–70 | 3·0 | 2·5 | | 2·9 | 1·1 | 5·7 | .. |
| 1870–80 | 1·9 | 0·8 | 0·9 | 2·4 | 1·2 | 2·8 | 1·3 |
| 1880–90 | 4·2 | 3·5 | 3·8 | 1·6 | 0·5 | 3·0 | 1·7 |
| 1890–1900 | 2·1 | 1·2 | 1·3 | 2·8 | 0·2 | 0·4 | 1·0 |
| 1900–13 | 1·1 | 0·4 | 0·6 | 1·6 | 0·2 | 4·2 | ±0·1 |
| 1870–1913 | 2·3 | 1·3 | 1·5 | 2·1 | 0·6 | 2·7 | 1·1 |
| 1913–29 | 0·8 | 0·8 | 2·1 | 1·6 | .. | −1·3 | 0·6 |
| 1920–9 | 2·0 | 1·5 | .. | 2·8 | 3·8 | 1·6 | 0·9 |
| 1929–38 | 2·1 | 1·7 | 2·1 | 2·7 | 1·8 | −4·0 | 1·3 |
| 1920–38 | 2·1 | 1·6 | .. | 2·8 | 2·8 | −1·2 | 1·1 |
| 1913–38 | 1·4 | 1·2 | 2·1 | 2·0 | .. | −2·3 | 0·8 |
| 1950–60 | 2·6 | 2·1 | 2·0 | 3·0 | 2·2 | 1·8 | 2·0 |
| 1870–1938 | 1·9 | 1·3 | 1·7 | 2·0 | .. | 0·8 | 1·2 |

Sources: Cols (1) and (2), C. H. Feinstein, 'National Income and Expenditure of the United Kingdom, 1870–1963', *London and Cambridge Economic Bulletin*, L (1964); col. (3), A. Maddison, *Economic Growth in the West* (1964); col. (4), K. S. Lomax, 'Production and Productivity Movements in the United Kingdom since 1900', *Journal of the Royal Statistical Society*, A122 (1959), and 'Growth and Productivity in the United Kingdom', *Productivity Measurement Review*, XXXVIII (1964); col. (5), E. H. Phelps Brown and S. J. Handfield-Jones, 'The Climacteric of the 1890s: A Study of the Expanding Economy', *Oxford Economic Papers*, IV (1952), and London and Cambridge Economic Service, *Key Statistics of the British Economy 1900–1966* (1967); col. (6), A. H. Imlah, *Economic Elements in the Pax Britannica* (Harvard U.P., 1958) and *Key Statistics*; col. (7), Feinstein, in *London and Cambridge Economic Bulletin*, L, and R. Stone and D. A. Rowe, *The Measurement of Consumers' Expenditure and Behaviour in the United Kingdom, 1920–1938*, II (1966).

than those experienced in the 1950s, and in comparison with the recent performance of European countries they were very modest indeed.

The growth of the economy was by no means uniform over each decade, as a glance at the detailed breakdown will show. Compared with the previous decade the 1870s were marked by relatively slower rates of growth. But in the following decade income rose sharply partly as a result of the favourable shift in the terms of trade; on the other hand, industrial production and productivity growth actually declined. After the 1880s most indices of growth tended to decelerate, the retardation being most marked and continuous in national income and industrial productivity. Though this trend continued more or less unchecked down to 1913 it is difficult to press the case for continuous retardation too strongly since not all indices conformed to the pattern exactly. For example, the rate of industrial growth rose in the 1890s compared with the previous decade whereas most other indices registered a further check. Again in the 1900s exports, with a growth rate of 4·2 per cent as against only 0·4 per cent in the 1890s, displayed a contrary tendency to most other indices. However, despite these exceptions a case can be made out for a slowing down in growth in the generation or so before 1914. In fact in the years 1900–13 the economy was probably growing more slowly than at any time since the beginning of modern economic growth in the late eighteenth century. The timing of the break in trend or climacteric in growth has been the subject of some debate in recent years. Some writers claim that it can be dated in the 1870s, but this may be difficult to reconcile with the rapid increase in national income during the following decade. Even in the case of industrial productivity, which maintained a downward trend for much of the period, it would be difficult to establish the turning point before the 1880s. It is possible that the initial break came even before the 1870s, but unfortunately the data is too fragmentary and unreliable to test such a hypothesis properly. Moreover, Table 1 shows that the break in growth tended to vary in time from series to series.

The First World War checked the growth of the economy. Altogether some six years of growth were lost as a result of the war and its aftermath, and it was not until 1920 that income and production returned to the levels of 1913. Since the early 1920s were relatively depressed it was some years before the pre-war levels were surpassed by any substantial margin, though productivity did rise quite sharply in this period. Yet despite this set-back, rates of growth over the period 1913–29, though lower than the long-term average before 1914, were similar to, or even higher than, those of the years 1900–13, the major exception being exports which failed to recover after the war. If the war years are excluded the performance is somewhat better. Income and production rose more rapidly than in the 1900s and compared favourably with the long-term trend before 1914. Even exports rose in the 1920s though the rate of growth was somewhat inflated due to the low level reached in 1920. But the most remarkable break in trend was in industrial productivity, which rose by 3·8 per cent compared with 0·6 per cent a year or less before 1914. A word of caution is required, since the data on which the productivity estimates are based may well exaggerate the break in trend. The pre-war figures are derived from Hoffmann's index of production which does not give sufficient coverage to those industries in which productivity was rising rapidly.[1] On the other hand, the inter-war estimates, based on the more comprehensive Lomax index, are adjusted to take account of unemployment. Furthermore, the use of 1920 as the base year tends to inflate the result since in that year productivity was probably on the low side. However, even if we alter the base year the rate of industrial productivity growth for the 1920s remains much higher than before 1914.

Despite a further check to the British economy as a result of the economic crisis of 1929–32, growth was vigorous in the 1930s and the level of economic activity soon exceeded that of 1929. Apart from exports which fell back sharply, rates of growth over the years 1929–38 compared very favourably with those prior to the war. Thus despite the black spots in the inter-war economy, notably the stagnation in exports and the heavy unemployment, economic growth was by no means negligible. Excluding exports, most indices of growth compared favourably with the long-term pre-war performance, and they were substantially better than those between 1900 and 1913. If the war years are included (1913–38) the achievement appears somewhat less favourable, though it was still better than that recorded for the immediate pre-war years.

How did Britain fare in comparison with other countries? The analysis of this question is somewhat more difficult owing to the limited amount of comparable data of a reliable nature. The discussion will therefore be confined to two sets of statistics, namely those for domestic output and industrial production. In Table 2 the growth rates of domestic output and output per man-hour are given for twelve countries including Britain. In both cases Britain performed badly before 1914. Between 1870 and 1913 output growth was well below the general average and from the 1890s Britain was near the bottom of the growth league table. But after 1913 Britain's relative position improved considerably. Over the period 1913–38 both output and productivity growth were higher than the average of all countries together. This relative improvement was most marked in the latter half of the period, i.e. 1929–38, when Britain secured a position in the top half of the league table. On the other hand, in the previous decade or so (1913–29) total output grew more slowly in Britain than elsewhere, though in terms of output per man-hour her performance was no worse than the general average. But only in the inter-war period were Britain's growth rates above average. Both before 1914 and again after the Second World War her performance

[1] Though if building is excluded the Hoffmann index is not seriously out of line with the more recent estimates of industrial production for this period (e.g. that of Lomax).

was worse than the average of the group of countries listed in Table 2.[1]

TABLE 2

Average Annual Rates of Growth of Domestic Output and Output per man-hour

| | *1870/71–1913* | | *1913–29* | | *1929–38* | |
|---|---|---|---|---|---|---|
| | *Output* | *Output per man-hour* | *Output* | *Output per man-hour* | *Output* | *Output per man-hour* |
| Belgium | 2·7 | 2·0 | 1·6 | 2·0 | −0·5 | 0·6 |
| Denmark | 3·2 | 2·6 | 1·8 | 1·7 | 2·1 | 0·4 |
| France | 1·6 | 1·8 | 1·6 | 2·8 | −2·2 | 1·6 |
| Germany | 2·9 | 2·1 | 0·3 | 0·8 | 3·9 | 2·1 |
| Italy | 1·4 | 1·2 | 1·8 | 2·3 | 1·6 | 3·2 |
| Netherlands | n.a. | n.a. | 3·3 | 2·6 | 0·1 | −0·3 |
| Norway | 2·2 | 1·8 | 2·8 | 3·0 | 2·9 | 2·2 |
| Sweden | 3·0 | 2·7 | 1·3 | 0·9 | 2·6 | 3·0 |
| Switzerland | n.a. | n.a. | 2·8 | 3·2 | 0·6 | 1·1 |
| U.K. | 2·2 | 1·5 | 1·6 | 2·1 | 2·3 | 2·1 |
| Canada | 3·8 | 2·1 | 2·4 | 1·3 | −0·2 | 0·0 |
| U.S.A. | 4·3 | 2·4 | 3·1 | 2·8 | 0·0 | 3·3 |
| Unweighted average | 2·7 | 2·0 | 2·0 | 2·1 | 1·1 | 1·6 |

Source: Calculated from A. Maddison, *Economic Growth in the West* (1964) pp. 201–2, 232.

The relative improvement after 1914 was less marked in the case of industrial production. Before 1914 Britain's industrial production grew more slowly than that of any other country for which data are available. From 1913 to 1929 there was some improvement in her relative position but again it was in the 1930s that the tide ran strongly in Britain's favour. With a growth rate of 3·4 per cent per annum between 1929 and 1937, she was one of the best industrial performers, surpassed only by Denmark and Sweden. By contrast the record of the 1920s was very poor indeed. Industrial production grew more slowly than in any other country and was less than half the average for Europe, a position which was relatively worse than that before the war. But the comparison is somewhat distorted by the aftermath of war. In 1920 European production as a whole was about one-third below the 1913 level whereas in this country it was more or less back to normal. Thus growth rates worked out on a 1920 base would tend to favour those countries in which recovery from the war was slow. A more satisfactory benchmark year would be 1924, the date when most countries had regained their pre-war levels of production. Over the period 1924–37 industrial production in Britain

[1] See D. H. Aldcroft, 'Economic Growth in Britain in the Inter-War Years: A Reassessment', *Economic History Review*, xx (1967) 313–14.

increased at a similar rate to that of Europe, though her performance was somewhat below that of the major industrial countries.[1]

Despite the improvement in growth rates after 1913 Britain's relative importance in the world economy continued to decline throughout the inter-war years. This of course was simply a continuation of the trend extending back into the third quarter of the nineteenth century. In 1870 Britain had accounted for nearly one-third (31·8 per cent) of the world's manufacturing production as against less than one-quarter (22·3 per cent) for her nearest rival, the United States. Within the next three or four decades Britain's predominating position was steadily undermined as a result of rapid industrialisation abroad. By 1913 she accounted for only 14·1 per cent of world production while America and Germany claimed first and second place with 35·3 and 15·9 per cent respectively. After the war the decline continued, though less rapidly, and by the end of the 1930s Britain was lying fourth, being surpassed by America, Russia and Germany in that order. The figures for shares in world trade in manufactured products tell a similar story, though in this case Britain's loss of importance was somewhat less sharp. In 1913 she was still the world's largest trader though Germany was not far behind. Nevertheless this was a very different position from that in 1880 when Britain had been twice as important as her nearest rival, France. Yet despite the check to exports after 1913 Britain held her position reasonably well so that by the end of the 1930s she still managed to equal Germany. But over the period as a whole (1880–1937) Britain's proportionate loss in world trade was greater than that for any other country (see Table 11, page 65).

A number of general conclusions may be drawn from this survey of long-term growth. Over the entire period Britain's relative position in the world economy declined rapidly, the decline being most pronounced before 1913. In view of the rapid development of Germany, the United States and later Russia and Japan, this loss was only to be expected since a pioneer country is bound to lose its relative position as other countries follow suit. But before 1913 the British economy was growing less rapidly than those of the major developing countries, and after the 1880s rates of growth of most indices tended to slacken off through to 1914. Despite the severe check to economic activity between 1914 and 1919 and again between 1929 and 1932 Britain's economic performance, apart from exports, in the inter-war years compared favourably with past trends. It is probable that in this period the slow growth trend of the couple of decades before 1914 was reversed, though growth was not

[1] Aldcroft, in *Economic History Review*, xx (1967) 313–14.

as rapid as in the middle of the nineteenth century or after the Second World War. On an international basis inter-war performance can be regarded as reasonably satisfactory, especially in the 1930s when Britain held a place near the top of the league table. But in relation to the recent performances of many western economies Britain's record of growth was very modest indeed throughout the period 1870–1939.

## Sources of Growth

The neo-classical approach to growth analyses the contribution of each main source of growth to the expansion of the economy. The three main sources are an increase in labour supply, capital accumulation and the 'residual'. The last is a catch-all category including everything which can account for a rise in output per unit of input, not only advances in new techniques but also managerial improvements, business organisation, a rise in average practice (in technology, entrepreneurial efficiency, etc.) towards the best practice known, educational improvements and the acquisition of new skills, narrowing the gap between the existing allocation of resources and the allocation that would maximise national output, reduction in restrictions on competition such as monopolies, restrictive practices in business and trade unions and tariff barriers, gains from economies of scale, and raising the degree of resource utilisation. Of these, technical advances are usually the most important but the influence of improvements in resource allocation and gains from economies of scale may also be substantial. We may exclude land and natural resources as an independent source of growth on the grounds that the stock of resources may be regarded as fixed unless capital is invested in resource improvement.

Growth may be achieved by increasing the inputs of labour and capital and/or by an improvement in the productivity of resources. If we increase one factor at a time this will involve a change in the relative factor mix (i.e. the capital/labour ratio). For example, the amount of capital employed per worker might be raised. This could mean either a duplication of the equipment used by each worker (e.g. supervising two machines rather than one) or, in a multi-sector economy, a shift of labour into the more capital-intensive sectors with a constant capital/labour ratio maintained in each. It is also possible to raise the level of output by increasing capital and labour inputs in the same proportion so that the capital/labour ratio is unchanged. On the other hand, the residual may be the sole source of growth with the labour force and the capital stock held constant. The normal course, however, will be for growth to be a product of simultaneous changes in all three variables. For instance, whether or not productivity improvements are accompanied by additions to the stock of resources depends very much upon the nature of the improvement. The application of major innovations, such as steam or electric power, will obviously require fairly large additions to the capital stock. Similarly, gains from economies of scale will clearly need factor inputs to be increased. On the other hand, productivity gains may result from, say, a reorganisation of existing plant and the work force without additional capital and labour. For example it has been suggested that the steep rise in output per man-shift in the German coal industry in the 1930s was brought about primarily by a much improved organisation of mining operations.[1]

Though economists still disagree about the relative importance of capital, labour and the residual, many recent empirical studies have shown the residual to be the most important. For the United States Solow estimated that 87 per cent of the increase in output per man between 1909 and 1949 could be attributed to the residual.[2] Aukrust found productivity improvements to be much more important in the growth of Western European economies in the 1950s than increments to the labour supply and capital stock, and this conclusion has been confirmed in a recent major work by Denison.[3] One drawback to these researches is the possibility that it may not be meaningful to make a clear distinction between capital accumulation and technical progress. Some economists argue that most new techniques will require new capital; in other words, most technical progress is 'embodied' in new machines. Even when old machines are replaced as they wear out, the replacement will be superior in efficiency and will incorporate technical improvements, so that it is gross not net investment which counts. Economists holding these views have developed models which make technical progress a function of the rate of capital accumulation. If this is valid, to apportion the growth in output per head between capital per man and the residual, as in the above studies, will understate the role of capital because most tech-

[1] G. C. Allen, 'Economic Progress, Retrospect and Prospect', *Economic Journal*, LX (1950) 467.

[2] R. M. Solow, 'Technical Change, and the Aggregate Production Function', *Review of Economics and Statistics*, XXXIX (1957) 320.

[3] O. Aukrust, 'Factors in Economic Development: A Review of Recent Research', *Productivity Measurement Review* (Feb 1965) and E. F. Denison, *Why Growth Rates Differ* (1968).

nical advances contained within the residual could not have taken place in the absence of capital accumulation.

Recently an attempt has been made to measure the contribution of capital, labour and the residual to the growth of the British economy over the past century. In a paper to the Manchester Statistical Society in 1964 Matthews calculated the growth due to changes in capital and labour by combining the two inputs in the ratio of 4:6 for the pre-1913 period and 3:7 for the inter-war years. The difference between the growth attributable to these two factors and the actual growth in output could then be ascribed to the influence of the residual. This work is only in the preliminary stages and consequently the breakdown of the figures before 1913 is not as detailed as one would wish. Nevertheless the results of these calculations, which are presented in Table 3, do suggest that the residual was an

TABLE 3

Annual Rates of Growth of Output and Input in the U.K.

| | *Real G.D.P.* | *Employment in man-years* | *Capital* | *Total inputs* | *Growth due to: Technical progress* | *Change in capital per man* |
|---|---|---|---|---|---|---|
| 1856–99 | 2·0 | 0·9 | 1·3 | 1·1 | 0·9 | 0·2 |
| 1899–1913 | 1·1 | 1·0 | 1·8 | 1·3 | –0·2 | 0·3 |
| 1924–37 | 2·3 | 1·2 | 1·7 | 1·4 | 0·9 | 0·2 |

Source: R. C. O. Matthews, 'Some Aspects of Post-War Growth in the British Economy in Relation to Historical Experience', *Transactions of the Manchester Statistical Society* (1964).

important factor governing changes in the long-term rate of growth. The stability of labour inputs is at once clearly apparent, while from the end of the nineteenth century through to the 1930s the rate of growth of the capital stock was remarkably constant. The result was that the combined contribution of capital and labour inputs to economic growth changed little over the period as a whole, despite the fact that the growth of output was substantially higher between the wars. This means that variations in the rate of economic growth were due largely to shifts in the residual element. Thus in the latter half of the nineteenth century the residual contributed around 0·9 per cent to the 2 per cent growth in output, whereas in the decade or so before the war, when the overall growth rate was halved, the residual element was negative. On the other hand, when the growth rate rose again in the inter-war years the contribution of the residual was similar to what it had been in the nineteenth century. Unfortunately, owing to the lack of adequate capital stock figures it is difficult to provide a more detailed breakdown of the figures which would enable us to locate more precisely the timing of the break in growth before 1913. However, tentative calculations on the basis of the Douglas capital stock figures do suggest that the contribution of the residual may have been checked in the 1890s.[1]

The relative stability in the rate of growth of labour and capital inputs over the period as a whole can be explained quite easily. Before 1913 the rate of employment growth was very similar to that of population. Although the rate of population increase declined after the war, employment growth remained relatively stable as a result of a rise in the proportion of the working age group in the population and, to a lesser extent, a higher level of employment participation by females in the 15–64 years age group. As for capital, in the pre-1914 period domestic investment was perhaps somewhat lower than it might have been owing to the large outflow of savings abroad. Conversely, that the rate of capital input was maintained in the inter-war years can be explained partly by the much reduced rate of foreign lending and partly by the rapid expansion in building activity. Moreover, although investment in the older industrial sectors was declining this was compensated for by the rapid accumulation in the newer industries and in the service sectors of the economy.

The above calculations may, of course, understate the role of capital in the growth process if capital is the vehicle of technical progress. Moreover, technical progress may be embodied in replacement investment. If this is so then the gross investment figures are the more relevant ones to look at. However, since the overall investment ratio was low and remained fairly stable it does not appear that much modification of our earlier conclusion is necessary. Between 1920 and 1938 gross fixed capital formation as a proportion of G.N.P. was 6·8 per cent compared with 5·8 per cent for the period 1870–1913. It is significant, moreover, that in the decade or so before 1913, when the residual's contribution to the growth of the economy was negative, the investment ratio was almost identical to that for the inter-war years. In other words, it is unlikely that capital contributed much more to growth, via embodied technical progress, than allowed for by net additions to the capital stock.[2]

[1] P. H. Douglas, 'An Estimate of the Growth of Capital in the United Kingdom, 1865–1909', *Journal of Economic and Business History*, I (1930).

[2] The embodied technical progress thesis would indicate that industries with a high rate of capital growth would show a high residual. However, Matthews found for the period 1924–37 a correlation coefficient between these two variables of 0·19 which is statistically insignificant.

## Innovation and Structural Change

If the residual was the main element in the long-term growth of the economy then it is important to determine more precisely how this was brought about. Probably the two most important components were shifts in resource allocation and technical improvement. The long-term growth of the economy may be determined to a considerable extent by the rate at which structural changes occur. Thus when inter-sectoral shifts of resources are taking place from low to high productivity sectors the overall growth of the economy will tend to be high. On this basis it would be possible to explain the buoyancy of growth in the inter-war years by the movement of resources towards the rapidly expanding newer sectors. Conversely, the retardation before 1914 might be attributable to the limited extent of structural change. Structural change may not necessarily be autonomous. Some structural shifts in the pattern of economic activity may be simply a response to the introduction of industry-creating innovations. New industries may arise as the result of the application of new technology, and these industries will tend to attract resources from those sectors with a relatively low rate of growth. Alternatively, structural changes may feature only to a limited extent. More important may be the flow of major innovations or the rate at which new techniques are applied throughout the economy *as a whole*, rather than the speed with which resources move from one sector to another.

To determine the process by which growth was generated we need to examine the structure of the economy and the rate and character of innovation over time. We shall confine our attention to two specific issues, namely the tendency for growth to slacken off in the couple of decades or so before 1914, and the subsequent recovery in the rate of economic expansion in the inter-war years. There has been considerable controversy in recent years as to the causes of the variations in growth during these periods. For the purpose of this analysis it will be convenient to treat the two periods separately.

### *Retardation before 1914*

Generally speaking, changes in the structure of the economy before 1914 were not very marked and did little to promote the expansion of the economy. Table 4 provides a breakdown of the main sectors via the distribution of the occupied labour force. These figures should be treated with caution, since they are only approximations. It can be seen that the main losses occurred in agriculture, while mining, transport and public and professional services recorded the most striking gains. On the other hand, manufacturing, in which the absolute level of output per head was considerably higher than in any of the other branches of activity, only increased its share of the labour force very marginally over the period 1871

TABLE 4

Distribution of the Occupied Labour Force in Great Britain (as percentage of total)

| | *Agriculture, forestry and fishing* | *Mining and quarrying* | *Manufactures* | *Building* | *Trade* | *Transport* | *Public and professional services* | *Domestic and personal services* |
|---|---|---|---|---|---|---|---|---|
| 1871 | 15·0 | 5·0 | 32·5 | 6·7 | 13·3 | 5·8 | 5·8 | 15·0 |
| 1891 | 10·9 | 5·5 | 32·7 | 6·1 | 15·6 | 7·5 | 6·8 | 15·6 |
| 1911 | 8·6 | 6·4 | 33·3 | 6·4 | 13·4 | 8·1 | 8·1 | 14·0 |

Source: Calculated from figures in P. Deane and W. A. Cole, *British Economic Growth 1688–1959* (1962). p. 143

to 1911. The same holds true if the reference period is limited to the years 1891 to 1911. It appears, therefore, that the shake-out of labour from agriculture involved a transfer of resources to those sectors which had a relatively low level of productivity.

In other words, shifts in resource allocation did not favour the rapid growth of the economy since they tended to occur between low productivity sectors. On the other hand, this does not rule out the possibility of favourable structural shifts within the main groups, particularly the industrial sector. Unfortunately, reliable data to illustrate this point are very scanty especially for service industries. The only available data over time are that for employment based on the persons enumerated as occupied in the Censuses of Population. There are, in addition, the findings of the first Census of Production which was taken in 1907. On the basis of these two sources it is possible to say something about the industrial sector (mining, manufacturing and building) which accounted for something under one-half of total employment in the period under review.

On the whole, inter-industry shifts in the structure of the labour force were relatively modest. What movements there were occurred mainly within or between the older staple trades rather than between old and new sectors of the industrial sector. The chief losses took place in textiles and clothing while the main gains were recorded in heavy staples, notably mining, engineering, shipbuilding and metals, and in public utilities. Though this represented a relative transfer of labour to industries with a higher average output per head than in the losing branches, it should be emphasised that some of these industries, more especially mining, were experiencing diminishing returns during this period. Such industries continued to attract resources because of the buoyancy of market demand—coal production, for example, was boosted by the steady growth in the export market. In terms of employment and output the total transfer had only a limited effect. A rough estimate made by Ashworth on the basis of the 1881 Census of Population and the Production Census of 1907 suggests that 7·8 per cent of the industrial employment and 12·6 per cent of the net output of industry in 1907 could be attributed to structural changes since 1881.[1]

The relative absence of major inter-industry shifts in resources meant that a few key staple trades dominated British industry throughout this period. Thus in 1907 coal, textiles, iron and steel and engineering accounted for about 50 per cent of net industrial output; these same industries also gave employment to one-quarter of the occupied population and supplied 70 per cent of Britain's exports.[2] Comparable data for earlier years are not available, but the weighting used by Hoffmann for his industrial output index in 1881 suggests that a similar group of trades accounted for between 45 and 50 per cent of total industrial output in that year.[3] Most of the industries within this group were heavily dependent on the export market. Coal, cotton, wool, linen and shipbuilding accounted for nearly 45 per cent of all exports in 1913. In some cases the proportion of output exported was very high indeed. Over 80 per cent of the cotton industry's output went abroad, 60 per cent of the machinery output, 57 per cent of the wool textile industry and 30 per cent of British coal output.[4] On the other hand, the newer, potential growth industries were very poorly represented and were much less dependent on the export market than the old staples. In 1907 they accounted for 6·5 per cent of net industrial output, 5·2 per cent of industrial employment and contributed 7·4 per cent of all exports, though without chemicals the export proportion was only 2·8 per cent.[5]

[1] W. Ashworth, 'Changes in the Industrial Structure: 1870–1914', in J. Saville (ed.), *Studies in the British Economy, 1870–1914*, special number of the *Yorkshire Bulletin of Economic and Social Research*, XVII (1965) 64.

[2] A. E. Kahn, *Great Britain in the World Economy* (1946) p. 67.

[3] W. G. Hoffmann, *British Industry, 1700–1950* (1955) pp. 18–19.

[4] B. R. Mitchell and P. Deane, *Abstract of British Historical Statistics* (1962) pp. 283–4, 304–6; Kahn, *Great Britain in the World Economy*, p. 68.

[5] Kahn, *Great Britain in the World Economy*, pp. 106, 109. The new industries included electrical machinery, electrical goods and apparatus, road vehicles, rayon, chemicals, and scientific instruments and apparatus.

Probably a more important influence on the growth of the economy was the rate of technical progress. Here there are two main possibilities which should be noted. It has been suggested that this period was characterised by an absence of large-scale innovations in maturing sectors combined with slow development in potential growth sectors based on new technology. In an article in 1952 Phelps Brown and Handfield-Jones[1] argued that the check to real income and productivity growth in the 1890s was due to the ending of the massive application of the techniques of steam and steel, and the delay in the intensive application of new techniques of electricity, the internal combustion engine and new chemical processes. Given the biased industrial structure of the economy it would seem that growth potential relied heavily on the large staples. As these were based predominantly on the techniques of steam and steel, this gives some support to the authors' argument. On the other hand, as shown in the essays in Section B, the argument is open to considerable criticism. It is more convincing to argue that technical progress in this period was slowing down over a wide sector of the industrial economy. Many of the older industries were slow to adopt new machines or processes of production, or they neglected organisational opportunities which would have brought economies and halted the tendency towards diminishing returns. The evidence on this matter is fairly abundant but need not be repeated here.[2] It suggests that a large part of British industry was technically backward,[3] and it is significant that the older industries, in which the rate of productivity growth was falling, were the ones which appear to have been most technically deficient.

It would appear, therefore, that unfavourable resource allocation and a lag in technical progress were mainly responsible for the downward shift in the residual in the late nineteenth century which in turn largely accounts for the retardation of the economy. Technical progress was probably the more important of the two, since unfavourable shifts in the economic structure were less pronounced in the period 1891–1911 than in the previous two decades. On the other hand, many unresolved points still remain. The timing of the break

[1] E. H. Phelps Brown and S. J. Handfield-Jones, 'The Climacteric of the 1890s: A Study of the Expanding Economy', *Oxford Economic Papers*, IV (1952).

[2] See the essays in Section B of this volume.

[3] A point recently confirmed by Landes in 'Technological Change and Development in Western Europe, 1750–1914', *Cambridge Economic History of Europe* (1965) vol. 6, ch. 5, p. 558. Not all branches of industry were technically stagnant of course. There were dynamic sectors in some industries, notably engineering, as Professor Saul has shown. See S. B. Saul, 'The Market and the Development of the Mechanical Engineering Industries in Britain, 1860–1914', *Economic History Review*, XX (1967) and 'The Machine Tool Industry to 1914', *Business History*, X (1968).

is still somewhat blurred and a final answer will not be possible until more and better information is available on certain aspects, especially on productivity and the capital stock. The absence of satisfactory data on the latter renders it impossible to provide a detailed breakdown of the contribution of the residual, and so we cannot determine its movements in the period from 1870 to the early 1890s. Since we do not know whether the residual was high or low in these years relative to earlier in the century, it is impossible to attempt a similar analysis for this period. Furthermore, little is known about the non-industrial sectors of the economy which accounted for about one-half or more of total output. Finally, as we have seen, not all economic indices moved in step and in the short run the divergence in movement was sometimes quite sharp. Thus considerable further research is required before we can hope to provide a final answer to the question of Britain's growth in this period.

### *The Inter-war Years*

Despite heavy unemployment and the relative stagnation of some of the old staple industries, the overall growth of the economy was fairly respectable in the inter-war period. In fact, as we have seen, it was a considerable improvement on the pre-war performance. This has been attributed to the favourable shift in the structure of economic activity, the most notable feature of which was the development of the new industrial sector based largely on inventions developed before 1914.

Structural changes were far more significant in this period than before the war. The main economy-wide changes are shown in Table 5. Three sectors, agriculture, mining and transport, declined in relative importance between 1911 and 1938, while the miscellaneous groups, including professional and domestic services, declined sharply up to 1921 and then rose slightly. The largest relative gains were in manufacturing and electricity, while building, and Government and defence, advanced less rapidly. However, these broad divisions do tend to hide significant changes occurring within the groups. For example, though the relative importance of transport as a whole declined, motor transport expanded rapidly in the inter-war years. Similarly, the expansion of the manufacturing sector was influenced to a considerable extent by the growth of the newer industries. Their contribution to net industrial output rose from 6·5 per cent in 1907 to 12·5 per cent in 1924 and 19·0 per cent in 1935.[1]

For purposes of inter-war growth analysis a distinction between

[1] Kahn, *Great Britain in the World Economy*, p. 106.

TABLE 5

Industrial Composition of the U.K. as percentage of Total Incomes from Employment

| | *1911* | *1921* | *1938* |
|---|---|---|---|
| Agriculture, forestry, fishing | 5·2 | 4·2 | 2·5 |
| Mining and quarrying | 7·0 | 7·0 | 4·7 |
| Manufacture | 28·0 | 31·6 | 32·0 |
| Building and contracting | 6·0 | 6·1 | 6·4 |
| Gas, water, electricity | 0·9 | 1·5 | 2·0 |
| Transport and communication | 23·2 } | 11·0 | 9·9 |
| Trade and commerce | .. } | 13·0 | 16·0 |
| Government and defence | 8·2 | 9·1 | 8·8 |
| Miscellaneous | 21·5 | 16·6 | 17·8 |

Source: P. Deane and W. A. Cole, *British Economic Growth, 1688–1959* (1962) p. 257.

the industrial and service sectors of the economy is useful. The first includes agriculture, manufacturing, building and electricity, while the second covers all services including trade and transport. In terms of both income generated and employment the two groups were roughly of equal importance. The big difference was in the shares of capital stock. Services accounted for over two-thirds of the capital stock in 1937 as against 31 per cent for the industrial sector. Moreover, between 1924 and 1937 the service sector increased its share of both employment and the capital stock.[1]

Despite the fact that the service sector absorbed one-half or more of the nation's total resources its contribution to output and productivity growth in the inter-war period was relatively modest. Between 1924 and 1937 the rate of input growth (capital and labour) in services was twice that in the industrial sector (2·0 compared with 0·9 per cent per annum), yet output growth was only half that of the latter sector, while productivity actually declined by 0·4 per cent per annum compared with a 2·4 per cent rise in the industrial group. On the other hand, the importance of the service sector should not be underrated. Though a low growth sector its contribution to employment was large, and no doubt welcome at a time of heavy unemployment. Most of the service industries increased their labour forces rapidly during these years; for example, the distributive trades and insurance, banking and finance accounted for nearly one-third of the total increase in employment of 3 million between 1924 and 1937.[2] Altogether, the service group expanded its share

[1] See J. A. Dowie, 'Growth in the Inter-War Period: Some More Arithmetic', *Economic History Review*, XXI (1968) 109.

[2] A. L. Chapman and R. Knight, *Wages and Salaries in the United Kingdom, 1920–1938* (1953) p. 18.

of total employment from 44·3 to 48·5 per cent over the period.

It is clear, however, that the industrial sector made the chief contribution to Britain's growth in terms of both output and productivity. There are some interesting differences between the subsectors. In terms of output and input growth the construction industry and electricity led the field whereas the contribution of mining and agriculture was relatively low. On the other hand, output per man rose slowly in construction and most rapidly in agriculture, while even mining had a creditable record in this respect. In both mining and agriculture employment fell sharply and this was partly responsible for the high level of productivity growth. Compared with some sectors the growth performance of manufacturing considered as a whole was fairly modest.[1]

In recent years considerable attention has been focused on the role of the newer industries. Most of them expanded rapidly in the inter-war years and they accounted for a steadily increasing share of total output and employment. These industries witnessed a constant stream of innovations and, under the influence of rapid technical progress and economics of scale, productivity rose substantially and prices were reduced.[2]

Nevertheless it is easy to exaggerate the contribution of the newer sectors to economic growth both in the long and short term. The new industries strictly defined could only have had a limited influence on economic growth in the early 1920s since their total weighting in the economy was still relatively small at that time. It is hardly conceivable, for instance, that the newer industries could have been responsible for the rapid rise in industrial productivity between 1920 and 1924 (at the rate of 5·6 per cent per annum). In part this high rate of growth reflected the rather low level of productivity attained at the end of the war but it was also due to the adoption of more efficient methods of production, as in engineering, and the shake-out of labour from many of the older industries which had previously been grossly overmanned. For example, output in the mechanical engineering industry rose by 6 per cent between 1920 and 1924 yet the labour force fell by no less than 46 per cent. Similarly in mining and quarrying production rose by nearly 19 per cent yet total employment fell slightly. In some cases, notably in engineering, improved efficiency resulted from experience derived from wartime production.

Though the relative importance of the newer sectors increased steadily during the inter-war period they were by no means the only ones in which expansion occurred. In fact as Table 6 shows, over the

[1] For the actual estimates see Dowie, in *Economic History Review*, XXI (1968) 108.

[2] Information on their development is contained in Section B.

years 1924–37 only one industry, mining, suffered a contraction in output, and only one other, drink, recorded a drop in productivity. But ranking the industries on the basis of their rate of output growth (col. 1, Table 6) the division into old and new sectors is brought out quite clearly. All the industries expanding at less than the general

TABLE 6

Annual Rates of Growth of Output, Output per man, Capital and Employment in Selected Industries 1924–37

| | *Output* | *Output per man* | *Employ-ment* | *Capital* | *Total input* | *Residual* |
|---|---|---|---|---|---|---|
| Electrical engineering | 6·3 | 0·7 | 5·6 | 3·8 | 4·5 | 1·8 |
| Vehicles | 6·2 | 3·3 | 2·9 | 3·7 | 3·1 | 3·1 |
| Electricity, etc. | 5·9 | 2·9 | 3·0 | 3·6 | 3·1 | 2·8 |
| Other manufactures | 5·4 | 3·7 | 1·7 | 0·9 | 1·4 | 4·0 |
| Non-ferrous metal manufactures | 4·9 | 2·5 | 2·4 | 1·2 | 2·0 | 2·9 |
| Metal goods, n.e.s. | 4·8 | 2·1 | 2·7 | .. | .. | .. |
| Timber and furniture | 4·8 | 3·3 | 1·5 | 2·2 | 1·6 | 3·2 |
| Building materials | 4·7 | 2·3 | 2·4 | −0·4 | 1·5 | 3·2 |
| Construction | 4·6 | 1·5 | 3·1 | 1·9 | 2·8 | 1·8 |
| Food | 3·9 | 2·1 | 1·8 | 0·4 | 1·4 | 2·5 |
| Tobacco | 3·5 | 2·9 | 0·6 | 1·8 | 1·0 | 2·5 |
| Precision instruments | 3·5 | 3·2 | 0·3 | .. | .. | .. |
| Chemicals | 3·1 | 1·7 | 1·4 | 1·5 | 1·4 | 1·7 |
| Ferrous metal manufactures | 3·0 | 2·2 | 0·8 | 0·4 | 0·7 | 2·3 |
| Paper and printing | 2·8 | 1·0 | 1·7 | 2·0 | 1·8 | 1·0 |
| Clothing | 2·1 | 1·7 | 0·5 | 1·9 | 0·9 | 1·2 |
| Mechanical engineering | 1·9 | 0·0 | 1·9 | 0·2 | 1·4 | 0·5 |
| Leather | 1·8 | 1·2 | 0·6 | 1·9 | 0·9 | 0·9 |
| Textiles | 1·6 | 2·4 | −0·8 | −0·9 | −0·8 | 2·4 |
| Shipbuilding | 1·2 | 2·6 | −1·4 | −0·9 | −1·3 | 2·5 |
| Drink | 0·7 | −0·2 | 0·8 | 0·4 | 0·7 | 0·0 |
| Mining | −0·4 | 2·4 | −2·7 | 0·5 | −1·8 | 1·4 |
| Manufacturing | 3·3 | 2·1 | 1·2 | 0·5 | 1·0 | 2·3 |
| Total industry | 3·1 | 2·4 | 0·7 | 1·1 | 0·9 | 2·2 |

Source: Based (with a few minor corrections and additions) on J. A. Dowie, 'Growth in the Inter-War Period: Some More Arithmetic', *Economic History Review*, XXI (1968) 110; and R. C. O. Matthews, 'Some Aspects of Post-War Growth in the British Economy in Relation to Historical Experience', *Transactions of the Manchester Statistical Society* (1964) p. 20.

average were old ones, while four of the major staple trades, mining, textiles, shipbuilding and mechanical engineering, were almost lowest in rank. The three fastest growers were all new industries, electrical engineering, electricity supply and vehicles, while chemicals and scientific instruments grew slightly faster than the general average. On the other hand, there was a fairly wide band of older industries, including building and related trades, metal manufactures, food and tobacco, which had rates of growth well above the average.

When we turn to productivity growth the division between old and new industries is less clear cut. Most rapidly expanding industries had high rates of productivity growth, though there were exceptions, notably in some of the new industries such as chemicals and electrical engineering, and in construction. Electrical manufacture was somewhat unique in that it had a very low rate of growth of output per head despite the fact that it was one of the fastest growing industries. This can partly be explained by the fact that the scope for mass production methods and economics of scale is limited in electrical engineering by the nature of the product; many products, especially heavy engineering equipment, transformers and generating plant, are built to individual specifications. However, some of the slow growing staple trades also had quite high rates of productivity growth, especially mining, shipbuilding, textiles, and iron and steel. Many smaller trades, such as cement, glass, non-ferrous metal manufactures and precision instruments recorded considerable advances in productivity. This can be explained partly by the fact that these industries were getting rid of their excess labour and partly because they gained from a high rate of technical progress. For instance, in mining, mechanisation advanced steadily throughout the period. The major exception here was mechanical engineering where productivity failed to increase. Again this poor performance was to some extent determined by the nature of the production process as in the case of electrical manufacture.

The old staple trades had little to contribute to employment growth. In most cases (the major exception was mechanical engineering) employment was either declining (e.g. mining and shipbuilding) or expanding below or around the average (e.g. drink, leather, clothing, and iron and steel). On the other hand, employment expanded rapidly in at least three new industries, and in a number of established trades including construction and metal manufactures. Few industries, however, had very high rates of capital accumulation except vehicles and electricity supply, and in the majority of cases the amount of capital per worker actually declined. Indeed in manufacturing, capital per employee fell at the rate of 0·7 per cent per annum, and even in the economy as a whole it only rose very slowly. This is a striking feature of inter-war economic history and points to the considerable improvement in productivity of the new capital installed.[1]

[1] C. H. Feinstein, *Domestic Capital Formation in the United Kingdom, 1920–1938* (1965) p. 56.

As a result of the relatively low rates of employment and capital growth, most industries experienced fairly modest increases in total factor inputs (we assume that labour's share was 0·7). The chief exceptions were the three fastest growing new industries, construction and non-ferrous metal manufacture, all of which had total input rates in excess of 2 per cent per annum. But in most industries, whether fast- or slow-growing, the expansion in output was determined more by the residual than by additions to the stock of productive factors. On the other hand, in two new industries (electrical manufacture and electricity supply) and also in construction, paper and printing, drink, and mechanical engineering, technical progress contributed less to the growth of output than did additions to the stock of capital and labour.

Thus, the improvement in the residual in the inter-war years was in large part due to shifts in resource allocation within the industrial sector and a fairly rapid rate of technical improvement which affected both old and new industries alike. Though growth was fairly widespread (especially productivity growth) it was centred on a group of interrelated sectors including the new industries, the construction trades, metal manufactures and non-ferrous metals. The repercussions of expansion in these industries helped to carry the rest of the economy forward.

# II The Business Cycle

## The Periodicity and Amplitude of Cycles

There are many different kinds of fluctuations in an industrial economy each of which exhibits quite separate characteristics, the most obvious being differences in periodicity. The most important of these fluctuations are, to name them after their investigators: the Kitchin cycle (3–4 years); the Juglar cycle (7–11 years); the Kuznets cycle (16–22 years); and the Kondratieff cycle (40–50 years). There is considerable statistical evidence to support the existence of the first three types of fluctuation, but the reality of the Kondratieff cycle, urged so forcibly by Schumpeter,[1] is in doubt. We shall concentrate on the Juglar, i.e. the standard business cycle. But economic fluctuations before 1914 are not fully comprehensible without reference to the longer Kuznets cycles related to fluctuations in building activity, migration and capital exports — all of which were dominant features in the development of the British economy in the half-century before the First World War.

The identification and measurement of business cycles is a task beset with complex problems even for modern periods for which statistical data are relatively abundant. One of the difficulties is that at any point of time, regardless of the phase of the cycle, some activities will be expanding while others will be contracting. The solution to this problem is to construct a diffusion index which measures the percentage of a given group of activities undergoing expansion at each stage of the cycle, and to plot the path of the cycle from such an index. Statistical materials before 1914, and possibly before 1939, are too scanty for such a technique. For the earlier period we lack unemployment statistics, apart from the trade union returns of a limited number of craft unions, and industrial output statistics are very imperfect. Different turning points result from the selection of different indicators. Burns and Mitchell used 'reference dates' calculated by taking the composite turning points revealed from consideration of a number of key indicators.[2] Here national income estimates are used as a guide to identifying cycles because they

[1] J. A. Schumpeter, *Business Cycles* (1939) 2 vols.
[2] A. F. Burns and W. C. Mitchell, *Measuring Business Cycles*, N.B.E.R. (1946).

enable us to calculate a rough measure of relative amplitude from cycle to cycle.

TABLE 7

Periodicity of Cycles, 1870–1938

| TROUGHS | | | PEAKS | | | PERIODICITY (*Years*) Trough to trough | | | Peak to peak | | |
|---|---|---|---|---|---|---|---|---|---|---|---|
| *a* | *b* | *c* | *a* | *b* | *c* | *a* | *b* | *c* | *a* | *b* | *c* |
| | | | 1866 | 1865 | 1866 | | | | 9 | 7 | 7 |
| 1867 | 1868 | 1868 | | | | 12 | 11 | 11 | | | |
| | | | 1875 | 1872 | 1873 | | | | 8 | 10 | 10 |
| 1879 | 1879 | 1879 | | | | 6 | 7 | 7 | | | |
| | | | 1883 | 1882 | 1883 | | | | 7 | 8 | 7 |
| 1885 | 1886 | 1886 | | | | 8 | 7 | 8 | | | |
| | | | 1890 | 1890 | 1890 | | | | 10 | 9 | 10 |
| 1893 | 1893 | 1894 | | | | 11 | 11 | 10 | | | |
| | | | 1900 | 1899 | 1900 | | | | 7 | 7 | 7 |
| 1904 | 1904 | 1904 | | | | 4 | 4 | 4 | | | |
| | | | 1907 | 1906 | 1907 | | | | 6 | 7 | 6 |
| 1908 | 1908 | 1908 | | | | 6 | 6 | 6 | | | |
| | | | 1913 | 1913 | 1913 | | | | | | |
| 1914 | 1914 | 1914 | | | | | | | | | |
| | | | 1920 | 1920 | 1920 | | | | 10 | 7 | 9 |
| 1921 | 1922 | 1921 | | | | 11 | 10 | 11 | | | |
| | | | 1930 | 1927 | 1929 | | | | 8 | 10 | 8 |
| 1932 | 1932 | 1932 | | | | — | 6 | 6 | | | |
| | | | 1938 | 1937 | 1937 | | | | | | |
| — | 1938 | 1938 | | | | | | | | | |

*a.* Real national income (Feinstein's estimates).
*b.* Unemployment. Up to 1923 based on trade union returns; from 1923 Ministry of Labour data (see Mitchell and Deane, *Abstract*, pp. 64–7).
*c.* Reference dates from Burns and Mitchell, *Measuring Business Cycles*, N.B.E.R. (1946).

Table 7 shows the turning-points according to these different measures (national income, unemployment and reference dates) for business cycles between the late 1860s and the end of the inter-war period. There was a marked trough in 1926, when industrial production fell by 5·3 per cent from the level of 1925, but this has been excluded, since it was accounted for entirely by the repercussions of the General Strike and formed no part of the Juglar pattern. 1907–8 is also something of an exception. Depression spread in late 1907 from the United States, and was induced there by a financial crisis rather than by endogenous cyclical forces. In spite of their exogenous origins,[1] the peak of 1907 and trough of 1908 are included in Table 7,

[1] This is despite Schumpeter's description of the crisis as an 'intermezzo' and 'not a depression in our sense at all'.

although their inclusion rather spoils the periodicity of pre-1914 cycles. Rostow solved the difficulty by explaining the cycle culminating in 1907 as a 'minor cycle', that is, marked by expansion in the foreign trade sector rather than by a boom in long-term investment and by full employment.[1]

Although turning points differ slightly according to the index used to measure fluctuations, this makes little difference to the periodicity of the cycles. Table 7 makes it clear that there is no obvious change in periodicity either within the period 1870–1914 or in comparing the fluctuations before 1914 with those between the wars. Apart from the impact of 1907–8 which is, as we have seen, a special case, the length of cycles however measured fell within the range 6–12 years with an average of eight years. In Table 8 we throw some light

TABLE 8

Relative Amplitude of Cycles, 1870–1938

| *Period of upswing* | *Change in real N.I. from trough to peak as % of previous peak* | *Annual rate of change in upswing (%)* |
|---|---|---|
| (*1*) | (*2*) | (*3*) |
| 1867–75 | 35·1 | 3·8 |
| 1879–83 | 10·8 | 2·6 |
| 1885–90 | 29·3 | 5·3 |
| 1893–1900 | 26·8 | 3·5 |
| 1904–7 | 11·3 | 3·6 |
| 1908–13 | 9·9 | 1·9 |
| 1921–9 | 24·8 | 2·8 |
| 1932–8 | 21·7 | 3·3 |

Source: Feinstein's estimates deflated by the Bowley cost of living index.

on the amplitude of successive cycles by estimating the change in real national income in each upswing relative to the level reached in the previous boom. Again, there is no marked contrast in pre-1914 and post-1918 experience, and no tendency for fluctuations to exhibit either increasing or decreasing intensity over time. Cycles differed in amplitude, of course. If we qualify the proportionate expansion of each upswing by its duration (i.e. refer to col. 3), we find that three upswings were below average intensity—the early 1880s, the years up to 1913 and the 1920s, and of these only the second was much below average. The only outstanding upswing in

[1] W. W. Rostow, *British Economy of the Nineteenth Century* (1948) pp. 33, 36–7, 38, 39–45.

the period, in terms of annual rates of income expansion, was that of the late 1880s.[1]

It seems reasonable to conclude that business cycles over the period 1870–1939 were broadly similar in terms of periodicity and amplitude, in the sense that there was no continuing tendency for cycles to become either shorter or longer or to become stronger or weaker. This is not to say that fluctuations before and after 1914 were essentially similar in other respects. For instance, the approximate equality of amplitude could have been largely fortuitous, reflecting compensating changes in the trend movements of different components of income. An example is the fact that the acceleration of industrial production between the wars was offset by falling net foreign investment. Moreover, each cycle exhibited its own special characteristics. Industries dominating the upswing varied from one cycle to the next; some fluctuations were export-oriented while others were based on domestic sectors I ; there was considerable variety between cycles in monetary and price experience and in employment fluctuations.

## The Role of Exports

Fluctuations in an economy as open as that of the United Kingdom between 1870 and 1939 cannot be explained by internal factors alone. British cycles can be understood only in terms of the inter-

[1] It should be remembered, of course, that movements in national income may not be parallel with movements in other indicators, such as industrial production. The relative strengths of successive business cycles might take on a different appearance if reliable industrial production indices were available for the period before 1900. For cycles after 1900, the Lomax index of industrial production indicates upswings of increasing intensity, as is shown below:

| *Upswing* | *Annual rate of change in industrial production (using previous peak as base)* |
|---|---|
| 1901–7 | 1·7% |
| 1908–13 | 3·1% |
| 1921–9 | 4·9% |
| 1932–7 | 7·1% |

Based on K. S. Lomax, 'Production and Productivity Movements in the U.K. since 1900', *Journal of the Royal Statistical Society*, A122 (1959).

Lomax's less precise index for the period before 1900 ('Growth and Productivity in the United Kingdom', *Productivity Measurement Review*, XXXVIII (1964) 6) suggests upswings of the order of 2·7 per cent for the years 1878–83, 3·6 per cent for 1886–91 and 4·8 per cent for 1893–9. Apart from the early 1880s these again point to the diversity of cyclical experience between income and industrial production.

action between the domestic cycle and events abroad.[1] Overseas influences include systematic movements such as recurrent cycles in the major overseas economies, and random elements such as crop disturbances, financial crises abroad and wars. The impact of the latter will vary in an unpredictable way from cycle to cycle, but the pattern of fluctuations in the world economy, and its impact on Britain, is likely to be influenced markedly by trends in world production and trade. Although world trade was expanding between 1870 and 1914 more slowly than before 1870, its upward trend nevertheless compared favourably with the stagnation of the inter-war period. The difference in experience in the two periods meant a change in the role of exports in British business cycles.

In the short run, as Cairncross first pointed out, home and overseas investment tended to move together before 1914, and the link between the two was the behaviour of exports. Ford has suggested that 'the *immediate* cause of fluctuations in British money incomes was fluctuations in merchandise export values, aided or impeded by fluctuations in home investment'.[2] It was also noted that new overseas issues fluctuations led those in exports by one to two years, thereby making a case 'for relating British cyclical fluctuations not only to variations in world market conditions and the domestic propensity to invest but to the varying pace of British overseas investment'.[3] There is something in this argument, especially since foreign lending led directly in many cases to the export of investment goods. But although induced exports of commodities almost certainly exceeded one-quarter of the invested capital (as estimated by Tinbergen) they were insufficient to effect the transfer of the capital. Ford himself admitted the possibility that both overseas issues and merchandise exports could have been responding to autonomous changes in economic activity abroad. Having pointed out the possible primacy of foreign lending, we shall henceforth concentrate on the relationship between merchandise exports and domestic fluctuations.

That exports had a crucial role in British business cycles in the nineteenth century has been emphasised by many observers, but pre-eminently by D. H. Robertson, Beveridge and Rostow.[4] But others

[1] For a clear statement of the need for this interaction and a demonstration of how it can be analysed see J. Tinbergen, *Business Cycles in the U.K., 1870–1914* (1956) ch. viii.

[2] A. G. Ford, 'Overseas Lending and Internal Fluctuations, 1870–1914', in J. Saville (ed.), *Studies in the British Economy, 1870–1914*, special number of the *Yorkshire Bulletin of Economic and Social Research*, XVII (1965) 25–6.

[3] Ibid., p. 30.

[4] D. H. Robertson, *A Study of Industrial Fluctuation* (1915); W. H. Beveridge, *Full Employment in a Free Society* (1944) appendix A; and W. W. Rostow, *British Economy of the Nineteenth Century* (1948).

have argued that the economy, at least up to 1900, was not 'export-propelled'.[1] These apparently opposing views are not necessarily inconsistent. The growth rate of exports was halved after 1870, and this fact made it improbable that exports could continue to act as a leading sector. But this does not rule out the possibility that fluctuations in exports could be of crucial importance at the turning points. Yet those who stress the interrelationships between the trend and the cycle would only expect exports to dominate upwings in periods when the secular trend rate of growth in exports was high. However, we must make a distinction between leading the recovery and dominating it. It would be possible for exports to show a repeated tendency to lead the economy out of slumps and yet to be swamped by growth in domestic sectors during the revival.

The argument for the predominance of exports in British economic fluctuations before 1914 has a number of separate strands. First, the business cycle was becoming international in character so that the effects of a marked change in the direction of economic activity (whether upwards or downwards) in a major economy could be transmitted to the U.K. economy through changes in the performance of her export industries. The maturity of the British economy, its slower rate of growth and the comparative stability of its structure and financial system meant that internal autonomous impulses were likely to be weaker than those imported from overseas, where economic development was more discontinuous and financial crises more common. This internationalisation of the business cycle showed itself most strongly in the links between primary producers and the industrial economies. For instance, it is easy to detect the influence of rice harvests of India on the export trade in cotton piece-goods. Moreover, all the turning points save one between 1890 and 1932 fell within the harvest seasons of the northern and southern hemispheres.[2]

Although it is easy to detect a relationship between fluctuations in a major market and the exports of a single industry (e.g. the United States and the Yorkshire woollen trade booms of 1867–70, 1879–81, 1886–90 and 1912–13), synchronisation of turning points in *total* exports with turning points in the domestic economy must be due to random factors *unless* the major parts of the world economy moved into booms and slumps together. According to Saul, the world economy was insufficiently integrated before the 1890s to make it

[1] The most recent exponent of this view is A. J. Brown, 'Britain in the World Economy, 1870–1914', in J. Saville (ed.), *Studies in the British Economy*.

[2] Beveridge, *Full Employment*, p. 303. These seasons fell between July and September and November to January respectively.

reasonable to speak of a world business cycle. Nevertheless there was a remarkably high co-variation of business cycles among the chief European countries (Britain, Germany and France), despite an assertion to the contrary by Lewis and O'Leary. Using the reference cycle technique Morgenstern has demonstrated the similarity of European cyclical experience between 1870 and 1914, though the United States economy moved in a different rhythm; however, by the inter-war period even the European economies became out of step with each other due to post-war readjustments and increased government intervention.[1] More recently, A. G. Ford has also cast doubt on the primacy of the United States in pre-1914 fluctuations by showing that exports to Europe were the main source of absolute fluctuations in export values, and synchronised more than exports as a whole with domestic turning points.[2] On the other hand, cycles in certain important extra-European economies followed a different course certainly before the 1890s, and the different parts of the world economy were not so interdependent as to establish exports as the most important single variable in the fluctuations of the British economy.

Secondly, it is sometimes argued that exports fluctuated more widely than other sectors. Beveridge was a strong proponent of this view, and initially tested the hypothesis on 1929–37 experience. However, this was a misconceived inquiry which could establish little, since exports were bound to fluctuate more widely at a time of severe international crisis when world cycles were more intense than those in Britain.[3] He followed this up with investigations into the pre-1914 period, which showed that textile industries fluctuated more widely than industry in general (though much less severely than construction and other capital goods industries), a fact to be explained by the dependence of textiles on overseas demand. Despite the quantitative importance of textiles in total exports, this finding is not conclusive evidence of the wider amplitude of fluctuations in total exports. The method used in the inquiry (measuring the standard deviation of indices of industrial activity in a limited group of sectors) is not above reproach. A more meaningful investigation would be to compare the amplitude of fluctuations in exports over Juglar cycles with the parallel fluctuations in national income. Such an exercise gives rise to certain difficulties. Turning points in exports sometimes differed from those in national income. Another problem

[1] O. Morgenstern, *International Financial Transactions and Business Cycles*, N.B.E.R. (1959) ch. 2.

[2] A. G. Ford, 'British Economic Fluctuations, 1870–1914', *Warwick Economic Research Papers*, 3 (1968) 16–17.

[3] T. C. Chang, *Cyclical Movements in the Balance of Payments* (1951) p. 126.

is how to measure fluctuations in exports. In Table 9 we measure the relative amplitude of cycles in exports in terms of both current values and volumes.[1]

TABLE 9

Relative Amplitude of Export Fluctuations, 1870–1938

| VALUES | | | VOLUMES | | |
|---|---|---|---|---|---|
| *Period of upswing* | *Change in export values from trough to peak as % of previous peak* | *Annual rate of change in upswing* (%) | *Period of upswing* | *Change in export volumes from trough to peak as % of previous peak* | *Annual rate of change in upswing* (%) |
| 1868–72 | 41 | 8·9 | 1864–72 | 67 | 6·6 |
| 1879–82 | 20 | 6·0 | 1879–84 | 29 | 4·7 |
| 1886–90 | 21 | 4·9 | 1885–90 | 21 | 3·9 |
| 1894–1900 | 29 | 4·3 | 1893–9 | 22 | 3·3 |
| 1901–7 | 50 | 7·0 | 1901–7 | 41 | 5·9 |
| 1908–13 | 35 | 6·1 | 1908–13 | 27 | 4·8 |
| 1921–4 | 7 | 2·3 | 1921–9 | 45 | 4·8 |
| 1926–9 | 10 | 3·0 | | | |
| | | | 1932–7 | 18 | 3·3 |
| 1932–7 | 21 | 3·9 | | | |

Sources: Up to 1913, A. H. Imlah, *Economic Elements in the Pax Britannica* (1958) Table 8, pp. 94–8; from 1920, London and Cambridge Economic Service, *Key Statistics of the British Economy, 1900–1962* (1963) Table G.

If we compare the amplitude of fluctuations in exports as given in Table 9 with that in national income in Table 8, the generalisation that export fluctuations were wider receives some support. This is certainly true of all cycles before 1914 with the exceptions of the late 1880s and the late 1890s. The first of these exceptions is somewhat surprising in view of Britain's preoccupation with international economic development (and hence high foreign lending) in the 1880s; the second exception is what we should expect in view of the marked domestic boom of the nineties. The divergence between national income and export fluctuations is particularly marked after 1900, reinforcing accepted views about the nature of Britain's growth at this time. Between the late 1890s and the outbreak of the First World War manufactured exports rose by over 70 per cent, while manu-

[1] It should be noted that our technique of measuring relative amplitude by the change from trough to peak as a proportion of the previous peak obviously ignores the downswings. There is some evidence that downswings in exports were stronger than in national income, since the latter tended to undergo 'ratchet' growth with very limited falls in national income during slumps and concentration of income expansion in the booms. This is, of course, consistent with the view that exports have greater cyclical sensitivity; what we must beware of, of course, is taking the rates of change in exports during upswings as an indication of secular export growth.

facturing output rose only by a quarter. Foreign lending revived (especially after 1905) at the expense of domestic investment, productivity growth slowed down and the distribution of income moved against labour (primarily because of unfavourable terms of trade). In the inter-war period the cycles in exports and in the economy as a whole were broadly similar in amplitude. The trend of exports was undoubtedly downwards, but when we allow for the marked contractions in 1925 and 1926 the rate of export expansion in the upswings corresponds closely to the rates of change in national income. This was in spite of a marked readjustment in the economy from exporting towards production for the home market.

The stress on the greater intensity of fluctuations in exports is not, therefore, unwarranted. However, whether this is necessary to establish the importance of exports is debatable. For instance, if we resort to accelerator models we would expect fluctuations in investment to be much wider than in exports (and home demand).[1] The relevant question in determining the influence of exports is whether absolute changes in export demand are greater than absolute changes in domestic demand. Even if the answer is 'yes', this may or may not mean wider fluctuations in exports. Whether exports fluctuate more than the economy in general would then depend upon the relative proportions of exports, home consumption and domestic investment in total income.[2]

A third argument for the importance of exports is that they led the economy out of slumps and into recessions. Although the annual turning points in Tables 8 and 9 show no tendency for exports to lead, a more detailed analysis gives general support to the hypothesis. For example, revival in the third quarter of 1879 was initiated by new orders, especially of rails, from the United States. Moreover, the fluctuations in individual industries before 1914 suggest that export industries revived earlier than other industries. The two main export groups, textiles and metal manufacturing, led in 1893 and again in 1908, in both cases a year before most other sectors turned upwards. Within each main export group the industries most

[1] Assuming, of course, that capital coefficients exceed unity.

[2] Tinbergen, however, argued that the acceleration principle was not very applicable to fluctuations in fixed capital in Britain before 1914. He found that the supply of both home consumer goods and export products was very elastic (*Business Cycles in the U.K. 1870–1914*, pp. 95, 96), suggesting that there was a good deal of spare capacity in British industry. Unless this was a constant proportion of total capacity, its existence weakens the usefulness of the accelerator as an explanatory factor in British economic fluctuations. The widespread excess capacity of the inter-war economy also suggests that the accelerator, at least at a macro-economic level, has limited application to fluctuations after the First World War.

dependent on overseas demand, such as cotton piece-goods and tinplate, turned earlier than others. Similarly, many of the downswings were triggered off abroad. The clearest case is the crisis of 1907 which spread from the United States. There are several other examples; exports led into the depression in 1873 and the first reversal in the upward trend in output in the early 1880s was due to falling exports connected with crises on the Continent. This repeated tendency for exports to lead lends support to Schumpeter's generalisation that U.K. 'cycles tended to shape in function of foreign business situations and her "crises" as well as financial booms to originate in foreign events'.[1]

This finding has to be qualified for inter-war fluctuations. Perhaps not surprisingly in view of the slow growth in world trade, exports did not lead the economy out of depressions between the wars. Admittedly, there was a mild revival of exports after the sterling devaluation of September 1931 but this did not start a general recovery, and revival was delayed for another year. Similarly a decade earlier in 1921, unemployment had reached its peak in May and June and signs of monetary stability were evident from July, yet major export categories (such as cotton piece-goods) failed to revive much before the end of the third quarter of the year.[2] On the other hand, exports played a major role in initiating downswings. Export collapse is relevant to an analysis of all three major downturns—1920–1, 1929–30 and 1937–8. However, the impact of exports was most clearly visible in 1929–30, when the export industries began to turn in March 1929 several months ahead of other sectors and the general downturn in the economy as a whole. In 1937–8 the recession was caused by both external and internal factors, but exports still led the way since they had already begun to fall slightly in the middle of 1937 while the recession was not general until the last quarter of the year. In 1920 domestic industries (particularly consumption goods industries) as well as exports declined at an early stage of the recession. But on the whole the generalisation holds that exports led into depressions between the wars but failed to lead out of them.

The increasing internationalisation of the business cycle, the wider amplitude of fluctuations in exports and the lead of exports over other indicators when economic activity changed direction (subject to the reservations noted above) are important features determining the character of British economic fluctuations between 1870 and 1939. They do not, however, establish a case for assigning

[1] Schumpeter, *Business Cycles*, p. 367.

[2] A. C. Pigou, *Aspects of British Economic History, 1918–25* (1947).

to exports a recurrent causal role in the cycles. For instance, even if exports led at the revival this does not necessarily imply that they dominated upswings. The substantial boom of the 1890s, for instance, was dominated by housebuilding and, to a lesser extent, by expansion in a fairly wide range of industries, mainly catering for the home market. The major export industries did not revive substantially until quite late in the boom. The revival of 1879–83, once under way, was dominated far more by shipbuilding, electricity company formation and other joint stock development than by exports. Most striking of all, economic recovery after 1932 was predominantly a home market revival, with industrial production expanding by more than 40 per cent over the 1929 peak compared with a decline in the volume of exports of 18 per cent. In more general terms, the marked difference in amplitude between British cycles and world cycles over the inter-war period (Britain experienced a sharper post-war boom and slump, a much weaker upswing in 1925–9, a relatively mild depression in the world slump and a more complete recovery after 1932) suggests that internal developments were the critical forces behind the economy's fluctuations. When we make allowances for the lower level of world trade before 1926 (relative to 1913), the export sluggishness of the 1920s was much more a consequence than a cause of Britain's difficulties in that decade. Between 1929 and 1938, the movement of exports was quite different from that of national income, and their belated revival shows a much closer correspondence with movements in the United States national income. The course of exports had only a marginal influence on the cycle of internal activity in the 1930s.

The role played by exports differed over time. It was greater before 1914 than after, reflecting the declining share of exports relative to G.N.P.[1] and the changes in the international economic environment. But the importance of exports in pre-1914 fluctuations varied from cycle to cycle. After 1900, the marked expansion in exports contrasted sharply with the stagnation of the domestic economy. An analysis of fluctuations for the 1900–14 period would have to devote considerable attention to exports and overseas investment compared, say, with an analysis of fluctuations in the previous decade. Over the period as a whole, however, fluctuations in domestic investment sectors (such as construction and engineering) dominated business cycles, and although shorter export cycles were detectable in the movement of exports of individual products (e.g. export values of cotton goods and yarn), these did not determine the

[1] The ratio declined from 19·8 per cent in 1913 to 14·9 per cent in 1929 to 8·2 per cent in 1938, A. Maddison, *Economic Growth in the West* (1964) p. 67.

course of activity in the economy as a whole as they had in the first half of the nineteenth century.[1] No convincing case can be made for the view that exports were the main causal variable in business cycles between 1870 and 1939. The most important function of the overseas trade sector was to stabilise the growth path of the economy before 1914 by moving inversely, in the long run, to internally generated fluctuations.

## Innovations, Technical Progress and the Cycle

The fluctuations of the 1870–1939 period occurred around an upward trend; real national income increased about three-and-a-half times over these seventy years, and real income per head rose by more than two-and-a-quarter times. The residual rather than capital accumulation was responsible for most of this growth, with the probable exception of the period between the 1890s and 1914.[2] If the residual accounts for the greater part of the growth in incomes, and if growth is concentrated in boom periods, then technical progress, and in particular innovations, may have an important impact on the business cycle. If growth and cycles are to be explained by the same single factor, there is a strong argument that the essential element of such an explanation is that there should be revolutionary advances in technique which occur discontinuously. From each major innovation (such as steam power, railways, electrification, the internal combustion engine) there will result a succession of investment booms based upon application of not only the main technical advance but also a cluster of minor innovations in a wide range of activities made possible by the major breakthrough. Since the commercial application of these innovations depends upon favourable economic conditions (a receptive capital market, optimistic expectations, etc.), this fact in itself leads to innovations taking place in swarms, usually in cyclical upswings. But there is a world of difference between showing discontinuity in innovations and demonstrating that innovations *cause* business cycles. Admittedly modifications can be made to an innovations theory which relieve some of the strain placed on the evidence. For example, such a theory need not conflict with the finding that booms and slumps are imported from abroad via changes in the rate of exports, since these changes may be

[1] A. D. Gayer, W. W. Rostow and A. J. Schwarz, *The Growth and Fluctuation of the British Economy, 1790–1850* (1953) vol. II, ch. i.

[2] See above, Section A, I.

explicable in terms of the exploitation of innovations abroad and the associated growth of markets. Moreover, the interrelatedness of innovations in different sectors of the economy and the possibility of 'echo-effect' fluctuations resulting from replacement of the original machines breaks the need for a link between an individual innovation and a particular cycle.

However, as the generality of the argument is increased, the role of innovation becomes blurred and dubious. For instance, in each major upswing one or two industries usually lead the way in the sense of leading at the lower turning point and/or experiencing the fastest growth in output and/or dominating net capital formation. But this is a characteristic of almost all business cycles, whether we subscribe to an innovational theory or not. It may be possible to discover the origins of these leading industries in an innovation applied years (possibly even decades) earlier or to explain an acceleration in their growth rate by, say, reductions in input costs which are in turn the consequence of innovation in other sectors, but can we then go on to argue that these innovations are, in a meaningful sense, the cause of the cycle? It is true that since the dominating industries of boom periods tend to be relatively new industries the booms can ultimately be traced back to the appearance of some innovation in the relatively recent past. It may also be true that, if a feature of booms is high investment rates in newer industries, the normal case will be for investment in new plant to incorporate minor modifications and refinements in production techniques rather than to mean the simple duplication of existing machines, and in this sense the boom may be associated with innovational activity. But these facts are consistent with virtually any explanation of cycles, and cannot be used as a support for the view that cycles are essentially fluctuations due to innovational activity.

Despite these unsettled questions, the innovations theory cannot be disposed of by facile generalised arguments. One such argument is that Britain's relatively poor productivity performance compared with other advanced economies rules out the hypothesis that technical progress could govern economic fluctuations. As shown in Chapter I, Table 2, the rate of growth in output per man-hour over the period 1870–1913 was low in Britain relative to the growth rates of her main competitors. But the comparative productivity performance of the economy as a whole is a limited guide to the role of innovation in the economy. The main reason for this is that in the two or three decades before 1914 there was in Britain a pause in resource shifts into industry so that rises in output per head were now dependent on *overall* productivity growth rather than on the rate of transfer of resources from low productivity sectors (such as agriculture) into high productivity sectors (particularly manufacturing) as was often the case abroad. Moreover, in the inter-war period the relative position of the United Kingdom in productivity performance improved somewhat (see Table 2). To the extent that this relative change reflected decreasing scope for intersectoral resource transfers in some countries abroad and an improvement in resource allocation in Britain, it provides partial support for the above explanation. However, the absolute rise in the British growth rate between the wars also reflects a higher overall trend in technical progress, and therefore a potentially more favourable environment in which to discover a relationship between innovational activity and economic fluctuations.

Similarly, it is dangerous to infer anything conclusive from the comparative stability of the capital/output ratio during this period. There was only one marked shift during this period, and that was over the First World War when the ratio rose from 3·8 to 4·9. Over the 1870–1914 period as a whole, the capital/ouput ratio varied between $3\frac{1}{2}$ and $4\frac{1}{4}$, a variation not much larger than the margin of error in the capital stock data;[1] though the average ratio was higher between the wars, it remained relatively stable. The absorption of capital associated with applying innovations might suggest that a high rate of innovations would result in a rising capital/output ratio. This is not necessarily the case. Technical progress may be capital-saving or labour-saving or both at the same time. A stable capital/output ratio is quite consistent with rapid innovations if technical progress is Harrod-neutral between factors.[2] Even if technical progress in a given sector is both capital-using and labour-saving, this may nevertheless be consistent with overall stability in the capital output ratio if shifts in demand favour less capital-intensive sectors. Thus to base any argument about the relative pace of innovational activity on the stability of, or changes in, the aggregate capital/output ratio is bound to be misleading.

A serious difficulty with the argument linking innovations with cycles is that it invariably stands on *a priori* generalisations supported by one or two (possibly unrepresentative) examples. The main trouble stems from the insuperable problems arising in any attempt to measure innovational activity. We need to make a clear distinction between invention and innovation, since inventions are of no

[1] Matthews, in *Transactions of the Manchester Statistical Society* (1964).

[2] Technical progress is Harrod-neutral when the rise in the capital/labour ratio required to hold the profit rate constant also causes the capital/output ratio to remain constant.

economic significance until they have been commercially applied. But it is even more difficult to measure innovational activity than inventive activity, mainly because we cannot satisfactorily separate out innovational investment from other forms of net investment (i.e. investment induced by rising demand) and from replacement investment. A measure of inventive activity will be only a very imperfect substitute. Here one of the main problems is how to evaluate the qualitative significance of each invention. The economic consequences of the internal combustion engine were many thousand times greater than many other technical discoveries which might count equally in any tally of inventions. This is one, among many, of the main defects of patent statistics. A sharp and steady rise in patents may consequently be consistent with a continuous decline in the rate of technical progress. Moreover some of the most significant innovations may not be patented at all, while others may have been first introduced abroad. For these reasons it is very doubtful whether any comparison of fluctuations in patents with fluctuations in business cycle indicators can yield meaningful results.

However, to test whether any relationship exists, patents sealed in the United Kingdom were compared with movements in fixed capital formation over the period between 1870 and 1938. The simplest result to support an innovations theory would be for patents to lead investment consistently. But there was no clear-cut result of this kind, and indeed the tendency was for capital formation to lead and patents to lag.[1] If patents were an acceptable indicator of innovational activity this result might seem to give a death blow to the innovational theory. However, this is not necessarily the case. Some observers, including Rostow, have argued that plant expansion and the introduction of new techniques have been characteristic features of the *later* stages of major upswings. If this were true, a tendency for patents to lag behind turning points in capital formation is not necessarily inconsistent with innovations having a role in business cycles. Moreover this interpretation caters for quite realistic lags (of up to a few years) between the sealing of patents and (where relevant) their commercial application. But the part played by innovation and technical progress in this situation would be a modified

[1] At the peaks patents led capital formation at the turn of the century (in 1899 as against 1902) and in the years before the war (in 1911 as opposed to 1913). The troughs in the 1900–13 period were widely apart in both series. On other occasions, however, both before 1900 and in the inter-war period, capital formation led patents at the turning points. At the troughs, capital formation turned in 1869 and patents in 1870, both turned together in 1886, and capital formation led again by two years in 1922 and by one year in 1932. At the peaks, capital formation led in 1866 (patents reached a peak in 1868) and in 1930 by one year.

one, in the sense that they would tend to influence the periodicity of cycles by prolonging the upswings, rather than by precipitating the turning points.

A common feature of many modern growth models is the assumption that the rate of technical progress is a function of the rate of investment.[1] This assumption reflects several notions, such as the view that 'learning' is a primary factor in increasing productivity and that most technical progress is 'embodied' in new machines rather than being on tap for application over a wide range of sectors and in existing as well as new plant. An inference of these models is that a precondition for an economy to have a high rate of technical progress is that it should also have experienced high investment rates. In fact, gross domestic capital formation[2] was quite low relatively to G.N.P. throughout the period under study, compared with both contemporary ratios abroad and with post-1945 British investment ratios. As shown in Chapter 1, gross non-residential investment averaged 5·8 per cent of G.N.P. in the period 1870–1913 and 6·8 per cent between the wars. Before 1913 a considerable proportion of personal savings and accumulated profits went for foreign investment, while in the inter-war period, despite a fall in the propensity to invest abroad, disinvestment in a number of stagnating sectors and very limited increases in plant in some others meant very little overall expansion in the ratio of G.D.C.F./G.N.P. Given the low investment ratios, it might be argued that the rates of technical progress would also tend to be low, thereby placing severe restrictions on the scope of technical advances as a determinant of economic fluctuations.

This argument, plausible though it appears, has the serious flaw that it would be valid only in a closed economy. In an open economy, and all the advanced industrial economies were open during this period, the rate of technical progress is not dependent upon the rate of investment alone, and is not determined by the extent of 'learning through experience'. The point is that innovations were often first discovered abroad, and introduced only later into the United Kingdom.[3] Relatively favourable conditions existed (before 1914 because

[1] For example, see N. Kaldor and J. A. Mirrlees, 'A New Model of Economic Growth', *Review of Economic Studies*, XXIX (1962).

[2] 'Gross' figures are more appropriate than 'net' because 'like-for-like' replacement rarely took place and is, indeed, incompatible with vintage capital models and the embodied technical progress concept.

[3] Examples include the dynamo (Z. Gramme, Belgium 1870), the Goodyear welter and chain stitcher (boots and shoes, U.S.A. 1872–3), the Northrop automatic loom (U.S.A.), the gramophone (E. Berliner, U.S.A. 1888–9), the electrolytic process for aluminium production (C. M. Hall, U.S.A., and P. Heroult, France), the internal combustion engine (Daimler, Maybach and Benz, Germany) and the

of the high degree of international economic interdependence and between the wars because of the growth of the international corporation and the spread of licensing agreements) for the transmission of technology between advanced countries, so that new techniques, and even new industries, could often be imported from abroad. Thus the modest investment ratios in the British economy were not a firm constraint on technical advances or on their potential impact upon business cycles.

Finally, heavy foreign investment before 1914 might be used as a reason for dismissing the effects of innovational activity in U.K. fluctuations. It is sometimes argued that the substantial diversions of accumulated savings abroad, especially in the 1880s and after 1905, reflected the dearth of investment opportunities at home. Schumpeter, for instance, argued that in the latter period there was 'so little public financing of domestic innovation' because there was 'not much to finance'.[1] From holding views of this kind, it is quite tempting to go further and rule out the innovational theories altogether as explanations of the British case. But such an argument requires very severe qualifications. In the first place, overseas investment was not continuously heavy throughout our period. Domestic investment was quantitatively much more important in the 1890s and the early 1900s, in the inter-war period (especially in the 1930s when net foreign investment was negative) and, to a lesser extent, in the 1870s. Even in the decades of heavy overseas lending, there were marked year-to-year variations in the relative importance of domestic and overseas investment. Secondly, even if overseas investment dominated a particular cycle this does not mean that innovational factors have to be excluded from consideration. It is clear that innovations may be applied abroad and yet have a marked influence on domestic cycles. For instance, one consequence of such innovations might be a rising demand for British exports. Alternatively, if innovations abroad were cost-reducing and applied in export sectors a common result was a favourable shift in Britain's terms of trade favouring income growth. Finally, as already suggested, innovations first introduced abroad could later be applied in Britain, though the circumstances in which such innovations might be linked to British overseas investment were probably very

---

diesel engine (Germany 1897) before 1914, and hot strip continuous rolling of steel (J. B. Tytus, U.S.A. 1923), the continuous casting of metals (S. Junghans, Germany 1927–32) and nylon (W. H. Carothers, U.S.A.) between the wars. These are a few of many examples. Most of those quoted are taken from J. Jewkes, D. Sawers and R. Stillerman, *The Sources of Invention* (1st edn, 1958).

[1] Schumpeter, *Business Cycles*, p. 430.

rare, in view of the very limited U.K. investments in overseas manufacturing.

The data deficiencies are so great and our understanding of the process of technical change and how it influences the level of economic activity so imperfect that even if the case for an innovations theory is valid it would be very difficult to establish conclusively. But the difficulties involved in substantiating such an explanation are not sufficient grounds for attempting to dismiss it out of hand by resorting to these superficial, and in some cases *a priori*, objections.

Nevertheless it is not easy, short of microscopic analysis of individual cycles, to offer firm evidence to support a strong positive association between innovations and business cycles. It is clear enough from the writings of Schumpeter and Sir Dennis Robertson that many of the upswings of this period were dominated by expansion in certain industries, or by the repercussions of basic innovations perfected and introduced earlier, or by meteoric expansions in one or two, usually minor and quantitatively insignificant, sectors. The international boom of the late 1860s and early 1870s was closely associated with continued railway building. If this is to be explained by innovational activity, we must refer to the 'carry-over' effects of innovation many decades earlier. There is no doubt that in Britain this boom was associated, especially in its later stages, with a rapid growth in iron production and in coal output. In both these spheres there were new technical developments, but the innovations introduced can scarcely be described as major. The steel innovations of the 1860s had limited impact, while the innovations in coal (deeper pits, mechanical fans, more efficient winding machinery and underground haulage methods, and the beginnings of mechanical coal-cutting) were part of a long continuous process of minor modifications and refinements rather than representing anything startlingly new. The long string of major innovations in shipbuilding—the screw, the steel ship, better boilers and the compound engine—is of recurrent importance in the post-1870 period but had more impact in the early 1880s than in the 1870s. The arguments attempting to relate the upswing of the late 1860s and early 1870s to innovational activity are therefore unconvincing.

The upswing of 1879–83 was dominated by steel. The development of cheap mass-produced steel was the major breakthrough, though the crucial innovations were more than two decades old. But the strategic importance of this development cannot be judged by the expansion of steel output alone. It brought about, though not immediately, a revolution in engineering increasing the efficiency of steam-driven machinery, machine tools, arms, and hydraulic machinery, and spreading new methods, such as greater standardisation and the use of more interchangeable parts facilitating mass production in several sectors. In the shipbuilding boom steel ships were produced in quantity for the first time. The electric lighting and telephone booms reflected quite recent innovations, but they were of future rather than present significance. The upswing of the early 1880s can therefore be related fairly directly to innovational activity, though the innovations to which it refers had mainly been introduced some years earlier. Yet, as we can see from Table 8, this upswing was relatively weak in the context of most pre-1900 booms, and the slower rate of income growth is not what we should expect to find in a boom associated with innovation. The upswing of the late 1880s was primarily a foreign investment boom, and activity in many domestic industries remained sluggish. It is difficult to connect this upswing with innovational activity, with the possible exception of innovations applied abroad.

The domestic boom of 1894–1900, though stronger, had little to do with innovations. Schumpeter described it as consisting 'of odds and ends'.[1] There was a marked expansion in electrical engineering, and its share in domestic investment rose from 0·4 per cent to 3·2 per cent over the decade. Most of the metropolitan electric lighting companies had been established by 1897, and in 1896 electric traction had been applied to the Underground. But the quantitative weight of such developments was still negligible by 1900. The bicycle boom fits the innovational theory quite well, though again the *initial* innovations had taken place many years before. The opening up of the South African gold-mines affected the British economy via increased exports to South Africa, but it was an 'innovation' only in the broad Schumpeterian sense. Although there were minor technological advances over a wide range of industries, the main carriers of the boom were old sectors of the economy little affected by new techniques, such as building, brewing and distilling. The upswing was also assisted by cheap money, yet easy money conditions did not stimulate much in the way of innovational activity.[2]

British economic fluctuations between 1900 and 1914 are largely explicable in terms of the impact of developments abroad. Exports and foreign investment governed the character of the cycle, and the flows of goods and capital were induced more by traditional developments (such as railway construction) than by new advances. Nevertheless, innovations in electric power in the transport and

[1] Schumpeter, *Business Cycles*, p. 381.

[2] For details of this upswing see E. M. Sigsworth and J. M. Blackman, 'The Home Boom of the 1890s' in J. Saville (ed.), *Studies in the British Economy*.

constructional booms of 1900 and 1907 and of oil fuel in 1912 were of some significance.[1] But in this period as a whole, all major domestic developments, whether related to innovational activity or not, were subordinate to and dominated by the impact of external events.

As is shown in the essays below,[2] there were many new technical developments and innovational activities generally between the wars, affecting not only the newer industries (such as electrical engineering, rayon and motor vehicles) but also the old (iron and steel, cement, machine tools and even coal). In part, these technical advances were stimulated by the war,[3] in part (especially in the newer sectors) they were concerned with the introduction of mass production techniques, and in part they reflected the beginnings of industrial research. The rate of growth in industrial production per man-year rose far above the pre-war levels (and was probably around 3 per cent per annum between 1920 and 1937).[4] Yet there is little evidence that the weak upswing of the late 1920s was associated with innovation. The new industries were still very small relative to total output, and the main expanding sector, building, which dominated the upswing up to 1928 was affected very little by technical developments. When housebuilding in the public sector slumped under the impact of declining subsidies, the later stages of the upswing were carried by some revival in exports induced by the much stronger booms experienced overseas. The new developments of the stock market boom in 1927–8 (films, greyhound racing tracks, gramophone records, rayon and plate glass) were only partially directly related to innovation, and made much more of an impact on the capital market than on real capital formation. Schumpeter argued that the shakiness of the world economy in the 1920s had been aggravated by the effects of agricultural innovation on primary producers which reinforced the tendency for world supply to run ahead of demand, due, among other things, to the slowing down of population growth in the industrial countries. However, it is difficult to link this factor with the cyclical performance of the British economy.

The general arguments hold up rather better for the 1930s. The revival of the new industries was a potent factor in the recovery after 1932.[5] But the expansion of these industries in this period was not noticeably associated with the *simultaneous* application of new inno-

[1] D. H. Robertson, *A Study of Industrial Fluctuation* (1915) pp. 159–62, 184–6.

[2] See below, Section B, 6, 7 and 8.

[3] As shown by R. S. Sayers, 'The Springs of Technical Progress, 1919–39', *Economic Journal*, LX (1950).

[4] London and Cambridge Economic Service, *Key Statistics of the British Economy, 1900–62*, Table D.

[5] See below, Section B, 7.

vations. Most of the important technological advances had been introduced in the 1920s (an exception was refinements in production methods for rayon staple fibre, which was manufactured only on a small scale before 1934–5) or earlier. The fundamental basic steps to which the majority of these industries can be traced, the internal combustion engine and electrification, had their origins far back in the nineteenth century. Moreover, there were other forces in the recovery which had little *directly* to do with innovation. These included the private housing boom which was an important stimulus especially before 1934, the high level of real incomes (partly the result of improving terms of trade) and the high propensity to consume of most of those in work. The recovery of the 1930s would not have been as strong without prior innovational activity, but the causal sequence from individual innovations to a particular cyclical expansion is obscure.

Professor Sayers was rather sceptical of the role played by innovations in inter-war business cycles. Since the motor car had less impact in Britain at this time than in the United States, there was no spectacular innovation in the inter-war period comparable with the impetus given by the railways to some nineteenth-century booms. However, he argued that innovation moderated the slumps of 1920–1, when shipbuilding activity was maintained higher than would otherwise have been the case because of technical changes in methods of propulsion and in hull design, and of 1930–1, when the introduction of new stainless steels held up activity relatively well in the Sheffield steel industry. From this he drew the conclusion that 'technical progress moderated slumps in two of their blackest spots—in shipbuilding and the steel industry, and it did relatively little to exaggerate the booms'.[1] But these examples are quantitatively insignificant, and scarcely form the basis of a general argument that innovations are more crucial in depressions than in periods of high activity.

This brief survey suggests that the verdict on an innovations theory to explain British economic fluctuations between 1870 and 1939 must be 'not proven'. There were cycles which were dominated by old-established sectors which had benefited very little from recent innovational activity. On the other hand, in several upswings new industries were significant carriers of revival. It was only very rarely, however, that rapid cyclical expansion in new sectors was accompanied by a *simultaneous* application of major innovations. More frequently, the key innovations had been introduced several years or even a few decades earlier. Although innovations can be made

[1] Sayers, in *Economic Journal*, LX (1950) 290.

responsible for subsequent booms by referring to the 'carry-over effects' concept, the difficulties of tracing the links can lead to tampering with the evidence to suit the theory. It might be argued, for instance, that if growth is concentrated in boom periods the discovery that a few rapidly expanding sectors dominate the boom is self-evident, following inevitably from the asymmetry of the growth process. Although the growth of rapidly expanding sectors can be ascribed to innovations at some time or other, the links are often too tenuous and too many years apart to support the innovations theory. Admittedly, if investment rates are high in the upswing some of the machinery installed will incorporate minor technical modifications, but these scarcely qualify as major innovations.

Business cycles and innovations are interdependent in the sense that all aspects of a capitalist economy are interdependent. But a more precise identification of the impact of innovation on the cycle is normally possible only when both the lag between invention and innovation, and the time span between the first introduction of a technical development and its widespread application throughout an industry, are short. Very few cases can be found where both conditions are satisfied. We do not deny that innovations and technical progress can play a significant part in determining the cyclical patterns of a modern industrial economy. But there is no strong argument for making innovations the essential *cause* of fluctuations. It is very difficult to support empirically the proposition that all major upswings and downswings are brought about by the ebb and flow of innovational activity. If technical progress is a major determinant of growth, and if growth takes place in spurts rather than at a steady rate, then it is very probable that there will be a strong, if hidden, link between technical progress and cycles. But there is no need to explain all fluctuations in economic activity in terms of discontinuities in the flow of innovations, *à la* Schumpeter. It is more plausible to treat the impact of innovational activity as random erratic shocks acting on the rhythm of economic activity, with the cyclical mechanism explained by variables other than technical progress.

## Building and Economic Fluctuations[1]

Fluctuations in building activity may have an important influence on fluctuations in economic activity as a whole, though the exact

[1] This section draws upon H. W. Richardson and D. H. Aldcroft, *Building in the British Economy between the Wars* (1968) chs. 1, 3, 12.

nature of the influence is complex and not easily understood. The main reason for the importance of building is its quantitative weight in total investment. In approximate terms, residential building accounted for up to 20 per cent of total domestic capital formation over the period 1870–1914 and for over 30 per cent between the wars; when non-residential building is included, the share of total building in investment is considerably higher. Moreover, investment in building fluctuates more widely than most other kinds of investment, and is not very sensitive to minor fluctuations in income. For these reasons, fluctuations in the economy as a whole are more likely to be influenced by movements in building than vice versa.

It is clear, however, that the relationship between building and business has not remained the same over time. In the first half of the nineteenth century building activity tended to synchronise with business cycles. From about the 1860s, however, fluctuations in building were detached from the Juglars and followed a course of their own. Non-residential building continued to move in line with other forms of investment, but housebuilding became subject to separate influences. Thus we can observe in the period 1870–1914 housebuilding cycles of greater periodicity and amplitude than business cycles; troughs are to be found in 1871, 1890 and 1912 with booms in 1876 and in 1898 (though the peak here continued into 1903). Building booms overlapped upswings in general economic activity, and continued to expand after the downturn in the economy as a whole. On the other hand, when building slumps did emerge they lasted much longer than the normal troughs of business cycles.

These long swings are not in evidence in the inter-war economy. Although this might in part reflect the brevity of the period and the distortions due to two world wars, the main reason for the non-existence of long building cycles is that conditions had fundamentally changed. The international economy no longer had much of an influence on building activity, primarily because the introduction of strict immigration controls in the United States and elsewhere meant a sharp reduction in international migration flows. Foreign investment was much lower, and there is no evidence that capital was diverted abroad from profitable employment at home in housebuilding. Indeed the flow of funds into building societies increased as fast in the 1920s as in the 1930s when the foreign loan embargo was in operation. The growth of the public sector in housebuilding and the replacement of investors in building by owner-occupiers financed by building society mortgages were important new features in the inter-war period which influenced the pattern and tempo of housebuilding activity. Perhaps most significant of all were the direct effects of the First World War. The war resulted in a massive housing shortage so that the severe fluctuations in housing demand that had dominated building cycles before 1914 disappeared. Instead, in the inter-war period there was a persistently high level of potential demand for houses subject to the constraints of income and the availability of finance.

In broad terms, the most striking aspects of an inter-war comparison between fluctuations in building and in the economy at large is their lack of correspondence in the 1920s and their similarity (at least in regard to the turning points) in the 1930s. The main causes of their opposite movements in the first post-war decade were exogenous, particularly changes in the level of government subsidies. Subsidised housebuilding (both public and private) accounted for about three-fifths of the houses built over the years 1920–9. The expansions in housebuilding in 1920–1, 1926 and 1927 were due to high subsidies, while the declines in 1927–8 and to a lesser extent 1921–2 are most easily explained by subsidy reductions. In the 1930s, the upswing in housebuilding differed in character from that in the general economy. There was a strong upsurge in 1932–4 followed by a flattening out of the housebuilding curve between 1934 and 1937; the recovery between 1932 and 1937 in the economy as a whole was steady and continuous, though the pace of recovery slackened temporarily in 1934–5. Looking at building fluctuations in isolation the most noticeable feature is the existence of two housing booms, the first based on subsidised building between 1925 and 1927 and the second based on private owner-occupier demand, stretching from 1933 to 1938.[1] The occurrence of two housing booms, one superimposed upon the other, suggests that the notion of long building cycles characterised by the familiar trough–peak–trough sequence is not strictly applicable to the inter-war period. There are theoretical reasons why building should fluctuate in cycles longer than the business cycle: the durability of the product; the importance of slow-changing demographic variables in the potential demand for houses; the length of production and reaction lags; the nature of expectations among builders, housing investors and house buyers; the independence of regional building fluctuations and its consequences for the national pattern. But there are other factors at work making building respond to different phases of the business cycle—mainly the impact on building of changes in building costs, interest rates and in real incomes. The interaction of these forces is very complex and even so provides only incomplete answers to the problem of the

[1] This boom slackened after 1934.

interrelationships between building activity and economic fluctuations. General economic trends in the economy and the institutional environment are also important, a point that can be illustrated by a brief discussion of the reasons for the long swing in building before 1914.

It used to be believed that the building cycle was 'a migration cycle in disguise', that a building slump in Britain was normally found in periods of high emigration and foreign investment and, conversely, booms occurred when emigration was low and most investment was being undertaken at home. Moreover, because these long-run flows of men and capital were linked (especially before 1890) to the development of the Atlantic economy, inverse building cycles were found in Britain and the United States.[1] More recently, this hypothesis has been modified. It has been recognised that the inverse relationship could, in part at least, be the result of accidental factors, that the argument neglected the important role played by internal influences on housebuilding, and that fluctuations in the numbers of emigrants were too small to account for the wide fluctuations in housing demand unless rural–urban migration was inversely correlated with emigration.

The transformation from the short pro-cyclical building fluctuations of the first half of the nineteenth century to the longer cycles of later decades can be explained by internal factors. The rise in the share of the middle class in total internal migration in the later part of the century meant that some migration was not constrained by the business cycle. Moreover, income levels were better maintained in depressions, while the absence of internal financial crises after 1866 and the development of new sources of building finance permitted building activity to continue *after* the upper turning point of the business cycle. Suburban housebuilding was increasing in importance, and this took place in the form of suburban waves lasting longer than the upswings in general economic activity. Regional

[1] It has even been argued that the 7- to 10-year periodicity of the business cycle might have been the accidental result of these inverse cycles in building, migration and investment, and that it 'derived mainly from the existence of two unsynchronised waves, each of roughly twice that duration, in home and foreign investment respectively' (R.C.O. Matthews, *The Trade Cycle* (1959) p. 220). While we accept that there is a degree of interdependence between the cycles of different periodicities in the economy (among which the building cycle is merely one), we find Matthews's conclusion unconvincing. A similar argument to that of Matthews stressing the causal influence of the United States transport–building cycle has been put forward by D. J. Coppock, 'The Causes of Business Fluctuation', *Transactions of the Manchester Statistical Society* (1959). For further analysis of Kuznets cycles see W. A. Lewis and P. J. O'Leary, 'Secular Swings in Production and Trade 1870–1913', *Manchester School*, XXIII (1955).

differences in the timing of peaks and troughs in building activity were considerable, a fact tending to lengthen the national cycle. The Atlantic economy thesis neglects the influence of domestic credit conditions, internally generated fluctuations in income, the speculative character of the industry and the operation of reaction lags, all of which had a more than negligible impact on fluctuations in building activity before 1914.

Whatever the causes of the pre-1914 building cycle, it is clear that fluctuations in building differed markedly from those in business activity generally. In some circumstances, the effect of building activity was to dampen fluctuations in the economy as a whole; in other circumstances, building had a destabilising influence. In the 1870s building reached a peak (in 1876) after the business cycle had turned downwards. Thus the building boom moderated the early years of the depression of the 1870s. The building slump developed quickly, and in 1879 only 86,000 houses were built as opposed to 130,800 in 1876. Between 1879 and 1895 housebuilding activity remained uniformly low. Throughout the 1880s domestic sectors of the economy remained fairly depressed and industrial growth was low. The rate of income growth was made respectable only by income accruing from rising foreign investment and other invisible exports and by improving terms of trade. The upswings of 1880–3 and 1886–90 in the economy had no impact at all on building (just as the later upswing of 1904–7 was associated with falling building activity), supporting the argument made earlier that building activity is insensitive to modest fluctuations in national income. The long and quite strong domestic boom of the 1890s coincided with an exceptionally vigorous building boom. The general upswing got under way first in 1893–4, but after 1895 housebuilding activity expanded rapidly (the number of houses built annually increased by about 75 per cent between 1895 and 1898) reaching a peak in 1898 but not showing much decline until after 1903. The building boom almost carried the upswing of the 1890s and was much more significant quantitatively than expansion in other sectors such as electrical engineering, brewing and the bicycle industry. Once again, moreover, housebuilding was maintained after the upper turning point (in 1900) and helped to keep the economy fairly stable in the early years of the century. From 1903, however, building activity slumped almost year by year up to and into the First World War; by the years immediately before the war the annual level of housebuilding had fallen to depths unknown since the 1860s. As in the 1880s, national income continued to expand only because of the boom in foreign investment and exports; but the rate of growth was much lower than experienced in the past, and it is very doubtful whether this fact and the gravity of the building slump can be entirely coincidental.

In the inter-war period, the upward trend in building was more noticeable than its cyclical path. Non-residential building fluctuated very sharply with deep depressions in 1920–2 and 1930–2 and strong revivals in 1926–9 and 1933–7, but since non-residential building was quantitatively smaller than housebuilding and since the movements in the two sectors tended to offset each other, the course of building activity as a whole was relatively even. Within housebuilding, there were strong inverse cycles in private and local authority building. These inverse cycles had stabilising consequences so that total building activity escaped the severe slumps experienced by individual sectors, leaving only two strong upswings in the mid-1920s and after 1932.

It is obvious that building activity is affected by certain key variables which move cyclically—real income, building costs and interest rates. Bernard Weber related the cyclical influence of these variables to their trend movements. For instance, he suggested that if the trend of real incomes is rising and is in reverse direction to the trend of costs and interest rates (conditions which approximate to inter-war experience) then building will tend to move pro-cyclically. We have called this hypothesis 'the Weber thesis'.[1] Interesting as it is, it does not fully predict what happened. Building tended to expand in the early phases of business revival between the wars, and to decline in the later stages. The relative falling off in building activity in the late 1902s and the mid-1930s is to be explained by factors not considered in the Weber model. But the rapid expansion of 1932–4 is consistent with the argument, if by real incomes we mean real wage incomes. Real earnings expanded fastest in 1930–1, interest rates fell most sharply between 1931 and 1933 and building costs between 1930 and 1932. Assuming a one- or two-year lag, these factors could have been crucial in the building boom in 1933 and 1934. A serious drawback of the argument is that it treats the relationship between building and economic activity as a one-way influence, ignoring the interdependence between the two, and the potential impact of building activity on the business cycle.

This impact may be of considerable importance for the explanation of business cycles. Before 1914 building often continued to expand after the upper turning point of the Juglar. On the other hand, it is often argued that building leads other sectors at the lower turning point. Any tendency for building to lead general activity is not

[1] See Richardson and Aldcroft, *Building*, ch. 11.

supported by the evidence before 1914, when exports seemed to be the normal 'lead' sector. In the 1920s, observation is obscured by the effects of the war and by the influence of changing subsidy levels on building. In the 1930s, however, building probably led the way out of the depression. The lower turning point in housebuilding is, in fact, found in 1928 before the depression developed, and private unsubsidised housebuilding expanded year by year after 1928. In 1932, building plans revived some months before signs of recovery in other sectors. But this merely suggests that depression forces do not adversely affect expectations in building as much as elsewhere, and any tendency for building to lead should not be taken to imply causal significance.

Similarly, the association between a housing boom and a general upswing in Britain in the 1930s (and the association between housing and overall booms in the United States in the 1920s) does not necessarily suggest a causal dependence of economic activity on building fluctuations. Other examples can be found which contradict the correlation; for instance, Japanese experience in the 1930s where the strongest upswing in the world developed without much of an expansion in building, or Sweden where building lagged behind the general recovery by over a year. Indeed, when there is an association between a building and a general boom this is usually because *both* respond to common stimuli, such as a sustained increase in real incomes or a favourable shift in expectations.

These negative conclusions do not imply that fluctuations in building activity had no influence on the business cycle. The lack of correspondence between building and business in the 1920s kept the economy on a fairly even course, because building investment usually expanded when industrial production declined (as in 1920–1, 1926 and 1930) while building tended to fall off when industrial production increased (as in 1921–2 and in 1928 and 1929). Only in the years 1922–5 did they move upwards together. In the 1930s, the private housing boom reinforced the early stages of general recovery in 1932–4 while the flattening out of housebuilding after 1934 had a dampening effect on the upswing in the economy at large; at the beginning of the decade the slight expansion in houses built between 1930 and 1932 moderated the slump. The general role of *housebuilding* in the 1930s was to act as a stabiliser, moving counter-cyclically and offsetting fluctuations elsewhere in the economy. At the same time, however, the rapid expansion in private residential building after 1932 facilitated, though it was not the sole cause of, recovery.[1]

[1] See below, Section B, 7, and H. W. Richardson, *Economic Recovery in Britain, 1932–39* (1967).

This discussion of the interrelationships between fluctuations in building activity and in the economy in the 1870–1914 period and between the wars makes it clear that there was no clear unidirectional causal relationship. Before 1914, building cycles were, to a great extent, independent of Juglars and their impact on the economy was determined by whether booms and slumps in the two generically different cycles coincided. The turning points in business cycles were brought about by factors other than building. On the other hand, a tendency for high levels of building activity to persist after the upper turning point in major upswings in the economy as a whole (i.e. in the early 1870s and the late 1890s) moderated the slumps which followed. Analysis of the interdependence between building and economic activity in the inter-war period is complicated by the effects of the First World War and by the entry of the government into housebuilding. The most general observation possible is that building activity, especially housebuilding, had a stabilising effect on general economic fluctuations. What is undeniable is that some consideration of building and its influence increases our understanding of the nature of business cycles during this period.

## Monetary Factors

It was once believed that monetary influences were the primary cause of fluctuations and that the business cycle was a purely monetary phenomenon. However, this view has been discredited for a long time, and intermittent attempts to rehabilitate monetary theories have never been fully successful. Nevertheless monetary forces may have considerable impact on the amplitude and periodicity of cycles. For instance, high (and rising) interest rates may discourage expansion in booms while low (and falling) interests rates may help create conditions favourable for revivals in slumps; in this way monetary movements will tend to have a stabilising effect. But the situation may be more complicated than this. If the supply of money for transactions purposes becomes inelastic in the later stages of an upswing, or if rising interest rates choke off investment, expansion may be checked or even reversed; in such circumstances the monetary factor acts as a ceiling. Moreover, because of the existence of lags, interest rates reverse and credit conditions change later than the turning points of the cycle itself. In their early stages, therefore, both the upswing and downswing may be reinforced by monetary factors. Thus it is possible for monetary forces to have a destabilising effect on economic fluctuations. To sum up, at its minimum, elasticity in the monetary system has an accommodating role in the cycle enabling the upswing, due to real forces, to be financed, while flexible monetary policies may be a necessary prerequisite of revival from a slump. Whether stabilising or destabilising tendencies predominate will depend on circumstances. In certain, probably rare, conditions, credit restriction may actually cause the recession.

Conditions in the period between 1870 and 1914 were favourable for a monetary policy to be effective. After 1866, there were no financial crises breaking after the upper turning point of the cycle, and thereby increasing instability. The government sector was small, and fiscal and debt management policies in their modern sense unknown so that the Bank of England could operate continuously with no fear of conflict with other aspects of policy. The Bank of England, in effect, kept the single reserve for the whole financial system, had an added degree of control over the money market by engaging in direct dealings with the public, and was willing to act as lender of last resort. The main instrument employed, Bank rate, was an effective means of control over the market, especially later in the period when it was supplemented by open market operations. The money market accepted changes in Bank rate as an indicator of changing conditions, and adjusted itself to these changes rapidly. Moreover, the economy as a whole adjusted to changes in credit conditions. First, a large part of business (especially that directly engaged in international trade) was financed by borrowed money, and commitments had to be revised with changes in interest rates. Secondly, for monetary policy to be effective changes in the volume of orders had to lead quickly to changes in the price of goods and of labour. Wages and prices were much more flexible than in later periods. Thirdly, recognition of Bank rate as an index meant that it affected business psychology and expectations.

The system had a serious potential drawback. International trade and finance were having an increasing influence on the monetary system. The equilibrating mechanism operated was a reliance on credit variations within a system of fixed exchange rates, and the maintenance of the convertibility of sterling into gold at the legal parity was the dominant objective of monetary policy. This meant that the main factor influencing changes in Bank rate was alterations in the Bank of England's reserve ratio in response to external drains and inflows of gold. Thus when Bank rate was raised and credit restricted, economic activity might contract at home for reasons connected primarily with the balance of payments situation and its effects on the Bank of England's reserves. However, the worst consequences of this situation were usually avoided because the Bank of England learnt how to shield the domestic economy by not correcting for minor temporary drains, or even by entering the gold market as an alternative to changing interest rates. On the other hand, the protection of reserves remained the overriding objective. The Bank was unwilling to accept the greater accumulations of excess reserves and the periodic declines in reserves that might have ensured internal stability. However, the situation was relieved by the fact that external flows of gold and reserves often offset internal flows. In the upswing, gold and/or silver were moved from the Bank of England's reserves into internal circulation to meet rising transactions demand. We would also expect to find an external drain of gold in the upswing, because of the effects of induced import demand on the balance of payments. Yet there was an increasing tendency for the United Kingdom to enjoy a net *import* of gold during the upswing, because high interest rates attracted funds from abroad. The changes in the Bank of England's reserves were consequently not as great as they might have been. Of course, in order to attract the necessary gold, interest rates were sometimes pushed up higher than warranted by domestic economic conditions.

Rostow assigned only a passive role to monetary measures in nineteenth-century economic fluctuations, arguing that 'the Bank, and the monetary system as a whole, would appear to have been an essentially negative element in the British trade cycles of this era'.[1] He pointed out, as D. H. Robertson had before him, that the early stages of the upswing were stimulated by a continued tendency for interest rates to fall. In the later stages credit tightened and both market interest rates and Bank rate rose. After the peak, however, interest rates continued to rise, but the Bank's discounts rose, often rapidly. Up to the upper turning point, the Bank of England helped to finance expansion by meeting the legitimate demands of trade; after the upper turning point its function was to meet a crisis in confidence by acting as lender of last resort. Rostow believed that the tightening of money markets and rising interest rates, although they reflected a monetary limit to expansion, were not material factors in inducing downturns because the supply of money was more elastic than the supply of other factors of production. This view is supported by Tinbergen's analyses which suggested the elasticity of supply of central bank credit was about 1·2.[2] Also, the increases in interest charges were modest relative to changes in other costs, and were

[1] Rostow, *British Economy*, p. 57.

[2] Tinbergen, *Business Cycles in the U.K.*, pp. 95–6.

unlikely to have had a serious adverse effect on the demand for credit.

Rostow's judgement that the Bank of England's role was entirely passive does not do full justice to the effectiveness of monetary policy at this time. Since Bank rate moved consistently upwards in the upswing and downwards in recessions, with the exception of the lags noted above, it acted in general terms counter-cyclically. The Bank of England did not consciously follow a stabilising monetary policy, since the state of its reserves consistently governed its actions. But these actions in response to changes in reserves nevertheless had, fortuitously, a stabilising effect. There was a strong inverse correlation between movements in Bank rate and the Bank of England's reserve ratios. These ratios also moved inversely with the business cycle, so that the gearing of Bank rate changes to the reserve ratio resulted in the positive correlation between Bank rate and domestic business cycle fluctuations required for a counter-cyclical monetary policy.[1] But this was an accidental, though welcome, by-product of the Bank's actions. Thus a rise in Bank rate in the upswing was aimed at attracting short-term funds and gold from abroad to meet an incipient gold loss; if the rise also checked domestic investment this was incidental. Although this incidental effect was very often consistent with the requirements of the economy, at other times (such as in 1907) it occasionally led to an undesirable disturbance of economic activity. Moreover, in downswings Bank rate was dropped not explicitly to moderate slumps but to increase earnings or to keep in touch with the money market. The main reason why monetary policy worked so well in this period was because there happened to be 'no major conflict between external stability and internal stability'.[2]

Interest rate changes varied in pace from cycle to cycle. In some cycles, interest rates, though still moving in the expected manner, moved rather sluggishly. Usually this sluggishness could be explained by exceptional circumstances. Thus in the downswing of the middle and late 1870s interest rates moved downwards and short-term funds became plentiful only very slowly. The delay was due to several factors: a non-commercial demand for gold, bank failures, political uncertainty, an intermittent drain of funds from London to the United States, and an adverse balance of payments problem in the years 1876–8. Conversely, in the 1890s money remained cheap for a long time despite the substantial domestic boom in the economy.

[1] A. I. Bloomfield, *Monetary Policy under the International Gold Standard: 1880–1914* (1959) pp. 29–40.

[2] Ibid., p. 38.

Here the main factors at work were the increased world supply of gold (the opening up of mines in South Africa), and heavy gold inflows into the Bank of England consequent upon United States financial policies.

In the inter-war period up to 1931 decisions on monetary policy were dominated as much by external conditions as they were before 1914; by the strain on the exchange rate up to 1925 pending the restoration of the gold standard, and between 1925 and 1931 by the strain on gold and exchange reserves. In the early part of the period the main precondition of restoring gold was to reduce the price level relative to the American. Since prices in the United States fell rapidly after 1920, this aim was difficult to achieve. It called for drastic credit restrictions, and interest rates were held at high levels long after the post-war boom had collapsed. Thus Bank rate which had been raised in November 1919 to 6 per cent to curb the speculative boom at home, was raised again to 7 per cent in April 1920 and kept at this level for a year, despite the fact that in the meantime the boom had collapsed. Interest rates remained high, despite the depths of the slump, even into 1922. Thus monetary policy was dictated by external events and by preoccupation with the exchange rate position, not by any concern with internal fluctuations. Similarly, between 1925 and 1929 the balance of payments surplus was insufficient to carry on investing abroad at former levels, and further reductions in prices were needed to make exports more competitive. The Bank of England sought to attract in foreign funds by relatively high interest rates, which had the secondary results of restraining home demand and keeping down prices. On two occasions only before 1931 were monetary measures employed with the dominant aim of influencing domestic levels of activity. These were the deflationary measures of 1919–20 introduced to control the boom which was about to burst of its own accord, and the reflationary steps taken in the winter of 1929–30 in an attempt to create conditions favourable to long-term investment, an attempt which failed because the world depression was developing too quickly for interest rate movements to counter its effects.

Over the 1920s as a whole, therefore, monetary factors had on balance a destabilising effect. Yet it is difficult to accept that they were a major depressant on the British economy. Interest rates (though higher than the average before 1914, in the 1930s and in the cheap money phase of the post-1945 period) were moderate compared with recent experience, and it is improbable that investment demand was sufficiently interest-elastic for many viable investment decisions justified by market conditions to be postponed. Sayers argued that the real deflationary forces at work were the depression in the export trades and the competition of imports, rather than high interest rates.[1]

In the second quarter of 1932 a cheap money policy was introduced to check an inflow of short-term capital and to facilitate the government's war loan conversion scheme, and this provided a favourable environment for recovery. Bank rate was, in fact, kept at 2 per cent between June 1932 and August 1939, and was consequently ineffective as a stabilisation instrument. Even in the later stages of the upswing in 1936 and 1937, the cheap money policy was not reversed (though there was some hardening of long-term interest rates and a marked deceleration in expansion of the supply of money). However, for most of the recovery period monetary influences were compatible with the demands of the economy. Cheap money had a favourable impact on building activity, making it easier for builders to get overdrafts, stimulating the demand for houses as an investment, and leading to reduced mortgage rates. It helped to drive institutional investors from the trustee into the industrial capital market, and it may have permitted the financing of some projects which would have been postponed at higher interest rates. But the building boom can be explained more easily by non-monetary factors, and there were important sources of finance for industrial investment other than the new issue market and the banks. Cheap money was necessary for a smooth recovery, but it was not the direct cause of revival.

It is a reasonable generalisation that over the period between 1870 and 1939 the primary criteria of monetary action were external conditions, particularly the state of the reserves, rather than domestic stabilisation. Even in the 1930s stabilisation of the exchange rates remained an objective of policy, through the creation of the Exchange Equalisation Account and restrictions on overseas lending insulated the economy more effectively from external influences. However, despite the dominance of external aims, steps taken by the Bank of England had relatively few adverse effects on the domestic economy. Indeed, monetary factors had a marked stabilising effect on the business cycle, especially before 1914. But this was a fortuitous by-product of measures taken on other grounds, not a conscious attempt to stabilise the level of economic activity in the United Kingdom. Only in the 1920s was monetary policy persistently at odds with the requirements of the domestic economy. But the harmful effects of credit restriction and high interest rates can easily

[1] R. S. Sayers, 'Bank Rate in the Twentieth Century', *Central Banking after Bagehot* (1957) p. 79.

be exaggerated. The causes of the economy's sluggishness are to be found outside the monetary sphere, and, in any event, it would not be fair to describe the 1920s in terms of complete stagnation.[1]

## Random Shocks

One of the main reasons why a single business cycle model does not provide a complete basis for the explanation of cycles is the fact that such a model cannot cope with all the variables at work in the economy at each moment of time. In particular, a system built upon such a model cannot take account of the unsystematic and unpredictable shocks that influence fluctuations. Tinbergen's econometric model of the U.K. business cycle between 1870 and 1914 revealed large unexplained residuals, which suggest that random shocks had some importance. As Frisch showed, random shocks may play a crucial role in economic fluctuations by keeping damped cycles inherent in the structure of economy oscillating.[2] Emphasis on such shocks does not require us to abandon the view that the economy exhibits an inherent tendency to fluctuate, i.e. that once key variables in the economy move in a certain direction there is a mechanism perpetuating this movement, and also that there are endogenous factors which may tend to bring upswings and downswings to a halt, and possibly to reverse them. It has sometimes been argued that economic fluctuations are *only* the result of random shocks, but mathematical tests of randomness do not yield a rhythm in economic activity that looks anything like a business cycle. However, if we accept that the economy tends inherently to fluctuate, however slightly, shocks can be important for perpetuating fluctuations. Moreover, they may in some cases play a critical part in reversing explosive upward and downward movements at the turning points.[3] For instance, in the later stages of an upswing when supply inelasticities are developing and expectations are beginning to waver, an adverse shock may easily start a downturn.

Shocks may sometimes affect the economy as a whole. They may lengthen the periodicity of the cycle by reinforcing the upswing or downswing, or they may shorten it by precipitating the turning

[1] See below, Section B, 6.

[2] R. Frisch, 'Propagation Problems and Impulse Problems in Dynamic Economics', *Economic Essays in Honour of Gustav Cassel* (1933).

[3] J. S. Duesenberry (*Business Cycles and Economic Growth* (1958)) assigns an important role to external shocks in his explanation of the turning points of business cycles.

point. The most violent shock within one period was, of course, the First World War. The fluctuations of the whole inter-war period show its effects to some extent, particularly in certain sectors such as building (as a result of the cessation of building activity during the war and the demographic disturbances). And it is clear that the violent fluctuations of the first three or four post-war years, the immediate post-war boom and the collapse which followed, were the direct result of the war itself. The other wars of the period, important shocks though they were, usually affected only a few sectors. The general financial stringency associated with the Boer War lasted only a short time, and its main impact was felt by shipping, coal and shipbuilding in response to a demand for increased tonnage for the conveyance of troops and supplies to South Africa. In 1898 Atlantic freights soared as a result of the effects of the Spanish–American War, and this recurred in the Near East in 1912 because of the Balkan Wars. In 1870–1 and again in 1900 manufacturers of khaki clothing in the West Riding profited from large orders. Finally, the growth in rearmament spending in the late 1930s reinforced the late stages of the upswing especially in iron and steel, engineering and shipbuilding.

Very often, shocks were associated with financial disturbances. Internal crises were rare during this period (even the repercussions following the failure of the City of Glasgow Bank in October 1878 had little effect on the economy), but financial crises abroad had more of an impact. For instance, the recession of 1907–8 was a complete distortion of the normal cyclical pattern resulting from a severe financial crisis in the United States. Industrial disputes were another source of shocks. The General Strike of 1926 and the associated seven-months coal strike reversed an upswing in industrial production, and was also responsible for the supernormal increase in activity in 1927, making up for ground lost in the previous year. Before 1914 the engineering disputes of 1897 and 1908 had had more than a marginal impact on the industry, while the transport strike of 1911 dampened activity in a number of industries, particularly the woollen trade. Tariffs can be regarded as another shock; for instance, the woollen industry incurred serious difficulties in the 1890s because of the raising of tariffs in the United States. Similarly British export growth in the 1920s was interrupted intermittently as a result of tariff increases abroad. Year-to-year crop fluctuations overseas also had an important influence on the cyclical behaviour of the shipbuilding industry and of the export industries generally.

This raises an important question. We have seen that fluctuations in exports were a key variable in British business cycles, especially before 1914. But how far were these export fluctuations due to random factors? By the late nineteenth century economic fluctuations were becoming more international in the sense that booms (and slumps) occurred simultaneously in many countries, yet a disaggregated analysis shows that different trades varied considerably in their experience according to economic conditions in their main markets. Crop fluctuations governed these conditions to a considerable extent and, if these were random, emphasis on the international transmission of business cycles from the United States (or Europe) may give a misleading impression of the determinants of fluctuations in British exports. Saul went so far as to argue that 'Political unrest and bad harvests played a powerful part' and that 'the attempt to fit the varied experiences of the British international economy to any regular recurrent pattern of events' was 'unconvincing'.[1] Tinbergen suggested that foreign investment and its impact on the British economy might be regarded as a random variable if investments in new countries were autonomous.[1] Moreover, innovations, sometimes an endogenous element in business cycle theory as in Schumpeterian analysis, may be treated as random shocks, occurring irregularly and, while not cyclical in themselves, sustaining fluctuations arising from inherent tendencies in the system to produce damped cycles. Indeed, exploring the relationship between technical progress and cycles from the standpoint of regarding innovations as erratic shocks may be a more fruitful and realistic approach than the more ambitious framework outlined by Schumpeter. These examples suggest that the boundary separating an 'innovations theory' or an 'exports theory' of the cycle from endogenous self-regenerating models disturbed by random shocks may be very thin indeed.

## Conclusions

The periodicity and amplitude of business cycles over the period 1870–1939 remained fairly constant. This is rather surprising in view of the marked differences in the pre-1914 and inter-war environments, and to some extent it must be regarded as the result of accidental factors. All business cycles are historical individuals, and their main features vary from cycle to cycle. The boom of the early 1870s was characterised by heavy foreign investment with high levels of

[1] S. B. Saul, *Studies in British Overseas Trade, 1870–1914* (1960) pp. 130, 133.
[2] Tinbergen, *Business Cycles in the U.K.*, p. 124.

induced home investment. The slump down to 1879 was serious but moderated by a housing boom. In the following decade there was a major revival in foreign investment and emigration. The minor boom of the early 1880s was dominated by new, primarily domestic developments, but the stronger upswing of the late 1880s was based upon expansion abroad, as shown by rapid income growth but low industrial growth. In the early 1890s the economy was severely depressed, with a slump in both home and foreign investment. From 1894 to 1895, however, a strong domestic boom developed based on a tremendous housing boom but affecting a wide range of domestic industries as well. Economic activity in the first few years of this century was rather unsteady, but held up by high levels of building activity even though the housing boom had reached its peak in 1898. However, from 1905 up to 1914 there was an explosive foreign investment and export boom, apart from a sharp interruption in 1907–8. Despite the high growth of staple exports and the rapid increase in invisible earnings, the period between 1900 and 1914 was one of low overall growth. In the inter-war period, there were marked fluctuations in the first post-war decade: an immediate post-war boom followed by a sharp severe slump, and then a relatively weak and unsteady upswing up to 1929, interrupted in 1926 by the effects of the General Strike. Export sluggishness, excess capacity in the formerly great staple industries, and high unemployment were dominant features of the decade. The depression after 1929, though severe in comparison with previous slumps, was mild relative to experience elsewhere in the world, and was caused entirely by external events. Revival after 1932 was based on the home market and was dominated by a building boom (especially in private residential construction) and by the expansion of new industries; its strength was assisted by policy measures which insulated the economy from continued depression forces abroad.

In view of the variety of these cycles, it is not surprising that economic fluctuations over the seventy years as a whole cannot be explained in terms of a single causal factor. Exports consistently led at both turning points before 1914, and at the upper turning point between the wars. Moreover, before 1914 the fluctuations in exports were more severe than in national income. Yet some of the strongest upswings of the period were domestically based, and it is misleading to treat exports as the main causal variable. Innovational activity and variations in the rate of technical progress had an important impact on the business cycle, but the links between specific innovations and individual fluctuations are obscure. It is more satisfactory to treat innovations as random shocks helping the economic system to continue oscillating. However, both exports and technical progress have an important place in any explanation of fluctuations over this period, and emphasis of their role offers hope of reconciling the trend and the cycle.

Building fluctuations had a sizeable impact on business cycles, but this varied from cycle to cycle before 1914 depending on whether or not booms and slumps in building and business coincided. But especially in the mid-1870s and in the early years of this century, high levels of building activity moderated slumps. Between the wars fluctuations in housebuilding had a marked stabilising effect on economy-wide fluctuations. Monetary measures, although dictated primarily by external circumstances and the Bank of England's reserve ratio as affected by gold and other flows, also helped fortuitously to stabilise internal fluctuations over this period, except in the 1920s. There is little evidence that monetary factors alone either triggered off recesssions or directly promoted revivals. No account of business fluctuations can be regarded as convincing without mentioning the influence of random shocks such as wars, financial crises, political disturbances, industrial disputes, sudden changes in commercial policy and other unpredictable factors. But the classification of a particular change as a systematic variable or as a random shock is sometimes a matter of dispute. Changes in the relative influence of the main causal factors over time and the obvious irregularity of shocks of quite different magnitudes suggests that the remarkable constancy in periodicity and amplitude of British business cycles over this period was largely accidental.

# III International Aspects

## INTRODUCTION

IT is impossible to understand the development of the British economy over the past two hundred years or more in isolation from its place in the world economy. Britain's rapid and profitable industrialisation took the form of heavy concentration of resources on a limited range of industries exporting high proportions of total outputs.[1] Because of Britain's relatively narrow resource base, this concentration was accompanied by heavy reliance on overseas sources for many raw materials, and specialisation had induced the transfer of resources out of agriculture at a faster rate than experienced by more 'balanced' economies, leading to a high dependence on food imports. Throughout the nineteenth century Britain was the pivot of the international economy, and interdependence between Britain and the rest of the world reached its peak in the 1870–1914 era. The T/Y ratio (i.e. the ratio of foreign trade to national income),[2] after growing steadily from about one-sixth at the beginning of the century, reached almost three-fifths by the 1870s, and fell little below this level up to 1914.[3] The T/Y ratio declined markedly in the inter-war period, but even in the depressed trading conditions of the 1930s the T/Y ratio remained higher than in the 1840s. Moreover, Britain's role in the world economy was by no means confined to commodity trade. She invested large sums abroad before 1914, varying in the range of 3–9½ per cent of G.N.P. or 30–65 per cent of total capital formation, and (if we include Ireland) contributed a gross total of about 10 million emigrants to countries outside Europe between 1870 and 1914.[4] And this was not all. Financial institutions and the money market of London dominated the financing of international trade, the Bank of England was the keystone of the international gold

[1] The proportion of coal exported increased from 13·4 per cent in 1870 to 32·8 per cent in 1913; over the same period the export fraction of cotton output increased from two-thirds to four-fifths, that of iron and steel products fluctuated between one-third and one-half, and that of wool tended to fall from two-fifths to one-quarter. Also, between 15 per cent and 20 per cent of the total ships built over the period 1870–1914 were sold to foreign owners.

[2] Foreign trade is defined here as domestic exports + imports + re-exports.

[3] See Table 10, col. 6.

[4] Net emigration, however, amounted to about 5 million persons.

standard, and sterling was the world currency. As a result of these factors, trading balances were settled multilaterally, and a world-wide multilateral system developed which fostered the growth of world trade in general and British trade in particular. It provided indirect protection against competition in markets outside Europe and the United States, and allowed Britain to lose ground in industrialising markets without having to face serious payments crises.

The international monetary system did not survive the First World War intact and worked imperfectly and inefficiently in the 1920s, before disintegrating into separate currency blocs. The flows of goods, labour and capital were weaker and more intermittent than before 1914. With the onset of the world depression international investment ceased. As a result of severe slumps in the 'regions of recent settlement' the direction of international migration was reversed. The primary producers ran into balance of payments difficulties, and the measures adopted to meet these resulted in exchange control, lack of convertibility and bilateral trading, all of which severely restricted the multilateral payments system. These changes in the international economy were reflected in movements in Britain's foreign trade and factor movements.

Statistics illustrating the growth of the economy's external sector before 1914 and how it reacted to the First World War and the depression are shown in Tables 10 and 11. They are mainly self-evident and it is unnecessary to comment in detail. It may be useful, however, to indicate a few general trends.

Over the period 1870–1914 the most impressive characteristic is the comparative steadiness of growth and expansion. There were fluctuations which are partially obscured by taking decennial averages rather than cyclical changes, though even in the decennial statistics some jerkiness is evident in the growth in foreign investment and emigration.[1] But the upward trend was uninterrupted. Although the import surplus widened absolutely, it remained more or less constant relative to the growth in trade, for exports increased almost as fast as imports. The break in trend in the rate of export growth had, in fact, occurred just before the beginning of our period.[2] Between 1870 and 1914 exports increased more or less steadily,

[1] The clustering of foreign investment activity in the 1880s (especially the latter half of the decade) and in the period 1905–14 is, of course, well known.

[2] Exports had increased at an annual rate of over 4½ per cent between 1820 and 1870; the rate of growth in the 1870–1914 period was halved, at 2·3 per cent. Saul argues that the mid-century rate of growth may have been exceptional because of vast railway building in Europe and the United States coupled with the immaturity of their heavy industries (S. B. Saul, *Studies in British Overseas Trade, 1870–1914* (1960) p. 34).

## Table 10

### Britain and the International Economy, 1870–1938

| | COMMODITY TRADE (1913 = 100) | | | | | | | | FOREIGN INVESTMENT | | | | | MIGRATION | |
|---|---|---|---|---|---|---|---|---|---|---|---|---|---|---|---|
| | *Imports* | *Exports* | *Re-exports* | *World trade in primary products* | *World trade in manufactures* | *T/Y (foreign trade as % of NI)* | *Merchandise imports surplus (current £m.)* | *Terms of trade (1913=100)* | *Current account balance (current £m.)* | *Income from overseas investments (current £m.)* | *Net foreign investment as % of G.N.P.* | *Accumulating capital abroad (£m.)* | | *Gross extra-European passenger movement of U.K. citizens (,000 annual average)* | *Net passenger movement (,000 annual average)* |
| | (1) | (2) | (3) | (4) | (5) | (6) | (7) | (8) | (9) | (10) | (11) | (12) | | (13) | (14) |
| 1870s | 35·9 | 35·1 | 45·5 | 31·2 | 32·1 | 59·8 | 94 | 92·4 | 50 | 53 | 3·9 | 1870 | 692 | 165 | 63 |
| | | | | | | | | | | | | 1875 | 1065 | | |
| 1880s | 47·2 | 48·2 | 63·4 | 41·2 | 42·6 | 59·0 | 94 | 87·3 | 75 | 75 | 4·9 | 1880 | 1189 | 257 | 180 |
| | | | | | | | | | | | | 1885 | 1497 | | |
| 1890s | 64·9 | 55·1 | 73·5 | 55·8 | 47·0 | 55·8 | 147 | 94·3 | 46 | 97 | 3·2 | 1890 | 1935 | 179 | 76 |
| | | | | | | | | | | | | 1895 | 2195 | | |
| 1900–13 | 85·3 | 76·8 | 84·7 | 81·6 | 76·3 | 54·8 | 156 | 97·9 | 91 | 145 | 5·4 | 1900 | 2397 | 315 | 166 |
| | | | | | | | | | | | | 1905 | 2642 | | |
| 1911–13 | 95·5 | 95·8 | 97·8 | 97·0 | 95·6 | 58·8 | 140 | 97·9 | 206 | 188 | 9·5 | 1910 | 3371 | 448 | 252 |
| | | | | | | | | | | | | 1913 | 3990 | | |
| 1920s | 103·1 | 72·1 | 85·5 | 97·8 | 88·9 | 49·3 | 328 | 126·2 | 122 | 234 | 2·4 | 1929 | 3738 | | 119 |
| 1930–8 | 117·4 | 57·4 | 64·1 | 110·7 | 81·7 | 33·9 | 340 | 145·4 | –26 | 185 | –1·0 | 1938 | 3692 | | –18 |

Sources: Cols (1), (2) and (3): up to 1913, A. H. Imlah, *Economic Elements in the Pax Britannica* (1958); from 1920, London and Cambridge Economic Service, *Key Statistics*; cols (4) and (5): F. Hilgerdt, *Industrialisation and Foreign Trade* (1945); col. (6): K. W. Deutsch and A. Eckstein, 'National Industrialisation and the Declining Share of the International Economic Sector, 1890–1959', *World Politics*, XIII (1961); cols (7), (8) and (9): up to 1913, Imlah, *Economic Elements*; from 1920, L.C.E.S., *Key Statistics*; col. (10): up to 1913, Imlah, *Economic Elements*; from 1920, Mitchell and Deane, *Abstract*; col. (11): based on C. H. Feinstein's estimates; col. (12): up to 1913, Imlah, *Economic Elements*; estimates for 1929 and 1938 based on Sir Robert Kindersley (*Economic Journal*, 1930 and 1939) but including estimates of unquoted investments; cols (13) and (14): L. Ferenczi and W. F. Wilcox (eds), *International Migration* (2 vols, 1929–31); inter-war estimates from *Board of Trade Journal*.

rather more slowly than G.N.P. but faster than manufacturing output.[1]

Exports may be a crucial leading sector in an economy's expansion and the phenomenon of export-led growth has received a good deal of attention from Kindleberger, Coppock and Lewis, among others.

TABLE II

Aspects of Britain's Trade, 1870–1938

A. RATES OF GROWTH

(*Percentage per annum*)

| | *Exports* | *Imports* | *G.N.P.* | *Manufacturing* |
|---|---|---|---|---|
| 1870–90 | 2·6 | 3·2 | 3·0 | 2·1 |
| 1890–1913 | 2·1 | 2·1 | 1·7 | 1·9 |
| 1913–25 | −1·9 | 1·1 | 0·2 | 0·9 |
| 1925–38 | −2·1 | 0·8 | 2·5 | 2·8 |

B. UNITED KINGDOM SHARES

(*Percentage*)

| | *World exports* | *World imports* | *World trade in manufacturing* | *World manufacturing production* |
|---|---|---|---|---|
| 1885 | 16·7 | 21·0 | 37·1*a* | 31·8*c* |
| | | | | 19·5*d* |
| 1913 | 13·9 | 15·8 | 25·4 | 14·1 |
| 1929 | 10·8 | 14·9 | 20·4 | 9·4*e* |
| 1938 | 10·2 | 16·8 | 19·1*b* | 9·2*f* |

*a.* 1883 *d.* 1896–1900
*b.* 1937 *e.* 1926–9
*c.* 1870 *f.* 1936–8

Sources: A. A. Maddison, 'Growth and Fluctuation in the World Economy, 1870–1960', *Banca Nazionale del Lavoro Quarterly Review*, xv (1962); B. Maddison, loc. cit., Hilgerdt, *Industrialisation*, and W. A. Lewis, 'International Competition in Manufactures', *American Economic Review*, Papers, 47 (1957).

Meyer showed that if the trend rate of growth in exports had not fallen then the rate of industrial growth between 1872 and 1907 could have been 4·1 per cent rather than the 1·75 per cent actually realised.[2] But the rate of export growth did fall off, and this fact coupled with the slight lag of exports behind G.N.P. make it most unlikely that exports were a leading sector in the long-run growth of

[1] The higher growth rate in G.N.P. than in manufacturing is explained by the growth in overseas investment income and invisible earnings abroad and by expansion of the service sectors at home.

[2] J. R. Meyer, 'An Input–Output Approach to Evaluating the Influence of Exports on British Industrial Production', *Explorations in Entrepreneurial History*, VIII (1955–6) 17.

the economy. This does not exclude the possibility that exports may have led the economy in the short-run out of slumps. In the inter-war period, the much slower growth in world trade and the troubles of Britain's export industries make the 'export-led' thesis even less applicable. On the other hand, it would be misleading to apply the logical converse—the case of exports as a lagging sector. For this to be relevant the growth rate of the economy would need to have been held down as a consequence of the poor export performance. But as we have seen the economy grew faster between the wars than before 1914. It may not be too fanciful to argue that the difficulties of the export staples facilitated this upward shift in the growth rate by forcing the transfer of resources into newer increasing returns sectors.

Although it is easy to infer rash conclusions of backwardness from Britain's declining share in world trade shown in Table 11, such inferences are grossly misleading. First, it was inevitable that her semi-monopolistic position of the 1860s could not be maintained for ever as industrialisation marched on in Western Europe and the United States. Secondly, her falling share in world trade reflected, among other things, the opening up of new countries outside Europe and the entry of increasingly large volumes of non-manufacturing products on to the world market. Apart from the rise in coal exports Britain could only expand her export trade in manufactured goods. Thirdly, Britain's share in world *trade* in manufactures declined much less steeply than her share in world manufacturing *production*. Moreover, it is dangerous to dwell too much on the commodity trade situation. The foreign challenge was not serious in capital exporting, shipping, the provision of insurance and in other financial services including short-term credits for financing international trade. There was a rising trend rate of growth in long-term lending overseas and, to a much lesser extent, in emigration. Finally, the strategic function of the United Kingdom in the development and working of the international economy was far more important than an examination of quantitative trade shares would suggest.

A striking feature of Table 10 is the marked contrast between pre- and post-1914 experience. In the inter-war period, the growth in imports slowed down, exports and re-exports fell drastically, and consequently the import surplus widened; foreign investment and emigration declined. But a distinction must be made between the 1920s and the 1930s. In the first post-war decade foreign investment was still important; new overseas issues averaged £123 million between 1922 and 1929. The current account balance held up fairly well considering the difficulties facing the export industries and the inelasticity of import demand. Net emigration remained high in comparison with those pre-war periods *not* characterised by heavy capital exports, especially in view of the growth of immigration controls abroad. In the 1930s, on the other hand, the economy had on average a current account deficit, repayments from abroad exceeded new issues and there was a net inflow of population. It was in this decade that Britain, like most other countries, turned inwards to seek domestic sources of expansion, though the withdrawal from the international economy was more marked with regard to factor movements than in commodity trade. Over the inter-war period as a whole, Britain's trading position was not as serious as the trade indices suggest. The continued rise in imports and the decline in exports were associated with parallel movements in world trade in primary products and in manufactures, and these co-variations reflected the commodity composition of imports and exports respectively. Of course, as the table shows, British import volumes rose more than world trade in primary products while export volumes declined more than world trade in manufactures, but the repercussions of these divergent trends on the balance of payments were moderated by the sharp and almost continuous improvement in the net barter terms of trade.

## Commodity Exports

The most important question relating to merchandise trade between 1870 and 1914 was how the British economy would face the difficulties posed by industrialisation abroad, initially in Western Europe and the United States but later in other parts of the world as well. In 1870, Britain's share in world manufacturing production was more than two-thirds of the combined shares of the United States, Germany and France (46·8 per cent); by 1913, this ratio had fallen to less than one-quarter, and manufacturing output in the United States alone was more than two-and-a-half times that in the United Kingdom.[1] As world industrialisation proceeded at a high rate (3·8 per cent per annum, 1870–1913),[2] the rate of growth of British exports was bound to be subject to pressure. This could be met in a number of ways. First, Britain could have developed new export categories and/or produced specialised and high-grade types of existing goods. This was the most effective long-term remedy, but it

[1] F. Hilgerdt, *Industrialisation and Foreign Trade* (1945) p. 13.

[2] Ibid., pp. 132, 134.

required a high propensity to innovate and a smooth transfer of resources from old-established into new sectors at home. A second possibility would have been to attempt to improve competitive ability in existing trading goods, i.e. to introduce sufficient productivity improvements to reduce costs by a margin large enough to hold on to markets being challenged. This alternative, though acceptable in theory, is subject to constraints. For instance, where the main markets are the domestic markets of industrialising countries, cost reductions by British exporters could be matched by the raising of tariffs. Moreover, it assumes that foreign competition takes the form of price competition, an invalid assumption in some cases. Where foreign competition took the form of direct selling methods and sales promotion, provision of after-sales service and lengthier credit terms, the response of British manufacturers and exporters had to go further than simple productivity advances in production methods, and required changes in business attitudes and in the organisation of the export trade. Business attitudes were deep-rooted and difficult to alter, and the organisational improvements very often required close co-operation among manufacturers and exporters, and their acceptance that the changes were necessary. The third solution to the challenge of industrialisation abroad was to continue to produce the same goods in more or less the same old way, but to redirect exports to new markets, possibly with the assistance of capital exports. This is, in effect, the short-run response. By postponing the need for innovation, productivity-raising measures and social change it stores up trouble for the future, making the readjustments when they do come, as they must, more painful. The simple fact that the number of new markets that can be opened up is finite makes it clear that a redirection of existing exports is no long-run solution.

Nevertheless, of the three courses of action this was the one on which most reliance was placed before 1914. Assisted by the continued growth in incomes and by the fact that new primary producing economies were developing at a rapid, if discontinuous, rate and were entering world markets, this response worked surprisingly well before 1914. But the underlying difficulties were masked, only to reassert themselves in the inter-war period. However, the problems facing exporters in the 1920s—the slow growth in world trade, the instability of income levels in the primary producing countries, and the effects of overvaluation after 1925—forced a new line of action on the economy. But despite the rapid rate of resource transfer into the new industries and their quite respectable export performance in the 1930s, Britain did not choose the first of the prescriptions outlined above. Instead, more resources were concentrated on domestic activities—housebuilding, a nation-wide electricity transmission system, new consumer durable industries catering for home demand, an expansion of service sectors generally, and the shopbuilding and public utility developments associated with suburbia. The T/Y ratio sank far below even its downward trend line.

The main trends in British overseas trade in the inter-war period cannot be described solely in terms of a decline in the importance of the foreign trade sector itself. There were also significant changes in the pattern of trade and in its direction. In the first place, the dependence on declining export categories (such as textiles) was reduced while expanding export commodities such as machinery, vehicles and electrical goods increased their shares in total exports. But the pace of readjustment looked less healthy when compared with what was happening abroad. Britain's share in the total exports of the ten leading industrial countries fell much more steeply between 1900 and 1938 in vehicles (48·0–20·7 per cent), metal manufactures (33·6–16·0 per cent), chemicals (28·0–14·7 per cent) and machinery (39·7–23·4 per cent) than in textiles (47·6–34·2 per cent).[1] Tyszynski's analyses indicated the same conclusion: that Britain's falling share in world trade in manufactures (according to his figures, a decline from 32·5 per cent in 1899 to 22·4 per cent in 1937)[2] was not primarily due to a commodity structure adverse to growth as much as to an inability to compete in old and new sectors alike.

Secondly, there were marked shifts in the relative importance of different export markets between the wars. With the exception of the decline of the United States market, these shifts were more extensive than those experienced before 1914. These shifts were due to many forces associated with the radical change in the international environment, but two predominated. Slow economic growth in Europe and increased restrictions on trade resulted in a sharp fall in intra-European trade particularly between the main manufacturing economies. Trade between the three most important manufacturing economies (Britain, Germany and France) fell to only 50 per cent of the 1913 level.[3] The other main development affecting the geographical pattern of the export trade was the breakdown of multilateralism and the consequent negotiation of bilateral trade agreements in the 1930s. The most important of these were with certain

[1] R. E. Baldwin, 'The Commodity Composition of Trade: Selected Industrial Countries, 1900–54', *Review of Economics and Statistics*, XL (1958). A slightly redeeming feature was the increased share in miscellaneous manufactures (from 18·9 per cent of the ten industrial countries' exports in 1900 to 20·1 per cent in 1938).

[2] H. Tyszynski, 'World Trade in Manufactured Commodities, 1899–1950', *Manchester School*, XIX (1951).

[3] I. Svennilson, *Growth and Stagnation in the European Economy* (1954).

TABLE 12
Geographical Distribution of British Exports, 1870–1938
(*Percentage*)

| | *N. and N.E. Europe* | *W. Europe* | *Central and S.E. Europe* | *S. Europe and N. Africa* | *Turkey and Mid. East* | *Rest of Africa* | *U.S.A.* | *British N. America* |
|---|---|---|---|---|---|---|---|---|
| 1870 | 5·5 | 13·7 | 11·4 | 6·5 | 8·0 | 2·3 | 14·2 | 3·4 |
| 1890 | 5·0 | 13·0 | 8·3 | 7·2 | 4·2 | 5·0 | 12·2 | 2·7 |
| 1910 | 6·7 | 11·4 | 10·2 | 6·0 | 4·3 | 8·0 | 7·3 | 4·7 |
| 1930 | 7·9 | 12·4 | 6·7 | 6·3 | 3·3 | 9·8 | 5·0 | 5·2 |
| 1938 | 11·8 | 8·5 | 7·0 | 4·4 | 4·6 | 13·2 | 4·4 | 5·0 |

| | *W. Indies* | *Central and S. America* | *Australia* | *N. Zealand* | *India* | *Rest of Asia* | *Western and Central Europe and U.S.A.* | *British Empire* |
|---|---|---|---|---|---|---|---|---|
| 1870 | 3·3 | 8·8 | 4·2 | 0·8 | 9·7 | 8·1 | 39·3 | 26·0 |
| 1890 | 2·2 | 10·8 | 7·5 | 1·3 | 12·7 | 7·5 | 33·5 | 33·1 |
| 1910 | 1·1 | 12·2 | 6·4 | 2·0 | 10·7 | 8·4 | 28·9 | 34·2 |
| 1930 | 1·2 | 9·5 | 5·6 | 3·1 | 9·3 | 8·0 | 24·1 | 39·7 |
| 1938 | 1·6 | 7·7 | 8·1 | 4·1 | 7·2 | 7·1 | 19·9 | 46·5 |

Source: Mitchell and Deane, *Abstract*, pp. 315–26.

Dominions (particularly Australia and South Africa), Scandinavia and certain parts of Eastern Europe. Accordingly, the ranking of these areas among British export markets increased noticeably. It should be noted that the growth in direct trade had substantial repercussions on the sources of imports too. For example, although the British Empire's share in U.K. exports rose from 39·7 per cent in 1930 to 45·6 per cent in 1938, its share of U.K. imports increased more, from 25·9 per cent to 37·9 per cent. The distribution of import surpluses altered drastically after the breakdown of multilateralism. In 1928, 90 per cent of Britain's import surplus arose out of trade with the United States and Europe while Britain enjoyed a sizeable export surplus (£78 million) from trade with the major exporting primary producers (Australia, Brazil, Malaya, Ceylon, China, India and the East Indies).[1] Six years later this had been converted to an import surplus, while the import surpluses with Europe and the United States had been more than halved. This represented a volte-face with earlier periods when rising import surpluses with industrial countries had been indirectly paid for by export surpluses with primary producers.

Some of these points can be emphasised by reference to statistics of the geographical distribution and commodity structure of British exports between 1870 and 1938 as given in Tables 12 and 13. The

TABLE 13

Commodity Distribution of British Exports, 1870–1938

(*Percentage*)

| | *Textiles* | *Metals* | *Machinery* | *Chemicals* | *Vehicles* | *Electl. Goods* | *Coal* | *Misc.* |
|---|---|---|---|---|---|---|---|---|
| 1870 | 55·8 | 14·2 | 1·5 | 0·6 | 1·1 | — | 2·8 | 24·0 |
| 1890 | 43·4 | 14·5 | 3·0 | 2·2 | 3·5 | — | 7·2 | 26·2 |
| 1910 | 36·5 | 11·4 | 6·8 | 4·3 | 3·8 | 1·0 | 8·7 | 27·5 |
| 1930 | 25·6 | 10·3 | 8·2 | 3·8 | 9·0 | 2·1 | 8·6 | 32·4 |
| 1938 | 18·8 | 10·3 | 12·9 | 4·7 | 7·0 | 2·8 | 8·6 | 34·9 |

Source: Mitchell and Deane, *Abstract*, pp. 304–6.

relative strength of the three remedies suggested for meeting the growth of competition abroad before 1914 (i.e. developing new export goods, improving competitive ability in existing markets, or redirecting old-established export commodities to new markets) should be reflected in these statistics. Adoption of the first solution should show itself in a rapidly changing commodity structure and a more stable geographical distribution; the second course of action would be associated with stability in both commodity and geographical structure; while the third would tend to be associated with a

[1] Hilgerdt, *Industrialisation.*

stable commodity structure and a changing geographical distribution. The evidence given in the tables is not clear cut, and its interpretation is subject to how far commodity and areal divisions are disaggregated; stability at these levels of aggregation might give way to rapid relative changes with a more detailed breakdown. For instance, the significant regional changes in export markets shown in Table 12 are lost when we look at the geographical distribution of exports by continents.[1] Europe, for example, included both advanced industrial countries and primary producing economies during this period, and the continent as a whole maintained its relative position in Britain's export trade. This was because lost markets in Western Europe and in Germany were in part compensated by increased trade with Scandinavia and south-east Europe.

Although Table 13 shows that the commodity composition of exports was changing, the rate of transformation was not fast enough for the most advanced industrial nation to keep ahead of industrialising rivals. Textiles still accounted for well over a third of total exports by the outbreak of the First World War, while the share in total exports of the newer categories (machinery, chemicals, vehicles, and electrical goods) stood at only 15·9 per cent in 1910. The share of metal manufactures, still a rapidly expanding sector at this time, actually declined. The fastest growing export category before 1914 was the old staple product, coal—an expansion, incidentally, which helps to explain the relative buoyancy in exports to Europe. Moreover, between 1900 and 1913 Britain's share in world exports declined much faster in newer categories (such as machinery, chemicals and vehicles) than in, say, textiles.[2] Furthermore, within these broad export categories Britain tended to specialise in the older lines rather than in the most recently developed products; the concentration on inorganic rather than organic chemicals, on locomotives and ships rather than on motor vehicles, and on textile and farm machinery rather than machine tools and electrical machinery, are obvious cases in point. In other words, the changes in the commodity structure of the export trade before 1914 are less favourable than appears at first sight. Although it is a question of degree, Britain was not developing new export lines fast enough to maintain her market shares in industrial markets.

[1] Saul's emphasis on stability in the geographical distribution of Britain's overseas trade largely stems from considering continents and other global aggregates. (S. B. Saul, 'The Export Economy', in J. Saville (ed.), *Studies in the British Economy*.)

[2] Baldwin's statistics for the exports of the ten leading industrial economies show that Britain's share fell 39·7–29·2 per cent, 28·0–22·9 per cent and 48·0–37·0 per cent in machinery, chemicals and vehicles respectively, but her share in textiles fell modestly from 47·6 per cent to 44·5 per cent.

Similarly, there is little evidence that Britain's hold over industrial markets was maintained in old-established export products, though experience varied considerably from industry to industry. Wool textile exports were the main sufferer from tariffs, the volume of exports falling by about 15 per cent between 1870 and 1900.[1] In iron and steel goods, on the other hand, Britain by the late nineteenth century could not compete effectively with American and German domestic production and exported to these countries mainly in periods of boom to supplement their home output. Cotton exports were hit hard by tariffs in certain industrial countries; for instance, exports of piece-goods to Italy slumped from a peak of 84·2 million yards in 1887 to 3.3 million yards in 1900.[2] But the cotton industry's export performance as a whole was not severely disturbed since the trade with industrial countries was relatively small, and foreign cotton industries were not efficient enough to compete in neutral markets. Failure to provide after-sales services of capital goods, poor responses to changes in consumer tastes, the inability to provide medium-term credit facilities, and downward inflexibility of export prices are, it is often suggested, evidence of Britain's declining competitive ability, but the evidence is ambiguous and difficult to interpret. However, the United Kingdom's relative export prices rose, it has been estimated, at an annual rate of 0·4 per cent between 1870 and 1914.[3] Finally, the continuous decline in the market share of industrial countries (i.e. the United States, Western and Central Europe) from 39·3 per cent of British exports in 1870 to 28·9 per cent by 1910 clearly controverts the view that Britain successfully maintained her position in industrial markets by improved competitive power.

By elimination, we are left with the third solution—the redirection of existing export categories to new non-industrial markets. The continued absolute growth in the exports of cotton goods from an average of £75·2 million in the period 1870–4 to £118·9 million in the period 1910–13 (the price levels were similar in both periods) is one indication of successful redirection; absolute expansion in other export lines provides others. But the clearest evidence for the success of the course adopted is found in the geographical changes in export markets shown in Table 12. The United States declined markedly in relative terms as a British export market, but the fall in the share of

[1] In fact, Britain increased her share of a falling total of world wool textile exports mainly by switching from worsteds to woollen goods.

[2] Saul, *Studies in Trade*, p. 150.

[3] J. Knapp and K. Lomax, 'Britain's Growth Performance: The Enigma of the 1950s', *Lloyds Bank Review* (Oct 1964) 19.

Western Europe was mitigated by rising coal exports (from an annual average of £9·5 million over the years 1870–4 to £43·1 million in the period 1910–13).[1] The declining relative importance of industrial markets was matched by expansion in certain primary producing markets over the period 1870–1914. Pre-eminent among these were Africa (particularly South Africa), Australasia and Central and South America. It is to be noted, however, that the growing importance of primary producing markets was not confined to those within the Empire. Apart from Latin America, the less developed parts of Europe and certain Asian markets became most important for U.K. exports. On the other hand, some Empire markets did not increase their ranking among British export markets; India's position remained relatively stable, that of the West Indies fell, while Canada's was also declining up to the post-1900 capital exporting boom. In fact, the Empire's share in U.K. trade actually fell between 1900 and 1913 for several reasons: prolonged slumps in South Africa and Australia, stagnation in cotton exports to India and successful foreign competition in newer export goods. Indeed, taking our period as a whole the Empire's share in British exports rose more between the wars than before 1914 (as shown in the last column of Table 12).

Of the choices before her in how to meet the challenge of industrialisation abroad, Britain selected before 1914 the least painful solution of developing new markets sheltered from competition for her major export lines. This method could not offer long-term security, partly because the absence of rivalry from other exporters in these markets was guaranteed only so long as the elaborate multilateral system existed and world trade continued to grow, partly because these markets would eventually want to industrialise themselves. More fundamental readjustments were forced on the economy after the First World War. These were necessitated by the stagnation in world trade, the imperfect functioning of the international economy and general overproduction in the basic nineteenth-century industries. Changes in the commodity structure of exports were consequently more radical than before 1914. Textiles' share was halved, metals, chemicals and coal retained stable shares of a reduced total, but the combined share of machinery, vehicles and electrical goods increased from 11·6 per cent of total exports in 1910 to 22·7 per cent in 1938.

[1] The sharp fall in the relative importance of Turkey and the Middle East as a U.K. export market between 1870 and 1890 is, of course, explained by entirely different reasons such as the shift of U.K. capital exports away from and slow economic growth in this region.

Moreover, as suggested earlier and as Table 12 confirms, the geographical shifts were greater than before 1914. The primary producing areas were throughout the period, but especially in its latter half, in difficulties. Their purchasing power was low because of falling export receipts, and they attempted to speed up their industrialisation in order to reduce their import dependence. Thus some of Britain's most rapidly declining markets were now found in Latin America and Asia, a decline accelerated by the growth of United States and Japanese competition respectively. The stagnation of the European economy meant falling export markets in industrial Europe. The largest upward shifts in export markets are to be observed only after 1930, and occurred in Northern Europe and Africa and, to a lesser extent, in Australasia and the Middle East. It is clear that the bilateral trade agreements negotiated at Ottawa and elsewhere were the main cause of these shifts. In other words, despite the fact that Britain's share in world trade in the twentieth century had declined both through failure to compete and an unfavourable commodity structure, the most striking features of Britain's export trade between the wars were stronger attempts to improve its structure and to maintain competitive ability if through commercial policy measures. Such attempts were unavoidable, since redirection was now ruled out for it can only succeed in periods of rapidly expanding world trade. The adverse effects of the partial failure of these attempts were reduced by contracting the foreign trade sector relative to the economy as a whole.

The continuous and marked decline in the proportion of British exports sold to the United States and industrial Europe (shown in the penultimate column of Table 12) is prima facie evidence that industrialisation abroad adversely affected the growth of Britain's overseas trade. Moreover, Professor Lewis's statistics show that whereas Britain's share in world trade in manufactures was halved between the early 1880s and 1937, that of the United States increased rapidly from 3·4 per cent to 17·3 per cent and Germany's share even rose slightly from 17·2 per cent to 19·7 per cent.[1] In the pre-1914 period, especially after the 1880s, Germany (and to a limited extent Belgium) made great strides in capturing European markets which were former preserves of Britain, especially in iron and steel goods. The entry of the United States into world markets occurred later, in the mid-1890s, and had fewer harmful effects on British exports, partly because her export structure was more complementary to than competitive with that of the United Kingdom, partly because

[1] W. A. Lewis, 'International Competition in Manufactures', *American Economic Review*, Papers, 47 (1957) 579.

American export growth was concentrated on certain areas particularly Canada and Latin America. Although British trade with these markets was substantial, she was able to expand faster in alternative primary producing markets. Industrialisation in the United States behind tariff barriers affected British exports to the American market far more than did increased U.S. competition in neutral markets.

The adverse consequences of industrialisation abroad are, because they are more noticeable than the benefits, easily exaggerated. Britain's relative position in world trade was bound to fall off, as other countries built up their industries.[1] Moreover, a large part of the decline in Britain's share in world trade was due to her inability to compete in iron and steel and engineering,[2] fields in which the United States and Germany had special advantages in natural resource endowment and technological leadership. Most important of all, the income effects of industrialisation in Europe raised import demand from the primary producers, who purchased high proportions of their import requirements from Britain. Moreover, rapid growth in incomes in industrialising countries stimulated the imports of manufactured goods, and these countries tended to expand their manufactured imports faster than other countries (though the composition of manufactured imports shifted more towards capital goods and luxury consumer goods).[3]

Up to 1914, continuous income growth and lack of strain on the balance of payments suggest that industrialisation abroad did not seriously hinder the growth of Britain's overseas trade. A conclusion on these lines is less certain for the inter-war period. The First World War led to the beginnings of industrialisation in many countries, and a very rapid acceleration in the rate of industrial growth in the United States and Japan. American competition was more serious because machinery and motor vehicles, fields in which her competition was most marked, were now two of the few expanding export categories. Japan and the new industrialising economies concentrated most on markets for textiles, still the largest U.K. export sector and the one in which her supremacy had scarcely been challenged before 1914. Normally, the growth of competitive pressure would have been a stimulus to readjustment. But the changes were, as a result of the war, very sudden, and the stagnation in world trade intensified the competition. In such conditions, the greater stickiness of export prices in Britain

[1] As Hilgerdt put it: 'It is axiomatic that a country which is a pioneer in industrial and commercial development should lose its relative position as other countries follow suit, even if it gains in absolute terms' (Hilgerdt, *Industrialisation*, p. 109).

[2] Had Britain retained her 1899 share in world trade in iron and steel and engineering, her share in world trade between 1899 and 1937 would have declined only from 32·5 per cent to 31·3 per cent rather than to 22·4 per cent.

[3] These are the key findings of Hilgerdt's classic study.

compared with other countries was a serious handicap. At the same time it was more difficult to expand sales to primary producers, because stagnation in European demand for primary products was not compensated for by rising demand in the United States with her lower import dependence. Lower export receipts in the primary producing economies not only made them less sturdy as export markets directly but forced them to industrialise faster. Finally, with the breakdown of multilateralism Britain lost part of her important primary producing markets to her younger competitors. Even so she was able to minimise these harmful effects by relying more on markets in the Empire which ensured her a degree of protection[1] and by paying for her necessary imports via a reduction in capital exports and some liquidation of capital assets abroad (though payment was greatly facilitated by the improvement in the terms of trade). Despite the more intense competitive effects of world industrial development on Britain in the inter-war period and especially in the 1930s, over our period taken as a whole Britain benefited rather than suffered from industrialisation abroad.

## The Costs and Benefits of Free Trade

For over sixty years of this period, Britain remained ostensibly a free trade country. 'Back door' protection was introduced with a gradual build-up of tariff legislation between 1915 and 1931, and some but not all the industries protected were important, but before 1931–2 the great bulk of British industry remained unprotected from foreign competition. The key element in pre-1914 commercial policy was the 'most-favoured-nation' system under which Britain made M.F.N. treaties with countries which enabled her to benefit as a third party from any tariff reductions offered by these countries to their trading partners. Tariff cuts were made in the interests of the parties directly negotiating, and these were often of little value to Britain if the structure of her exports differed strongly from the other country involved, but nevertheless the system kept discrimination against British exports at a minimum. Of the major trading countries, Britain alone adhered to free trade. There had been a fairly strong movement towards liberalisation of trade in the 1850s and 1860s, apart from in the United States where

[1] According to Schlote, the Empire's share of U.K. exports in 1932–4 exceeded 70 per cent for paper, fell in the range 60–70 per cent for soaps, books, motor vehicles, beer, tobacco products, non-ferrous metals, cutlery, and pharmaceutical products, and within the range 50–60 per cent for electrical goods, paint, pottery, locomotives and rolling stock, spirits, ships' hulls and iron goods (W. Schlote, *British Overseas Trade from 1700 to the 1930s* (1952) p. 102).

tariff legislation was introduced during the Civil War, but this was reversed with the price decline of the 1870s and the entry of overseas cereal supplies on to the European market. New tariffs, usually at increasingly higher rates, were introduced intermittently by most important trading countries in the forty years before 1914.[1] In these circumstances, an important question is whether the retention of free trade in Britian was economically justified.

Given certain assumptions, it might be possible to evaluate the effects of the free trade system in Britain over a prescribed period in terms of the measurement of its quantitative costs and benefits. It would be beyond our scope here, however, to do more than list the costs and benefits supplemented merely by an intuitive assessment of their relative importance.

The argument that free trade meant a loss of government revenue (customs duties fell from over 32 per cent of import values in the early 1840s to between 5½ per cent and 7 per cent over the 1870–1914 period) is, of course, specious. Unless the foreign supplier paid all the import duty, a precondition of which is that the long-run elasticity of supply was zero, import taxes would have been paid by domestic consumers. If the revenue had been required by the government to contribute towards the costs of administration, defence, etc., other taxes could have been deployed just as effectively.

A stronger case for protection might be made on the basis of the effects of free trade on British agriculture. Agricultural output did not expand at all between 1870 and the 1930s, compared with an annual rate of growth of over 2½ per cent between the late 1930s and the mid-1950s.[2] Crop production, in fact, declined markedly. The rate of transfer of labour out of agriculture proceeded at a high rate so that by 1920 only 5·9 per cent of the labour force were employed on the land, a proportion that would certainly be considered too low by supporters of the 'balanced economy' thesis. Wheat prices by 1894 had dropped to about a third of the level of twenty years before, and some might argue that price declines of this magnitude constituted a case for protection if British farmers were to survive. These arguments are unconvincing. The failure of agricultural output to grow was the price to be paid for the gains from specialisation in manufacturing, and has to be assessed relative to these gains rather than studied in isolation. Moreover, stagnant overall output

[1] Examples include the tariffs of Germany in 1879–80 and 1902, France in 1892 and 1910, the United States in 1890 and 1897, Italy in 1878–9 and 1887 and Switzerland in 1891 and 1906.

[2] See the rates of growth given in M. Fg. Scott, *A Study of United Kingdom Imports* (1963) p. 104. See also Schlote, *British Overseas Trade*, pp. 59–60.

reflected marked shifts within different agricultural sectors away from those branches of agriculture in which Britain could not compete towards those in which her comparative disadvantage was least, such as dairying and market gardening. The shift of labour from agriculture to industry meant a movement from low to high productivity sectors which raised national income and real earnings. The strategic argument for a larger agrarian sector was weak in a period of relative peace, in a world where there were many alternative, highly competitive suppliers of primary products and at a time when Britain had a majority share of the world's shipping capacity. As for the fall in wheat prices in the Great Depression period, the prices of other cereals fell less steeply, and the prices of meat and dairy products fell less than the aggregate price level. Moreover, cheap wheat prices meant cheap bread, an obvious benefit to low income consumers at home which freed considerable purchasing power for buying domestic goods. Furthermore, we should note that meat and animal products ranked high in the expanding categories of imported foods, and yet domestic production of these goods also increased. This fact suggests that the growth of these imports was not the result of the absence of protection but of population growth and rising incomes in Britain.

But the main weakness of regarding the effects of free trade on agriculture as a major social cost is that it ignores what the consequences of a tariff on wheat and other foodstuffs would have been. As we have seen, the primary producing countries played the key role in keeping Britain's export trade in a healthy state before 1914 by providing compensating markets for those lost by industrialisation abroad. A tariff on wheat (or on other foods produced overseas) would have cut the foreign sterling earnings of these important buyers of British goods, had an adverse long-run effect on income levels in the primary producing countries by forcing down the world price of the protected commodities, and might have invited retaliation. As it was, the buoyant demand for imported food in Britain sustained British exporters and made it easier for borrowing countries to make their interest payments on U.K. capital.

Was the faster growth in imports than in exports and its implications for the balance of payments a cost of free trade? We think not. The faster growth in imports must be kept in perspective. In the 1870s and 1880s imports did expand faster than exports, but not appreciably; between 1890 and 1913 imports and exports advanced at the same rate.[1] Between 1870 and 1914 the merchandise deficit obviously widened in consequence, but its increase was more abso-

[1] See Table 11.

lute than relative. It gave rise to no balance of payments difficulties because of the substantial earnings on services, and interest and dividend receipts from overseas. In the inter-war period, on the other hand, imports continued to grow (though much more slowly than before 1914) while exports declined rapidly. Even so the balance of payments remained in surplus in the 1920s, and over the inter-war period as a whole never became a serious source of trouble for the domestic economy—mainly because of the rapid improvement in the terms of trade. Most important of all, however, the continued growth in imports reflected not the lack of protection but the resource needs of the British economy and the demand for imported food.

One aspect of the growth in imports which cannot primarily be explained in terms of economic necessity is the rise in the imports of manufactured goods. These accounted for 5½ per cent of total imports in 1860, 17·3 per cent in 1880, almost 25 per cent before the First World War and 29·4 per cent by 1930. In the last thirty years before 1914, food imports grew at an annual rate of 2 per cent, raw materials by 1·8 per cent and manufactures by 3·4 per cent. Once again, however, we should be very careful about the implications to be drawn from such facts. Many of the manufactured imports were complementary to rather than competitive with domestic production; the goods either could not be produced in Britain at all (usually because of natural resource scarcities) or they could only be produced at uncompetitive costs. Examples include petroleum products, certain non-ferrous metal goods, and wood and timber products. Even when imported goods were competitive with the home product it does not follow that they were undesirable. Imported consumer goods often reflected rising real incomes and the widening of consumer choice, and the greater variety offered by domestic and imported brands meant a higher level of welfare. Imported capital goods which in the trade statistics might appear competitive with home-produced goods were frequently not; instead, there was often extreme specialisation so that if a domestic manufacturer wanted a certain machine for a specific purpose there would sometimes only be one producer in the world, and whether that producer was British or foreign would be largely accidental. Specialisation of this kind was very common in several products—machine tools and synthetic dyestuffs are merely two examples. Moreover, even though manufactures were a high and rising proportion of total imports, imports were in most cases only a small fraction of home-produced sales on the home market. In 1935[1] manufactured

[1] Admittedly, general protection had been in operation for three years so that imports were lower than they would have been under free trade.

imports plus duty amounted to only 8 per cent of home produced sales.[1]

The growth in manufactured imports cannot of itself be regarded as a price to be paid for free trade. A more serious argument is that the absence of protection explains the slower development of new industries in the United Kingdom. Britain relied heavily on imports before 1914 for chemicals, synthetic dyestuffs, scientific instruments, electrical machinery and motor-cars. It is arguable that a system of infant-industry tariffs could have promoted a faster expansion before the First World War. But it is difficult to generalise. In some cases, like synthetic dyestuffs, protection against imports was necessary to develop the industry. In others, the high import levels may have reflected 'an inability or unwillingness to strike into new lines or to master new skills'.[2] In some fields, motor vehicles is probably one example, tariff protection could have had the effect of making firms less efficient and even more unwilling to change. It is important to recognise that the infant-industry tariff argument does not necessarily require a general abandonment of free trade. In fact between 1915 and the mid-1920s most of the new industries received some form of tariff protection (motor vehicles, dyestuffs, other organic chemicals, magnetos, rayon, etc.). If we accept the argument that tariffs on older industries are likely to delay reorganisation and technical advance, by 1932 a general tariff was almost irrelevant for the protection of individual industries since most of the growth industries in the economy were already protected. The tariff's main virtue was then to reduce the *total* import bill, and thereby to divert purchasing power into the home market where it could be spent on new houses and consumer durables.

The benefits derived from free trade were real enough but difficult to measure. No doubt Britain enjoyed considerable gains from international specialisation. She was able to buy food and raw materials from the cheapest source of supply. Many of the export sectors, at least in the early decades of the period, benefited from scale economies which would not have been enjoyed as fully if trade restrictions had been imposed. This argument applies whether British exporters had to face tariffs abroad or not, the main point being that the growth of exports was stimulated most before 1914 by rising demand in the new overseas countries. This demand was maintained at high levels because incomes in these countries were sustained by Britain's

[1] The highest shares were 29 per cent for leather and fur, 25 per cent for chemicals and 22 per cent for paper. It is improbable that Britain had a comparative advantage in any of these fields.

[2] Saul, *Studies in Trade*, p. 37.

willingness to import primary products regardless of the consequences for British agriculture. Moreover, it was Britain's willingness to tolerate a rising merchandise import surplus which freed her from the competition of European industries in these new overseas markets. The open market in Britain was the key to the functioning of the world-wide multilateral payments system which developed, centring on the United Kingdom, after 1870. Increasing competition, particularly from domestic suppliers, lost markets to Britain in Western Europe and the United States, and trade deficits with these areas widened. On the other hand, British exports to many primary producers, but particularly to India and Australia, expanded faster than imports from these countries, so that Britain had substantial export surpluses; India alone financed more than 40 per cent of Britain's total deficits. The industrial countries of Western Europe bought raw materials and foodstuffs from the overseas primary producers, and ran up heavy import surpluses with these countries. By exporting to primary producers, by supplying shipping, insurance and banking services, and by her interest receipts, Britain was able to pay indirectly for her import surplus with industrial countries and allow these countries to finance their primary product imports.

This multilateral system protected Britain from strong industrial competition in primary producing countries—a protection which Professor Saul has called a 'paradox of free trade'. It was the most substantial benefit conferred by free trade on the British economy before 1914. However there were signs of strain in the multilateral system even before 1914. The fall in U.S. food imports after 1900 led Britain to look for alternative wheat and meat supplies in Argentina and Canada. This resulted in import surpluses with these areas and a smaller deficit with the United States, and it was more difficult to adjust to the changing pattern of settlements. In the inter-war period, the strains became serious. Many of the overseas countries with whom Britain had export surpluses were now developing their own industries; moreover competition from other industrial countries had intensified even in these markets. Although the multilateral payments system survived in the early 1930s, its special benefits for British exports had largely been dissipated. Nevertheless, to meet the international economic problems of the inter-war period tariff protection by Britain was an irrelevancy.

To the extent that free trade fostered trade expansion, Britain gained indirectly through increased receipts from shipping, financial and insurance services. Britain's share of the world merchant shipping fleet remained relatively stable at slightly over one-third of the total between 1870 and 1914.[1] The income from the supply of shipping services averaged £50·8 million in the period 1871–5 rising to an average of £93·1 million, 1906–14, while the income from insurance and trade services rose rather more slowly, from £49·3 million to £71·8 million over the same period.[2] Although shipping could be subsidised, insurance and financial service sectors could not easily be protected by countries. But Britain supplied these services not because she retained free trade but because she had specialist qualifications and a substantial comparative advantage in these fields. It is difficult to believe that had Britain resorted to protection before 1914, the receipts from these services would have been lost to her. When British control in the supply of these services declined in the inter-war period, the main reason was the stagnation in world trade (though foreign shipping lines were subsidised more heavily than before 1914). Britain's share in world shipping fell to 29·6 per cent in 1929 and to 26·5 per cent in 1937. After protection had been adopted, there was no sudden downward shift in income from shipping, insurance and trade services. Earnings were low in the depression but they revived quite strongly later in the 1930s. We doubt whether free trade added much to the growth of international trading services supplied by Britain, apart perhaps from keeping a rather higher share of the world's carrying trade in British hands before 1914. In general, however, the expansion of receipts from these services reflected the growth in world trade and Britain's singular qualifications for supplying them, rather than a windfall gain from her free trade policy.

Imlah has suggested that the retention of free trade had favourable effects on the domestic economy in that it 'allayed class bitterness and promoted national unity', thereby contributing to national security.[3] This argument can easily be exaggerated. Although free trade avoided regressive tariffs on imports, many goods were subject to excise duties which were regressive in their effect. Free trade may have hindered the growth of domestic monopolies, and therefore restricted the scope for exploiting consumers. On the other hand, imported food was cheap and this was a material factor in the growth of real wages during the late nineteenth century. But it is dangerous to ascribe all the growth in real incomes and the expansion of output to free trade, as Imlah almost suggests.

To sum up, neither the benefits nor the costs of free trade were as

[1] See D. H. Aldcroft, 'The Mercantile Marine', in D. H. Aldcroft (ed.), *The Development of British Industry and Foreign Competition* (1968) p. 327. In 1911, the U.K. share was almost four times larger than that of her nearest rival, Germany.

[2] Imlah, *Economic Elements*, pp. 73–5.

[3] Ibid., pp. 187–8.

substantial as some accounts suggest. The prosperity of Britain under free trade does not necessarily imply that this prosperity was due to free trade, and the weakening of Britain's position in the international economy long before free trade was abandoned suggests the falseness of such a *simpliste* view. The chief benefit was the indirect protection given to Britain in overseas markets by the multilateral payments system which functioned so well before 1914 because of Britain's 'open door' for imports. The main cost was the failure to give initial protection to newer industries on which the long-run solution of Britain's problems in the international economy depended. However, infant-industry duties before 1914 would not have required an overall departure from free trade.

By the early 1930s, on the other hand, protection had ceased to be very relevant to curing Britain's difficulties because most of the new industries were already protected. Its justification in 1931–2 was as part of a policy package designed to insulate the domestic economy from further depression impulses from overseas. The results of general tariff protection were hardly impressive. Imports of newly protected goods declined no more than those of other goods. There is no evidence that the tariff raised employment, output or productivity. It probably raised prices, particularly by making price-rigging easier. The bulk of the improvement in the terms of trade took place before the tariff was introduced. As a tactical weapon, tariffs diverted Britain's trade into different channels without increasing it. Thus our suggestion that the benefits of free trade have been overestimated cannot be read to infer that we extol the coming of protection.

## Foreign Investment

Britain's overseas investment activity before 1914 was an important aspect of her role in the international economy. Her dominance in investment was far greater than in commodity trade; almost one-half of the international investments outstanding in 1913 were U.K. owned. Moreover, her relative decline in the inter-war period was more dramatic in the capital exporting field. The growth and decline can be illustrated by referring back to Table 10. Before the second half of the nineteenth century British overseas investment had increased only slowly; Imlah estimated total accumulations of overseas capital of less than £100 million in 1825 and of less than £210 million in 1850.[1] It was not until later in the 1850s, however,

[1] Imlah, *Economic Elements*, pp. 70–1.

that overseas investment became of continuous significance to the balance of payments. The importance of foreign investment within our period at least up to 1914 is clear from Table 10. Between 1870 and 1914 the total of British overseas capital increased almost six-fold. But although the growth was continuous it did not occur at a steady rate. The rate of expansion was much more rapid in the 1880s and after the early years of this century than in the seventies and nineties. But even in the decades when capital formation was oriented towards the home economy, an average of about £50 million (assuming that *ex post* foreign investment is represented by the current account balance) was invested abroad, a sum equal to between 3 per cent and 4 per cent of G.N.P. On the other hand, the experience of the years immediately before 1914 when the rate of foreign investment was about £200 million per annum and almost 10 per cent of G.N.P. was not typical, but meant a marked acceleration of the pace of the capital exporting boom of the previous years.[1] Apart from the last few years of the pre-1914 era foreign investment was almost always less than the income receipts from capital already placed abroad, though the two amounts were very similar in the 1870s and 1880s. This suggests that investment income from abroad could have been, indirectly, the main source of new overseas investment funds, though this income especially after 1890 also helped to meet the deficits on trade and services. In the peak period 1911–13, investment income was equal to about 8½ per cent of national income.

Another aspect of the development of the international economy before 1914 was that capital outflows from Britain were closely associated with outflows of men. Thus, as Table 10 shows, the peak decades for capital exports were also peak decades for net emigration. To some extent, fluctuations in foreign investment and emigration can be regarded as a reflection of intertemporal shifts in relative economic opportunities between Britain and the main borrowing countries. Generally speaking, the main capital importing areas (the regions of recent settlement) were also the main areas absorbing labour. Canada, for example, in the period 1900–14 imported about £300 million of capital and absorbed about a million immigrants from Britain. Immigration associated with capital imports was of some benefit to borrowing countries. It kept down costs during investment booms by making the labour supply functions in borrowing countries much more elastic. It also helped to sustain the booms when they were beginning to wane because the inflow of population

[1] For a detailed analysis of British overseas issues before 1914 see M. Simon, 'New British Portfolio Foreign Investment, 1865–1914', in J. H. Adler (ed. for I.E.A.), *Capital Movements and Economic Development* (1967).

increased capital requirements for housing, public utilities and services. On the other hand, the direct effects of emigration from the United Kingdom may have been harmful. Most emigration clustered in boom periods, thereby accentuating labour scarcities at home.

Table 10 also illustrates the changes in overseas investment after the First World War. Although Britain continued to invest substantial sums abroad in the 1920s, the rate of foreign investment was much lower relative to overseas investment income and to G.N.P. than at any time since before 1870. Moreover, new investments abroad scarcely made up for the liquidation of capital assets abroad via the sale of overseas securities during the First World War (and, to a much lesser extent, via defaults in the post-war period). In the 1930s net foreign investment became negative and the balance of payments showed, on average, a current account deficit. Britain's accumulated capital abroad was, in fact, declining, and repayments exceeded new overseas issues by a considerable margin. Income from previous overseas investments, on the other hand, continued to hold up surprisingly well. The reversal in the direction of net international capital flows, which had been unchanged for well over a century, was accompanied by a net immigration of population into Britain. Although there were policy influences at work (foreign loan embargoes in Britain and decisions not to import capital in borrowing countries), the main factors behind the changed direction of capital and labour movements were relatively depressed conditions persisting abroad and more buoyant economic conditions and the presence of new investment opportunities in Britain.

Apart from growth in the total of British overseas investments and fluctuations in its rate of increase, there were marked changes in its geographical distribution and in its character and type. Before 1870 the main areas of investment had been Europe and the United States. In our period Europe declined in absolute importance (for example, between 1875 and 1913 U.K. investments in Europe fell by 50 per cent, while elsewhere they increased fivefold), and though the western regions of the United States continued, especially in the 1880s, to absorb British capital the United States relied increasingly on domestic accumulation. After 1870 more than two-thirds of British overseas investment went to the regions of recent settlement, i.e. the areas developed primarily by immigrants from Europe; apart from the United States, this meant the British Dominions and South America. However, the favoured areas changed over time. In the 1880s, the United States, Australia and the Argentine predominated; in the following decade when overseas investment was low South Africa was the sole area of activity; after 1900 Canada, the

Argentine and Brazil absorbed most of Britain's capital exports. Thus most of the pre-1914 investment by Britain in Australia took place before 1900, and especially within the period 1885–93; between 1904 and 1911 there was actually a repatriation of capital to Britain.

By 1913, according to Feis's breakdown[1] over 47 per cent of British quoted investments overseas were in the British Empire, and almost all of this in Canada, Australia, India and South Africa. Only about 5½ per cent of British Imperial investments were in the colonies (particularly in West Africa and the Straits Settlements). Of the remaining 53 per cent in foreign countries, about 75 per cent was invested in the American continent equally distributed between the United States on the one hand and Latin America on the other. Investment in Europe accounted for less than 6 per cent of Britain's international investments in 1913, and fully one-half of this was in Russia, and was consequently lost after 1917. The inter-war changes in geographical distribution can be observed from the breakdown in 1930. The negative foreign investment of the 1930s made little difference to the distribution, since the main areas receiving new capital, the British Dominions, also made most of the capital repayments. By 1930 the Empire's share had risen to almost 59 per cent. Again the Dominions had been the main beneficiaries of the increase, though the relative rankings between areas had changed. Australia was now the most important area, India and Ceylon had surpassed Canada, and investments in South Africa had declined. Within the reduced foreign total, the changes were rather more marked. Latin America now accounted for well over one-half of Britain's non-Imperial investments. The share of the United States had slumped drastically (from 20·0 per cent in 1913 to 5·5 per cent in 1930 of Britain's *overall* overseas investments), mainly because of the massive sale of United States investments in the First World War to obtain foreign exchange. The other noticeable change was the rise in Europe's share, primarily because Britain had participated in the loans to Europe in the 1920s.[2] Over the period as a whole, the rising relative importance of the British Dominions was obviously the most marked geographical change, although the increase in the Dominion share was intermittent and jerky before 1914. The reasons for the rise in Dominion investments were that, after the industrialisation of Western Europe and the United States, they were among the most rapidly developing regions of the world economically and that

[1] H. Feis, *Europe the World's Banker, 1870–1914* (1930) p. 23.

[2] Europe's share in the total had risen from 5·8 per cent in 1913 to 7·9 per cent in 1930 despite the liquidation of British investments in Russia (R. Kindersley, 'British Foreign Investments in 1932', *Economic Journal*, XLIII (1933) 199–200).

investment there incurred much lower risks than elsewhere. This greater security was confirmed by granting Empire government loans trustee status under the Colonial Stock Act of 1900.

In the pre-1914 period most British overseas investments went into Empire and foreign governments, railways (whether publicly or privately owned) and public utilities. The 1913 breakdown revealed about 30 per cent of total British capital abroad in central and local government stocks, over 40 per cent in railway companies and about 5 per cent in other public utilities. Of the remainder, investment in raw materials production and in banking and finance was rather more important than in commerce and industry. However, the pattern was extremely varied. Over the period 1870–1914, investment in foreign governments was becoming less popular relative to Dominion government and railway securities. Within Imperial investments apart from governments and railway companies, there were huge direct investments in mining in South Africa, short- and medium-term loans from export–import companies in West Africa to peasants engaging in production for export, and investment in the Indian jute industry. This last example was not typical, since very little investment from Britain went into competitive manufacturing overseas. Indeed, commerce and industry as a whole (including sectors complementary to as well as competitive with Britain's industrial structure) accounted only for 5½ per cent of Britain's overseas investments in 1913, and at the inter-war peak in 1930 its share was only 6·9 per cent. Although relatively small, industrial investments were increasing. Even so, only a third of inter-war capital exports could be described as 'industrial' even in the broadest sense, i.e. including finance, raw materials, etc. The share of government and municipal securities also rose between the wars, exceeding well over 42 per cent by the 1930s, paralleled by a decline in the share of railway securities to less than 24 per cent. Outside government bonds, there was some preference for investment in equities rather than bonds, and this was especially marked in oil companies, banks, mining, rubber, tea and coffee plantations. Declining equity returns were the main factor in the fall in overseas investment income in the world depression—investment income in 1933 was 40 per cent lower than the average for 1925–30. Subsidiary factors included the conversion of overseas debts to lower interest rates (over £363 million converted between 1932 and 1936) and losses through defaults (£60 million in the period 1931–4).

Interesting questions are why Britain became the great nineteenth-century foreign lender and why her capital export capability was markedly reduced after the First World War. An answer to the first question contains several strands. Her early start in industrialisation and consequent monopolistic position enabled her to accumulate savings at a rapid rate from which, once the domestic railway network had been built, a surplus became available for investment abroad. The high degree of concentration on manufacturing required Britain to import a rising share of her primary product requirements from abroad, and this resulted in a commodity import surplus. This negative trade balance facilitated the payment of interest and dividends on previous investments via borrowing countries exporting primary products to Britain. At the same time, the growth of capital exports was accompanied by the development of sophisticated capital and money markets based in London. The key position of London as the pivot of international money markets eased considerably the initial stages of a transfer of capital exports from Britain by permitting an outflow of bullion from and an inflow of short-term capital to London. However, the main transfer of capital was achieved by rising exports, though the extent to which the association between capital and commodity exports was due to the adjustment mechanism rather than a response to common forces (e.g. overseas railways required capital for their finance and rails and rolling stock for their construction) is difficult to estimate. In either event, Britain's ability to export to the non-industrial countries, and the freedom from competition there guaranteed by the multilateral pattern of settlements, allowed capital exports to be transferred smoothly. Moreover, political factors (the possession of a large Empire which was a low-risk investment area, military and diplomatic prestige, an international outlook) made overseas investment more attractive and safer than it would have been for, say, a militarily insignificant, inward-looking nation.

After the First World War Britain's capability to meet the world's demand for capital was much reduced. The surplus available for capital export had been cut down by a widening commodity import surplus due to difficulties in the export trade (particularly of cotton piece-goods) and by the fall in the real value of overseas interest and dividend receipts. Savings rates were lower than before 1914, and in the post-war boom domestic industries competed for the available capital. The margin between the average yield on all foreign securities and on gilt-edged securities had narrowed compared with the pre-1914 position. Moreover, there was intermittent interference with the freedom to invest overseas. There was an embargo operated during the war up to 1919, in 1924–5 pending the return to the gold standard, and an unofficial partial foreign loan embargo was operated in 1930 and made more stringent in 1931. In the 1920s interest rates were sufficiently high to deter many overseas borrowers; the price of new *foreign* government borrowing was up to 7–8 per cent. The United States was a much stronger competitor as an overseas lender than before 1914 and expanded capital to a much wider range of countries; furthermore, the cost of borrowing was for many countries considerably lower in New York than in London. Nevertheless, many countries still found it profitable to borrow in Britain—most of the British Empire, Argentina and some European countries. In view of these difficulties, the average rate of overseas investment in the 1920s was surprisingly high.

The most important question of all refers to the effects of Britain's foreign investment on her borrowers and on herself. To answer it in depth is far beyond our scope and only a few generalisations will be made. British capital undoubtedly assisted economic development in the regions of recent settlements. It enabled countries to develop rapidly and to build up their social overhead capital with the aid of imported capital goods without being troubled by persistent balance of payments deficits. Knapp argued that British capital was relatively unimportant to the growth of new countries because it was exceeded in quantity by repayments.[1] The argument is unconvincing. It neglects the fact that British capital had a crucial initiatory role in economic development. It raised incomes, and it was this subsequent increase in incomes which enabled repayments to be made. In Australia in the 1880s and in Canada in the 1900s capital imports exceeded 10 per cent of national income and amounted to about 50 per cent of domestic capital formation. However, in relatively advanced countries such as the British Dominions domestic capital formation provided a sizeable base for investment (meeting the demands for replacement investment, for example), with capital imports from Britain often playing a supplementary role, though accounting for much of the fluctuations in total investment. In colonial countries, on the other hand, domestic investment was very low. But British capital failed to initiate broadly based economic development in colonial territories, but merely opened up a few lines of trade with Europe via investment in harbours, plantations, mines, and railways from production points to the ports, or developed administrative centres. Foreign investment usually created only a highly capitalised commercial enclave in otherwise underdeveloped economies.

It is sometimes argued that U.K. overseas investments 'exploited' colonial territories. Leaving aside the emotive connotations associated with the word 'exploitation' and the difficulties involved in defining the term objectively, the argument is unimpressive. As we

[1] J. Knapp, 'Capital Exports and Growth', *Economic Journal*, LXVII (1957).

have seen, the bulk of British overseas lending went to the British Dominions and to other relatively rich countries rather than to the underdeveloped economies of today, and into government or railway bonds rather than into direct investments in mining, manufacturing and primary production. Where direct investments were made, no matter how limited were their repercussions on the colonial economy as a whole, they at least created employment opportunities for indigenous workers which would not otherwise have been present. A far more serious charge against British overseas investment was not that of exploitation but a crime of omission, i.e. the failure to pump *enough* capital into colonial economies and the preference for the safe returns obtainable in the regions of recent settlement.

The benefits to the lender, both from a national and the investors' points of view, were beyond doubt before 1914. Although some investors lost large sums, especially when they had invested in unstable European, Middle Eastern and Latin American governments, defaults were relatively rare. The average rate of return, varying between 4½ per cent and 6 per cent over the 1870–1914 period as a whole—though with tremendous variations according to type and character of the investment[1]—was rather higher than on domestic loans. It is impossible to quantify the national benefits, but they were substantial. Much of British exported capital went, directly or indirectly, into transport and communications or non-competitive productive enterprises. This made for a permanent improvement in the purchasing power of borrowing countries and a stimulus to British exports.[2] British investment in overseas railways and port facilities generated considerable external economies resulting in cheaper imports into the United Kingdom and enlarged gains from trade. The paradox of higher levels of purchasing power for borrowing countries and cheaper imports for Britain is explained by the fact that the main element in her improving terms of trade was the fall in transoceanic freight costs, while some of the sharpest reductions in primary production costs were found in countries such as the United States not as heavily dependent on British capital. Moreover, falling costs were in many cases fully compatible with rising receipts

[1] For example, in the 1870s yields on government bonds averaged 5·5 per cent varying from −6·0 per cent in Peru to +14·5 per cent in Portugal, and yields on railway investments averaged 6·7 per cent falling within the range of 2·1 per cent in Canada and 9·3 per cent in United States rails. The rates of return on land companies, colonial banks, foreign banks and telegraph cables averaged 16·0 per cent, 12·4 per cent, 5·7 per cent and 5·3 per cent respectively (R.I.I.A., *The Problem of International Investment* (1937) pp. 117–18).

[2] The degree of stimulus varied. Capital exports from Britain to Canada were followed by heavy Canadian purchases of United States goods, while investment in India and Latin America induced exports from Britain to a greater extent.

because of increased output coupled with productivity gains. Finally, the growth path of the British economy before 1914 was more stable than it would otherwise have been because the long-run inverse correlation between foreign investment and home investment meant that the export of capital could be regarded almost as an automatic stabiliser.

The evidence for the argument offsetting these advantages, that British industries (especially newer industries) were starved of capital in the decade before 1914, is sparse. Indeed most of the evidence available points the other way, supporting Cairncross's thesis that foreign investment was a 'sink' absorbing excess capital unable to find a use at home. Saul, for example, has shown that capital shortage was not one of the motor industry's more serious handicaps before 1914.[1] Many late nineteenth-century concerns, particularly outside the manufacturing sector, had difficulty in finding outlets for their excess funds. On the other hand, the argument is not fully settled. There are difficulties involved in the definition of capital shortage, the problems of small and new firms were more intractable than those of well-established large firms, and for the former the crucial question was not the availability of capital as such but whether it could be obtained at tolerable rates of interest.

The nature of international investment and its effects on borrowing and lending countries were less conducive to stable growth in the world economy in the inter-war period than before 1914. The links between capital exports and commodity exports were much less noticeable. The role of the world's chief lender had passed from Britain to the United States. Not only was New York less experienced as an international financial centre, but the United States was less suited to the role of creditor in the sense that she was unwilling to receive all her interest payments in the form of commodity imports. A substantial proportion of her investment went to Europe as part of a reconstruction programme, and much of it was not invested productively in the sense of improving capacity to export and thereby assisting the payment and transfer of interest and dividend receipts. Although British overseas investment was still oriented far more to the primary producers than to Europe, the position of the primary producing economies was less secure than before 1914—mainly because of technical progress in agriculture on the one hand and falling rates of population growth in the western world on the other. Short-term capital movements were more important than in the late nineteenth century and destabilising speculative activity became common, partly because under the gold exchange standard

[1] S. B. Saul, 'The Motor Industry before 1914', *Business History*, v (1962).

foreign exchange was held as reserves in addition to gold and partly because the existence of more than one major financial centre enabled funds to be shifted from one centre to another. In the 1930s long-term international investment almost disappeared; the United States was preoccupied with internal problems after the depression, in Britain the employment of capital at home was more profitable than abroad, and the major debtor countries (their balance of payments difficulties aggravated by adverse terms of trade, the collapse of world trade and the breakdown of multilateralism) reacted against overseas borrowing.

## The International Monetary System

The international monetary system of the late nineteenth century (based on permanently fixed exchange rates, a gold bullion standard and a close substitutability between sterling—in which the bulk of international trade was conducted—and gold) evolved naturally as countries went on to gold after choosing different metallic standards. But the process was a slow one; although completed in Western Europe by the 1870s monometallism was not established in the United States until 1900. As a system for international balance of payments adjustments, the gold standard worked smoothly for a number of reasons. Sterling was strong and readily available as a result of Britain's surplus. In slumps low levels of capital exports from Britain were compensated for by deficits on current account. Sterling surpluses were always returned to the international pool and imbalances were cushioned by longer trade credits. It was possible, therefore, for balance of payments disequilibria to be settled by movements of gold and sterling and by the effects of gold movements on domestic economies rather than by exchange rate variations. Conditions in the international economy and internally were favourable. The classical assumptions of relatively free trade (and, by inference, high price elasticities of demand in international trade) and a high degree of factor mobility were more nearly realised than in later periods. The rate of world economic development was steady enough, though lower than before the 1870s, for adjustments to be achieved without severe deflationary effects. After 1890 there was a broad synchronisation of business cycles between countries. This meant the direction of change in economic activity was normally the same in all countries at any one time, so that massive reserves were not required to fulfil a buffer function. Britain functioned as the centre of the international economy with a gold reserve in the region of $1\frac{1}{2}$ per cent of G.N.P. There were no symptoms of the destabilising speculation that developed between the wars. 'The world had to regard suspension of gold payments and a depreciation of sterling against gold as unthinkable. And this it dutifully did.'[1] The substantial inter-country flows of long-term capital enabled the developing countries of the period to maintain long-term current account deficits so that adjustment was often necessary only in the long run. There was a high degree of co-operation among central bankers under the leadership of the Bank of England to take the actions necessary for gold flows to bring about the appropriate adjustments in the balance of payments; in other words, they reinforced price and income effects with interest rate changes, and internal monetary supplies were linked to gold movements. The gold standard equalised international and national prices. As a consequence of these factors, the gold standard was operated with total gold and exchange reserves that were equal to only 20 per cent of world imports. Britain was able to act as the pivot of the system, because her invisible income (accruing from financial, insurance and shipping services) enabled her to escape balance of payments difficulties.

Internal conditions also facilitated the working of the system. Booms never got out of hand because internal drains of gold to the public in the upswings led to increases in the discount rate which had a stabilising impact on economic activity. The booms were mild enough, therefore, to be accommodated by the permissible fall of reserves and by short-term borrowing from abroad. The price adjustments necessary to eliminate deficits were achieved because wages were more flexible to changes in demand than in more recent periods. Moreover, they were reinforced by income effects which made up for the fact that observed price changes after gold flows were too small to bring about full correction of the balance of payments.

Because of these unique circumstances, the international economy was remarkably stable before 1914. There was no shortage of international reserves to slow down world economic growth and trade, exchange rates remained fixed, and no country developed chronic balance of payments problems compelling action adverse to international economic development.

The smooth functioning of the international monetary system did not persist into the inter-war period. This was partly the result of changes in the world economy. The First World War had interrupted free convertibility and had disrupted trade channels, and the pre-1914 structure proved impossible to restore in its original form.

[1] A. J. Brown, in J. Saville (ed.), *Studies in the British Economy*, p. 59.

The basic preconditions of relatively free trade and high factor mobility no longer existed. Tariffs were used as remedies for depression and exchange difficulties, and countries altered them more frequently than when their sole purpose was to guarantee permanent protection. Immigration controls were introduced in the major population absorbing centres and, as we have seen, a much higher proportion of international investment failed to add to export capacity in borrowing countries. Economic conditions in the primary producing economies were more unsteady than before 1914. The pre-1914 international economy had functioned efficiently because Britain's balance of payments position was sound and because international exchange rates reflected relative costs between countries. The decline in U.K. exports and wartime losses in investment income required price adjustments in the British economy that were too difficult to achieve. Although the rise in the commodity import surplus did provide the rest of the world with exchange reserves, the balance of payments was subject to increasing strain. After 1925, short-term borrowing was used to finance long-term overseas lending, a factor which became a source of trouble in 1931. The drastic post-war alterations in exchange rates such as the deliberate undervaluation of the French franc in 1926, often to achieve national objectives rather than to assist the automatic working of the international monetary system, aggravated balance of payments disequilibria and led to losses of confidence in the system. It became profitable to speculate on the instability of external currency values.

In these circumstances, the obstacles in the way of smooth operation of the international monetary system were great. But the system of the inter-war period was not that of before 1914, and was less able to bear the strains upon it. Because of wartime and post-war gold shortages, holdings of foreign exchange (mainly pounds, dollars or short-term sterling and dollar assets) supplemented gold as international reserves. Reserves were increased relative to gold; for example, during 1927 and 1928 about 40 per cent of the international reserve holdings of European central banks consisted of foreign exchange. Nevertheless, there was a lack of liquidity of international reserves. Co-ordination among central bankers was very imperfect compared with before 1914, and there was little confidence in the system. A high proportion of the foreign exchange reserves of many countries were not, in fact, owned by them but were borrowed at short term. The synchronisation of business cycles between countries was reduced compared with pre-1914 days, and consequently more reserves were needed to act as buffers against the impact of overseas fluctuations. Worst of all, the international monetary system was now concentrated on three centres, London, New York, and to a lesser extent Paris, rather than on London alone. More foreign balances are needed for clearing with multiple centres. Moreover, the existence of three centres greatly increased the scope for speculative activities: borrowers and investors could take advantage of interest rate differentials; and, more seriously, it became profitable for countries to speculate on exchange rate movements by converting one reserve currency into another without risking much of a deterioration in their reserve positions. Finally, the growth of New York made the state of the United States economy the critical factor in influencing the stability of the world economy. New York bankers had less experience in international monetary matters, and the New York money market was more susceptible to domestic influences than London. For instance, the inflow of funds into New York in 1928 to take advantage of the stock market boom made it impossible for New York to function as a short-term international lender. In view of the United States' unwillingness to tolerate an import surplus, the supply of dollar exchange to the rest of the world depended upon a steady flow of American lending. Since the rate of outflow of capital from the United States was related to the level of economic activity in the United States, the effectiveness of the working of the international monetary system became increasingly dependent on internal fluctuations in the United States.

The system did not survive the effects of the post-1929 world depression. It worked very imperfectly up to 1931, attempts were made to prop it up in the years 1931 to 1933, but after 1933 international co-operation was at a minimum. Britain's leadership of the international monetary system had been challenged in the 1920s. After 1931 by devaluing sterling and by resorting to tariffs, foreign loan controls and other restrictive devices, she abdicated control. Severe depression in the United States prevented New York from taking over Britain's former role. There was no world-wide monetary standard, for the reconstruction attempts of the 1933 World Economic Conference were left in ruins by devaluation of the dollar—an action taken for domestic rather than balance of payments reasons. The multilateral payments system was severely restricted, and was replaced by exchange control, inconvertibility and bilateral channelling of trade. The flow of long-term international investment ceased, and world trade stagnated because of low levels of economic activity and high tariffs.[1] Industrial countries turned to internal

[1] By the late 1930s, however, there was some recovery in world trade due to economic recovery in many countries and to a moderate policy of trade liberalisation, initiated by the Cordell Hull Reciprocal Trade Agreements Act of 1934.

solutions to their difficulties, involving insulation and self-sufficiency measures. The self-correcting international monetary system and adjustment mechanism of the late nineteenth and early twentieth centuries and Britain's key role as its centre had gone for ever. However, the breakdown of the international economic system and the collapse in world trade in the 1930s was an aberration from rather than a continuation of the trend. After the Second World War, a new international economic system was constructed, world trade revived and Britain rediscovered a role, though now more a subsidiary than a central role, in the world economy.

# SECTION B

# 1 Retardation in Britain's Industrial Growth, 1870–1913

## I

It is now generally accepted that there was a slowing down in the rate of economic growth in the United Kingdom after 1870. There is not the same measure of agreement, however, as to its extent or its causes. The problem has received much attention in recent years but if one tries to synthesise the results one is struck not so much by the mass of material as by the confusing and inconsistent picture which emerges from a study of it. There are two main difficulties: the definition of the problem and the interpretations to be put upon it. In regard to the first, there are several questions which need to be answered. Is the British experience to be studied as one support for the general hypothesis of retardation in mature economies or merely as an instance of a temporarily lower trend rate of growth resulting from a special set of historical circumstances? What do we understand by the rate of economic growth? If we refer to the rate of growth of industrial production the results are very different from examination of the rate of growth of gross national product or of real income per head. To give one instance, in so far as retardation is verifiable it seems to date from 1870 in regard to industrial production but from the 1890s in the case of G.N.P. Is the retardation indisputable? The available statistics are not beyond reproach, and are little more than rough, incomplete estimates. Moreover, the slowing down indicated by some time series is relatively slight.

Once retardation is established, the difficulties involved in interpreting its causes are even more serious. The nature of the problem is such that one can carry on adding cause upon cause until one has a very long, impressive, but meaningless list. There are so many arguments possible that comprehensiveness is scarcely profitable. The first aim of any inquiry must be to try to assess the relative weight to be given to the main elements in the situation, but this is not made any easier by the fact that causes fall into three groups: theoretical arguments rooted in analysis of the nature of the growth process; economic causes based on a study of the prevailing historical situation, particularly of Britain's changing role in a developing world; non-economic, primarily sociological factors. These three categories have no common denominator, and any attempt to assess their relative importance is bound to be inconclusive. The most reasonable approach would seem to be to put forward a number of *not* mutually exclusive hypotheses, which must then stand or fall by their commonsense logic and by their compatibility with accumulated historical knowledge. Finally, another cause of confusion is that in the writings the problem of deceleration has often become entangled with the separate (though not unconnected) problem of the Great Depression (1873–96); obviously, the causes of a declining rate of industrial growth are not the same as the causes of a secular price fall.

## II

The aim of this paper is twofold: first, to point out some of the questions raised by existing interpretations of Britain's deceleration in the period 1870–1913; secondly, to elaborate a new (or rather hitherto little stressed) hypothesis which it is believed does not exclude other explanations but helps to clarify them. As a preliminary, however, some consideration must be given to what we understand by retardation. Three main indicators may be chosen: the rate of growth of industrial production, the rate of growth of gross or net national product (national income) and the rate of growth of income *per capita*. The choice between these will closely depend upon the purpose of the inquiry. Industrial production will be the most valuable index if one is concerned with questions of industrial efficiency, entrepreneurial activity, changes in the structure of exports, the effects of industrialisation overseas and the like. If one is seeking to understand developments in the whole economy (including the growth of the service trades and expansion in the public services, etc.) the national income will be more appropriate. Changes in real average incomes *per capita* are probably the best guide to the extent of economic growth in its truest and most important sense—as an indicator of changes in living standards (though the question of income distribution demands caution in the use of such an index). The different indicators do not move together and therefore to speak of retardation in economic growth in the late nineteenth century without further explanation may be meaningless.[1] Several factors may

[1] The following apparently contradictory statements illustrate this: 'But in the case of Britain it is likely that industrial deceleration after the early seventies went some way beyond the normal rate of retardation that must be expected in the overall rates of growth of mature industrial societies' (J. Saville, 'Mr. Coppock on the Great Depression: A Critical Note', *Manchester School*, XXXI (1963) 69) and 'We might conclude therefore that the period of most rapid sustained growth in the British economy took place in the last thirty or forty years of the nineteenth century' (P. Deane, 'Contemporary Estimates of National Income in the Second Half of the

account for divergence between industrial output and income growth: movements in the terms of trade, the extent of incomes from overseas investments and other 'invisibles', variations in the rate of population growth and the rates of expansion in non-industrial sectors of the economy such as the service industries or primary agriculture. Thus, real incomes may rise rapidly even when industrial growth is decelerating as in the 1880s.[1]

There is a strong case for concentrating on retardation in *industrial* growth. This enables the British case to be used to examine the general proposition of inevitable retardation in mature industrial economies, and in any event the controversy over causation has referred much more to slowing down in the rate of industrialisation than in the rate of income growth. Can the existence of deceleration in the rate of growth of industrial production be established? The basic data must be the Hoffmann index.[2] In this paper his index of industrial production *including* building will be used; by adjusting with double moving ten year averages Hoffmann smoothed out the effect of short-term fluctuations. In previous studies the index excluding building seems to have been preferred, perhaps because Hoffmann's estimates have often been used in studies of cyclical fluctuations for which this index, being uncorrected, is more appropriate. For the analysis of long-term retardation, however, it seems more logical to use the adjusted index which includes building. The criticism that building should be left out as it moves more in line with other trends, emigration and foreign investment, for example, has little merit since building is an integral part of industrial activity; recent investigations suggest that building fluctuates more with the trend of domestic activity than was once thought.[3] The Hoffmann index has often been criticised but it is the only one available. The main objection to his estimates has been that they are based on raw material inputs alone and they therefore tend to underestimate

---

Nineteenth Century', *Economic History Review*, IX (1956–7) 460). However, these statements are not necessarily incompatible since the first refers to the rate of industrial growth and the second to average real income per head. On the other hand, the contemporary estimates of average income growth compiled by Miss Deane, are not fully consistent with other data (e.g. S. Kuznets, *Economic Development and Cultural Change*, V (1956)) or with the evidence of retardation in real wages.

[1] See Table 1. Hoffmann suggested that low growth rates for industry between 1870 and 1890 were balanced by high growth rates for services (W. G. Hoffmann, *British Industry 1700–1950* (Oxford, 1955) p. 216).

[2] Ibid., Table 54 B.

[3] H. J. Habakkuk, 'Fluctuations in House Building in Britain and the United States in the Nineteenth Century', *Journal of Economic History*, XXII (1962); S. B. Saul, 'House Building in England 1890–1914', *Economic History Review*, XV (1962–3).

industrial expansion in the late nineteenth century when methods of production became more 'roundabout' and the contribution of net output substantially greater.[1] In spite of this, the Hoffmann index has shown a good fit with the more recent estimates of A. R. Prest and J. R. Stone and D. A. Rowe for consumers' expenditure and of K. S. Lomax for production movements (apart from the war years in the former cases and the period 1919–21 in the latter), so it remains fairly satisfactory. It remains likely, however, that the index will accentuate any retardation evident in the period 1870–1913 up to 1907 (in that year the first Census of Production was available and improvement in the weighting and quality of indicators may have been carried out). The decennial rate of increase in industrial production is given in Table 1: for the twentieth century the more refined estimates of K. S. Lomax have been used,[2] and the annual average growth rates are given in Table 2.

The estimates in Table 1 suggest that the dating of 1870 as the watershed after which Britain's industrial growth fell off seems justified, but the usual implication that deceleration was either steady or progressive is not corroborated here. Industrial production before 1870 grew at a rate of about 35 per cent per decade, then fell to a rate of 20–25 per cent, but the lower rate of the late nineteenth and early twentieth century was not uniform. Table 1 points to two periods when industrial expansion was very moderate, the 1880s and even more so between 1900 and 1919 (the absolute fall in output during the First World War is, of course, easily accounted for). Thus the evidence does not conform to the widely held impression of retardation being concentrated in the Great Depression period 1873–96, for expansion was slower after 1900 than before.[3] Apart from these two periods, the modest falling off in the rate of growth was not very surprising. Saville's argument that this 'went some way beyond the normal rate of retardation that must be expected' is open to question.

[1] This criticism has been put the following way: 'In a developing economy with new methods of production and increasing fabrication the ratio of input to net output is unlikely to remain constant. It is practically certain that the ratio of input to net output will fall. If input indicators are used the index will, over the period in which increased fabrication occurs, tend to have a downward bias and therefore will underrate the trend in output or consumption.' (J. B. Jefferys and D. Walters, 'National Income and Expenditure of the United Kingdom 1870–1952, International Association for Research in Income and Wealth, *Income and Wealth*, Series v (1955) 11.)

[2] K. S. Lomax, 'Production and Productivity Movements since 1900', *Journal of the Royal Statistical Society*, A122 (1959).

[3] It should be pointed out that comparison with the Hoffmann index excluding building shows that stagnation in building played a major role in the relative slowing down after the late 1890s. For an illustration of what conclusions may be drawn from this, see G. Maynard, *Economic Development and the Price Level* (1962) p. 178.

TABLE 1

Percentage Change per Decade in some Indicators of the Rate of Economic Growth in Britain

| | *Industrial production* | *Real gross National product* | *National income per capita* | *Population* | *Real wages* |
|---|---|---|---|---|---|
| 1830s | 40 | 32 | | 13·4 | |
| 1840s | 35 | 22 | | 12·5 | |
| 1850s | 39 | 21 | | 11·1 | |
| 1860s | 33 | 23 | 28 | 12·7 | |
| 1870s | 23 | 28 | 11 | 13·9 | 26 |
| 1880s | 16 | 50 | 39 | 11·2 | 21 |
| 1890s | 24 | 22 | 11 | 12·0 | 11 |
| 1900s | 9 | 12 | 5 | 10·3 | −6 |
| 1910s | −5 | 5 | −1 | 4·6 | −2 |
| 1920s | 21 | 5 | 5 | 4·7 | 19 |
| 1930–7 | 19 | 20 | 19 | 3·1 | 5 |

One would have expected a high rate of growth in the early stages of industrialisation when the basic industries were being established and the economy's infrastructure (particularly the railways) being built; when the rate of growth fell off this was not an unhealthy phenomenon which needed wild allegations of the economy's 'failure' but the natural course of events. This is *not* the same argument as that which stresses inevitable and continuing retardation in a mature industrial economy. Rather it points to an abnormally high rate of expansion in the early decades of industrialisation to be followed by lower growth rates which may then vary upwards or downwards according to the changing economic environment, these later phases not necessarily being characterised by further retardation. Indeed, the British case is a poor choice for the demonstration of continuing and inevitable retardation for, as Table 2 indicates, industrial growth has taken place at an *accelerating* rate in this century. Of course, it might be argued that this reversal of trend is to be

TABLE 2

Average Annual Rate of Growth in Manufacturing (percentage)

| | *U.K.* | *U.S.A.* | *Germany* | *France* | *World* |
|---|---|---|---|---|---|
| 1900–13 | 1·7 | 5·3 | 4·7 | 2·5 | 3·0 |
| 1920–37 | 2·9 | | | | |
| 1946–62 | 3·6 | | | | |

accounted for by exceptional circumstances, and that the 'law of retardation' still holds. But a general 'law' can have so many exceptions that it ceases to have any real meaning. There is certainly no evidence of progressive deceleration even in the period before 1914, for the rate of expansion in the 1890s was slightly higher than in the 1870s. What does require explanation is the very slow industrial growth of the 1880s and of the period 1900–13. In general, however, to search for causes of the declining rate of industrial growth after 1870 is likely to be much less fruitful than examining the reasons for the high rate of growth before that date.

Attention was drawn above to the possible divergence between rates of growth of industrial production and the rate of growth of national income and national income *per capita*. Looking at the long-term position, it is perhaps surprising that the acceleration in industrial growth after 1913 as compared with before contrasts with the continued deceleration in the annual average growth rate of aggregate real national product, which was 2·4 per cent over the period 1870–1913, but dropped sharply to 1 per cent in the war and inter-war period, and even in the period 1938–50 was only 1·6 per cent, still much below the 1914 level.[1] Even before 1913 there was a similar lack of correlation (or rather inverse correlation) between these rates. In the 1880s the lower rate of industrial growth was matched by the highest rate of growth of national income *per capita* over the 1860–1914 period (though the improvement in real wages of the 1870s may have fallen off slightly). On the other hand, both industrial and income growth were characterised by very slow expansion in the 1900–13 period. These facts may be relevant to a discussion of the exceptional deceleration of these two periods.

## III

It has been suggested that it is inappropriate to view British economic development in terms of a high rate of growth up to 1870 and a low growth rate afterwards, and to search for 'causes' responsible for the change in trend. But indiscriminate accumulation of causes of deceleration has been a favourite pastime of economists and economic historians. Hoffmann, for instance, points to three particular factors apart from a natural tendency towards retardation—changes in commercial policy (especially the effects of continued free trade in throwing the domestic market open to foreign competition), the slowing down in the rate of Britain's export growth consequent upon industrialisation overseas, and the increased costs of certain raw materials such as coal.[2] Saville suggests several retarding influences: the adverse effects of the early start and the 'obsolescence' problem

[1] R. W. Goldsmith, 'Financial Structure and Economic Growth in Advanced Countries', in N.B.E.R. *Capital Formation and Economic Growth* (1958) p. 115.

[2] Hoffmann, *British Industry*, pp. 214–15.

on the rate of investment and innovation; the slow development of facilities for technical education; the handicap to capital formation of cheap and plentiful labour; an unequal income distribution retarding the demand for standardised consumer goods and hence restricting the exploitation of mass production methods; the imperfections of the capital market for domestic industry; and the prosperity of the late nineteenth and early twentieth centuries which dampened the incentive to change.[1] Habakkuk indicates a similar range of arguments—entrepreneurial deficiencies (both economic and sociological), an unfavourable factor endowment (cheap labour again), poor market prospects, slow progress of standardisation of British manufactures, the 'early start' thesis, a custom-bound society.[2] It is as if each authority were trying to outbid the other in the number of 'causes' which he can score. The favoured candidates appear to be: the inevitable nature of retardation, the effects of industrialisation abroad, the 'early start' handicap, the low rate of technical progress and the declining calibre of entrepreneurship. It is not denied that these influences were present to some degree in the British economy in the late nineteenth century; what is doubtful is that any of them can be shown to be 'causes' of retardation in any real sense. Apart from the main difficulty (that is, giving each factor in a catalogue of causes the relative weight it deserves), it is in many cases impossible to generalise about the validity of the factor itself. It may be useful to examine some of these 'causes' briefly to show how difficult it is to draw firm conclusions; for this purpose some systematisation will be useful.

Before doing this, it is relevant to inquire into the appeal of running down the performance of the British economy in the late nineteenth century. It seems as if economic historians are determined to represent the development of the British economy after the first flush of industrialisation in terms of progressive decline and failure. This attitude probably springs from the apparently unfavourable comparisons with growth rates in other industrial countries in the late nineteenth century; the evidence shows that the rate of growth of income per head was much lower in Britain than in the United States, Germany and even France.[3] But the step from such a

[1] J. Saville, 'Some Retarding Factors in the British Economy before 1914', *Yorkshire Bulletin of Economic and Social Research*, XIII (1961).

[2] H. J. Habakkuk, *American and British Technology in the Nineteenth Century* (Cambridge, 1962), ch. vi.

[3] Between the 1860s and 1914, national product *per capita* showed an average increase of 12·5 per cent per decade in the United Kingdom compared with 21·6 per cent in Germany and 27·5 per cent in the United States (for France the percentage growth per decade averaged 16·3 per cent over the nineteenth century as a whole),

comparison to propositions about Britain's relative stagnation to be accounted for by defects in the social and economic structure is by no means a logical one. Because the other industrial countries were starting from much lower levels it would have been surprising had their growth rates been similar to that of the United Kingdom.

The possible causes of retardation may be classified under three heads. The first covers the theoretical, *a priori* arguments which attempt to show that deceleration is inevitable in a mature industrial economy; this may be called the Law of Retardation argument. The second is a very broad category indeed, comprising all the economic and historical influences which might emerge from a comparison of the United Kingdom with the newly industrialising economies. These include the slowing down in population growth, a lower rate of technical progress (resulting from the early start or from a declining propensity to make new innovations), the effects of industrialisation abroad on British exports, the character of capital formation (either a too low overall level or too high a proportion being diverted to overseas lending), the effects of low profitability in British industries during the Great Depression period, and so on. The last group consists of the non-economic or sociological causes; prominent among these are decline in entrepreneurial ability (perhaps due to industrial nepotism, the inferior status of business relative to other professions, immobility in the social structure) and changes in the attitude of society as a whole (possibly the loss of 'growthmindedness' after mid-Victorian optimism collapsed). The lines between these groups are clearly not hard and fast: the law of retardation is rooted in economic trends such as the effects on the individual economy of the widening of the world's production base; arguments of too few innovations rely on opinions about the character of entrepreneurs; if British society became less growth-oriented in the late nineteenth century this was bound up with economic developments, such as the revulsion against free trade ideals in Europe and contemporary attitudes to the Great Depression. A detailed analysis of any of these explanations is far beyond the scope of this paper, and only the briefest comments will be made on some of the more popular explanations. If these comments are adverse, this does not mean to imply that the arguments are thereby disposed of. The aim is relatively modest; to indicate a few of the difficulties involved in explanations which rely on *a priori* reasoning, on comparisons with developments in the United States and Germany, or on sociological generalisations.

---

S. Kuznets, 'Quantitative Aspects of the Growth of Nations', *Economic Development and Cultural Change*, v (1956).

The hypothesis of retardation in total industrial output follows from the inevitable retardation of individual industries. As has often been pointed out, a logistic curve is most representative of a real description of an industry's expansion—a rapid increase in the early stages of an industry's existence, followed by a phase when the growth rate is lower, and ultimately succeeded by a period of absolute decline. The rate of growth of an industry is bound to fall off for a number of reasons.[1] First, there is the simple fact that a high growth rate cannot be maintained for ever. 'It is a natural development, and almost a truism, that the rate of expansion of industry, measured in per cent, must decline during the course of an industrialisation process. A rapid percentage increase in the beginning of an industry's existence cannot continue indefinitely without retardation, as otherwise production would soon reach completely abnormal figures.'[2] There is a tendency for technical progress to slacken as an industry expands; cost reductions in a new industry are limited by the character of the technological basis of the industry itself, and once the initial break-through is made, further refinements will tend to yield diminishing marginal cost reductions.[3] Merton's investigations in the 1930s showed that there is a skewness in the rate of innovation in a given industry weighted heavily towards the early phases of its growth.[4] Again, as technical progress advances, many particular improvements are merely new ways of producing existing products; in the absence of a rapid resurgence of demand for these products, this will make for natural retardation in individual sectors. Similarly, the spread of industrialisation throughout the world will tend to retard growth in a given industry in any one economy. Exhaustion of raw materials may ultimately exert a dragging influence on an industry's growth curve. Finally, on the demand side, retardation will follow from the fact that as products age the level of demand for each individual product (other than replacement demand) will tend to reach saturation point and rising real incomes cannot stave off this point indefinitely.

Retardation in individual industries does not necessarily imply

[1] The pioneer works on the problem of retardation date from the 1930s; prominent among them are S. Kuznets, *Secular Movements in Production and Prices* (New York, 1930); A. F. Burns, *Production Trends in the United States since 1870*, N.B.E.R. (1934); R. Glenday, 'Long Period Economic Trends', *Journal of the Royal Statistical Society*, CI (1938), and Hoffmann's standard work originally published in Germany in 1939.

[2] L. Jorberg, *Growth and Fluctuations of Swedish Industry, 1869–1912: Studies in the Process of Industrialisation* (Lund, 1961) p. 66.

[3] W. W. Rostow, *The Process of Economic Growth* (Oxford, 1953) p. 102.

[4] R. K. Merton, 'Fluctuations in the Rate of Industrial Invention', *Quarterly Journal of Economics*, XLIX (1934–5).

retardation in the economy as a whole because slowing down effects may be eliminated by the appearance of new fast growing industries. 'In "maturing" individual industries it is, of course, not uncommon to find slackening of growth rates, frequently after periods of increasing rates of growth in output. But there have always existed new as well as maturing developments, and hence the proportionate rate of growth of aggregate output has so far shown no clear-cut signs of slackening.'[1] On the other hand, the very appearance of new industries will increase the obstacles to growth in old-established industries. In many instances new industries produce goods which are substitutes for existing products and which therefore exert a direct influence on the growth rate for such products. They will also compete with the older industries for factors of production and their competition will be effective as their high productivity gains will enable them to pay higher prices for their inputs. Most important of all, deceleration follows from the fact that both the birth rate of new industries and the death rate of old industries are low, thus biasing the industrial structure towards old industries; since the aggregate growth rate is but a weighted average of the growth rates of individual industries the rate of increase of output in a mature economy will therefore tend to slow down. The point is that older industries will not be entirely eliminated unless there is complete product substitution; the mere proliferation of products suggests that the old industries will continue in existence. Further growth in these industries will depend on demand factors, particularly the rate of population growth and the level of average incomes; historical experience in industrialised countries suggests that after the early phases of industrialisation the birth rate tends to fall (though often the fall is merely temporary), and the income effect on *old* industries is also likely to diminish.[2]

Yet it is difficult to give the authority of a law to these retarding factors. They express only a *tendency* to decelerate, and retarding effects may be outweighed by special historical conditions such as the opening up of new markets, or by a high birth rate of new industries. Moreover, the case for inevitable retardation has up to the present not been substantiated by experience in that the growth rates of mature industrial economies have not displayed any continuing tendency to decline. Admittedly, there is evidence for growth rates after technological maturity to be lower than during early indus-

[1] W. Fellner, *Trends and Cycles in Economic Activity* (New York, 1956) p. 65.

[2] J. F. Weston. 'The Influences of Stages of Development on Growth Rates', American Statistical Association, *Proceedings of the Business and Economic Statistics Section* (1961) pp. 68–9.

trialisation, but the high growth rates of an industrialising economy are to be accounted for by rapid expansion in the leading sectors, by urbanisation and by the construction of a transport network. Once this period of exceptional growth has passed away further retardation has not been evident.

The secular stagnationists of the 1930s gave much emphasis in their analysis of retardation to the slowing down of population growth. This factor, however, has never received more than passing mention in explanations of Britain's declining rate of industrial growth. One reason for this is that the inter-census statistics indicate that the falling off was slight (see Table 1), though Hoffmann argues that if Ireland is excluded 'a certain similarity in the two patterns of growth for population and for industrial output is now evident—in both cases a period of rapid growth followed by a period of less rapid growth'.[1] A second reason is that French experience provides the classic case for an analysis of the relationship between the slow growth of population and industrial output, and the United Kingdom material is much less suitable for such an analysis. Nevertheless, it is interesting that according to Table 1 the periods of slow industrial growth (the 1880s and after 1900) are also the periods when population expanded the least. Although one factor in this may have been high emigration connected with the heavy foreign investment of these periods it also suggests some interaction between population and industrial growth. It is well known that this interaction is mutual, not only that changes in the rate of growth of population influence the rate of growth of industrial output but also that changes in the rate of growth of industrial output influence population changes. But whereas the latter is a long-term effect, that as industrialisation proceeds there may be a socio-culturally induced fall in the birth rate, a slowing down in population growth may influence industrial expansion in the short run by marginally restricting the home demand for consumers' goods,[2] by affecting the level of building construction, or by reducing the rate of investment perhaps through its effect on entrepreneurial expectations.[3] On the whole, it

[1] Hoffmann, *British Industry*, p. 214.

[2] An objection to this argument might be that smaller families increase the proportion of disposable income with positive effects on consumers' expenditure. This objection, however, is much more appropriate to the twentieth century when the multiplicity of goods especially consumer durables gave more opportunities for disposing of surplus income. In the nineteenth century aggregate consumers' expenditure was much more a direct function of the size of the population, and any income above subsistence was more likely to be saved.

[3] For an interesting analysis of the relationship between population and industrial growth, see United Nations, *The Determinants and Consequences of Population Trends* (New York, 1953) chs xiii and xiv.

seems doubtful that the slowing down in population growth was extensive enough to have much influence on the rate of industrial growth, though it might have had an indirect effect via the rate of capital formation. A comparative investigation of the British, French and German situations after 1870 showed that Germany, which experienced the largest increase in population in this period (especially after 1890), consistently invested a higher percentage of her national income than either France or the United Kingdom.[1]

A common argument is that which states that the rate of technical progress was lower in Britain than in the new industrial economies and suggests that this is a major factor in explaining retardation. The argument is not fully convincing. The declining productivity in the coal industry was the exception rather than the rule, and the stock example in iron and steel, tardiness in the adoption of the Gilchrist-Thomas basic process, might be explained by the fact that British steelmakers had by the time the new process came to light invested heavily in Bessemer plants, and a changeover would have been uneconomic. The difference in efficiencies was probably very small, the case for the basic process being founded not so much on greater operative efficiency as on more effective resource use, that is, cutting down imports and using domestic phosphoric ores. Again, one would have expected technical progress to be greater abroad where industries were still relatively young. Finally, there is no aggregate statistical evidence to support the view that technical progress in Britain was much lower. Even if the argument could be substantiated, is there necessarily a close relationship between high productivity and high output growth? Admittedly, a much higher rate of technical progress would enable an economy to expand more easily relative to the availability of factors of production. But the problem to be explained is not why the British economy expanded at a slightly lower rate than the newcomers but why the annual growth rate was half, or less than half, that abroad (see Table 2); the 'technical progress' argument scarcely seems relevant to this. In *a priori* terms, there is no reason why the British economy should not have been able to prevent the growth rate from falling by extending capacity on existing lines, even if techniques employed were not the most recent. For this argument to have any substance at all it is necessary to relate it to international competition. If productivity levels were lower in Britain than abroad this could have resulted in higher price levels for British exports, which might then have lost ground to the industrial products of other countries. But the proportion of British exports going

[1] L. Goldenberg, 'Savings in a State with a Stationary Population', *Quarterly Journal of Economics*, LXI (1947) 40–65.

to markets where they faced serious competition from other exporters was relatively small; many of the largest markets were in the Empire where competition was virtually non-existent. As for British exports to industrial countries, disparities in costs due to productivity differentials could have had little effect compared to the high level of tariffs, and indeed Britain's role in these markets was often merely to act as a marginal supplier in times of high demand.[1]

A corollary to the above argument is that which relates to entrepreneurial ability. The opinion that by the late nineteenth century British entrepreneurs, taken as a whole, were less dynamic, less adaptable and less efficient than their counterparts abroad or their forerunners at home is now a commonplace.[2] The basis for this opinion is still rather narrow, and the available material is not comprehensive enough to permit the generalisation that the quality of entrepreneurs in Britain was markedly inferior to that in the United States or Germany. Apart from isolated fragments, the only detailed information is that put forward by Miss Erickson in her study of the steel and hosiery industries.[3] Because this information is primarily statistical relating to age, education and social background it does not throw direct light on the capabilities of entrepreneurs, and of course refers to two industries only. Does it necessarily mean that because a businessman is elderly, has inherited the business from his father, or has social ambitions, he is therefore inefficient? Were *all* these deficiencies peculiar to British entrepreneurs and to them alone?

A balanced discussion of the pros and cons of the case for entrepreneurial decline is given by Professor Habakkuk in his investigation into British and American technology.[1] He acknowledges that there are objections: 'the argument ignores, or at best does not explain, the curious patchiness of English business performance in this period. The rapidity of technical advance, in shipbuilding and in the open-hearth sector of the steel industry, for instance, show that the second generation of entrepreneurs in family firms could be conspicuously successful.[5] On the whole, however, Habakkuk seems

[1] This was especially true of the exports of capital goods, S. B. Saul, *Studies in British Overseas Trade 1870–1914* (Liverpool, 1960) pp. 142–3.

[2] An early instance of the argument was put by Marshall some sixty years ago: 'her [U.K.] imports of electrical plant and aniline dyes show that the hold on industrial leadership is insecure, and can be retained only by renouncing the easy self-complacency engendered by abnormal prosperity in the third quarter of the last century' (A. Marshall, *Official Papers*, 'Memorandum on Fiscal Policy of International Trade' (1903) p. 408).

[3] C. Erickson, *British Industrialists, 1850–1950: Steel and Hosiery*, N.I.E.S.R. (1959).

[4] Habakkuk, *American and British Technology*, ch. vi, pp. 189–220.

[5] Ibid., p. 194.

to think that there were entrepreneurial deficiencies and that these were important. His arguments in support of this view are not entirely satisfactory. He suggests that the social structure of Britain and the state of public opinion were less favourable than the American to entrepreneurship, in regard both to the recruitment of ability and to the full exertion of ability once recruited. He points to the social standing of the professions as against business in England and draws the conclusion: 'The wider the circle from which a country draws its businessmen, the more likely it is to produce great entrepreneurs.'[1] This is only true if one assumes that the pool of talent in a country is so small that the existence of competing opportunities elsewhere (for example, in the professions) can severely limit the quality of entrepreneurs coming forward. The concept of a small static élite is difficult to maintain. If a large proportion of the middle class is attracted to the professions, the entrepreneurs will be recruited from other classes. In any event, many of the successful businessmen in both Britain and the United States were men of low stock, and in Britain's case these would have been barred entry to the law, the church and the civil service. Another of Habakkuk's arguments is that British entrepreneurs were less capable because Britain was in a later phase of industrialisation: 'The drive inside the individual entrepreneur to expand his concern, to make the most of opportunities, is greatest in the early stages of industrialisation and loses some of its force once an industrial society has been created.' This is not self-evident, and is plausible only if related to either the 'early start' thesis or to degeneration in family firms. Finally, Habakkuk relates entrepreneurial deficiencies to the performance of the British economy: 'But the abundance of entrepreneurial talent in the United States was the consequence rather than the cause of a high rate of growth; and it was the slow expansion of English industry which accounted for the performance of English entrepreneurs in the later nineteenth century not vice versa.'[2] But given some relationship between the speed of technical progress and the rate of growth of output, and as he had earlier argued that entrepreneurial deficiencies may have accounted for less technical progress in Britain than in the United States, the reasoning appears almost circular. It would seem that the arguments of entrepreneurial failure in the United Kingdom have been given undue prominence relative to supporting evidence. If such a case is to be justified, it is necessary to explain why the economy which produced the most dynamic entrepreneurs in the first half of the nineteenth century produced the most inefficient in the second.

[1] Ibid., p. 191.
[2] Ibid., p. 213.

The 'early start' thesis is an attractive explanation of retardation in that it is comprehensive; it can take account of the low rate of technical progress, entrepreneurial backwardness and other interpretations of a declining rate of growth. At the root of the argument is the assumption that as an industrial economy matures it may develop rigidities which make it difficult to adapt to new techniques, changes in market situations, and so on. For example, the survival of old-established, durable but still fairly efficient machinery may make it uneconomic for a firm to adopt the latest innovations and techniques; a particular innovation will not be introduced unless it is estimated that total costs (including depreciation charges on the new machines) will be reduced. The old economy may suffer from a lack of standardisation, especially of inputs from engineering to other industries, as a result of having developed its industries piecemeal. It may have expended vast sums of money on ultimately unworkable technical discoveries, making costly mistakes which latecomers can avoid. The greatest rigidities of all may be in men's minds; the entrepreneurs of the early starter may become so accustomed to the monopoly position that falls to the industrial leader that they cannot adjust to the new situation when conditions of international competition develop. Ames and Rosenberg have tried to explain the assumptions and logical reasoning involved in the argument and concluded that the importance of the early start has been exaggerated.[1] But their arguments were by no means conclusive, and were vitiated by a comparison of the highly industrialised early starter with the agricultural low-income country (or in the authors' theoretical exercises, Westland industrialising after 1700 and Eastland after 1900). Using this basis for comparison they argue 'that the oldest and most advanced countries possess *on balance* far greater flexibility and capacity for change than predominantly agricultural low-income countries'.[2] This is stating the obvious. The critical basis for comparison is the highly industrialised early starter (such as Britain) and the highly industrialised latecomer following within a few decades of the leader (such as the United States or Germany); it would be difficult to disprove that 'transition costs' were greater in the former than in the latter case.

An obvious element influencing Britain's rate of industrial growth in the late nineteenth century was the expansion of industrial production abroad. Professor W. A. Lewis,[3] and following him

[1] E. Ames and N. Rosenberg, 'Changing Technological Leadership and Industrial Growth', *Economic Journal*, LXXII (1963).

[2] Ibid., p. 29.

[3] W. A. Lewis, *Economic Survey 1919–39* (1949) p. 74.

D. J. Coppock,[1] both suggested that Britain's retardation was exogenously determined by the growth of industry overseas, and can there fore be explained in terms of a declining trend in British exports. It was found that there was a strong correlation between output and export growth in Britain's major industries in the nineteenth century and a tendency for both rates to fall off after 1870.[2] Schlote found that the annual average rate of growth of United Kingdom exports was only 2·1 per cent between 1870 and 1890 and 0·7 per cent in the 1890s compared with 5·3 per cent between 1840 and 1860 and 4·4 per cent in the 1870s,[3] and another observer concluded that 'if exports had continued to grow in the last quarter of the century as in the third, English industrial output would have more than maintained the rapid pace of the earlier years'.[4] The main causes of retardation in exports were a drastic fall in the propensities to import from Britain of Western Europe and the United States as industrialisation advanced in these areas and the fact that Britain's compensation in agricultural, particularly Imperial, markets was insufficient because incomes were growing less rapidly in the primary producing than in the industrial economies. It seems most unlikely that this emphasis on retardation in exports *explains* the slowing down in industrial growth as against indicating the form which it took. This is because the spread of industrialisation to new areas is an ever-present danger for mature industrial economies; in normal circumstances the problem is met by changes in the structure of the advanced economy towards expanding and relatively untried fields of production. In the late nineteenth century, the declining rate of both output and export growth in Britain reflected not so much the growth of industrialisation abroad as the low rate of structural change at home. This leads on to an analysis of why structural change between industries did not compensate for retardation tendencies.

## IV

The hypothesis advanced here is the simple one that the retardation in Britain's industrial production after 1870 reflected the exceptionally low rate of structural change achieved during this period. The structural lag was to be explained up to the 1890s by the fact that

[1] D. J. Coppock, 'The Climacteric of the 1890s: A Critical Note', *Manchester School*, XXIV (1956).

[2] Ibid., p. 28.

[3] W. Schlote, *British Overseas Trade from 1700 to the 1930s* (Oxford, 1952) p. 42.

[4] J. R. Meyer, 'An Input–Output Approach to Evaluating the Influence of Exports on British Industrial Production in the late Nineteenth Century', *Explorations in Entrepreneurial History*, VIII (1955) 12.

there were no new high growth industries leading the economy while the more recent growth industries, steel and engineering, were already facing strong competition overseas. After the late 1890s important new industries were being developed in the world economy, but their growth in Britain was restricted by a number of circumstances which made investment in them seem uneconomic. This explanation is not completely new, and has been hinted at on many occasions; Musson, for example, suggests that the falling off in the rate of growth is to be explained by the lack of 'immense new technological innovations'.[1]

The argument requires certain assumptions. First, that there is discontinuity in the flow of major (that is, industry-creating) innovations. It is necessary to the hypothesis that after the innovations in steel, the development of the steamship, and technological advances in machine tools which fostered the engineering industries in the 1850s and 1860s there was a lull before the major innovations of the 1890s made possible the growth of the motor-car, electrical engineering, rayon and other new industries. The second assumption is that new industries enjoy the highest rates of growth and are virile enough to influence the aggregate rate of growth. The skewness of technical advances in a given industry,[2] and the role of high elasticity of demand for new products support this. Also, historical experience suggests that the differential in the growth rates of old and new industries is substantial enough for newer industries to assert themselves in overall output statistics at a fairly early stage. Thirdly, it assumes that long-established industries in the economy are unable to maintain their high growth rates of the past; theoretically, that old industries tend to grow slowly is the converse of the thesis that new industries grow rapidly. In the late nineteenth century British economy mass steel production and other capital goods industries in the engineering field could hardly be included in the category of old or declining industries. That these industries failed to emerge as new growth sectors was due to a chance historical factor—that Western Europe and the United States were industrialising during this period. The character of the industrialisation process in these areas was such that their leading sectors were not textiles but the very industries on which the United Kingdom relied at that time, and the new

[1] A. E. Musson, 'British Industrial Growth during the "Great Depression" (1873–96): Some Comments', *Economic History Review*, xv (1962–3) 531.

[2] This does not necessarily mean that the rate of technical progress within a given industry will decline progressively. An old-established industry with a modest technological performance may sometimes be transformed by new revolutionary innovations. An example is the current technological revolution in the steel industry based on the adoption of new oxygen-using processes.

economies were, as a result of more favourable resource endowment and the timing of innovations in steel, better placed than Britain to exploit them.

The absence of leading sectors in the British economy after 1870 meant that her growth rate was liable to fall. Leading sectors derive their momentum from autonomous impulses, such as new technological inventions, the discovery of new resources or independent growth in foreign demand. At the same time they must have direct effects on other sectors by giving rise to demands for new inputs or by improving the flow of intermediate goods to purchasing industries (i.e. by backward and forward linkages), and also indirect external economy effects on the growth rate via their impact on the social structure, changes in economic organisation, etc.[1] Growth sectors of this kind were conspicuously absent in the post-1870 period as compared with, say, the inter-war period when new leading sectors helped to speed up industrial growth (in spite of heavy unemployment) especially in the recovery period after 1932.[2] The analysis may be applied to the 1870–1913 period as a whole, though less forcibly after the 1890s; in the decade or two before the First World War the technical conditions for exploiting the new innovations had been created but market possibilities remained unfavourable. The character of the Great Depression of 1873–96, on the other hand, fits very well with the thesis of low structural change in the sense that cyclical fluctuations of the era took the form of short upswings (1880–2 and 1887–90) and much longer downswings (1873–9, 1882–6 and 1890–6). 'In periods when great new industries are rising to maturity over several decades, it is likely that booms will be very vigorous and carried to high points, and depressions will be short-lived. And similarly in periods when great new industries have reached their maturity and ceased to grow, and equally important new industries have failed to take their place, it is likely that booms will be less vigorous, prosperity relatively short-lived, and depressions deep and prolonged.'[3]

It was shown above that within the longer period 1870–1913 there were two phases of exceptionally slow industrial growth, the 1880s and after 1900. One notable feature is that the rate of growth of in-

[1] For an analysis of the implications of this statement, see W. W. Rostow, 'The Problem of Achieving and Maintaining a High Rate of Economic Growth: A Historian's View', *American Economic Review*, Papers, 50 (1960); and S. Kuznets, 'Notes on the Take-off' in International Economic Association, *Economics of Take-off into Sustained Growth* (1963) pp. 28–30.

[2] See H. W. Richardson, 'The Basis of Economic Recovery in the 1930s', below, Section B, 7.

[3] G. Terborgh, *The Bogey of Economic Maturity* (Chicago, 1945) p. 24.

come was substantial in the 1880s but very moderate indeed after 1900. This high rate of income growth in the 1880s illustrates the point that slow industrial growth does not necessarily mean stagnation. More significant is the fact that both periods were characterised by heavy foreign investment. Exports of capital were consistently high in the 1880s, averaging £61·6 million in the years 1881–5 and £87·6 million a year between 1886 and 1890. In the early years of the twentieth century foreign investment was very moderate, but the annual average in the period 1906–10 was £145·8 million and £206·1 million between 1911 and 1913.[1] This made a substantial contribution to the increase in income in at least three ways: by financing cost-reducing transport innovations abroad and thus improving the terms of trade, by promoting the export industries (unfortunately not new growth industries), and by adding to Britain's invisible receipts. It is a reasonable inference that the slow industrial expansion and the high foreign investment of the 1880s and the period 1900–13 were not pure coincidence, for the higher rates of industrial growth in the 1870s and 1890s were accompanied by low levels of capital export. Table 3 provides the basic data which hints at the nature of the relationship between home and foreign investment. It is clear that a low rate of capital formation cannot explain the slow industrial growth of these periods, for capital formation (as a percentage of G.N.P.) was almost as high in the 1880s and after 1900 as in the 1870s, and much higher than in the 1890s. On the other hand, retardation may have been associated with low *domestic* capital formation, as this was somewhat lower in the 1880s and in the period 1904–13. At the same time, the proportion of foreign investment to gross domestic capital formation was exceptionally high in both these periods. In a statistical sense, therefore, foreign investment was at the expense of domestic investment. But home and foreign investment are not interchangeable quantities: there is no guarantee that if capital is prevented from going abroad it will be employed at home or vice versa. It may be more accurate to say that capital went abroad in these periods because given the prospective rates of return it could not be profitably employed at home, and because conditions abroad permitted foreign investment. It is sometimes argued that capital exports in the late nineteenth century were at the expense of domestic investment in the sense that the British economy was so geared to foreign lending that profitable domestic opportunities suffered. There is more justification for Cairncross's view that foreign investment was a 'sink' for unemployable capital,

[1] A. H. Imlah, *Economic Elements in the Pax Britannica* (Harvard U.P., 1958) pp. 73–5.

a *pis aller*, the alternative being a shortfall of investment below savings and hence lower income.[1] Britain's propensity to export capital in the second half of the nineteenth century had its limits as shown by the reactions against foreign lending after the collapse of the overseas railway boom in 1873 and the Baring crisis in 1890. Despite the fact that the London capital market was so deeply concerned with foreign lending, it may still be argued that foreign investment went abroad in such large quantities only because of the absence of suitable investment opportunities at home.

Supporting evidence may be found for this argument. Some of the speculative domestic ventures of the early 1880s did not suggest

TABLE 3

Capital Formation and Overseas Investment

| | *Gross domestic capital formation as % of G.N.P.* | *Foreign investment as % of G.D.C.F.* | *Total C.F. as % of G.N.P.* |
|---|---|---|---|
| 1870–9 | 10·5 | 44·0 | 15·1 |
| 1880–9 | 9·2 | 62·1 | 14·9 |
| 1890–9 | 9·7 | 36·7 | 13·3 |
| 1900–9 | 10·6 | 41·6 | 15·0 |
| 1904–13 | 9·4 | 75·6 | 16·6 |

an investing class willing to risk money only overseas. The substantial and not firmly based investment booms in the notorious 'single ship companies', electric utilities and hotels indicate a search for profitable investment outlets at home.[2] Similarly, the not inconsiderable investment boom in 1893–5 in the bicycle industry gives some impression of what might have happened had there been important new industries developing at this time. Had there been industry-creating innovations in the late nineteenth century the foreign/home investment ratios would certainly have been different. It should be noted that this structural argument does not exclude other interpretations of retardation. For example, if it can be shown that technical progress expressed in terms of labour productivity was lower in this period, this could largely be accounted for by the absence of new *high productivity* industries.

The analysis cannot be applied as easily to the situation after 1900. By that time the rate of innovation had moved upward again,

[1] In Cairncross's words: 'Is it certain that, if there had been no convenient "sinks" for British capital in foreign countries, the income from which that capital was produced would ever have been created?' A. K. Cairncross, *Home and Foreign Investment 1870–1914* (Cambridge, 1953) p. 232.

[2] For evidence on this see H. A. Shannon, 'The Limited Companies of 1866–83', *Economic History Review*, IV (1933).

and the technical base for the development of the new twentieth-century growth industries had been laid down. American experience suggested that even by the early 1900s the new industries could be developed, yet the post-1900 period in Britain was characterised by further retardation and even heavier overseas investment. This lag cannot be satisfactorily explained by arguments based on lack of effective demand for new products. Although average income levels did not permit much exploitation of the market for motor vehicles before 1914 as compared with the United States, the substantial quantities of imports of newer types of goods, such as synthetic dye-stuffs and electrical appliances, proved that there was a market for the new industries in the United Kingdom.[1] Foreign investment is once again the key to the situation. The prospective yield of capital abroad was high enough to outweigh the moderate impact which domestic market opportunities might have had on the demand for new products and the yield of capital in new industries. The new domestic ventures contained a considerable element of risk which contrasted with the almost complete security and yet reasonable return offered by government and state borrowers in the British Dominions.[2] Moreover, an important effect of foreign investment was to boost British export industries, which meant the traditional staple industries.[3] Thus the low rate of structural change in British industry was matched by sluggishness in the changing structural pattern of British exports. [4]This expansion in old-established exports

[1] Saul, *British Overseas Trade*, pp. 37–8, states that high on the returns of imports from Germany in 1913 were chemicals (£1·9 million), synthetic dyestuffs (£1·7 million) and scientific instruments (£700,000), while from the United States imports of scientific instruments (£1·4 million) and motor-cars and parts (£1·5 million) were important. The small proportion of total 'new' exports reflects the slow development of these industries before 1914. Saul lists the following new exports:

| | |
|---|---|
| electrical goods | £5·39 million |
| motor-cars and parts | £4·36 million |
| scientific instruments | £1·83 million |
| motor-cycles | £990,000 |
| disinfectants and insecticides | £507,000 |
| artificial silk | £327,000 |
| celluloid manufactures | £237,000 |
| asbestos manufactures | £105,000 |
| aeroplanes | £47,000 |

Altogether these totalled only £13·79 million, or 2·6 per cent of net exports.

[2] The status of these loans had been made more secure than ever as a result of the Colonial Stock Act of 1900.

[3] W. A. Lewis, 'International Competition in Manufactures', *American Economic Review*, Papers, 47 (1957) 578–87.

[4] H. Tyszynski, 'World Trade in Manufactured Commodities, 1899–1950', *Manchester School*, XIX (1951) and R. E. Baldwin, 'The Commodity Composition

meant that the old industries appeared relatively more attractive than the new to the domestic investor. This harmed industrial growth, for the impact of overseas lending on the growth rates of the staple industries was moderate compared with the *potential* effects of expansion in the new. The appeal to investors of prospects in the new industries did not fully reflect the range or size of opportunities offered. When the twentieth-century industries later grew to maturity demand factors and input–output patterns reinforced the growth of one with the growth of another, and the new industries formed an interdependent sector. But many of these stimuli came within the field of external economies which were not, and could not, be taken into account by the pre-1914 investor. He was favoured by high yields, or moderate yields with security, from investing abroad, while the staple industries appeared profitable. In order for there to have been less overseas investment and a more intensive development of the new industries the pre-1914 generation would have had to make real sacrifices in terms of current income. Thus, explanation of retardation in terms of lagging development of the newer industries implies no criticism of the business and investing classes of the period, for this lag resulted from the fact that of the possible investment outlets of the time the new industries *appeared* to be the least profitable.

## V

This article stems from dissatisfaction with the direction of emphasis in recent attempts to explain Britain's declining rate of growth in the late nineteenth century. Interpretation of British economic history seems to have been marred by a tendency to describe industrialisation before 1870 in terms of dynamism and energy, as the classic case of economic growth, but development after 1870 in terms of complacency, relative backwardness and lack of adaptability. The contrast is far too sharp to be convincing. This tendency has been especially marked in explanations of Britain's industrial retardation. The favoured arguments, such as a decline in the calibre of entrepreneurs or a too low rate of technical progress, are generalisa-

of Trade: Selected Industrial Countries 1900–54', *Review of Economics and Statistics*, Supplement, XLI (1959). The share of textiles in total British exports fell only very slightly from 38·3 to 37·6 per cent of the total in the period 1900–13, while there was no relative expansion in the two main expanding groups: machinery and vehicles (Baldwin, Table A—1, p. 60). At the same time Britain was maintaining her share of world textile exports (this fell slightly from 47·6 to 44·5 per cent between 1900 and 1913), whereas her share of world machinery exports fell from 39·7 to 29·2 per cent and of vehicles from 48·0 to 37·0 per cent, due to her failure to expand as fast in the newer categories (Table A—3, p. 63).

tions drawn from a few scattered instances which cannot be confirmed by present knowledge. The myopic preoccupation with the search for defects in the economic structure of Britain in the late nineteenth century has resulted in a distorted view of British economic growth as a whole and has thrown the deceleration after 1870 out of perspective.

The upshot of the above argument is to suggest that the declining rate of growth after 1870 cannot be studied in isolation but only in the light of the periods that preceded and followed the years 1870–1913. There are strong theoretical reasons why the rate of growth in an individual industry should fall off sooner or later, but this does not necessarily mean retardation in the economy as a whole. Any *tendency* for the aggregate rate of growth to decelerate may be (and usually is) outweighed by compensating forces. The retardation after 1870 can best be explained by referring to the preceding period; the rate of growth was high between 1780 and 1870 because during this time the basic industries were being developed, the transport system built, urbanisation extended and the most consequential technical advance of the time, steam power, applied to a range of industries. Once these tasks neared completion, awaiting some new major technological solution, the growth rate was bound to fall. This did not mean inevitable retardation since after the First World War growth started to accelerate again. This suggests that the 1870–1913 era was exceptional in the history of the United Kingdom as an industrialised society as a period of much slower growth, for if any tendency towards retardation is very often offset by other influences why was this not the case in the late nineteenth century?

Yet it is doubtful that one needs to resort to sophisticated sociological arguments or to hazy generalisations of comparative industrial inefficiency to interpret the uniqueness of this period. If one will accept the hypothesis of discontinuity in the flow of major innovations (defined as innovations responsible for the establishment of completely new industries), then Britain's industrialisation process is exceptional as one during which there was a period (two or three decades after 1870) when the birth rate of new industries in the British economy was very low indeed. It is well known that new industries make a contribution to productivity growth out of all proportion to their share in output, and that they have a marked effect on the overall rate of growth. Although there were many opportunities for technical progress and introducing refinement in methods of production in the late nineteenth century there were no new major domestic investment outlets. Steel and engineering were the only important growth industries in the second half of the nineteenth century, and Britain's performance in these was affected by their simultaneous exploitation in Germany and the United States. The opportunities for structural change from low to high growth industries were more limited in this period than ever before or since.

This hypothesis required elaboration to explain the two 'depressions' of the period (as far as the rate of growth is concerned), the 1880s and this century up to 1913. That these periods were characterised by heavy overseas lending has been suggested as the most relevant factor. The high level of foreign investment in the 1880s indicated that profitable investment opportunities were not available at home, and the somewhat unsound ventures of 1881–3 suggest an unsuccessful search for such opportunities. But while the 1880s fall directly within the scope of the hypothesis as a period of dearth between spurts of industry-creating innovations, the years after 1900 do not, for by this time the new major innovations were known and were being exploited abroad. For British investors, however, the opportunities for investing abroad were a much more attractive proposition. Potential returns on capital showed a clear order of priorities: first, foreign investment; secondly, investment in the staple industries (staple exports being stimulated strongly by foreign investment between 1905 and 1913), with prospects in the new industries a poor third. Overseas countries were demanding both capital and goods, and the prosperity accruing to the British economy made the new investment outlets at home seem risky and uneconomic. On the other hand, the substantial imports of newer types of goods suggest that there were opportunities (that is, potential home demand) which could have been exploited even at this early date. But many of these opportunities fell within the category of external economies, and hence were outside the scope of the individual investor's time horizon. Since a higher rate of investment in the new industries before 1914 would have involved a loss of current real income for the sake of the future this would have required an altruism beyond what one could expect of the generation's investors. Industrial expansion was slow because prosperity in the staple industries meant only moderate growth compared with the high growth *potential* of newer industries. Foreign investment was possibly of great advantage to the British economy in the forty years before 1914, but it is important to note that it made a far greater contribution to the growth of national income than to the rate of growth of industrial production.

This interpretation of the phase of retardation in Britain's industrial production is tentative. But it may be argued in its favour that it places the late nineteenth century in its wider setting and is compatible with accepted notions of what one understands by the industrialisation process. It does not ask us to fall back on imperfectly understood if plausible sociological arguments which founder on attempts to explain the acceleration in industrial growth of more recent decades; nor does it require belief in the shaky assumption of an irrevocable break of trend after 1870. On the other hand, as an aggregative explanation emphasising changes in the structure of the economy as a whole, it is bound to gloss over unresolved questions about the position of individual firms and industries. But only the microscopic and hence gradual accumulation of evidence can permit generalisation on these points. Until this is possible we should be wary of dogmatising on lack of adaptability and entrepreneurial decline. There may have been signs of technical backwardness, entrepreneurial failure and slow readjustment in some firms and industries, but it is suggested that their effects were marginal.

# 2 The Problem of Productivity in British Industry, 1870–1914

It is now generally accepted by most students that the period 1870–1914 saw a retardation in British economic growth. The rate of growth of nearly all the major economic indices—exports, total output, industrial production and productivity—diminish or decelerate in the late nineteenth and early twentieth century. Table 1 presents

TABLE 1

Rates of Growth of Production and Productivity in the U.K., 1860–1913 (percentage per annum)

| | *Rate of growth of industrial production (incl. building)* | *Rate of growth of industrial productivity per man year* | *Rate of growth of total output per man-hour* |
|---|---|---|---|
| 1860–70 | 2·9 | 1·1 | n.a. |
| 1870–80 | 2·3 | 1·2 | 0·9 |
| 1880–90 | 1·6 | 0·5 | 3·8 |
| 1890–1900 | 2·8 | 0·2 | 1·3 |
| 1900–13 | 1·6 | 0·2 | 0.6 |

Sources: A. Maddison, *Economic Growth in the West* (1964) p. 232; K. S. Lomax, 'Growth and Productivity in the United Kingdom', *Productivity Measurement Review*, XXXVIII (1964) 6; E. H. Phelps Brown and S. J. Handfield-Jones, 'The Climacteric of the 1890s: A Study of the Expanding Economy', *Oxford Economic Papers*, 4 (1952) 294.

the key data in summary form. If the dimensions of the retardation are fairly clear cut, the explanations of the problem are far from settled. In recent years a spate of learned articles has appeared on the subject with the result that there are now a variety of possible explanations for Britain's poor economic performance.[1] It is not the intention here to review all this literature or discuss all the possible

[1] Some of the problems and literature are discussed in D. H. Aldcroft, 'The Entrepreneur and the British Economy, 1870–1914' below, Section B, 3, and 'Technical Progress and British Enterprise 1875–1914', below, Section B, 4. Recent discussions include: A. E. Musson, 'British Industrial Growth During the "Great Depression" (1873–96): Some Comments', *Economic History Review*, XV (1962–3); D. J. Coppock, 'British Industrial Growth During the "Great Depression" (1873–96): a Pessimist's View', *Economic History Review*, XVII (1964–5) and Musson's 'Reply', in the same issue; J. Saville (ed.) *Studies in the British Economy, 1870–1914*, special number of the *Yorkshire Bulletin of Economic and Social Research*, XVII (1965); H. W. Richardson, 'Retardation in Britain's Industrial Growth, 1870–1913', above, Section B, 1; C. Wilson, 'Economy and Society in Late Victorian Britain', *Economic History Review*, XVIII (1965) and W. Ashworth, 'The Late Victorian Economy', *Economica*, XXXIII (1966).

alternatives which have been presented. The chief aim in fact is to concentrate attention on one particular aspect of the problem, namely the decline in industrial productivity. This variable has been regarded by some economists as the key element in the general economic retardation or 'climacteric' of this period, though reasons for the lag in industrial productivity are far from clear. Most of this paper will be devoted to a critical discussion of the major causal factors which have already been suggested and the presentation of an alternative.

First let us take a closer look at the productivity data. An index of industrial productivity based on the Hoffmann industrial production data has been worked out for the years 1860–1914.[1] Compound annual rates of growth have been computed on the basis of this index and presented in Table 2 together with series for individual industries for which data were available. These show that apart from the early 1860s which were affected by the cotton famine, the growth of productivity was fairly high and sustained down to the end of the 1870s, but in the following decade a sharp break in trend occurred. Thereafter productivity grew only very slowly down to 1914, though there were temporary sharp upswings especially in the late 1880s and to a lesser extent in the later 1890s. A clearer picture emerges of the long-term trend if the short-term fluctuations are smoothed out by averaging. Thus in the last quarter of the nineteenth century and the first decade of the twentieth (i.e. 1880/1–1909/10) the annual average percentage increase in productivity works out at about 0.25 per cent compared with 1·87 per cent in the period 1865/6 to 1879/80 (Table 2, col. (4)). If the coal industry is included the growth of productivity in the latter period is almost negligible, 0·09 per cent per annum. The industries most affected appear to have been cotton, coal, iron and steel, brewing, railway traffic and possibly general engineering (see Table 2).

On the basis of the data at present available it would seem beyond dispute that industrial productivity grew much more slowly in this period compared with the years either before or after.[2] In fact in no

[1] See Phelps Brown and Handfield-Jones, in *Oxford Economic Papers*, IV (1952).

[2] The Hoffmann industrial production index, on which the productivity rates are based, has been criticised by a number of scholars for its inaccuracy. In fact, however, the recent reworking of the data suggests that the margin of error is quite small. The biggest discrepancies lie in the building sector (which we have excluded from our calculations) and in the later part of the period, that is from 1890 onwards when insufficient account was taken of the newer industries. Adjustments to take account of this factor would tend therefore to raise slightly the productivity rates for the later years but would not affect to any great extent the long-term trend of decelerating growth. Comparisons of the Hoffmann index and the Lomax index of industrial production over the long period suggest that the differences are generally quite small (see Table 2, cols (1) and (2) ).

TABLE 2

Average Annual Growth Rates of Production and Productivity (Quinquennial averages)

| | *Ind. production (Hoffmann, excl. building)* | *Ind. production (Lomax, incl. building)* | *Productivity (all industry)* | *Productivity (excl. coal)* | *Gross stock of plant and machinery (Feinstein)* | *Exports (Imlah)* | *Coal* | *Cotton* | *Iron and steel wares, machinery and tools* | *Pig-iron and steel* | *Brewing* | *Shipbuilding* | *Railway traffic* |
|---|---|---|---|---|---|---|---|---|---|---|---|---|---|
| | (1) | (2) | (3) | (4) | (5) | (6) | (7) | (8) | (9) | (10) | (11) | (12) | (13) |
| 1860/61–1864/65 | 1·54 | 2·0 | 0·44 | −0·16 | 1·47 | 0·24 | | 0·1 | | 0·48 | | 21·2 | 4·3 |
| 1865/66–1869/70 | 3·25 | 2·9 | 1·8 | 2·4 | 0·91 | 6·5 | | 8·64 | | 1·54 | | 2·92 | 2·23 |
| 1870/71–1874/75 | 2·42 | 3·9 | 1·62 | 1·5 | 1·51 | 2·18 | −6·0 | 2·8 | | 1·4 | | 5·12 | 1·53 |
| 1875/76–1879/80 | 2·44 | 1·0 | 1·16 | 1·72 | 1·59 | 3·82 | 4·46 | 2·58 | | 5·1 | | −0·24 | −1·0 |
| 1880/81–1884/85 | 0·78 | 0·5 | −0·55 | −0·58 | 1·12 | 1·7 | 0·02 | −1·26 | −2·1 | 0·46 | | −0·78 | −1·1 |
| 1885/86–1889/90 | 3·24 | 2·8 | 1·72 | 2·2 | 1·06 | 4·14 | −0·7 | 3·88 | 2·06 | 4·58 | 1·54 | 13·86 | 0·41 |
| 1890/91–1894/95 | 0·48 | 1·8 | −1·07 | −0·69 | 1·49 | 0·02 | −1·72 | 0·14 | −2·72 | −1·38 | −0·2 | −6·36 | −1·52 |
| 1895/96–1899/1900 | 2·72 | 3·9 | 1·42 | 1·41 | 2·65 | 1·1 | 1·49 | 1·08 | 2·05 | 5·98 | 2·63 | 6·26 | 1·02 |
| 1900/1–1904/5 | 1·08 | 1·2 | −0·54 | −0·14 | 2·75 | 4·4 | −0·96 | 1·92 | 2·18 | 0·93 | 0·93 | 1·22 | −0·58 |
| 1905/6–1909/10 | 1·02 | 0·6 | −0·46 | −0·71 | 1·75 | 4·18 | −1·62 | −3·34 | −0·14 | −0·04 | −0·76 | −3·16 | 0·78 |
| | | | | | Long-term Growth Rates | | | | | | | | |
| 1860/61–1879/80 | 2·4 | 2·5 | 1·3 | 1·4 | 1·4 | 3·19 | | 3·6 | | 2·13 | | | 1·59 |
| 1865/66–1879/80 | 2·7 | 2·6 | 1·5 | 1·87 | 1·3 | 4·17 | | 4·47 | | 2·66 | | 2·6 | 0·92 |
| 1870/71–1879/80 | 2·43 | 2·45 | 1·4 | 1·61 | 1·55 | 3·0 | −0·2 | 2·69 | | 3·15 | | 2·44 | 0·27 |
| 1880/81–1909/10 | 1·55 | 1·8 | 0·09 | 0·25 | 1·6 | 2·59 | −0·62 | 0·41 | 0·34 | 1·75 | 0·29 | 1·9 | 0·17 |
| 1880/81–1889/90 | 2·01 | 1·65 | 0·58 | 0·81 | 1·09 | 2·92 | −0·34 | 1·31 | 0·22 | 2·52 | 0·51 | 6·5 | −0·35 |
| 1885/86–1909/10 | 1·7 | 2·1 | 0·21 | 0·41 | 1·94 | 2·97 | −0·7 | 0·54 | 0·68 | 2·10 | 0·46 | 2·4 | 0·02 |
| 1890/91–1909/10 | 1·33 | 1·87 | −0·16 | −0·03 | 2·16 | 2·43 | −0·7 | −0·05 | 0·34 | 1·4 | 0·15 | −0·51 | −0·08 |

Sources: Cols (1), (3), (4) and (7)–(13) are based on W. G. Hoffmann, *British Industry 1700–1950* (1955 ed.) and E. H. Phelps Brown and S. J. Handfield-Jones, 'The Climacteric of the 1890s: A Study of the Expanding Economy', *Oxford Economic Papers*, IV (1952); col. (2) on K. S. Lomax, 'Growth and Productivity in the United Kingdom', *Productivity Measurement Review*, XXXVIII (1964); col. (5) on data kindly supplied by Dr C. H. Feinstein of the Department of Applied Economics, Cambridge University; col. (6) on A. H. Imlah, *Economic Elements in the Pax Britannica* (1958).

other period of British economic history has the level of productivity growth been so low for such a prolonged period. Comparison with the post-war period is instructive as a glance at Table 3 will show.

TABLE 3

Average Rate of Productivity Increase (percentage per annum)

| | |
|---|---|
| 1860–70 | 1·1 |
| 1870–80 | 1·2 |
| 1880–90 | 0·5 |
| 1890–1900 | 0·2 |
| 1900–13 | 0·2 |
| 1920–37 | 3·0 |
| 1950–60 | 2·2 |

Source: E. H. Phelps Brown and S. J. Handfield-Jones, in *Oxford Economic Papers*, IV (1952) 294, and London and Cambridge Economic Service, *Key Statistics of the British Economy 1900–1962* (1963) p. 9.

Moreover, by all accounts Britain's productivity performance was very poor compared with that of the other major industrial countries. In the United States the trend rate of growth of industrial productivity in manufacturing industry was around 1·6 per cent per annum in the period before 1914 and in Germany possibly as high as 2·6 per cent.[1]

Obviously such a prolonged period of very low productivity growth requires some explanation. No doubt a large number of factors could be assembled which had some bearing on the matter but for the sake of simplicity we shall confine our attention to three possible causal factors, which are as follows: (*a*) the theory of leading innovations, (*b*) capital accumulation and exports, and (*c*) technical progress. The reasons for reopening the inquiry into productivity stem largely from a nagging dissatisfaction with existing explanations that is those under heads (*a*) and (*b*). In a short paper such as this it will be impossible to do full justice to the question. The main task will be that of outlining some of the chief objections to the theories put forward and suggesting a possible alternative.

The leading innovation argument was put forward by Phelps Brown and Handfield-Jones in their original article of 1952. Briefly they maintained that the productivity check was caused by the diminishing effect of technological innovation and not because of a check to capital accumulation. In particular the 1890s ('the climacteric') saw the ending of the massive application of the techniques of steam

[1] John W. Kendrick, *Productivity Trends in the United States* (1962) p. 152.

and steel and a delay in the widespread adoption of the new techniques associated with electricity, the internal combustion engine and new chemical processes.

The weakening of the innovation effect is a persuasive argument and not without a certain amount of validity. It is by no means a new argument. As early as 1929 Kuznets maintained that there was a law of diminishing effect of technological improvement[1] and recently Richardson has referred to the 'discontinuity in the flow of major innovations' as a causal factor in the retardation in industrial growth of this period.[2] But the leading innovation theory is not a very satisfactory explanation of the productivity lag, since the argument as outlined by Phelps Brown is not fully consistent with the data and because it leaves a number of questions unsolved. While not rejecting the hypothesis entirely, therefore, it is necessary to outline a few of the more serious objections to the argument.

In the first place it is difficult to find evidence for the dramatic ending of the innovation effects of steam and steel. Steel, for example, had only just begun to take hold in the 1880s—since before that date it had been too expensive to use extensively—and its widespread application came in the next two decades. As late as 1885 Britain was turning out more puddled iron than steel. Its widespread application therefore only really began in the last decades of the nineteenth century, and though the growth of steel production diminished slightly after 1900 the figures certainly do not suggest that there was not much scope for the extension of steel after the 1880s. Between the early 1880s and 1895 U.K. steel production had more than doubled and by 1910 it had almost doubled again.[3] It seems hardly plausible, therefore, to suggest that the steel effect had been worked out by or in the early 1890s.

Steam power is a more difficult proposition because of the unsatisfactory nature of the statistics. What evidence we have, however, suggests that the really massive application of steam power came in the late nineteenth and early twentieth century, contrary to what is often supposed. In the 1880s it is true there does seem to have been a check to its growth but after that steam power in industry appears

[1] S. Kuznets, 'Retardation of Industrial Growth', *Journal of Economic and Business History* (1929) 549.

[2] H. W. Richardson, 'Retardation in Britain's Industrial Growth, 1870–1913', above, Section B, 1.

[3] U.K. steel production in million tons:

| | |
|---|---|
| 1880 | 1·29 |
| 1895 | 3·26 |
| 1910 | 6·37 |
| 1914 | 7·84 |

to have increased more rapidly than before. The quantity of fixed industrial steam power in use in the U.K. rose from 500,000 horse power in 1850 to 2 million in 1880 and then increased to over 9 million in 1907. These figures probably exaggerate the true position in the later period, however, since the data for 1907 is from the Census of Production whereas the figures for earlier years are based on Mulhall's incomplete survey of steam power in industry.[1] Nevertheless it does seem that the application of steam power was by no means insignificant in this period and this conclusion is supported by recent findings in this field.[2] Moreover, if we take account of the fact that electrically driven motive power was being applied fairly rapidly to industrial operations from 1900 onwards[3] then we would be almost certainly justified in saying that industrial motive power increased more rapidly in the two decades or so before 1914 than in the earlier period.

It is doubtful, therefore, whether steam and steel, especially the latter, came to an end in the late nineteenth century. In any case did steel have such an enormous impact upon productivity growth as the authors imply in their analysis? And if it did its effects must have been telescoped into a very short period in view of the fact that the steel age had only just begun in the early 1880s. Even if we accepted the argument there are still a number of unresolved points. Productivity is said to have received a check around 1885; if so one would have expected steam and steel to have been played out around the early 1880s. But this certainly was not true of steel, as we have already shown. The force of this argument is strengthened moreover if, as the data in Table 2 suggests, the turning point in productivity was around 1880, or alternatively in the 1870s as Coppock suggests.[4] Furthermore, how is it possible to explain the fact that the check to productivity was not associated with a similar check to capital accumulation? There is, of course, no reason to suppose that capital and growth are highly correlated, but as Coppock points out one would expect perhaps some rough association between the two since 'it is difficult to see why the pace of capital accumulation should

[1] M. G. Mulhall, *Dictionary of Statistics* (4th ed., 1899) pp. 545, 809.

[2] Coppock suggests that the average annual growth in steam power per head in U.K. manufacturing was of the same order of magnitude as in the United States between 1870 and 1907, that is 3·1 as against 3·3 per cent per annum. D. J. Coppock, 'Mr. Saville on the Great Depression: A Reply', *Manchester School*, XXXI (1963) 177. See also D. S. Landes in the *Cambridge Economic History of Europe*, vol. vi, pp. 327–8.

[3] By 1912 the proportion of motive power driven electrically in mining and manufacturing was around 25 per cent.

[4] D. J. Coppock, 'The Climacteric of the 1890s: A Critical Note', *Manchester School*, XXIV (1956).

continue unchecked when a period of massive innovation had ceased'.[1]

Finally we might add that the theory implies that productivity growth is determined largely by the application of one or two large-scale techniques and that when these are exhausted the inevitable result is a sharp break in productivity. In effect this is a version of the leading sector argument, the importance of which has been vastly overrated since Rostow produced his stages theory of growth. Although the impact of leading growth sectors is obviously important in the initial stages of a country's development one must be wary about overstressing their role in productivity growth in relatively mature economies. In the inter-war years, for example, productivity in British industry rose rapidly yet it would be misleading to suggest this was brought about mainly by leading new sectors based on electricity and the internal combustion engine. Certainly these sectors were important in raising productivity levels, but they were by no means the dominant influence, and it is clear from recent studies that productivity growth would have been considerably lower in this period had the gains not been spread fairly widely throughout the industrial economy.

The steam/steel or leading sector explanation of the productivity check is thus of somewhat doubtful validity. An alternative explanation has been put forward by Coppock which runs as follows.[2] If exports are regarded as an autonomous variable then the decline in the rate of growth of exports explains a decline in the rate of growth of production and in the required rate of investment. And given a reduction in the rate of investment a decline in the rate of growth will follow. In short, he says, the decline in productivity in the U.K. after the 1870s and its low level compared with the United States and Germany is to be found in the low rate of capital accumulation in industry brought about by a check to the growth in exports.

On both theoretical and empirical grounds this explanation is open to criticism. The chief causal factor is the decline in the investment variable yet no very convincing evidence is produced to substantiate this point. Admittedly the data on capital investment in industry are very limited for this period; the main source is the Douglas estimates for the growth of the capital stock in the U.K. (1865–1909).[3] After excluding farmers' and railway capital Coppock finds that the average rate of growth of (mainly) industrial capital between 1875 and 1914 is of the order of 2·3 per cent per annum. This of

[1] Ibid., p. 22. [2] Ibid.

[3] P. H. Douglas, 'An Estimate of the Growth of Capital in the United Kingdom 1865–1909', *Journal of Economic and Business History*, 2 (1930).

course tells us very little since we do not know what the rate of increase is before 1875. The Douglas figures do show, however, that the increase in capital in the decade 1865–75 was twice as great as that for any subsequent decade. It is largely on this information that the author bases his conclusions, yet there are a number of points which require clarification before the argument can be accepted.

The downturn in Coppock's productivity estimates does not in fact correspond with the timing of the check in the growth of the capital stock. In fact at the very time when capital is supposed to have grown most rapidly the productivity growth rate had already fallen substantially from 2·5 per cent to 1·2 per cent (1854/60–1861/5 to 1867/5–1866/74.[1] This lack of agreement in timing surely requires explaining. If there is a positive link between capital and productivity growth one would expect to see a significant downturn in the capital index either before or during the 1865–75 decade and not afterwards, unless there is some unexplained lagged response which has to be accounted for.

Even if the downturn in capital growth after 1875 could be used to explain the break in productivity, it still could not explain why productivity growth remained so low right down to 1914. Certainly it seems unlikely that the capital variable can account for the long-term course of productivity. According to Douglas the check to capital growth was halted in the middle of the 1880s and from then to 1914 assumes a constant rate of growth of 1·5 per cent per annum. Yet over the whole period productivity hardly increased at all. How is this to be explained? Does it in fact mean that the investment rate must always be above a certain level (in this case 1·5 per cent per annum) before any substantial increase in productivity can be achieved? This hardly seems plausible judging from the experience of later years. Between 1924 and 1938 output per wage earner in British industry rose by one-third or more despite the fact that there was virtually no net addition to the capital stock during the period. Prior to 1913 almost the reverse was true; between the early 1890s and 1913 the capital stock rose steadily yet there was hardly any gain in productivity.[2]

In order to try and clarify this point reference was made to more recent estimates for capital stock. The general conclusion to be drawn from the new data is that there was no serious check to capital investment in this period. For the economy as a whole the investment ratio fell off slightly in the 1880s but thereafter rose, and it would be

[1] Coppock, in *Manchester School*, XXIV, 12.

[2] We shall demonstrate below that there was no real check at all to capital accumulation during this period.

difficult to argue that the downturn had more than a marginal effect on productivity growth.

A more detailed breakdown for the industrial sector alone was made by computing the rate of growth of the stock of plant and machinery (mainly though not entirely used in industry) from estimates made by Feinstein.[1] These estimates are fairly crude but it was thought that over the long term they would serve as a reasonably reliable guide as to the rate at which industry was adding to its stock of capital. It was found that there was no clear-cut correlation between productivity growth and additions to the capital stock of industry. In fact in less than half the number of observations did the growth of plant and machinery move in the same direction as productivity. Indeed the most striking feature is that when productivity growth was lowest (1890/1–1909/10) the stock of plant and machinery was increasing most rapidly while the reverse was true for the period 1865/6–1879/80 (see Table 2, cols (4) and (6)).

The lack of a positive association between investment and productivity will occasion no surprise to those familiar with current growth theory. In recent years economists have become increasingly sceptical of the importance once attached to capital as a growth producing agent. Various attempts—both theoretical and empirical—have been made to show the importance of technical progress as opposed to capital accumulation in the growth process.[2] While it is possible that the trend of opinion has swung too far in the opposite direction it remains nonetheless true, as Professor Williams has recently pointed out, that 'productivity growth is not a mechanical function of the investment rate'.[3] Even Coppock himself has been forced to admit in a later work that he originally placed too much emphasis on capital accumulation *per se* as a growth producing agent.[4]

One of the reasons for the confusion about the causal relationship between growth and investment arises from the fact that attempts have been made to draw conclusions from capital estimates never designed for the specific purpose in question. For one thing there is no satisfactory index of the growth of capital in manufacturing and even more important there are no statistics relating to the rate of replacement investment. The latter may well be the key variable,

[1] Thanks are due to Dr C. H. Feinstein of Cambridge University for providing these data. He is, however, in no way responsible for the use made of the figures.

[2] See, for example, Odd Aukrust, 'Factors of Economic Development: A Review of Recent Research', *Productivity Measurement Review* (Feb 1965).

[3] B. R. Williams, 'Prices and Incomes', *District Bank Review* (Jun 1965) 2.

[4] D. J. Coppock, 'British Industrial Growth During the Great Depression (1873–96): A Pessimist's View', *Economic History Review*, XVII (1964–5) 393, note 3.

however, for if replacement investment embodying technical progress is running at a fairly high level productivity may well increase quite rapidly irrespective of what is happening to the total capital stock. Conversely, a low rate of replacement investment or even a high rate which is devoted to static techniques may produce a low productivity growth even though net additions to the capital stock are substantial. It may well be that this is the crucial factor in understanding the productivity lag before 1914. Obviously it will not be possible to prove this point statistically since the relevant data are not available, but a more subjective approach will suggest that this is a correct hypothesis.

Before tackling this problem it is necessary to deal with the other main component of the capital theory of the productivity lag, namely exports. According to Coppock exports play a major independent role since they affect the rate of investment. Regardless of the fact that we have cast doubt upon the alleged investment lag, it is doubtful whether exports can be accorded this special role. Certainly there is a check to the growth of exports in the later nineteenth century compared with decades prior to 1860 but the decline is by no means continuous. Yet if exports affect productivity growth through investment, one would expect a fairly continuous association between the two variables. But in the period 1900–13 when productivity growth was at its lowest, exports staged a remarkable recovery from the trough of the 1890s and grew more rapidly than at any time since the late 1860s (see Table 2, col. (6)). Again over the long period 1885/6–1909/10 exports grew at a rate (2·97 per cent per annum) comparable with that for the years 1860/1–1879/80 but the rates of productivity growth were vastly different, 0·21 per cent as against 1·3 per cent in the earlier period (see Table 2, cols (3) and (6)). Moreover, the inter-war years provide no support for the hypothesis that the export component plays a major independent role. During this period exports never regained their pre-war level yet productivity advanced more rapidly than in the past half century.

Since the pattern of export growth is not entirely consistent with that of productivity it would seem to be misleading to regard exports as a major causal factor of the productivity lag. Perhaps a more accurate approach would be to suggest that the line of causation ran the other way, that is from the economy to exports, thereby relegating exports to a dependent variable. This argument has been expressed most forcibly by the American economist Kindleberger[1] and it has certainly much to commend it. There are at least three good

[1] See C. P. Kindleberger, 'Foreign Trade and Economic Growth: Lessons from Britain and France, 1850–1913', *Economic History Review*, XIV (1961–2).

reasons for accepting this argument as being the correct one. In the first place lower productivity in British industry compared with other countries (especially the United States and Germany) would result in relatively higher price levels for British goods and hence make British exports less competitive and foreign products more competitive in the home market. This is certainly the case with iron and steel, for example, the price of which rose substantially between 1883 and 1910 at a time when American and German steel prices were falling.[1] Secondly, the structure of British industry tended to be overcommitted to producing basic goods, e.g. rails and textiles, the demand for which was bound to diminish over time, and ill-adapted to producing newer goods the market for which was expanding rapidly. Moreover, Britain's export organisation was geared to selling traditional goods to primary producers and neglected the rich and expanding markets of industrial Europe and America.[2] Finally, there is plenty of evidence to suggest that British export orders were being lost in this period because of poor sales techniques, though it is impossible to attach any precise quantitative significance to this factor.[3]

Much more could be said about the current theories of the productivity climacteric but the above comments are sufficient to illustrate some of their defects. Neither the capital theory nor the leading innovations theory provide a fully satisfactory explanation of the productivity lag. In the light of recent data it seems very unlikely that there was any significant check to the rate of capital accumulation either in the economy as a whole or in the industrial sector alone, while the alternative hypothesis lays too much stress upon the application of one or two large techniques, the particular details of which we have cast doubt upon. The main defect of the current analysis, however, is that it lays insufficient stress upon the widespread and complex nature of technical progress as a source of productivity growth. The failure to appreciate the vital role of technical progress would be all right if it could be assumed that there were no technical backlogs and little delay in the utilisation or adoption of productivity-raising techniques. But this is an assumption divorced from reality. We shall argue therefore that investment was not unduly low in British industry during this period but that it was mis-allocated; that is, new investment was concentrated too heavily in the basic or old sectors of the industrial economy or, alternatively, replacement investment

[1] T. J. Orsagh, 'Progress in Iron and Steel: 1870–1913', *Comparative Studies in Society and History*, III (1960–1) 219–21.

[2] By 1913 something like 70 per cent of British exports went to primary producers.

[3] For details see D. H. Aldcroft, 'The Entrepreneur and the British Economy, 1870–1914', below, Section B, 3.

was either insufficient or of a traditional type. The second of these points is probably by far the more important. Too frequently replacement investment was devoted to static techniques and as a result it produced a delay in the utilisation of known productivity-raising or best practice techniques.[1] In this analysis technical progress (used in the widest sense of the term) is regarded as the key factor in productivity growth, and capital as a partially dependent variable. The importance of the whole concept has been emphasised by Salter in a recent work on productivity analysis: '. . . the delay in the use of new methods is extremely important in productivity analysis; it cannot be neglected, or even relegated to a minor role. . . . An understanding of productivity movements must include an analysis of the reasons for this delay in the utilisation of new techniques and an appreciation of the forces which determine the rate at which new methods displace old.'[2]

Obviously in a short paper such as this it will be impossible for a number of reasons to provide full evidence to support the above arguments. In the first place this paper merely represents some of the early findings of a fairly long study into productivity growth which is still being carried out. Secondly, much of the analysis is at the industry or micro-level and not all industries have yet been covered, while thirdly, it would be impossible in the space available to produce the more detailed data which lie behind the central argument. Nevertheless it is practicable to illustrate the above hypothesis as briefly as possible.

Recent work at the macro-level has been carried out by R.C.O. Matthews and his colleagues which tends to confirm our earlier suspicions about the important role of technical progress in growth. Matthews attempted to allocate the growth derived from the main factor inputs, i.e. labour, capital and technical progress (or residual) for the British economy during the past century. It is true that the

[1] The strong emphasis on the role of replacement investment is not misplaced. Replacement investment may well be the chief vehicle of productivity growth when net additions to the capital stock are low providing that this investment embodies the latest techniques. This situation is typical of the inter-war years when high productivity growth was accompanied by a low investment rate. Colin Clark has outlined the position clearly in his *National Income and Outlay* (1937) p. 262. 'The very rapid expansion in productivity at the present time is taking place at a time of heavily diminishing capital accumulation. . . . Without new investment the replacement of obsolete capital . . . appears to give all the necessary scope for the introduction of technical and organizational improvement and to bring about the rapid increase in productivity under which we are now living.' The same phenomenon occurred in the United States in the 1930s. See A. H. Hansen, *Monetary Theory and Fiscal Policy* (1949) p. 111.

[2] W. E. G. Salter, *Productivity and Technical Change* (1960) p. 49.

study refers to the whole economy rather than just the industrial sector with which we are mainly concerned, while in terms of time periods it is insufficiently disaggregated. Nevertheless it does seem to show that in the late nineteenth century through to 1913 it was the technical progress factor which accounted for the fall in the rate of growth. In fact the whole of the fall in the rate of growth of gross domestic product per man-year after 1899 was due to the technical progress function, while in the inter-war years when it recovered the rate of growth resumed a more normal course.[1]

At the micro-level there is abundant evidence to suggest that over a fairly wide sector of British industry best practice techniques were very slow to mature. New techniques of manufacture and improved methods of organisation which would have raised productivity were adopted only slowly. A few examples will illustrate this point more clearly though detailed examination cannot be made here.[2] The check to productivity in the coal industry might have been avoided had mechanisation been adopted more rapidly.[3] Similarly, the cotton industry neglected new machinery in spinning and weaving,[4] while many criticisms have been made about the technical backwardness of the iron and steel industry.[5] Technical failings were also apparent in certain branches of the engineering industry, the tinplate trade and even the railways. In fact many of Britain's major industries were technically unprogressive especially compared with their foreign counterparts and it is significant that in almost all industries which were known to be technically backward the rate of productivity growth was falling off. As Landes has recently commented: 'The worst symptom of Britain's industrial ills . . . was the extent to which her entrepreneurship and technology was defensive. She was no longer in the van of technical change; instead, even the best of her enterprises were usually being dragged in the wake of foreign precursors, like children being jerked along by important adults.'[6]

It is true of course that we still need to know more about many

[1] R. C. O. Matthews, 'Some Aspects of Post-war Growth in the British Economy in Relation to Historical Experience', *Transactions of the Manchester Statistical Society* (1964).

[2] See Section B, 3 below.

[3] A. J. Taylor, 'Labour Productivity and Technological Innovation in the British Coal Industry, 1850–1914', *Economic History Review*, XIV (1961–2).

[4] M. T. Copeland, 'Technical Development in Cotton Manufacturing Since 1860', *Quarterly Journal of Economics*, XXXIII (1909).

[5] T. J. Orsagh, 'Progress in Iron and Steel: 1870–1913', *Comparative Studies in Society and History*, III (1961).

[6] D. S. Landes, 'Factor Costs and Demand: Determinants of Economic Growth', *Business History*, VII (1965) 26.

individual industries and it would be misleading to argue on the basis of existing information that all industries experienced a lag in the application of new techniques. Some branches of industry appear to have been quite progressive.[1] On the other hand, it does appear that there was considerable scope for raising productivity in some of the major sectors had best practice techniques been applied more extensively. These industries accounted for a considerable share of Britain's industrial output in this period and it is inevitable that they exerted a significant drag on the overall rate of productivity growth. This is not to suggest that the productivity decline could have been halted completely but rather that the rate of productivity growth would not have been so low had the pace of innovation been more rapid, and had Britain's resources not been concentrated so heavily in those industries which were growing less rapidly than the newer sectors of the economy.[1] This line of reasoning seems to fit more closely with the facts that the theories which have been presented so far.

The most difficult problem however is to explain why the pace of technical innovation declined in this period. There are several possibilities though it is difficult to find one which is applicable generally. One suggestion that has frequently been raised is that of an exhaustion of technological opportunity. The major innovations thesis runs along these lines and recently the argument has been related more explicitly to the British pig-iron industry. McCloskey argues that the levelling off and slight fall in productivity in the pig-iron industry between the late 1880s and 1914 can be attributed to the fact that Britain had exhausted the current technology.[3] But this explanation is open to several criticisms. If, as he suggests, Continental practice was superior to the British around 1900 it is difficult to see how Britain could have exhausted all the technological opportunities at that time. Secondly, though the basic techniques in blast furnace practice had probably been perfected by the 1890s there were still many small improvements to be made which should have provided scope for some improvement in productivity. Thirdly, the argument tends to neglect improvements in productivity which can be achieved through better organisation and more efficient methods of production. Finally, even if the technological ceiling had been reached in this sector it would be difficult to apply this explanation to those industries whose technological boundaries were still infinite.

[1] See the studies in D. H. Aldcroft (ed.), *The Development of British Industry and Foreign Competition*, 1875–1914 (1968).

[2] This structural defect became more important in the early twentieth century.

[3] Donald N. McCloskey, 'Productivity Change in British Pig Iron, 1870–1939', *Quarterly Journal of Economics*, LXXXII (1968).

A second possibility is that the slower rate of growth of output in many of the older industries led to a reduced rate of investment and hence a lower rate of technical advance and this in turn would affect the rate of productivity growth. Temin, in fact, places a great deal of stress on this point with reference to the iron and steel industry.[1] It is true that the rate of productivity advance does tend to vary with rate of output growth but it is doubtful whether this holds true for all industries at all times. Some industries whose output fell during the inter-war years, for example, experienced quite respectable rates of productivity growth. The coal industry is an obvious example.

The third major explanation is the entrepreneurial one, namely that technical advances were neglected because of some failing on the part of businessmen. There is certainly a considerable amount of written evidence, by both contemporary and later writers, relating to their neglect of new techniques. It is difficult to say exactly how much importance should be attached to this factor though it certainly appears that it has more general relevance than the previous two reasons. On the other hand, it would be inaccurate to suggest that enterprise was lagging in all sectors or that it was the only reason for the slowing down in technical advance. Moreover, equally important in this context are the factors which motivated businessmen's decisions and an analysis of these provides greater insight into the determinants of technical progress. It is to these questions which we must now turn.

[1] P. Temin, 'The Relative Decline of the British Steel Industry, 1880–1913', in H. Rosovsky, *Industrialisation in Two Systems* (1966).

# 3 The Entrepreneur and the British Economy, 1870–1914

## I

In the last two or three decades much new work has appeared on the period 1870 to 1914 which has tended to confirm earlier suspicions that, while the British economy was growing fairly rapidly in absolute terms, its relative position *vis-à-vis* the world economy was deteriorating and that British industrial and commercial performance left much to be desired. British rates of growth of production, exports and productivity were slower in this period than in the early Victorian years, and compared unfavourably with growth rates abroad, especially with those of Germany and the United States.[1] In their quantitative assessments of the British economy most economists have been more concerned with analysing the changes in growth rates and economic variables and accounting for such changes in terms of their interaction without examining fully the basic factors which motivate changes in the variables themselves.[2] But as Kuznets has recently pointed out it is difficult to explain the course of economic change purely in terms of economic variables given the wide variety of other conditioning factors which must be taken into account.[3] Undoubtedly there are many factors, both economic and non-economic, which affected the course of British economic history in this period, but one of these in particular, that of British enterprise, has so far received comparatively little attention. The chief purpose of this article is to put forward the hypothesis that

[1] See, for example, E. H. Phelps Brown and S. J. Handfield-Jones, 'The Climacteric of the 1890s: A Study of the Expanding Economy', *Oxford Economic Papers*, IV (1952); E. H. Phelps Brown and B. Weber, 'Accumulation, Productivity and Distribution in the British Economy, 1870–1938', *Economic Journal*, LXIII (1953); D. J. Coppock, 'The Climacteric of the 1890s: A Critical Note', *Manchester School*, XXIV (1956); J. R. Meyer, 'An Input–Output Approach to Evaluating the Influence of Exports on British Industrial Production in the late Nineteenth Century', *Explorations in Entrepreneurial History*, VIII (1955); D. C. Paige *et al.*, 'Economic Growth: The Last Hundred Years', *National Institute Economic Review*, XVI (1961).

[2] Two useful correctives have been written. See W. A. Lewis, 'International Competition in Manufactures', *American Economic Review*, Papers, 47 (1957) and J. Saville, 'Some Retarding Factors in the British Economy before 1914', *Yorkshire Bulletin of Economic and Social Research*, XIII (1961).

[3] S. Kuznets, 'Quantitative Aspects of the Economic Growth of Nations: VI, Long-Term Trends in Capital Formation Proportions', *Economic Development and Cultural Change*, X (1961) 56.

Britain's relatively poor economic performance can be attributed largely to the failure of the British entrepreneur to respond to the challenge of changed conditions.

Although little is known about the origins and activities of British business leaders in this period[1] (and for this reason the subsequent analysis will of necessity be highly impersonal) there is ample evidence, in both contemporary and recent literature, to suggest that British businessmen were weighted down by complacency, conservatism and antiquated methods from the 1870s onwards.[2] Thus in 1902 McKenzie wrote:[3] 'If our workmen are slow, the masters are often enough right behind the times. In spite of all recent warnings, there is a stolid conservatism about their methods which seems irremovable. Even great houses which have the name of being most progressive, often enough decline to look into new improvements.' Four years later Shadwell, in his *Industrial Efficiency*,[4] echoed the same refrain, while in 1915 Veblen decided that Britain was paying the penalty for having been thrown into the lead and that British industrialists were burdened with 'the restraining dead-hand of their past achievement'.[5]

Much of the contemporary literature possibly tended to exaggerate the true position, yet Hoffman writing in the early 1930s was hardly less severe in his condemnation of British industrialists and merchants.[6] More recently two American authors, Landes and Hoselitz, have remarked on the apparent failure of British enterprise in this period,[7] while Musson in his reappraisal of the Great Depression has made some equally critical remarks about British enterprise.[8]

[1] See C. Erickson, 'The Recruitment of British Management', *Explorations in Entrepreneurial History*, VI (1953) 63.

[2] Toynbee wrote critically of British industrialists: 'If one were to single out the point in which Great Britain has been most at fault one would put his finger on the conservatism of our captains of industry who have idolised the obsolescent techniques which had made the fortunes of their grandfathers', *A Study of History* (abridged), p. 330, quoted in J. Jewkes, 'The Growth of World Industry', *Oxford Economic Papers*, III (1951) 9, note 4.

[3] F. A. McKenzie, *The American Invaders* (1902) p. 230.

[4] A. Shadwell, *Industrial Efficiency* (1906) vol. 2, esp. p. 453.

[5] T. Veblen, *Imperial Germany and the Industrial Revolution* (1939 ed.) p. 132.

[6] R. J. S. Hoffman, *Great Britain and the German Trade Rivalry, 1875–1914* (1933) esp. p. 80.

[7] D. S. Landes, 'Entrepreneurship in Advanced Industrial Countries: The Anglo-German Rivalry', *Entrepreneurship and Economic Growth*, papers presented at a conference at Cambridge, Massachusetts, (Nov 1954); B. F. Hoselitz, 'Entrepreneurship and Capital Formation in France and Britain since 1700', *Capital Formation and Economic Growth*, a report of the National Bureau of Economic Research (Princeton U.P., 1955); cf. H. Whidden, 'The British Entrepreneur: 1899 to 1949', *Change and the Entrepreneur* (Harvard U.P., 1949) p. 43.

[8] A. E. Musson, 'The Great Depression in Britain, 1873–1896: a Reappraisal', *Journal of Economic History*, XIX (1959) 199–228.

Moreover, studies of individual business firms confirm the belief that entrepreneurial initiative and drive were flagging particularly before 1900.[1]

It would appear therefore that the British entrepreneur had lost much of the drive and dynamism possessed by his predecessors of the classical industrial revolution. In a short article it will be impossible to treat the subject as extensively as one would wish. It is intended therefore to analyse four aspects which are relevant to the question in hand—technological progress, methods of production, scientific research and technical education, and commercial methods. Having demonstrated the shortcomings of Britain's entrepreneurs under these heads an attempt will be made in the last section to account for their deficiencies.

## II

It is suggested that technical progress is a more important factor in economic expansion than capital accumulation. Though relationships do exist between industrial growth and investment there is no close correlation between the two and it is not possible to explain differences in the rate of growth between countries simply in these terms. The statistics relating to Britain, America and Germany for the period 1870–1914 do not, for instance, permit such facile generalisations.[2] At one time it was fashionable to argue that capital was the major source of growth, but it has since been realised that high rates of investment do not necessarily produce high rates of growth and vice versa. Given favourable market opportunities faster growth can of course be achieved by increasing investment in existing techniques (e.g. the duplication of production facilities), but eventually there comes a time when additions to the capital stock yield diminishing returns. When this stage is reached only the willingness to invest in new technology will produce an acceleration in the rate of growth. Then capital accumulation is no longer an independent variable, but is determined by the rate of technical progress. In other words, in the long run although technical change will be facilitated and have wider repercussions with more capital formation it is technical progress which in the final analysis generates changes in the investment

[1] See especially, C. Wilson and W. Reader, *Men and Machines: A History of D. Napier and Son, Engineers Ltd., 1808–1958* (1958) p. 56; S. Marriner, *Rathbones of Liverpool, 1845–73* (1961) pp. 128–31; F. E. Hyde, *Blue Funnel: A History of Alfred Holt and Company of Liverpool from 1865–1914* (1957) p. 55; and W. G. Rimmer, *Marshalls of Leeds, Flax-Spinners, 1788–1886* (1960) pp. 252–3.

[2] See Kuznets, in *Economic Development and Cultural Change*, XI (1961); and 'Population, Income and Capital', *Economic Progress*, ed. L. H. Dupriez and D. C. Hague (1955) pp. 37–9.

variable and which is the major force producing growth. There is a further point in the argument to consider. Technical progress includes more than the use of new machines and the adoption of new processes; it can in the widest sense of the term cover a whole host of improvements such as better methods of organisation and the use of more skilled labour. In fact it is relatively easy to raise productivity by using existing resources in a more efficient manner, for as Professor Williams points out 'there is tremendous scope for growth through better industrial housekeeping'.[1] And since better resource utilisation requires little or no additional outlay in capital it follows that capital accumulation need play no part in raising growth rates. Thus, even in the short run, technical progress can hold the key to faster growth. Empirical investigation has shown that these assumptions are largely correct. Cairncross, Salter and Kuznets, to name only a few, have demonstrated the importance of technical progress as opposed to capital accumulation as a determinant of growth.[2] In a study of the American economy Urquhart found that technical change was the most important single factor in raising productivity between 1850 and 1950.[3]

If this hypothesis is accepted, then we are obliged to show that Britain's rate of technical progress was inferior to that of either Germany or America. For the moment we will abandon the all-embracing concept of technical progress and concentrate our attention on the adoption of new machines and processes to produce both old and new products.

The evidence suggests that Britain lost her former technological leadership in a number of industries. The failure to adopt new techniques, that is new machinery and other cost-reducing innovations, as rapidly as our competitors was one of the chief reasons for the fact that British export price indices were generally above European and American levels and ultimately for the decline in the rate of growth of the economy.[4] A few examples will serve to illustrate this point.

[1] B. R. Williams, 'Technical Innovation: The Key to Faster Growth', *The Times Review of Industry* (Dec 1962) 5.

[2] A. K. Cairncross, *Factors in Economic Development* (1962) esp. p. 107; W. E. Salter, *Productivity and Technical Change* (1960) p. 98; S. Kuznets, *Six Lectures on Economic Growth* (1959) p. 30. For useful summaries of the position see Williams, in *The Times Review of Industry* (Dec 1962); and C. Clark, *Growthmanship*, Hobart Paper 10 (1962).

[3] M. C. Urquhart, 'Capital Accumulation, Technological Change and Economic Growth', *The Canadian Journal of Economics and Political Science*, 25 (1959) 423.

[4] See C. P. Kindleberger, 'The Terms of Trade and Economic Development', *The Review of Economics and Statistics*, XL (1958) 77; and K. Martin and F. G. Thackeray, 'The Terms of Trade of Selected Countries, 1870–1938', *Bull. of the Oxford University Institute of Statistics*, X (1948) 376.

Between 1886 and 1913 Britain lost her position as leading producer and exporter of iron and steel.[1] In a recent comparative study Orsagh has shown that not only did Britain have a lower rate of conversion of pig-iron into steel than either America and Germany but also that between 1883 and 1910 German and American prices of iron and steel fell by 20 and 14 per cent respectively while British prices were roughly one-third higher.[2] This deteriorating position can be attributed largely to the failure of British iron and steel makers to keep abreast of modern developments. Although steel capacity more than doubled in the couple of decades before 1914 there was no significant change in technical practice. Britain was slow to modernise her plant[3] or to adopt new processes for steelmaking and coking. The more extensive use of the 'direct' process of steelmaking (that is liquid pig conversion direct to steel) could have resulted in considerable economies, while the adoption of by-product recovery ovens for coking would have permitted greater utilisation of waste gases and by-products. Yet in 1913 less than 28 per cent of the iron intended for steelmaking was sent in liquid form to the converters, whereas as early as 1900 some 75 per cent of German steel was made by the direct process.[4] Similarly in modern methods of coking Germany was well ahead; in 1909, 82 per cent of her coke was produced in by-product recovery ovens compared with only 18 per cent in Britain.[5] In fact at nearly every stage of the productive process British manufacturers lagged behind their rivals with the result that '... few British works, if any, are modern throughout in equipment and practice, with coking ovens, blast furnaces, steel furnaces and rolling mills adjacent to one another, and making full use of waste gases'.[6] No doubt the difficulties of the industry were enhanced by the shifting pattern of and deterioration in coal and ore resources, but personal deficiencies are alone responsible for the failure to adapt. As Orsagh says: 'A lack of *enterprise* was responsible for the

[1] For details see J. C. Carr and W. Taplin, *History of the British Steel Industry* (1962) pp. 230–5; and T. H. Burnham and G. O. Hoskins, *Iron and Steel in Britain, 1870–1930* (1943) pp. 30–1.

[2] T. J. Orsagh, 'Progress in Iron and Steel; 1870–1913', *Comparative Studies in Society and History*, III (1960–1) 219–21.

[3] In the 1890s Andrew Carnegie told British steelmakers what he thought was wrong with their trade: 'Most British equipment is in use twenty years after it should have been scrapped. It is because you keep this used-up machinery that the U.S. is making you a back number', quoted in F. Thistlethwaite, *The Great Experiment* (1955) pp. 211–12.

[4] D. Burn, *The Economic History of Steelmaking, 1867–1939* (1961 ed.) p. 222, note 4.

[5] Carr and Taplin, op. cit., p. 211.

[6] Committee on Industry and Trade, *Survey of Metal Industries*, H.M.S.O. (1928) p. 27.

continued existence of small, relatively inefficient, independent works; just as a lack of enterprise was responsible for the failure to innovate at a more rapid pace. The British entrepreneur, to judge by his behaviour, was unlike his German and American counterparts.'[1]

The iron and steel industry was not, of course, the only culprit. The failure to adopt labour-saving machinery in the coal industry was partly responsible for the decline in productivity from the 1880s onwards. In 1924 only 19 per cent of British coal output was cut by machinery compared with 70 per cent in America where productivity rose by 50 per cent between 1890 and 1914.[2] Admittedly the less favourable geological structure of British mines and the existence of a plentiful supply of cheap labour hardly provided an incentive to mechanise, but as Taylor points out, 'The achievements of Scotland and West Yorkshire, modest as they may seem by American standards, are sufficient to suggest that the explanation of the slowness of innovation in Great Britain is to be sought as much in the entrepreneurial as in the strictly technological field.'[3] In the tinplate trade the position was much the same, particularly after 1891 when the Americans made rapid progress in this field. 'Like that of the British coal industry, the prosperity of the tinplate industry was founded on unchanged organisation and unaltered technique. The lessons of the post-McKinley depression went unregarded and little was done to develop marketing facilities, to improve technique, to lower costs, or to adapt the structure of the industry to improve its competitive ability.'[4] Similarly the adherence to traditional techniques in the cotton industry was accompanied by diminishing returns. In contrast the efficiency of the American cotton industry increased considerably in this period because of the greater willingness to adopt new machinery, particularly the automatic loom which reduced weaving costs by about one-half.[5] Even shipbuilding is open to criticism for much of the equipment in British yards was less advanced than that in America or Germany, and indeed by 1939 the industry was badly out of date.[6] In fact, generally speaking, by 1914 there was hardly a

[1] Orsagh, in *Comparative Studies in Society and History*, III, 30.

[2] *Report of the Royal Commission on the Coal Industry (1925)*, Cmd. 2600 (1926) p. 122. The proportion mechanically conveyed was even smaller.

[3] A. J. Taylor, 'Labour Productivity and Technological Innovation in the British Coal Industry, 1850–1914', *Economic History Review*, XIV (1961–2) 58.

[4] W. E. Minchinton, *The British Tinplate Industry, a History* (1957) p. 71.

[5] M. T. Copeland, 'Technical Development in Cotton Manufacturing since 1860', *Quarterly Journal of Economics*, XXIII (1909) 144–7.

[6] S. Pollard, 'British and World Shipbuilding, 1890–1914: A Study in Comparative Costs', *Journal of Economic History*, XVII (1957) 436; L. Jones, *Shipbuilding in Britain* (1957) p. 90.

basic industry in which we held technical superiority except perhaps pottery.[1]

The position would not have been so bad had the lag been confined simply to the basic industries, but in fact we were behind in developing the new industries. It was foreign enterprise, and not British, which contributed most to the development of chemicals, machine tools, scientific instruments, motor-vehicles and electrical manufacture. By 1914 Britain was easily surpassed by America or Germany in these industries and often we were dependent on those countries for a substantial proportion of our domestic consumption of these commodities. The performance of the chemical industry was perhaps the most disappointing, since Britain had once been the dominant producer. In the latter half of the nineteenth century, however, our position was rapidly undermined and by 1913 this country accounted for only 11 per cent of world production compared with 34 per cent for America and 24 per cent for Germany, while Germany's exports of chemicals were nearly twice those of Britain. The worst branch was synthetic dyestuffs in which Germany had virtually a world monopoly and supplied Britain with some 90 per cent of her total consumption.[2] The position of the other industries gives little grounds for satisfaction. Needless to say the comparative neglect of the new industries was particularly unfortunate since these were the potential growth industries and had an important part to play in the economy. Moreover, the resultant over-commitment to the basic industries was an important factor intensifying the difficulties of the British, and particularly the Scottish, economy in the inter-war years.

## III

One of the reasons for the slow progress made in both the old and new industries was the lack of appreciation by industrialists of the importance of science and technology and its application to industry. This was particularly true in the case of such science-based industries as iron and steel, chemicals and electrical engineering, the progress of which was dependent to a large extent upon scientific and

[1] English potters, though conservative themselves, were often decades ahead of United States potters in the adoption of better methods. An ingenious reason for the less satisfactory progress in America has been put forward by one writer, in that many of the workmen and managers came from England to the United States and 'in the process of transplanting English processes and attitudes in American industrial soil, the undesirable features seemed to take root more vigorously than the desirable ones', H. J. Stratton, 'Technological Development of the American Pottery Industry', *Journal of Political Economy*, XL (1932) 668.

[2] I. Svennilson, *Growth and Stagnation in the European Economy* (1954) pp. 165, 290, 292–3.

technical expertise.[1] But the fact was that British economic supremacy had been built up by a nation of 'practical tinkerers'[2] and British industrialists were strikingly reluctant to depart from 'rule-of-thumb' methods and seemed even proud of the fact that they carried out little original research or employed few technicians. 'The only research British entrepreneurs would readily sponsor was that which led quickly to immediate and practical results. They thought in terms of training clever mechanics rather than engineers, and laboratory analysts instead of chemists.'[3] As late as 1904 a leading Sheffield steelmaker was saying that there was a feeling in the industry that young men with engineering and science degrees had spent too much time in theory to have the necessary workshop experience and that degrees stood in the way of obtaining good positions in the industry.[4] This attitude was typical of most British industries[5] and it stands out in sharp contrast to that of abroad, particularly Germany, where '. . . one of the most fundamental and important causes of the present prosperity of the German nation is the close relations which exist in that country between science and practical affairs'.[6] Indeed, much of the success of Germany (and to a lesser extent America), especially in the newer industries, can be attributed to the systematic and organised application of science to industry, the thorough system of technical education under state auspices and the co-operation between academic institutions and industry.[7] As one director of a German iron and steel works pointed out: 'We can compete and make profits because of the scientific basis of our manufacture and the technical education of our workpeople . . . every one of our foremen and managers has had two years' special education at the cost of the firm—a technical and scientific education.'[8]

[1] As early as the 1870s the 'lack of a highly intelligent class of workmen to carry out the practical details was held responsible for the fact that many valuable inventions in the steel industry had been abandoned in England', H. J. Habakkuk, *American and British Technology in the Nineteenth Century* (1962) p. 154.

[2] Landes, in *Entrepreneurship and Economic Growth*, p. 8.

[3] J. J. Beer, *The Emergence of the German Dye Industry* (1959) p. 20.

[4] C. Erickson, *British Industrialists: Steel and Hosiery, 1850–1950* (1959) p. 36.

[5] See W. H. G. Armytage, *A Social History of Engineering* (1961) p. 214; F. A. Wells, *The British Hosiery Trade: Its History and Organization* (1935) p. 182; S. B. Saul, 'The American Impact on British Industry, 1895–1914', *Business History*, III (1960) 24.

[6] E. D. Howard, *The Cause and Extent of the Recent Industrial Progress of Germany* (1907) p. 145.

[7] But in Britain, 'The phenomenal wealth of the British middle classes throughout the nineteenth century led to the development of a highly individualistic science organised seriously, but somewhat chaotically, by men of science themselves, including an unprecedently large number of wealthy amateurs', J. Bernal, *Science and Industry in the Nineteenth Century* (1953) p. 142.

[8] S. J. Chapman, *Work and Wages*, pt I, *Foreign Competition* (1904) p. 78.

Britain had little to compare with the scale and provision of university and technical education in Germany[1] which ultimately provided an army of technicians and scientists for the new science-intensive industries. Just before the First World War Britain had only 9,000 full-time students compared with around 58,000 in Germany, a figure not reached in this country until 1938. In addition, Germany had 16,000 polytechnic students, whereas there were only 4,000 taking comparable courses in Britain.[2] In view of these figures it is not surprising that German industry was able to recruit a far larger number of scientists than British industry. In 1901, for example, there were some 4,500 trained chemists employed in German works compared with fewer than 1,500 in the United Kingdom, and the ratio of university graduates in German and British chemical works was in the range 4 to 1. Moreover, German chemists were generally superior in training and quality than their British counterparts.[3] Similarly, it was estimated that in 1912 eleven polytechnic schools were supplying German industry with 3,000 engineers per annum.[4] By contrast in Britain the annual number of students graduating with first and second class honours in science and technology (including mathematics) in universities in England and Wales was only 530 and but a small proportion of these had received any training in research.[5] Yet even this was probably an improvement on what had gone before. In 1872 a British deputation visiting Germany and Switzerland found that all the universities and colleges in England together contained less students taking up research and the higher branches of chemistry than a single German university, that of Munich.[6]

Britain's backwardness in technical education is not difficult to explain. For one thing there was, as we have already noted, a widespread indifference among British manufacturers to the value of employing properly trained workers, no doubt partly on account of the fact that they themselves, apart from a few notable exceptions

[1] Marshall reckoned that, apart from Scotland, British education lagged behind that of Germany in some respects by more than a generation. A. Marshall, *Industry and Trade* (1919) p. 97.

[2] D. S. L. Cardwell, *The Organisation of Science in England* (1957) p. 156. It was estimated that in 1900 the number of day students per 10,000 population was 5·0 in the United Kingdom, 7·9 in Germany and 12·8 in the United States.

[3] W. M. Gardner, *The British Coal-Tar Industry* (1915) pp. 222–3; *Report on Chemical Industry in Germany*, Cd. 430 (1901) pp. 38 ff.

[4] H. Hauser, *Les Méthodes Allemandes d'Expansion Economique* (Paris, 1915) p. 43.

[5] *Report of the Committee of the Privy Council for Scientific and Industrial Research for the Year 1915–16*, Cd. 8336 (1916) p. 8.

[6] S. Smith, *The Real German Rivalry* (1916) quoted in Marshall, *Industry and Trade*, p. 97, note 1.

such as Lowthian Bell, had no more than a limited knowledge of science, and partly because the skilled craftsmen available satisfied their limited requirements. It was this lack of support for such education which 'goes far to explain the relatively slow progress in technical instruction compared with Germany'.[1] There is, of course, the other side to the question. It can be argued that it was the deficiencies of the British educational system as a whole which were at fault. In particular, the neglect of scientific studies in public schools and elementary schools and the failure to organise a system of secondary education until the turn of the century produced generations of employers who were in no position to appreciate the importance of qualified men. Furthermore, since for much of the nineteenth century the basic educational system in Britain left much to be desired, it is plausible to assume that there were relatively few industrial workers who had received sufficient elementary education to enable them to benefit from a course in technical instruction.

Whatever the line of causation there can be no doubt that poor educational facilities were ultimately responsible for the paucity of properly qualified men in industry and this in turn limited the range of opportunities open to British businessmen. It also provides an explanation as to why so little basic industrial research was carried out in this country compared with Germany where 'the mutual interaction between research and manufacture became extraordinarily close'.[2] The Germans made every effort to break down the basic raw materials in order to find new derivatives which could be utilised for the manufacture of new products. Such painstaking and persistent research by highly qualified technologists and scientists enabled Germany to exploit her resources fully and to acquire superiority in a wide range of industries including engineering, chemicals and precision instruments.[3]

People in Britain were not oblivious to the fact that this country was falling behind in technical education and scientific research. In fact the fear of German competition produced increasing demand for some improvement[4] and from the 1880s onwards some attempt was made both by the government and industry to remedy the

[1] S. F. Cotgrove, *Technical Education and Social Change* (1958) p. 28; see also Cardwell, *Organisation of Science*, p. 167.

[2] R. A. Brady, 'The Economic Impact of Imperial Germany: Industrial Policy', *Journal of Economic History*, Supplement (1943) p. 117.

[3] This point is brought out clearly by Beer, *German Dye Industry*; see also L. F. Haber, *The Chemical Industry during the Nineteenth Century* (1958).

[4] For this influence and its effects see the excellent article by G. Haines, 'German Influence upon Scientific Instruction in England, 1867–1887', *Victorian Studies*, I (1958).

situation. Nevertheless, progress was painfully slow and by the early twentieth century much lost ground remained to be covered. Firms were often too small to carry out adequate research even if the value of applied science had been fully appreciated, while industrial leaders still tended to regard technically trained people with scepticism. By 1914 fewer than 10 per cent of the steel industry's leaders had either technical school training or university education in science.[1] It was not until the demands of the first scientific war (or the 'engineers' war', as Lloyd George called it) made action imperative that any really serious attempt was made to fill the deficiency in this field.

## IV

As we pointed out earlier, capital accumulation is not necessarily the ultimate determinant of growth. Identical values of capital may in fact contribute to widely different amounts of product depending upon the way in which that capital is utilised. The Americans and later the Germans were to show that it was not just capital intensity or the volume of resources alone which were responsible for greater output and high efficiency, but the utilisation of the various factors of production, and above all capital, in the most economical way possible that was the clue to their success. Large-scale mass production of standardised goods secured maximum output at minimum costs. 'Probably in no other country in the world', wrote the Board of Trade *Journal* in 1901, 'is the principle of division of labour carried out to a greater extent, or with greater success, than it is in the United States. That the results obtained justify the theory is too evident everywhere to be disputed.'[2] Failure to emulate such methods where possible meant that in some industries British costs were unnecessarily high. This put Britain at a competitive disadvantage in world markets and ultimately resulted in loss of foreign orders.[3]

The uneconomical use of resources was most apparent in those industries which were slow to adopt modern methods of production and organisation, notably machine tools and engineering in which Britain rapidly lost ground to her rivals. As *The Times Engineering Supplement* observed as late as 1915 the organisation and methods of production in some of these factories was almost as defective as the machinery.[4] Britain, the pioneer of machine tools, was rapidly

[1] Erickson, *British Industrialists*, p. 39.

[2] Quoted in R. H. Heindel, *The American Impact on Great Britain* (1940) p. 222.

[3] For examples see *The Engineer* (7 Apr 1899) and B. C. Browne, 'Our American Competitors', *National Review* (Jun 1899) 568–80.

[4] *The Times Engineering Supplement*, 28 May 1915.

out-distanced by America and by the 1880s it was said that the price of machine tools in the United States had fallen to half that of the equivalent British tools.[1] From that date onwards Germany made rapid strides in this field too and by 1913 her exports of machine tools were four times greater than those of Britain.[2] The secret of the American and German success in machine tools was due to the fact that they concentrated on the production of large quantities of one or two standard tools in large, highly specialised and efficiently equipped plants. In contrast, in Britain a very large number of relatively small and inefficient firms existed producing a multiplicity of articles and some of them 'seemed to take a pride in the number of things they turn out'.[3] Costs of production in Britain could have been reduced appreciably if many of the older works had been well planned on a large scale, equipped with plant of the most efficient kind and if the character of the production had been standardised. But in fact there was 'generally an absence of totally new works with an economic lay-out', and it was not until the war 'opened the eyes of manufacturers to the advantages of manufacturing in large numbers instead of ones and twos',[4] that British machine-tool makers made any serious attempt to streamline their methods of production.[5]

An important factor which inhibited the development of cheap motor-car production in this country was the excessive number of small firms producing innumerable designs of cars. Before 1913 nearly 200 makes of car had been placed on the market and of these over 100 had disappeared.[6] In a recent, excellent article[7] Saul has illustrated the weaknesses of the early firms in the industry. A large number of small firms, each producing their own individual products and with 'a disastrous inability to see the technical as well as the commercial side of the American approach', made little

[1] H. J. Habakkuk, *American and British Technology in the Nineteenth Century* (1962) p. 107.

[2] *Engineering* (11 Sep 1914) 335.

[3] *Report of the Departmental Committee on the Engineering Trades after the War*, Cd. 9073 (1918) p. 10.

[4] Ibid., p. 8 and *Report of the Engineering Trades (New Industries) Committee*, Cd. 9226 (1918) p. 18.

[5] See *Engineering* (14 Mar 1919) 355–8. Shortly after the war twelve of the main firms in the industry pooled their manufacturing interests in an attempt to apply the principle of mass-production by standardising design and limiting the range of tools produced by each firm. The scheme achieved considerable success and great improvements in workshop organisation were effected by it. For details see *The Times Trade Supplement*, 21 Aug 1920, p. 605 and 4 Feb 1922 (Industrial Yorkshire Section) p. 15.

[6] G. Maxcy and A. Silberston, *The Motor Industry* (1959) p. 12.

[7] S. B. Saul, 'The Motor Industry in Britain to 1914', *Business History*, v (1962) 22–44.

attempt to combine to adopt more efficient methods of production. As Saul observes: 'The vital absentees from the British industry were the men with a deep knowledge of modern machine tools and the production methods that went with them. The American industry, in marked contrast, had many such engineers. . . . In Britain the engineers were obsessed by the technical product rather than by the technique of production.' Britain therefore failed to produce a cheap popular car largely because of the wasteful use of resources. By 1914 no manufacturer had managed to produce more than one car per man per annum. Yet as early as 1904 Ford was producing 1,700 cars with 300 men.[1]

Similar complaints were made about other industries, namely that antiquated methods of production hampered progress. The success of the German electrical industry, for instance, was attributed to the fact that production of electrical apparatus was consolidated in the hands of some few influential syndicates, which, with branches in almost all countries of Europe and well organised selling facilities were able to take the lead in nearly every department of electrical manufacture. The cheapness and excellence of certain German products made in immense numbers to standardised forms and patterns was said to be a barrier to successful rivalry in this country, where quantities of such articles ordered were relatively small and where almost every electrician required his own sizes and patterns.[2] Likewise the early American electrical manufacturing industry was surprisingly modern in its methods of production and organisation.[3]

It may of course be contended that the larger home market, especially in America, gave greater scope for mass production techniques. This argument can, however, be carried too far. In some cases, e.g. the car industry, the size of the market was important though it did not necessarily constitute the vital force in determining methods of production. If anything it was the nature of the market rather than its size which was the crucial factor.[4] But regardless of favourable market opportunities there is no getting away from the fact that American employers and their workers were far more willing to accept new methods of procedure to improve efficiency than their British contemporaries. The tinplate industry provides a useful illustration of this point. When the Americans began to produce their own tinplate the market for it was considerably less than the British one. Yet by the early 1890s American tinplate workers

[1] Ibid., 43–4.

[2] *The Times Engineering Supplement* (29 Jan 1915) 13; (29 Oct 1915) 192.

[3] H. C. Passer, 'Electrical Manufacturing Around 1900', *Journal of Economic History*, IV (1952) 394.

[4] See below.

were producing more from each mill than their Welsh counterparts, not because they had different machinery but simply because the productive facilities were organised in a more efficient manner. 'A Welsh emigrant', it was said, 'would have recognised the machinery of an American mill in 1890, but he would have been a stranger to its arrangement and operation. Therein lay the contribution of American industrial technology to the manufacture of tinplate.'[1]

## V

The reduced rate of industrial growth has been attributed by some writers to the fall in the rate of growth of exports. Meyer, in an input–output analysis, concludes that the total effect, indirect as well as direct, of a decline in export growth upon the U.K. economy was more than sufficient to account for the slower rate of industrial production.[2] Coppock[3] arrives at much the same conclusion and suggests that this reduced the incentive to invest. On the other hand, Kindleberger, in a recent paper, argues that this hypothesis is incorrect since it assumes that the pattern of exports would remain unchanged and concludes that 'the causation ran from the economy to exports, rather than the other way'.[4] Whatever the line of causation the fact is that Britain suffered a relative decline in her rate of growth of trade and this ultimately must have affected her pattern of industrial growth. By 1913 Britain's share of world trade in manufactures was 25·4 per cent compared with 37·1 per cent in 1883; between these two dates Germany increased her share from 17·2 per cent to 23 per cent and the United States from 3·4 per cent to 11·0 per cent.

To some extent this decline was inevitable for a number of reasons: the increasing industrialisation abroad, the relative stagnation of trade during the Great Depression, the erection of tariff barriers and the use of unfair commercial practices by foreigners. But to attribute everything to these factors would be misleading. Nor would it be totally correct to accept without qualification Lewis's proposition that the British export organisation was overcommitted to selling textiles, rails and consumer goods to primary producers and less suited to selling steel and machinery to the rich and expanding

[1] C. W. Pursell, 'Tariff and Technology: The Foundation and Development of the American Tinplate Industry, 1872–1900', *Technology and Culture* (summer 1962) 280.

[2] Meyer, in *Explorations in Entrepreneurial History*, VIII (1955) 17–18.

[3] Coppock, in *Manchester School*, XXIV (1956).

[4] C. P. Kindleberger, 'Foreign Trade and Economic Growth: Lessons from Britain and France, 1850–1913', *Economic History Review*, XIV (1961–2) 293–8.

markets of Europe.[1] It is true that Britain shared less in the expansion of the European market in this period and concentrated more of her exports on the Empire, though by 1911–13 her share of exports going to Empire countries was no more than in the middle of the nineteenth century.[2] On the other hand, the Americans and Germans were just as adept at exploiting the protected European market as they were at gaining entry to the markets of the more underdeveloped countries where traditional goods were most in demand. Thus in a group of fifteen manufactures British exports to protected foreign markets between 1895 and 1907 increased by 44 per cent while those of Germany and America increased by 125 per cent and 500 per cent respectively. The same exports to identical markets in the British Empire registered an increase of 91 per cent for Britain as against 129 per cent and 359 per cent for Germany and the U.S.A. During this period American manufactured exports to Empire countries increased at a faster rate than those of Britain, especially to the British West Indies and Canada. By 1913 America was slightly ahead in the West Indies and her exports to British North America were about three times greater than those of Britain.[3] Again, while German exports to Europe rose faster than Britain's (1890–1913), and by 1913 Germany was selling more to nearly every European country (and to America) than Britain, she was also expanding her trade more rapidly with many underdeveloped countries, e.g. Russia, Latin America and Turkey.[4] Thus by 1913 Germany monopolised the Russian market, her exports to that country being almost four times those of Britain.[5]

In so far as Britain was committed to selling traditional goods in traditional markets it stemmed from the character of her production, namely the failure to shift resources from the older basic industries into new lines of production as rapidly as America or Germany. According to Tyszynski's calculations Britain was on balance a net loser in the share of world trade gained in new products over the period 1899–1937.[6] But even more important was the failure all

[1] W. A. Lewis, 'International Competition in Manufactures', *American Economic Review*, Papers, 47 (1957) 583.

[2] Kindleberger, in *Economic History Review*, XIV (1961–2) 296.

[3] Heindel, *The American Review*, pp. 143, 174, 167.

[4] Hoffman, *German Trade Rivalry*, pp. 132 ff.; see also R. Schüller, 'Die Handelspolitik Grossbritanniens', *Zeitschrift für Volkswirtschaft, Sozialpolitik und Verwaltung* (1908) pp. 149–78; E. Crammond, 'The Economic Relations of the British and German Empires', *Journal of the Royal Statistical Society*, LXXVII (1913–14) esp. pp. 788–91.

[5] J. E. Gay, 'Anglo-Russian Economic Relations', *Economic Journal*, XXVII (1917) 316–17.

[6] New products include chemicals, electrical goods, motor vehicles and industrial equipment. H. Tyszynski, 'World Trade in Manufactured Commodities, 1899–1950', *Manchester School*, XIX (1951) 290.

along the line to adapt commercial procedure to meet the needs of the time. Industrialists and traders were not only finding it difficult to sell new goods in new markets but they were also finding increasing difficulty in selling traditional goods in established markets. If Britain was behind the times in technique and methods of production she was even further behind the times in her selling methods. 'In marketing, as in manufacturing, England was clinging, in a changing world, to methods and types of organisation which had been formed in the days of her supremacy.'[1]

The weaknesses of the English commercial system were emphasised in the Diplomatic and Consular Reports. Few of these reports praised British commercial ingenuity. In fact the general opinion among the consuls stationed abroad was that to maintain commercial supremacy British firms and traders would have to adapt themselves more to the requirements of their customers. Some of the main criticisms included the disinclination of traders to supply cheaper goods, to study the customers' wishes properly or to adopt the metric system in calculations of weights, measures and currency. As the consul reporting from Naples declared: 'It can never be too impressed upon British trade that all goods for sale on the Continent should be marked in metres and kilogs., and all catalogues sent to the Continent should be in a language "understanded of the people".'[2] Another frequent complaint made was the scarcity of British trade representatives abroad. British commercial travellers were generally few and far between and in some countries, for example Spain, the *bona fide* British traveller was almost unknown.[3] For example, the number of travellers entering Switzerland in 1899 on behalf of Britain was a mere 28 compared with 3,828 for Germany and 1,176 for France.[4] Nor was it unusual for the British travellers, few as they were, to be ignorant of the customs and languages of the countries they represented. 'It is pitiable', remarked Her Majesty's Consul at Naples, 'to see the British commercial traveller stumbling along with an interpreter, while his German competitor is conversing fluently, and one is still more sorry for him when his patterns and samples are marked with British weights and measures.'[5] Other criticisms included the poor packing of goods and inadequate credit facilities, many British firms finding it difficult to

[1] G. C. Allen, *British Industries and their Organization* (1935 ed.) p. 19.

[2] Chapman, *Work and Wages*, pt I, pp. 250–1.

[3] *Opinions of H.M.'s Diplomatic and Consular Officers on British Trade Methods Abroad*, C. 9078 (1899) XCVI, p. 6; *Diplomatic and Consular Reports*, nos. 4772 and 4776, Cd. 5465 (165/169) (1911) p. 6.

[4] Chapman, *Work and Wages*, pt I, p. 253.

[5] *Opinions of H.M. Diplomatic Officers*, C. 9078, p. 6.

compete with foreign firms which were backed by their own trade banks.[1]

On the other hand much of the success of Germany and America in the export field was based on their efficient sales policies. They paid as much attention to selling and distribution as they did to production. By organising foreign commerce, establishing direct-selling agencies and sending highly qualified travellers all over the world to ferret out openings for business they virtually created their own markets. The whole commercial policy of Germany was said to be directed towards the encouragement and extension of foreign trade. There were a number of organisations such as the Commerce Defence League and the Export Bureau of the German Export Bank which sent German agents abroad and supplied information on foreign markets to member firms.[2] Some of the larger American firms established nation-wide systems of sales agencies and employed salesmen who were technically competent.[3] In contrast the British approach was essentially conservative and individualistic, and at times apathetic and indifferent. There was a general lack of co-operation among British manufacturers for marketing purposes while the small scale of the typical firm rendered it difficult to establish selling organisations and agencies for dealing with foreign markets. For distribution purposes British firms relied heavily on the traditional merchanting system which all too frequently provided an inadequate reflection of the needs of her customers. British firms and merchants seemed almost hostile to the adoption of intensive and dynamic selling methods of their competitors which so clearly paid results.

On the other hand, it was alleged that the system of commercial intelligence was more efficient in America and Germany than that provided by the British Government for traders in this country. The foundation for this criticism is somewhat slender. Britain's consular service improved considerably in this period, particularly after 1899 when the Board of Trade established its Commercial Intelligence Branch which provided an ever-increasing supply of information in the interests of British trade.[4] But as Platt has shown in a recent

[1] *Diplomatic and Consular Report*, no. 5004, Cd. 6005 (177) (1912) p. 33.

[2] Watchman, 'Some New Facts about German Commercial Tactics', *National Review* (Mar 1910) 83–6; H. Birchenough, 'The Expansion of Germany', *Nineteenth Century* (Feb 1898) 189.

[3] See Passer, in *Journal of Economic History*, IV (1952) 392; E. M. Bacon 'Marketing Sewing Machines in the Post Civil War Years', *Bulletin of the Business Historical Association* (Jun 1946) 90–4.

[4] *Report to the Board of Trade by the Advisory Committee on Commercial Intelligence*, Cd. 4917 (1905) pp. 3–4.

article,[1] it was more often the case that British firms did not avail themselves of the services of the Department to the extent they might have done. In 1913 it was estimated that only just over 1,500 firms took full advantage of the Board of Trade's information.[2] Platt suggests that the major reason for this neglect was the fact that British manufacturers 'already enjoyed the advantage of a considerable network of commercial agencies abroad'. This may well be true, but it in no way lifts the burden of responsibility from British manufacturers, for it was these very institutions which were slow to adapt themselves to the changing needs of the time.

It is not improbable that British commercial deficiencies were one of the main reasons for the failure to acquire new markets and the loss of old customers. As late as 1912 it was reported from Romania that 'There is no doubt, were proper representation to be secured, that British merchants would increase, instead of losing, the trade they already do with the country in machinery, textiles, ironwork, paints, chemicals, clothing, hats, boots, machine and other tools . . . merchants might do worse than pay a personal visit to the country.'[3] Orders and markets were lost through the wilful neglect by British firms and traders to cater for the needs and wants of their customers.[4] For example, in 1883 New Zealand ordered 20 locomotives from England only two of which were delivered at the end of eighteen months. The order was subsequently transferred to an American works in Philadelphia. Here they were not only completed in three-and-a-half months but the finished product was better suited to the New Zealand railways and cost £400 each less than the English ones.[5] Many instances can be given to show how the Germans beat the English merchants by adapting their wares to the wants and prejudices of the customers. To quote just one example. The Brazilians disliked the black paper in which English needles were wrapped and therefore the Germans offered inferior needles in bright red paper and captured the entire market.[6] Nor was the question of ornamental packing as unimportant as it might seem, for it was alleged that 'a large proportion of the remarkable growth of the

[1] D. C. M. Platt, 'The Role of the British Consular Service in Overseas Trade, 1825–1914', *Economic History Review*, XVI (1963) 494–512.

[2] *Report on the System of British Commercial Attachés and Commercial Agents*, Cd. 3610 (1907) p. 2; *Report to the Board of Trade by the Advisory Committee on Commercial Intelligence*, Cd. 6779 (1913) p. 5.

[3] *Diplomatic and Consular Report*, no. 5102, Cd. 6665 (60), (1913) pp. 7–8.

[4] See A. Lambert, 'Neglecting Our Customers', *Nineteenth Century* (Dec 1898) 940–56.

[5] E. B. Dorsey, *English and American Railroads Compared* (1887) p. 105.

[6] Howard, *Cause and Extent*, p. 90, note 1.

export trade of Germany is attributed by many authorities to the tasteful decoration of their goods by enterprising manufacturers'.[1]

## VI

In the foregoing analysis we have demonstrated the existence of entrepreneurial sluggishness over a wide sector of Britain's industrial economy. A more difficult task is to explain why entrepreneurs behaved in the way they did. Some of the reasons, notably the attitudes adopted towards education and research, have already been touched upon. In a general article of this nature it will be impossible and even inappropriate to dwell upon all the specific factors relating to each industry. Consequently attention will be focused on the more important factors of general applicability.

First of all we may say that the general economic climate or public opinion in Britain was not conducive to change or to the acceptance of new ideas to the same extent as in America where 'society in the nineteenth century was basically predictable for innovations in producers' goods because it was not a society hostile to cheaper and better methods of production',[2] or as in Germany where efforts on the part of manufacturers were envisaged as a struggle for the 'rebirth and unity of the Fatherland'.[3] Part of the lethargy of British manufacturers may be explained by the lack of response from the demand side. In general Americans, and to a lesser extent Germans, were more responsive to change, that is they were more willing to purchase large quantities of standardised and relatively cheap goods rather than 'aristocratic goods of high individual quality'.[4] Society, or in other words demand, was, at least in America, as Habakkuk has observed, more malleable and less stereotyped than in this country and could therefore be moulded more easily to the pattern most appropriate to high rates of growth.

But it would be unwise to lay too much stress on market opportunities as Habakkuk has done, for lack of response from the demand

[1] C. 9078 (1899) p. 6.

[2] W. P. Strassmann, *Risk and Technological Innovation: American Manufacturing Methods during the Nineteenth Century* (1958) p. 185. Sawyer stresses the importance of social and cultural factors in economic development: 'Both the prevailing creed and the open structure of society were surely mightily at work in the development of this era, in the release and channeling of men's energies', J. E. Sawyer, 'The Social Basis of the American System of Manufacturing', *Journal of Economic History*, XIV (1954) 369.

[3] Landes, in *Entrepreneurship and Economic Growth*, p. 19.

[4] E. Rothbarth, 'Causes of the Superior Efficiency of U.S.A. Industry as compared with British Industry', *Economic Journal*, LVI (1946) 386.

side was certainly not the sole explanation. Demand can be stimulated from the supply side by the initiative of manufacturers through the introduction of new products or by energetic selling methods. Yet in these respects British industrialists took the line of least resistance and were extremely reluctant to accept the challenge of new conditions. It is quite evident that many entrepreneurs adopted a very complacent attitude towards their businesses, particularly on the commercial side where the 'take it or leave it attitude' has persisted even up to this day.[1] Was this because they were drunk with the achievements of their past performance and were content to live on their ancestral capital? Was Veblen right when he suggested that Britain was burdened with the restraining dead-hand of her past achievement and that the maturing British economy and social structure brought recourse to conspicuous waste?[2] Support for his hypothesis is not lacking. 'We are suffering from a surfeit of commercial and maritime prosperity', a contemporary wrote in 1902, 'a prosperity which has been our monopoly for so long that we are unable to realise that it must inevitably be threatened, and may conceivably be taken away from us.'[3] Recent historians have intimated that the accumulation of sufficient wealth was inimical to progress since it allowed the pursuit of leisure interests outside the business.[4] Burn, in his study of the steel industry, lays considerable stress on the 'indolence and apathy engendered by phenomenal success', and the corrupting influence of fortune on heirs to an industrial dynasty.[5] As succeeding generations of businessmen began to acquire new interests and sought to advance themselves in society, the restless strive to maximise profits ceased. In South Wales 'the tinplate maker had little incentive to pursue wealth. With a modest sum it was comparatively easy to become a prominent member of local society and to enjoy a comfortable standard of living. . . . The tinplate makers of South Wales were therefore easily satisfied and had little incentive to expand production or to attain leadership in the industry.'[6] Landed estate, the great status symbol of the nineteenth

[1] See *The Guardian*, (10 Jun 1962).

[2] Veblen, *Imperial Germany*, pp. 131–43.

[3] Y. Capel, 'England's Peril', *Westminster Review* (Feb 1902) 963. This point has been confirmed as regards the shipping industry by S. G. Sturmey in his recent book *British Shipping and World Competition* (1962) p. 399.

[4] Thus referring to the Rathbone family Miss Marriner writes: 'The family had made sufficient wealth to allow them to pursue their own interests and they were not keen enough to try to adapt their methods to new conditions', Marriner, *Rathbones of Liverpool*, p. 131. Cf. Landes, in *Entrepreneurship and Economic Growth*, p. 19; and Rimmer, *Marshalls of Leeds*.

[5] Burn, *Steelmaking*, pp. 298–301.

[6] Minchinton, *British Tinplate*, p. 106.

century, became the most coveted possession of Victorian entrepreneurs. Hence business affairs tended to become of secondary importance as second and third generations moved from the 'furnace to the field'.[1] In engineering the Boultons, in linen the Marshalls, in cotton the Strutts and in brewing the Bests, all attempted to raise their social standing in this way. As Thompson says, 'Clogs to clogs in three generations was matched as a piece of folklore by the saying that the third generation makes the gentleman'.[2]

Whether this theory would bear general application remains to be seen, but it has been suggested that at least in a technical sense Britain was handicapped by an early start.[3] Briefly the argument is that technical innovation was more expensive in Britain because of the greater cost of writing off accumulated plant and equipment, and innovation in one sector or process often created bottlenecks which could only be relieved by innovation throughout the remaining sectors. In other words, capital was highly interrelated and this made it difficult to replace single components of a productive process on a one-at-a-time-basis.[4] Thus modernisation in the cotton industry was hampered by the unsuitability of many sheds for highly mechanised equipment.[5] The unprogressive nature of British railways in this period[6] has been attributed to the fact that much of their capital was highly interrelated. Limits were set to the increase in the size of locomotives, coaches and waggons by the height of bridges, the short radius of curves and by the whole layout of stations, docks and works. The chairman of the Caledonian Railway was not exaggerating when he said 'there is not, at the present time, a single shipping port, iron and steel work, or gaswork, or any work in Scotland, capable of dealing with a waggon of a carrying capacity of 30 or even 20 tons of coal, and there are not half a dozen collieries in Scotland whose

[1] A. Briggs, *Victorian Cities* (1963) p. 69.

[2] F. M. L. Thompson, *English Landed Society in the Nineteenth Century* (1963) pp. 129–31.

[3] There is an extensive literature on this subject. See F. J. R. Jervis, 'The Handicap of Britain's Early Start', *Manchester School*, XV (1947) 112–22; M. Frankel, 'Obsolescence and Technical Change in a Maturing Economy', *American Economic Review*, XLV (1955) 296–314; C. P. Kindleberger, 'Obsolescence and Technical Change', *Bull. of the Oxford University Institute of Statistics*, XXIII (1961) 281–97; and E. Ames and N. Rosenberg, 'Changing Technological Leadership and Industrial Growth', *Economic Journal*, LXXIII (1963) 13–31.

[4] Ames and Rosenberg, in *Economic Journal*, LXXIII, 13–31.

[5] Salter, *Productivity*, p. 85.

[6] According to Paish 'Our railways have been content to go on working by the antiquated methods of thirty or forty years ago, and have neglected to take advantage of the experience of the American lines', G. Paish, *The British Railway Position* (1902) p. 12.

appliances for separating coal are capable of admitting a waggon of the height of a 30 ton waggon'.[1]

It cannot be denied that there is much truth in this argument, but it seems extremely doubtful whether it could serve as a general explanation as to why progress in British manufacturing industry was slower than in other countries. First because it implies that manufacturing technique must have been at a very primitive stage in America and Germany for them to have had any great cost advantage over Britain when contemplating the introduction of new methods or machinery. Secondly, it tends to ignore the fact that plant and equipment were older in this country which should in theory have provided an added incentive to scrap. And lastly, it would seem to imply that innovation in one process, e.g. cotton spinning, would be more expensive and difficult in Britain because of the resulting repercussions on other branches of the productive process. But there seems to be no obvious reason why capital should have been more highly related in this country than elsewhere.

A more convincing argument is the one regarding the different endowment of factors of production. The lag in the utilisation of new techniques can be regarded partly as a reflection of an economy's supplies of factors of production relative to its labour force. Thus, according to Salter, 'When real investment is cheap relative to labour, standards of obsolescence are high and the capital stock is up to date; when real investment is dear, rapid adjustment is uneconomic and the capital stock consists largely of outmoded equipment'.[2] In America the abundance of land and scarcity of labour stimulated industry to install labour-saving machinery or use capital-intensive techniques whereas in Britain factor endowments favoured accumulation with existing techniques.[3] In other words, a widening of capital was more appropriate in the British case rather than a deepening of capital as in America, though in the latter case there is some doubt as to the extent of the capital-deepening process.[4] In a number of industries the different costs of factors of production can account for the rate of growth in capital equipment. Taylor, for instance, has noted that cheap labour hardly provided an adequate incentive to technical change in the coal industry.[5] In turn cheap coal retarded research into fuel economy and delayed the introduction of electri-

[1] Ibid., p. 117.

[2] Salter, *Productivity*, p. 69.

[3] See Rothbart, in *Economic Journal*, 386 and Habakkuk, *American and British Technology*, p. 141.

[4] On this point see A. Hansen, 'Economic Progress and Declining Population Growth', *American Economic Review*, XXIX (1939) 7.

[5] Taylor, in *Economic History Review*, XIV 63.

city as a new source of power. Again the main reason for the more rapid adoption of ring spindles and automatic looms in the American cotton industry was because they were more economical of labour and hence more suited to the American conditions than the British.[1] Similarly it can be argued that the relative abundance of skilled craft labour in this country compared with America made it less imperative for British manufactures to adopt automatic machinery and mass production methods. The cost incentive apart, it is important to remember the differing attitudes of American and British labour towards technical change. The American worker was far more receptive to new ideas and actually abetted the process of technical change,[2] whereas 'an English workman finds it almost impossible to imagine that the adoption of labour-saving methods could result in higher wages and more employment'.[3] Although the introduction of new methods and machinery in Britain does not seem to have met with quite the same amount of opposition from employees as during the first half of the nineteenth century, it does appear that the lack of enthusiasm and the difficulty which manufacturers met in reducing piece-rates to the extent warranted by the increased productivity due to labour-saving machinery made British manufacturers less willing than their counterparts across the Atlantic to introduce new machinery and methods.[4]

One factor of relevance which we have not discussed in any great detail is the structure of the firm. The typical unit in British business was often the small firm dominated by family control. This tended to limit the flexibility of management and reduce the ability of firms to acquire the means to undertake large-scale expansion. Dr Sturmey has shown how the domination of family control bred conservatism in shipping resulting in an industry 'heavily biased towards maintaining the *status quo* and ill-adapted to showing flexibility to meet the enormous changes of the inter-war period'.[5] Rimmer, in his study of Marshalls the flax-spinners, lays great stress on this point. He maintains that the relative decline of the Leeds flax industry was not simply due to tariffs, imported flax and high wages but 'more important was the neglect, indifference, defeatism, even open hostility within firms based on the family'.[6] The difficulties of the small firm are well known. The wartime committee on

[1] Copeland, in *Quarterly Journal of Economics*, XXIII 129–57.

[2] Strassmann, *Risk*, p. 186.

[3] Chapman, *Work and Wages*, pt I, pp. 176–7.

[4] Habakkuk, *American and British Technology*, p. 136; see also E. H. Phelps Brown, *Growth of British Industrial Relations* (1959) pp. 94–6.

[5] Sturmey, *British Shipping*, p. 397.

[6] Rimmer, *Marshalls of Leeds*, p. 253.

scientific research observed that '. . . the small scale on which most industrial firms have been planned is one of the principal impediments in the way of the organisation of research, with a view to the conduct of those long and complicated investigations which are necessary for the solution of the fundamental problems lying at the basis of our staple industries'.[1] That the small firm was at a comparative disadvantage is not generally disputed; the important point is to establish why this was so. It may be argued that the tradition of self-financing contributed to the prevalance of small and medium-sized plants in many industries which in America and Germany were organised in large undertakings, and this in turn can explain why in certain fields British industry was less productive and progressive than American and German industry.[2] On the other hand, it cannot be argued that it was a shortage of capital as such that kept firms small or that the London capital market, with its concentration on gilt-edged and foreign issues, was unaccustomed to financing domestic issues.[3] The success in raising finance of companies which secured a public quotation, such as Brunner Mond and Co., Lever Brothers[4] and some of the steel companies, refutes this latter point.[5] Rather the line of causation was the other way round. Domestic capital went into gilt-edged and foreign issues not because of the inability of the capital market to finance home industrial issues but because of the paucity of domestic issues in which to invest or because English firms were on too small a scale to attract the issue houses. Firms remained small through lack of finance only in so far as family entrepreneurs were reluctant to enter the capital market for fear of letting in 'foreign' control.[6] Only this can explain why by 1914 nearly 80 per cent of British companies were private ones, the dominant feature of which was the absence of any appeal to the

[1] Cd. 8336, (1916) p. 25.

[2] See Hoselitz, *Capital Formation*, p. 331.

[3] This is the point Lewis and Saville make. See also H. Foxwell, 'The Financing of Trade and Industry', *Economic Journal*, XXVII (1917).

[4] In 1894 ,when Levers issued their first block of capital to the public, four times the amount required was subscribed. By 1911 the firm had raised £6¼ million in the market. C. Wilson, *The History of Unilever* (1954) I, pp. 45 and 122.

[5] Saul in his article on the early motor industry comes to much the same conclusion. In their book on *The Stock Exchange* (1962), Prof. E. V. Morgan and W. A. Thomas make no suggestion as to the inefficiency of the Stock Exchange in this respect. On the contrary, they state rather proudly that 'the combination of Stock Exchange and promoters provided a system which gave birth to many companies still flourishing today and which, in the twenty years prior to 1914, channelled more than £1,000 million of investment into British industry and commerce' (p. 139).

[6] Cf. Sturmey, *British Shipping* pp. 397–8. Even after companies became public there was sometimes a noticeable reluctance to offer shares to the public. See J. H. Clapham, *An Economic History of Modern Britain* (1930–8) vol. 3, p. 204.

general public. This reluctance to share control may also explain why the banks played relatively little part in the long-term financing of industry notwithstanding the conservative nature of the banks themselves. In this respect British manufacturers were obviously at a disadvantage with their competitors, particularly Germany where the link between the banks and industry was especially strong. Nor was the question merely one of long-term finance. Time and again British industrialists and traders lost ground to their competitors because of their poor credit facilities for which the banks were partly to blame. As one witness to the Committee on Shipping and Shipbuilding after the war put it:[1] 'Our experience is that there is a want of elasticity and lack of enterprise in our British banks which have hampered us, especially in dealing with foreign customers. We have found that foreign banks are much more helpful to their clients in assisting their enterprises.'

In some cases, particularly where development was interdependent, a lag in one industry retarded the progress of others. The late development of the aluminium industry can be partly attributed to the electrical lag, while the slow growth of motor-car production explains why the most intensive phase in the development of the British rubber industry was about a decade later than in America.[2] Likewise the manufacture of electrical products was dependent upon the extension of the power supply which was held up for a time by the vested interests of the municipalities in gas. Occasionally, too, unfavourable legislation made things more difficult. The absence of a compulsory working clause in the British patent law until 1907 led to the exploitation of many inventions abroad especially in the field of chemicals.

Obviously it would be difficult—probably impossible—to find a single answer even for one industry, to account for the unprogressive behaviour of British industrialists in this period. There is a host of interrelated factors, general and specific, economic and non-economic, which have a bearing on the matter and it would be rash to conclude that any one of them had a preponderating influence. Nevertheless, the force of tradition dies hard with the British people and this more than anything else seems to have influenced the outlook and actions of British industrialists and their employees. So long as it was possible to make an honest penny British entrepreneurs were content to jog along in the same old way using the techniques and methods which their ancestors had introduced. As one American

[1] Cd. 9092 (1918) p. 30.

[2] W. Woodruff, 'The Growth of the Rubber Industry of Great Britain and the United States', *Journal of Economic History*, xv (1955) 383.

commented after observing skilled Welsh tinplate workers, 'They know their business but when you ask them why they do a certain thing in a certain way they say, "Because my father did it, and my grandfather before him", and therefore they think they have to do it in the same way.'[1] Fifty years of industrial pre-eminence had bred contempt for change[2] and had established industrial traditions in which the basic ingredients of economic progress, science and research, were notably absent. And the longer this change was delayed the more difficult it became for manufacturers to sanction and their workers to accept a break with established practice.

## VII

In concentrating our attention on the role of the entrepreneur we have ignored many of the factors which influenced the rate of growth of the British economy between 1870 and 1914. This is not meant to imply that such factors were of no importance. Some of them, such as the impact of the Great Depression, tariffs, population changes, and government activity, probably had an important bearing on the more favourable outcome of economic change abroad than in Britain. Nor must we forget the fact that Britain's relative decline was partly inevitable, since it was inconceivable that she could maintain her early nineteenth century growth rates indefinitely or that she could retain her commanding role in the world economy in the face of rapid economic progress elsewhere. As a League of Nations study pointed out: 'It is axiomatic that a country which is a pioneer in industrial and commercial development should lose in relative position as other countries follow suit, even if it gains in absolute terms.'[3]

On the other hand, what we have tried to illustrate in this article is that changes in economic variables stem largely from entrepreneurial decisions. In so far as these decisions and the action arising from them were inconsistent with the needs of the time, then to that extent British growth indices compared less favourably with those of our competitors. The relationship is a simple one depending on our working hypothesis adopted earlier that technical progress (in the

[1] Pursell, in *Technology and Culture* (summer 1962) 280.

[2] In 1930 a governmental report noted that 'the very success of the Lancashire cotton industry in developing efficient methods in the conditions of the past . . . is today responsible in part for a disinclination to explore new possibilities and try new methods, many of which have already been exploited with success, for example, in the southern parts of the United States and in Japan', *Report of the Committee on the Cotton Industry*, Cd. 3615 (1930) para. 39.

[3] League of Nations, *Industrialization and Foreign Trade* (1945) p. 109.

widest sense of the term) is one of the major determinants of economic expansion. In this period innovations, technical advances, economies of scale and factor substitution were confined to a small sector of the economy and were slow to mature. The effects on productivity movements were adverse, unit costs were raised and rates of growth retarded. The conclusion, therefore, is inescapable: that the British economy could have been made more viable had there been a concerted effort on the part of British enterprise to adapt itself more readily.

Fortunately certain considerations can be put forward to redeem the entrepreneur's character. There can be no suggestion that entrepreneurial dynamism was non-existent at this time. Progressive types such as Lever and Beecham and some of the early manufacturers in the car and chemical industries would make a suggestion such as this untenable. In fact it is possible to argue that there was far too much individual enterprise and insufficient co-operative action between firms and industries.[1] Moreover, it seems likely that entrepreneurial lethargy was more evident before 1900 than afterwards. By the turn of the century foreign competition had awakened the interest of some industrialists and in the decade or so before the First World War some attempt was being made to recover lost ground.

Many of the points raised in this article have been of a highly controversial nature and the conclusions offered are at best tentative. Much further research is required into the history of individual firms and industries before a final judgement can be passed. Nevertheless, something will have been achieved if it stimulates inquiry into some of the more neglected aspects of our industrial and commercial history of this period.

[1] The early motor-car industry provides a typical case. Of the 393 firms founded before 1914, 280 had ceased to exist by that date. Saul, *Business History*, v 23.

# 4 Technical Progress and British Enterprise, 1875–1914

## I

SEVERAL attempts have now been made to chart and explain the retardation in British growth rates in the latter part of the nineteenth century. Statistics relating to the growth of national income, exports and industrial productivity all show a distinct tendency to decelerate in this period. The growth rates in this country compare unfavourably with those registered abroad especially in America and Germany. Perhaps the most alarming feature was the lag in British manufacturing productivity; the rate of growth of output per worker fell continuously throughout this period.[1] To explain the poor performance of British growth indices the unprogressive nature of British entrepreneurs during the years in question has been sometimes cited. Much evidence has also been produced to show that British industrialists were technically far less dynamic than their major competitors. In particular, it has been alleged that they failed or were slow to adopt cost-reducing innovations or new methods of production and selling and that they were reluctant to acknowledge the value of technical education and scientific research.[2] How far these deficiencies were responsible for the lag in British growth rates is difficult to determine. Obviously there is a strong connection between the two since technical progress (in the widest sense of the term) is, in the long run, one of the main determinants of growth. The purpose of this paper is not to traverse already explored territory however superficially it may have been covered, but rather to try and offer some general explanations as to why British industrialists were reluctant to innovate in the period under review.

In a general paper it will, of course, be impossible to deal with all the diverse factors which motivated the actions of British businessmen. Indeed, to do so would defeat the main aim which is to try to establish some factors of general applicability which explain the course of technical progress. Four major themes will therefore be

[1] Over the period the annual rate of growth of productivity in manufacturing industry was less than half the American and possibly one-quarter the German. For details see M. Frankel, *British and American Manufacturing Productivity* (1957) Table 17, p. 103, and D. J. Coppock, 'The Climacteric of the 1890s: A Critical Note', *Manchester School*, XXIV (1956) 23–4.

[2] For a general review see D. H. Aldcroft, 'The Entrepreneur and the British Economy, 1870–1914', above, Section B, 3.

considered. We shall start by examining the validity of the 'early start' thesis and the associated question of 'interrelatedness'. Having shown that there are serious weaknesses in this argument an attempt will be made to show how factor supplies, structural rigidities in industrial firms and market opportunities influenced investment decisions and determined the rate of technical progress. No attempt will be made to review technical developments in every industry but particular reference will be made to some of the basic industries for it was these which appear to have been technically the most backward.

## II

The 'early start' and 'interrelatedness' theories have gained wide currency in recent years though there is still a considerable difference of opinion among scholars as to their effects on technical progress.[1] The argument runs as follows. The latecomer to industrial development is said to have an advantage over the early starter since the former can benefit from the mistakes of the pioneer and is in a better position to adopt the latest techniques without incurring the heavy cost of writing off accumulated plant and equipment. Furthermore, since capital is often highly interrelated or complementary it acts as a drag on technical development in the country with an accumulated stock of capital, since it is rather more difficult to replace single components of a productive process on a one-at-a-time basis. The only real alternative in this situation, therefore, is to innovate at all stages of production which, of course, is costly in terms of capital and may ultimately act as a deterrent to innovation. Several examples have been used to illustrate these points. The country which industrialised later could perceive more readily the advantages to be gained from standardising plant and equipment once Britain had made the initial mistakes. On the railways, for example, no other country allowed the riot of individuality to occur with regard to the different types of axle boxes, tyres, springs and hand-brakes. British railways had no less than 200 types of axle boxes and over 40 variations of the ordinary wagon hand-brake.[2] Alternatively, when

[1] For the controversy the following sources should be consulted: F. J. R. Jervis, 'The Handicap of Britain's Early Start', *Manchester School*, XV (1947); M. Frankel, 'Obsolescence and Technical Change in a Maturing Economy', *American Economic Review*, XLV (1955) and the 'Comment' by D. F. Gordon, ibid., XLVI (1956); C. P. Kindleberger, 'Obsolescence and Technical Change', *Bull. of the Oxford University Institute of Statistics*, XXIII (1961) and E. Ames and N. Rosenberg, 'Changing Technological Leadership and Industrial Growth', *Economic Journal*, LXXII (1963).

[2] *Report upon the Standardization of Railway Equipment*, Cd. 9193 (1918) pp. 2–3; see also E. Ames and N. Rosenberg, in *Economic Journal*, LXXI 19.

contemplating the introduction of new methods the cost of scrapping old plant may deter manufacturers from making changes. The reluctance of British steelmakers to adopt the by-product recovery ovens for coke production or for that matter the Thomas process of steelmaking, has been attributed to the fact that they were already committed to beehive coke ovens and the Bessemer process. Similarly, the reason why Scottish ironmasters did not make the switch to steelmaking was because they had concentrated their resources on ironsmelting. The 'interrelatedness' argument has been most forcibly expressed by Frankel. He argues that the slowness of innovation in steel, cotton, and railways in particular, was due to the fact that technical changes in one department required fundamental changes throughout the dependent stages of production. In the cotton industry, for example, the adoption of the automatic loom was inhibited by the fact that it would have required alterations in the designs of weaving sheds and changes in the methods of production preliminary to weaving.[1]

While in theory the argument about the early start and interrelatedness sounds very plausible, and is not without a certain element of truth, it does not stand up very well to critical analysis. Even the empirical data used to support the thesis is often shaky, and it is possible to show that other factors were more important in determining the pattern of technical progress than the disadvantages of the early start. The argument certainly cannot be used, in either a specific or general sense, to explain the slower rate of technical progress in this country as compared with abroad, unless the countries with which the comparison is made were exceptionally backward at the time in question. But we know that both Germany and America were, by the latter part of the nineteenth century, already powerful industrial countries; originally they had borrowed much of their technology from Britain and hence had a considerable backlog of old plant and equipment to write off when contemplating the introduction of new techniques. Take the cotton industry as a case in point. Originally both America and Britain developed their cotton industries with the same technology, yet in the decades after 1860 the American cotton industry rapidly out-distanced the British in the introduction of ring spindles and automatic looms. Now, is there any obvious reason to suppose that it was easier for the American manufacturers to demolish the old technology, especially in weaving, since the automatic loom did not come into commercial use until the 1890s by which date the Americans had almost as much outdated plant and equipment to write off as their British counterparts? The

[1] M. Frankel, in *American Economic Review*, XLV 311–13.

answer of course is in the negative. If anything, one would have expected the British cotton industry to have been in the forefront of technical progress; the fact that its equipment was somewhat more antiquated than that of the American industry should in theory have provided an added incentive to scrap the plant and reinvest in new processes. Nor can we accept Frankel's interrelatedness argument as a factor inhibiting change in cotton, or in any industry for that matter except possibly the railways. The validity of this hypothesis rests upon the assumption that capital was more highly interrelated in Britain than elsewhere, which is quite incorrect. Britain may have had a large proportion of her resources tied up in old plant and technology, but it does not follow that her problems of interrelatedness were any the greater. In fact in the case of the cotton industry which Frankel uses as his stock example, there is reason to believe that American manufacturers faced greater difficulties in this respect owing to the highly integrated nature of the cotton works. And as we shall see below it was the wide discrepancy in factor supplies that facilitated the remechanisation of the American cotton industry.

Nor do other industries provide much support for the 'early start' thesis. The slow adoption of mechanised methods in the coal and footwear industries certainly cannot be attributed to this factor. Neither can the technical backwardness of the steel industry be accounted for on these grounds alone, for as Orsagh has pointed out, Britain, Germany and the United States were on a relatively equal footing around 1870.[1] The same argument applies to intermediate or ancillary processes. Coke, for example, was made exclusively in beehive ovens in all three countries in 1880; yet 82 per cent of Germany's coke was made in by-product recovery ovens by 1909 as against only 18 per cent in this country. Perhaps even more significant was the fact that America's performance was as bad as Britain's in this respect.[2] Even in the case of the railways, it can be argued that it was not interrelatedness but the opposition of the private wagon-owners, the nature of the traffic, the attention paid to service rather than economy, and the power-complex of the railway leaders which really inhibited technical progress.[3]

[1] T. J. Orsagh, 'Progress in Iron and Steel; 1870–1913', *Comparative Studies in Society and History*, III (1960–1) 229.

[2] J. C. Carr and W. Taplin, *History of the British Steel Industry* (1962) p. 211.

[3] See C. H. Grinling, *The History of the Great Northern 1845–1902* (1903 ed.) xii-xiii. Dow suggests that had Watkin (chairman of the Manchester, Sheffield and Lincolnshire Railway) been less obsessed with the aggressive expansion of his railway empire more attention might have been given to the consolidation and improvement of the property he already controlled. G. Dow, *Great Central, II, Dominion of Watkin, 1868–1899* (1962) p. 164.

An acceptance of this argument, moreover, would require satisfaction on a number of unresolved points. If, as alleged, innovation in these industries was hindered by such difficulties, why was shipbuilding not affected in the same way? Secondly, how does one account for differential rates of technical progress when making comparisons which do not involve Britain, for example, the relative speed of adoption of new coke ovens in America and in Germany? Can it not be argued that Germany and America were really in much the same position as Britain and they, too, should have come up against the same sort of problems, at least in certain sectors of the economy? For as Ames and Rosenberg point out,[1] 'if retardation is inevitable in a mature country, it is, presumably, inevitable for the followers as well as the leaders'. Yet no one has suggested that America incurred these disabilities, either in this period or later. Why not? Does the handicap only apply to the first starter and if so why? These questions will have to be answered before the protagonists of the early start can convince us of its validity.[2] A further point may also be considered. It is a well-known fact that technical progress need not necessarily be costly in terms of capital; the reorganisation or streamlining of production facilities or the adoption of some small improvement, for example, electric lighting in the works, may cost very little and yet be the cause of considerable gains in productivity. In such cases, therefore, the cost of scrapping accumulated plant and the problem of interrelatedness do not really enter into the question. How then do we explain the slowness with which British firms adopted American techniques of production in, say, engineering and machine tools?

Perhaps at this point we might try and get the best of both worlds and accept Kindleberger's proposition that 'there may be a penalty in the early start if institutions adapt themselves to a given technology and if static patterns of capital replacement develop as habits'.[3] A type of institutional interrelatedness, such as the entrenched position of the private wagon-owners on the railways, may develop and eventually inhibit progress. However, it is only fair to point out that this sort of situation was probably peculiar to the railways, owing to the division of ownership of the capital stock. It is really Kindleberger's second point which requires further elaboration. In effect this is nothing more than a repetition of the 'tradition' argument, that manufacturers were content to carry on investing in existing tech-

[1] E. Ames and N. Rosenberg, in *Economic Journal*, LXXII 29.

[2] Another objection is that the theory tends to assume a rather static business world in which the deficiency of the established firms is not counterbalanced by the entry of new firms. Such an assumption is, of course, quite invalid.

[3] C. P. Kindleberger, in *Bull. of the Oxford University Institute of Statistics*, XXIII 282.

niques simple because they had proved so successful in the past. Veblen was the first to suggest that the phenomenal success of British industrialists had deadened their initiative[1] and much evidence has been subsequently brought forward to support his statement. An official report on the cotton industry in 1930, for example, remarked how 'the very success of the Lancashire cotton industry in developing efficient methods in the conditions of the past . . . is today responsible in part for a disinclination to explore new possibilities and try new methods, many of which have already been exploited with success, for example, in the southern parts of the United States and in Japan'.[2] Critics might argue that this is merely an illustration of the early start thesis. Basically it is, the main difference being that it places little emphasis on the cost of scrapping old plant or the problem of interrelatedness. It simply asserts that manufacturers' investment decisions were bound by tradition and nothing more. But we are still faced with the problem of explaining why British entrepreneurs should be more traditionally-minded and hence content to jog along in the same old way. This aspect will be dealt with more fully when we come to discuss the structure of the firm.

For the moment we must draw together the threads of the above argument. In so far as the force of tradition determined the actions of British industrialists, then the early start may have placed Britain at a disadvantage, though there is no reason to assume that tradition-mindedness need necessarily increase as an economy matures. It may also be conceded that there may be some validity in the early start and interrelatedness theories when considering determinants of the rate of technical progress within a single country. In the 1930s Merton asserted that the problem of sacrificing accumulated capital in established industries 'may partially account for the relative decline in the rate of technological change as industry becomes more firmly established'.[3] But this cannot be used, save in exceptional circumstances, to explain differences in the rate of technical progress between countries which are at similar stages of development. By the late nineteenth century, America and Germany were not so far removed from Britain on the economic time-scale for them to have had significant 'late-starter' advantages. Thus, until it can be shown that the difficulties of writing off past capital and the problems of interrelatedness were significantly greater for the more mature economy, we may conclude that Britain was not seriously handicapped by her

[1] T. Veblen, *Imperial Germany and the Industrial Revolution* (1939 ed.) p. 132.

[2] *Report of the Committee on the Cotton Industry*, Cd. 3615 (1930) para. 39.

[3] R. K. Merton, 'Fluctuations in the Rate of Industrial Invention', *Quarterly Journal of Economics*, XLIX (1935) 466.

role as pioneer. On the contrary, in terms of pure economic theory it can be argued that the mature economy is in the best position to advance the pace of technical progress. Perhaps, then, Jewkes was not very wide of the mark when he suggested that the theory made little sense in its crudest form, for, if correct, 'the happiest position for any country would be that in which no start had ever been made at all'.[1]

III

Having cast doubt upon the validity of much of the early start thesis, we must now find some alternative to put in its place. Could it be that the relative abundance of factors of production retarded the rate of technical progress by reducing the incentive to invest in factor-saving techniques? We know from past experience that the pattern of technical progress in any one country will be determined to a great extent by the availability of the main factors of production, and the way in which they are combined for productive purposes will depend on their supply relationships and relative prices. Hence '... relative factor endowments and therefore relative factor prices may be expected to be critical in determining the choice of productive techniques'.[2] Thus if one factor is scarce relative to another then the techniques of production employed will be such as to minimise the use of the scarce factor. Land, for example, was scarce relatively to labour in Britain in the Industrial Revolution, so farming techniques were biased in favour of increasing productivity per acre rather than the productivity of labour. In nineteenth-century America labour was expensive compared with capital and therefore the accent was on capital-intensive or labour-saving techniques; whereas the opposite was true of Japan and hence labour-intensive

[1] J. Jewkes, 'The Growth of World Industry', *Oxford Economic Papers*, IX (1951). It could of course be argued that Britain's concentration on the heavy staple industries created structural rigidities and made it difficult to shift resources to newer lines of development. But there is no evidence to suggest that the newer industries were held up by lack of resources, either of labour or capital. The problem of these industries was not that they did not develop but that they progressed too slowly. There are a number of reasons to account for this, one of which is the smallness of many of the firms and the unscientific approach which they adopted to the techniques of production. For a recent appraisal of their development see S. B. Saul, 'The American Impact on British Industry, 1895–1914', *Business History*, III (1960) and 'The Motor Industry in Britain to 1914', *Business History* V (1962) and H. W. Richardson, 'The Development of the Synthetic Dyestuffs Industry before 1939', *Scottish Journal of Political Economy*, IX (1962).

[2] N. Rosenberg, 'Neglected Dimensions in the Analysis of Economic Change', *Bull. of the Oxford Institute of Economics and Statistics*, XXVI (1964) 67. On this point see also W. E. Salter, *Productivity and Technical Change* (1960) and C. Kennedy 'Induced Bias in Innovation and the Theory of Distribution', *Economic Journal*, LXXIV (1964).

techniques were more popular. The position is a little less clear as regards the Continent but it is probable that a relative scarcity of raw materials (especially fuel) and a fairly abundant supply of labour facilitated the adoption of those methods which reduced the quantity of materials required per unit of output.[1] The position in late nineteenth-century Britain was somewhat different, however, for apart from land, which could hardly be classed as an important factor of production as far as industry was concerned,[2] all factors were plentiful and there was no significant abundance or shortage of one factor relative to another. How then did manufacturers react to this situation and what effect did it have on the type of investment decisions they made?

Evidence suggests that because factor supplies were abundant they were used indiscriminately or wastefully, there being little incentive to economise in the use of one factor in terms of another. Cheap coal, for instance, helped to retard the adoption of fuel-saving techniques. In 1938 a speaker at the Institution of Electrical Engineers recalled that when he joined the railways at the beginning of the century, 'the price of locomotive coal was still so low that the majority of railways did not consider it worth while to undertake research on the locomotive considered as a heat engine, with a view to more economical design. The saving of coal, so important to the continental railways, who had to import much or all of their fuel, was of little importance in England.'[3] The iron and steel industry was equally negligent in this respect and was certainly far behind its continental competitors (especially Germany) in the matter of fuel conservation. Scottish ironmasters were said to follow a policy of 'suicidal prodigality' in using natural resources,[4] while even in the large steel firms where the fuel bill was an important item in total costs it was the exception to find an organised staff devoting their whole time to fuel consumption.[5] In fact many steel firms, unlike their German counterparts, had not even an approximate notion of their heat losses.[6]

[1] Initially, of course, a relative shortage of capital favoured labour intensive techniques.

[2] Except in so far as a shortage of land within urban centres restricted the expansion or redesign of industrial works. There is little evidence on this point and we can only suggest that any difficulties of this sort were being eliminated by improvements in local transport facilities which enabled manufacturers to re-locate their plants in less congested surroundings. See G. C. Allen, *The Industrial Development of Birmingham and the Black Country, 1860–1927* (1929) p. 142.

[3] Quoted in K. H. Johnston, *British Railways and Economic Recovery* (1949) p. 142.

[4] R. H. Campbell, *Carron Company* (1961) p. 237.

[5] *Final Report of the Coal Conservation Committee*, Cd. 9094 (1918) app. v, 78; see also D. L. Burn, *The Economic History of Steelmaking, 1867–1939* (1961 ed.) pp. 211–12.

[6] *The Times Engineering Supplement* (Sep 1919) 278.

Even in shipping, where fuel economy was supposed to be vital, the marine steam engine used coal 'with a prodigality to contemplate which is humiliating'. The work done by the best engines did not exceed 7½ per cent of the force latent in the coal which they consumed, the remainder of the force being wasted in the furnaces and boilers, in the exhaust and steam and by friction in the machinery and propeller.[1] Again, the availability of cheap coal after 1914 acted as a barrier to the adoption of oil for deep sea propulsion duties. Although greater attention began to be paid to fuel economy in the early twentieth century when coal became somewhat dearer, the wastage still remained enormous. Shortly before the end of the war, the Coal Conservation Committee estimated that, had the current coal consumption been used economically, it would have produced three times the amount of power and that manufacturing industry alone would have saved £27·5 million on its fuel bill.[2]

The most economical means of applying power to industry is the electric motor but by 1912 only one-quarter of the motive power used in manufacturing and mining was electrically driven. Again it can be argued that the availability of cheap coal and cheap gas delayed the widespread adoption of electric power in industry, though it was not the only reason. The inefficient method of electricity generation kept the price of electricity at a relatively high level while, until the turn of the century, the high cost of electrical plant was not offset by savings in fuel costs. Thus it was not until towards the First World War that the cost advantage became sufficiently attractive to induce many manufacturers to change over to electric power. This was unfortunate in a way, since the adoption of electricity often led to a redesigning of works and factory layout on more efficient lines which resulted in greater productivity.[3]

Apart from coal it seems unlikely that other industrial raw materials were so plentiful as to affect the course of technical progress, though the ease with which some could be acquired from abroad may have lessened the urgency of economising in their use.[4] On the other hand cheap labour probably constituted the greatest barrier to the adoption of mechanisation and new techniques.[5] The classic

[1] *Third Annual Report of the Chamber of Shipping of the United Kingdom* (13 Feb 1880) 38.

[2] Cd. 9084 (1918) pp. 9–11.

[3] I. C. R. Byatt, 'The British Electrical Industry, 1875–1914' (Oxford D. Phil. thesis, 1962).

[4] It could conceivably be argued that the relative ease with which British steelmakers could obtain non-phosphoric ores from abroad made them less inclined to utilise native phosphoric ores for the basic process of steelmaking.

[5] See J. Saville, 'Some Retarding Factors in the British Economy before 1914', *Yorkshire Bulletin of Economic and Social Research*, XIII (1961) 56.

case is the coal industry. The failure to make much headway in mechanising the mines before 1914 can be attributed almost entirely to the fact that coal-owners hardly ever ran short of labour. It is interesting to observe, moreover, that when wages and prices rose and temporary labour shortages developed the desire to mechanise became more apparent.[1] Similarly the cotton manufacturers were not under the same pressure as their American counterparts to introduce labour-saving devices such as the ring spindle and the automatic loom, which reduced the cost of labour by one-half. By 1919, half the looms in use in the States were of the automatic type, whereas Britain had only just begun to introduce them. Other factors, such as the nature of the product, no doubt helped to delay its adoption in this country, but the abundance of cheap labour was probably the major reason for the slower rate of technical progress in the British cotton industry compared with the American.[2] Coal and cotton were not the only industries which were affected in this way. In a number of other industries—hosiery, footwear, steel and the railways—there was not the same incentive to introduce labour-saving techniques as there was in America.[3] It may also be suggested that the relative abundance of cheap skilled craft labour in this country compared with America delayed the introduction of automatic machinery and mass production methods especially in engineering and car assembly plants.[4] Conversely, of course, it can be argued that the shortage of highly qualified scientists and technicians limited the range of opportunities open to British businessmen. This is particularly true in the chemical field where the 'want of encouragement of the chemist' was responsible for the failure to develop certain branches of chemical manufacture.[5]

The same sort of argument can be applied to the capital side. According to Marshall, English manufacturers had access to larger and cheaper supplies of capital than anyone else[6] and during the

[1] A. J. Taylor, 'Labour Productivity and Technological Innovation in the British Coal Industry, 1850–1914', *Economic History Review*, XIV (1961–2) 63; see also A. R. Griffin, *The Miners of Nottinghamshire*, vol. I—1881 to 1914 (1955) p. 177.

[2] M. T. Copeland, *The Cotton Manufacturing Industry of the United States* (1912) ch. iv *passim*.

[3] On footwear and hosiery see P. Head, 'Industrial Organization in Leicester 1844–1914: A Study in Changing Technology, Innovation and Conditions of Employment' (Leicester Ph.D. thesis, 1960) 89, 91–3, 118, 128 and 155.

[4] See H. J. Habakkuk, *American and British Technology in the Nineteenth Century* (1962) p. 185; cf. S. B. Saul, in *Business History*, v 36.

[5] This point in confirmed by H. W. Richardson, loc. cit.; J. J. Beer, *The Emergence of the German Dye Industry* (1959) and L. F. Haber, *The Chemical Industry during the Nineteenth Century* (1958).

[6] *Memorandum by Alfred Marshall on the Fiscal Policy of International Trade*, H.C.321 (1908) paras 62 and 80.

period there seems to have been no strong tendency for the labour supply to vary significantly in terms of capital. For most of the time the aggregate capital coefficient remained fairly stable, which suggests that there can have been no marked trend towards capital-saving techniques.[1] This point is less easy to verify, but what evidence we have does tend to confirm the fact that manufacturers were under no great pressure to economise in the use of capital. In the cotton industry, for example, the continental manufacturers economised in capital and the Americans in labour but the English seemed to have saved precious little. It is true that, after about 1860, the slant of technical change tended to be capital-saving but there does not appear to have been a noticeable shift in favour of capital-saving techniques.[2] Neither did the productivity of capital in iron and steel advance very rapidly if we may judge from the blast furnace performance; after 1890 output per blast furnace rose much more slowly than that of either Germany or America and technical practice in the industry as a whole hardly changed at all up to 1914.[3] One would not go so far as to suggest that the productivity of capital did not rise at all in some industries or that there was no attempt to use capital-saving techniques, but simply that the abundance of capital (like the abundance of labour in the opposite context) provided no strong incentive to employ techniques which were clearly capital-saving or adopt new methods of production which might have a similar effect. Yet there was tremendous scope for improving the efficiency of capital (and labour), especially in engineering, machine tools and the motor-car industry, if American methods of production had only been adopted. That this was not done to any great extent may be attributed to the fact that British industrialists never had to face the problem of saving either capital or labour, simply because both factors were so plentiful. The tinplate industry provides an even more graphic illustration of this point. The Americans, when they began producing tinplate in the 1890s, adopted the same stock of capital as used by the Welsh tinplate makers. Yet they made such startling innovations in the way in which they organised the production processes that within a few years they were producing much more per unit of capital and labour than their Welsh counterparts.[4] By 1910, America was producing the same amount of tinplate

[1] R. Bićanić, 'The Threshold of Economic Growth', *Kyklos*, xv (1962) 23.

[2] M. Blaug, 'The Productivity of Capital in the Lancashire Cotton Industry during the Nineteenth Century', *Economic History Review*, XIII (1961–2) 360.

[3] T. H. Burnham and G. O. Hoskins, *Iron and Steel in Britain, 1870–1930* (1943) p. 145.

[4] W. E. Minchinton, *The British Tinplate Industry, a History* (1957) p. 69.

as Britain with a labour force of just over one-quarter the British.[1] As Pursell says 'a Welsh emigrant would have recognised the machinery of an American mill, but he would have been a stranger to its arrangement and operation'.[2]

The above argument does not, of course, provide a foolproof explanation of the slower rate of technical progress in British industry compared with abroad. There are obviously many exceptions to any generalisation. Nevertheless there is sufficient evidence to suggest that factor supplies were such as to give little incentive to innovate in one particular direction. There was certainly no wide discrepancy in the supply or price of different factors of production, as there was in America, which would have given rise to the intensive use of one in terms of another. Thus we may assume that the situation encouraged industrialists to make neutral investment decisions[3] rather than ones with a distinct factor-saving bias. This does not mean that technical progress was completely static or that factor productivities did not increase but simply that innovation was less rapid than it might have been under different factor supply conditions. It is more than just coincidence that the very industries in which technical progress was particularly slow—cotton, coal, tinplate and iron and steel—should be the ones where trends towards economising in any one factor of production were least apparent.

The implications for growth are important but cannot be explored fully here. A few tentative suggestions may be put forward. Since the factor-supply situation lessened the incentive to adopt innovations with a strong factor-saving element, the rate of technical progress in British industry was slower than it might have been. Now assuming that technical progress is one of the main determinants of economic growth,[4] we can argue that the effect was to dampen growth rates,

[1] F. W. Taussig, 'Labour Costs in the United States Compared with Costs Elsewhere', *Quarterly Journal of Economics*, XXXIX (1925) 106.

[2] C. W. Pursell, 'Tariff and Technology: The Foundation and Development of the American Tinplate Industry, 1872–1900', *Technology and Culture* (summer 1962) 280.

[3] That is investment which has no distinct factor-saving bias either labour, capital or resource. This is slightly different from the neutral technical improvements of the Harrod model. See John E. La Tourette, 'Technological Change and Equilibrium Growth in the Harrod–Domar Model', *Kyklos*, XVII (1964) esp. 221.

[4] This, of course, is still a very debatable point among economists, though many would now agree that capital accumulation *per se* has lost some of its appeal as a growth factor. Analytically it can be shown that under long-run dynamic conditions investment is a dependent variable, the nature of which is determined by technical progress. Even in the short-run the latter may remain the independent variable on account of the fact that not all technical progress involves the formation of capital. See B. F. Massell, 'Capital Formation and Technological Change in United States Manufacturing', *Review of Economics and Statistics*, XLII (1960) 182–8.

especially productivity. Furthermore, we may hazard the suggestion that indiscriminate innovation[1] was less fruitful in terms of growth than technical progress with a built-in factor bias. American investment with its strong labour-saving bias tended to raise the productivity of both labour and capital—since in the frantic attempt to save labour American machines were pushed harder—and hence was more productive in terms of factor inputs than British investment with its non-factoral bias. Moreover, the absence of a strong factor inducement to determine investment decisions often meant that British industrialists continued to invest in existing techniques. Note for instance the steel industry where, in the couple of decades before the war, there was no significant change in technical practice despite the fact that steel capacity more than doubled in the period.

## IV

The fact that British manufacturers tended to maintain existing techniques cannot of course be attributed solely to the availability and cheapness of factor supplies. In part this course of action can be explained by the structure of British industry and the ingrained attitude of the typical entrepreneur.

The small unit often dominated by the family or association of friends predominated in British industry up to 1914. Sargent Florence suggests that the relative decline of British industry between 1880 and 1930 may well have been due to the fact that the large proportion of its output was controlled by family heads 'reacting less keenly to higher profit and reinvesting less of that profit'.[2] Some would dissent from this view but evidence continues to grow in its favour. Many firms which passed into second and third generations became markedly less dynamic, especially in cases where the descendants had sufficient wealth to allow the pursuit of interests outside the business and the acquisition of social recognition.[3]

The Rathbone family, for example, 'had made sufficient wealth to allow them to pursue their own interests and they were not keen enough to adapt their methods to new conditions'.[4] Burn in his study of the steel industry lays considerable stress on the 'indolence and apathy engendered by phenomenal success' and the corrupting influence of fortune on heirs to an industrial dynasty.[5] It is not sur-

[1] That is non-factor biased investment.

[2] P. Sargent Florence, *Logic of British and American Industry* (1953) p.320.

[3] See H. Whidden, 'The British Entrepreneur: 1899 to 1949', *Change and the Entrepreneur* (Harvard U.P., 1949) p. 43.

[4] S. Marriner, *Rathbones of Liverpool, 1845–73* (1961) p. 131.

[5] D. L. Burn, *Economic History of Steelmaking*, pp. 298–301.

prising to learn therefore that the founding generation was most successful in innovation.[1] The same sort of thing seems to have happened in the tinplate industry.[2] Businessmen sought to raise their social standing by investing in land, participating in politics or diverting their energies to a whole host of other liberal pursuits.[3] As a result they had less time for business matters and hence were less inclined to explore new fields or adopt new methods, being content to carry on along traditional lines. The decline of the great Tennant chemical works in the later nineteenth century was in no small part due to the fact that the second and third generation had become so tied up with extra-mural activities that they neglected the business. John Tennant, the descendant of the original founder, 'refused to be a slave to his business and travelled far and wide on horse-back. He was a *bon vivant* and had many convivial friends, to whom he was a generous host.'[4] Marshalls, the Leeds flax spinners, came to an end in 1886 for similar reasons.[5] Few shared the same fate but there were many business leaders of family firms who displayed similar characteristics with the result that their industrial interests suffered.[6] Even when outside interests were not so predominant there seems to have been a noticeable reluctance to innovate on the part of already established firms. Woodruff draws attention to the 'peculiar unwillingness' of those who led the early rubber companies to seize the new opportunities bound up with the developments in road transportation at the end of the nineteenth century. He says the older companies were more concerned with expanding sales of existing products rather than opening up markets for new ones and 'it required a new combination of inventive talent and commercial skill, new vision and imagination, to ensure the technical advance bound up with the development of the pneumatic tyre industry'.[7]

[1] C. Erickson, *British Industrialists; Steel and Hosiery 1850–1950* (1959) p. 165.

[2] W. E. Minchinton, *British Tinplate*, p. 106.

[3] See F. M. L. Thomson, *English Landed Society in the Nineteenth Century* (1963) pp. 129–31.

[4] *Enterprise: An Account of the Activities and Aims of the Tennant Group of Companies* (1948) p. 132.

[5] W. G. Rimmer, *Marshalls of Leeds, Flax-Spinners, 1788–1886* (1960) esp. pp. 252–3.

[6] For examples see C. P. Kindleberger, *Economic Growth in France and Britain 1851–1950* (1964) pp. 124–33 and T. J. Byres, 'The Scottish Economy During The Great Depression 1873–96, with Special Reference to the Heavy Industries of the South-West' (Glasgow University B. Litt. thesis, 1963).

[7] W. Woodruff, *The Rise of the Rubber Industry during the Nineteenth Century* (1958) pp. 182–3. A further point of similar consequence is worth considering. Some entrepreneurs took on business commitments outside their original field and were eventually unable to devote their attention properly to any one undertaking. Sir Edward Watkin and Sir Alfred Jones (the shipowner) certainly took on more than

Whether wealth, past success, or hankering after social prestige fostered a spirit of apathy among British businessmen and made them reluctant to innovate or whether the British entrepreneur was basically a different animal from his American and German counterparts is difficult to say. His time and spatial horizons were certainly more limited and in attitude and outlook he resembled the Frenchman rather than the German or American. He did not think big or strive to make money for the sake of doing so for 'the unrestrained pursuit of profit was not generally recognised as the end of human endeavour'.[1] The British manufacturer was obsessed with short-run possibilities and when things became difficult he took the line of least resistance and did not stop to consider the long-run implications of his actions. Thus when markets became tight in Europe and America in the last quarter of the century, he diverted his wares to the Empire and to primary producers rather than compete with more dynamic foreign rivals. And when profit margins were under pressure he sought to reduce the cost of his most variable factor, labour, not by economising in its use but by reducing wage rates. Wage-cost reduction was the short-term alternative to long-term technical economies and as such provided an easy way out for manufacturers in difficulties.[2] The long-term 'technological rationality' (to use Landes' phrase) of the German industrialist did not feature in the British entrepreneur's calculations. The German industrialists (and one may add the American) had, according to Landes, a longer time horizon and included in their estimates exogenous variables of continuing technical change which their British competitors held constant.[3] Moreover, we may argue that the German and American industrialists often sought technical change for its own sake whereas the Englishmen scorned anything new until it was tried or proven.[4] There was a curious unwillingness to scrap machinery, however old

they could manage and accordingly their business interests suffered. Dow, *Great Central*, II 100, 104, 252–3 and *Royal Commission on Shipping Rings*, Evidence, vol. III, Cd. 4670 (1909) qtn. 5201. It would be interesting to find out how many businessmen fell into this category and what effect it had on the rate of technical progress.

[1] W. E. Minchinton, *British Tinplate*, p. 106.

[2] See F. A. Wells, *The British Hosiery Trade: its History and Organization* (1935) p. 198. Reworking an earlier point we may argue that had the labour supply been less plentiful and had labour objected more strongly to reduction in their remuneration, relative wage costs would have been higher and this in turn would have forced manufacturers to seek other ways of reducing their costs.

[3] D. S. Landes, 'The Structure of Enterprise in the Nineteenth Century: the Case of Britain and Germany', *Extrait des rapports du XIe Congrès International des Sciences Historiques*, v (Stockholm, 1960) 121.

[4] E.g. the case of steel, see Orsagh, in *Comparative Studies in Society and History*, III 228.

it might be, and some firms were prepared to hang on to it until it practically fell to pieces. The directors of the Sun Mill Cotton Company, for example, admitted that much of their equipment was out of date but contended that it was 'as good as the new' and hence were not prepared to throw it away.[1]

It may of course be argued that this kind of attitude was probably inevitable given the nature of the British firm. Small family-dominated firms—and even large ones for that matter—tended to become insular and parochial in outlook, and inertia and conservatism soon set in after the first flush of victory.[2] Sturmey in a recent study has shown how close-knit family-controlled cliques in shipping bred conservatism and reaction to change and resulted in an industry bent on maintaing the *status quo* and ill-adapted to meeting the difficult conditions of the inter-war years.[3] And the fact that firms were small meant that they had neither the resources nor the talent (e.g. technically trained personnel) with which to investigate and apply new techniques of a costly nature. As Taylor has pointed out, it was the predominance of small units in the coal industry which 'militated against technical experiment and innovation'.[4] That firms remained in this awkward position was partly their own fault. Most of them were extremely reluctant to call upon outside sources to finance expansion or admit talented 'new men' to the fold for fear of disrupting the family clique or relinquishing independent control.[5] When the rubber interests of Moulton and Spencer were merged in 1891 the two families made sure that they retained control of the capital since neither party was 'inclined to trust their business to a stranger'.[6] Possibly, then, as Landes suggests, the conditions of supply determined the policy of these firms. The ease with which capital could be secured through private channels was sufficient to satisfy the limited aspirations of British enterprise. 'The absence of powerful investment banks and the availability of local resources, within and without the enterprise go far to account for the persistence of traditional patterns of business organisation and behaviour

[1] R. E. Tyson, 'The Sun Mill Company Limited—a study in Democratic Investment, 1858–1959' (University of Manchester M.A. thesis, 1962) 261.

[2] See, for example, G. B. Sutton, 'The Marketing of Ready Made Footwear in the Nineteenth Century: A Study of the firm of C. & J. Clark', *Business History*, VI (1964).

[3] S. G. Sturmey, *British Shipping and World Competition* (1962) p. 397.

[4] A. J. Taylor, in *Economic History Review*, XIV 64.

[5] See for example, B. H. Tripp, *Renold Chains: A History of the Company and the Rise of the Precision Chain Industry, 1879–1955* (1956); cf. Minchinton, *British Tinplate*, p. 107.

[6] P. L. Payne, *Rubber and Railways in the Nineteenth Century: A Study of the Spencer Papers* (1961) pp. 49 and 205.

into the twentieth century.'[1] Had capital been more difficult to come by privately, such firms would probably have been forced into the market for their cash. This, in the long run, might have had a salutary effect on their whole performance.

Of course one would not go so far as to say that all small firms were unenterprising or that all firms were governed by lethargic family groups of second and third stock. One has only to mention the names of Pilkingtons and J. & P. Coats to realise that sweeping generalisations of this sort can be very dangerous.[2] Still it is interesting to note that the really successful firms, or ones that retained their momentum, were those that were devoid of ancestral domination and/or prepared to let in outside talent. In steel, for instance, family dynasties were far less prominent among the innovating firms[3] and the individual histories of Carron Company and Vickers tend to confirm this conclusion.[4] But such conclusions must for the moment border on the speculative, for until we know more about the histories of individual firms, a precise statement of fact is impossible. Nevertheless it is more than likely that future research will reveal a heavy preponderance of firms dominated by relatively unenterprising family cliques.

We may suggest, then, that the routine element in replacement, to which Kindleberger has drawn attention,[5] was determined in part by the attitudes inherent in the typical British firm. The success of past methods, the diversion of entrepreneurial energy into outside activities and the obsession of maintaining family connections[6] caused many firms to continue to invest in static techniques in preference to exploiting the new technological possibilities which were being made available at the time.

## V

Insufficient attention has perhaps been paid in the past to the way in which market forces affect the pattern of technical progress. Yet the size, structure and profitability of the market may be very important in determining the nature and rapidity of the advances made along

[1] Landes, in *XIe Congrès des Sciences Historiques*, p. 114.

[2] T. C. Barker, *Pilkington Brothers and the Glass Industry* (1960) and M. Blair, *The Paisley Thread Industry* (1907).

[3] C. Erickson, *British Industrialists*, p. 165.

[4] R. H. Campbell, *Carron Company;* J. D. Scott, *Vickers: A History* (1962). The Consett Iron and Steel Company also provides an interesting case study. See *Business History*, VII (1965).

[5] C. P. Kindleberger, *Economic Growth*, p. 154.

[6] The same sort of thing was apparent in landed estate. See C. S. Orwin and E. H. Whetham, *History of British Agriculture 1846–1914* (1964) p. 66.

the technological front. It would seem that the large and fast-growing American home market provided greater scope for mass production techniques and product specialisation than that of the British. The unique degree of specialisation attained by the American machine tool industry was due in no small part to the vast expansion in the demand for the final products of that industry. Moreover, the fact that the machine tool industry constituted 'a pool or reservoir of skills and technical knowledge' and 'because it dealt with processes and problems common to an increasing number of industries it played the role of a transmission centre in the diffusion of the new technology' throughout the entire machine-using sectors of the economy.[1] The same effect was not apparent in Britain for the scale and structure of the market was less conducive to the adoption of mass production techniques and this in turn limited the demand for certain machine tools. Indeed, the market was so narrow for some tools that it was impossible to manufacture them economically, and demand had to be satisfied from abroad.

Size of market was perhaps not so important, except in so far as the volume of demand for certain commodities was so small as to render production uneconomic. Rather the crucial factor appears to have been the nature of the market or what Professor Saul has called the 'social depth' of demand. The Americans, and to a lesser extent the Germans, were more willing to purchase standardised products and this facilitated the adoption of mass production methods in which the limitation of product variety is of strategic importance. On the other hand British society, with its more rigid class distinctions, was less inclined to accept standardised consumption patterns and continued to demand 'aristocratic goods of high individual quality'.[2] Thus the absence of a strong demand for products of a high degree of uniformity discouraged manufacturers from adopting modern methods and new techniques, especially those which involved the production of large quantities of standardised commodities. The implications of this pattern of demand have been outlined by Frankel: 'Differentiation helps to divide and sectionalise the market, aids establishment and preservation of high-cost, unenterprising producers, creates resistances to innovations that depend for their success on large-scale output and consumption, and encourages undue research and promotional efforts in areas of style and fashion.'[3]

[1] N. Rosenberg, 'Technological Change in the Machine Tool Industry, 1840–1910', *Journal of Economic History*, XXIII (1963) 425–6.

[2] E. Rothbarth, 'Causes of the Superior Efficiency of U.S.A. Industry as compared with British Industry', *Economic Journal*, LVI (1946) 386.

[3] M. Frankel, *British and American Manufacturing Productivity*, p. 74.

This argument is particularly relevant, of course, to the engineering and motor trades which offered the greatest scope for high mass production techniques. But it also affected the rate of technical progress in other trades. The reason why machinery was more readily adapted to cutlery production in Germany than in England was because the trade of the former was concentrated on cheap goods which could be produced in quantity, whereas the latter aimed at producing the best articles possible.[1] Similarly the dearer fabrics produced by British cotton manufacturers were less suited to the new technical processes which were being used in America at this time. This is particularly true of the printing trades, where the British emphasis on style and quality did not facilitate the use of American machines designed to produce large quantities of standardised patterns.[2] Finally, it can be argued that the adoption of technical improvements by British railways, e.g. the use of larger wagons, was hindered by the fact that they were obliged to satisfy the individual wants and requirements of the traders and passengers.

One should, however, be careful about laying all the blame on the demand side. To some extent it was up to the manufacturers themselves to 'educate' the public into accepting articles of a more homogeneous nature. The British market was no doubt less plastic than that of Germany or America but its potentialities were great had it been tapped more assiduously. In other words the market for standardised products still remained latent or unopened and the failure to exploit it properly before 1914 may be simply due to the unwillingness of manufacturers to shift from the known to the unknown. A new kind of market was developing for flint glass at this time but 'the masters preferred to satisfy the market for high-grade wares, produced by traditional methods, rather than to aim at securing a share of the growing demand for cheaper qualities by a reorganisation of their plant and productive processes'.[3] In effect, we have now arrived back at the original point of departure where we discussed the impact of tradition. It is difficult to disentangle cause and effect in this matter, that is whether the blame should be laid on the supply or the demand side. There seems to be an equally good case for saying that industrialists were more interested in technical perfection and craftsmanship than in techniques of production and this, in turn, led to the failure to exploit new types of demand. Lanchester, one of the few of the early motor manufacturers to attempt to use modern methods of production, recalls how reluctant craftsmen were to work

[1] G. I. H. Lloyd, *The Cutlery Trades* (1913) p. 348.
[2] M. T. Copeland, *Cotton Manufacturing*, p. 99.
[3] G. C. Allen, *Industrial Development of Birmingham*, p. 221.

to standardised instructions. 'In those days', he said later, 'when a body builder was asked to work to drawings, gauges or templates, he gave a sullen look such as one might expect from a Royal Academician if asked to colour an engineering drawing'.[1]

What one has to consider above all, however, is not so much the size or the structure of the market but whether it offered sufficient inducement in terms of profit for manufacturers to contemplate making changes in their techniques. In this context the absolute level of profits is not important; rather it was the past trend of profits and the marginal increment of profit which might be earned by introducing new techniques that were the determining factors. Since it seems fairly certain that profit margins were being squeezed in the latter quarter of the nineteenth century, it was only to be expected that manufacturers would be disinclined to make large investments in applying new techniques unless the expected rate of return was substantial. But with falling profit margins, increasing foreign competition in home and export markets and rising tariffs abroad British entrepreneurs, with their short-run horizons, could only anticipate low returns. In other words the market did not provide the type of security which manufacturers required before they would consider changes in techniques. The Royal Commission on the Depression of Trade and Industry was struck by the way in which business confidence had been weakened by narrowing profit margins and difficult trade conditions and how this, in turn, had lessened the capitalist's willingness 'to embark his capital in productive enterprise'.[2] Several witnesses before the Tariff Commission hastened to explain that the uncertainty of the market in the past had made them reluctant to innovate. A firm of machinery manufacturers stated that 'in their experience improvement in steel works has been very much held back owing to the continual fear of United States steel being dumped on the home market. The result is an indisposition to keep plant up to date.'[3] Similarly woollen manufacturers complained that the steady erosion of profit margins over the past thirty years, due to increasing competition at home and abroad, had made conditions less secure and it was more difficult to attract capital for modernisation and efficiency.[4] Martin Albrecht, a Leeds woollen merchant and manufacturer, admitted that many firms in Leeds were running obsolete machinery but he said 'they cannot go and lay out £20,000

[1] P. W. Kingsford, *F. W. Lanchester: A Life of an Engineer* (1960) p. 49.

[2] *Final Report of the Royal Commission on the Depression of Trade and Industry*, C. 4893 (1886) pp. xiv–xv.

[3] *Report of the Tariff Commission*, vol. 4. *The Engineering Industries* (1909), para. 117.

[4] *Report of the Tariff Commission*, vol. 2. *The Textile Trades, Part 2. Evidence on the Woollen Industry* (1905) paras 1376, 1449, 1453, 1456–8.

and bring their machinery up-to-date without some security that they are going to be able to run it when they have done it'.[1]

The reaction of British businessmen to the less favourable market conditions was an unhappy one and merely served to accentuate their difficulties in the long run. They failed to recognise the significance of the challenge to their monopoly and instead of making adjustments along the technical front, they searched for the easiest escape routes in the insured markets of imperialism, in tariffs, restrictive practices, employers associations and wage cost reductions.[2] Tariffs and foreign competition encouraged British industrialists to shift to producing those goods and to selling in those markets where competition was least severe but which, at the same time, provided the least stimulus to technical change. By 1914 nearly 70 per cent of our exports went to primary producers, but, as such, could be regarded as nothing more than a residuary legatee of the home market. For however important and large this export component might be, the demand from agricultural and Empire markets could not produce the same kind of incentive to adopt sophisticated techniques as the rich and expanding markets of Europe and America.

It is probable then that the conditions of the market had a much greater psychologically depressive effect on British businessmen than is often supposed. For much of the period confidence in the market was low, even though demand was still growing fairly rapidly. But serious inroads were being made into former British markets by foreign competitors and this helped to accentuate the loss of confidence. In contrast, the American and German markets were much more buoyant and both quantitatively and qualitatively provided a greater stimulus to the adoption of new techniques and new methods. On the other hand, when (e.g. in the decade before the First World War) and where market conditions were more favourable, British businessmen, as Habakkuk has observed, were just as dynamic as the Americans.[3]

This paper is only a modest and preliminary attempt to explore in a general manner some of the more important factors which helped to retard the rate of technical progress in British industry in the late nineteenth and early twentieth centuries. Much historical spadework remains to be done before a final assessment can be made. In the past far too much emphasis has been placed on the early start and interrelatedness theories as an explanation of Britain's technical deficiencies. In fact, so often has this explanation been used that one

[1] Ibid., para. 1761.

[2] See W. W. Rostow, *British Economy of the Nineteenth Century* (1948) p. 89.

[3] H. J. Habakkuk, *American and British Technology*, p. 213.

wonders when it will cease to be applicable and why other countries never seem to fall foul of it to the extent that Britain is alleged to have done. We would be inclined to agree, therefore, with Professor Kindleberger's assertion that 'big theories of economic growth fail to account for the complex facts of life'. Hence we have suggested that there were more powerful and subtle factors at work which delayed the adoption of new techniques. In particular it would appear that factor supplies and costs, market opportunities and the structural features of the British firm deserve greater weight than historians and economists have been prepared to accord them. These by no means exhaust the possibilities but at least they will provide more fruitful routes for further inquiry than the early start theory.

# 5 Over-commitment in Britain before 1930

I

THE 'early start' thesis and the proposition that it handicapped Britain's industrial progress in the late nineteenth and early twentieth centuries has received a fair amount of attention over the last decade.[1] The usual approach to the early start problem is to discuss obstacles to new technological developments *within* mature industries in the economy (i.e. an *intra*-industry approach), particularly to examine how far the existence of original durable equipment in the staple industries (textiles, iron and steel, shipbuilding, and so on) slowed down the introduction of new techniques into these industries or other sectors linked directly with them. The objective in this article is to analyse the extent to which the early start proved a handicap when it became necessary to transfer resources to new industries based on major innovations of the late nineteenth century (an *inter*-industry approach). It is argued, therefore, that the extensive development of an old industrial structure with a high concentration of employment within a few long-established industries may make adjustments to *new* technology in other industries more difficult. At first sight there might appear no problem at all; classical analysis would indicate a fairly smooth transfer of labour and capital from old sectors to new at a rate determined by differences in the respective returns on capital and prices offered to factors of production. In a perfectly competitive world this would be so, but the heavy and traditional reliance on a narrow industrial base made for serious imperfections in competition. Although less obvious than the intra-industry aspect, the inter-industry one could be said to be the more

[1] The most important examples are I. Svennilson, *Growth and Stagnation in the European Economy* (1954); M. Frankel, 'Obsolescence and Technological Change in a Maturing Economy', *American Economic Review*, XLV (1955) 296–319; D. Gordon, 'Comment' and M. Frankel, 'Reply', ibid., XLVI (1956) 646–56; J. Saville, 'Some Retarding Factors in the British Economy before 1914', *Yorkshire Bulletin of Economic and Social Research*, XIII (1961) 51–60; C. P. Kindleberger, 'Obsolescence and Technical Change', *Bull. of the Oxford University Institute of Statistics*, XXIII (1961) 281–97; H. J. Habakkuk, *American and British Technology in the Nineteenth Century* (1962) ch. vi. Most interesting of all is the critical examination found in E. Ames and N. Rosenberg, 'Changing Technological Leadership and Industrial Growth', *Economic Journal*, LXXII (1963) 13–31. A few comments on their analysis are made in an appendix to this article.

important. This is because in periods of rapid world industrial development the ability of the early starter to keep pace in old industries is less crucial than the capacity for adjustment and transfer of resources to new industries. Technical progressiveness cannot be equated with competitive power because technically less efficient firms may be the low-cost producers if their equipment has already been paid for (their costs are not inflated by heavy depreciation charges), so a lag in the rate of technical progress in old-established industries is unlikely to slow down the aggregate growth rate as much as sluggishness in the new. In the new industries, on the other hand, failure to keep pace must mean competitive backwardness.

With regard to structural readjustment in the British economy, the accepted view is that from the late nineteenth century but especially in the inter-war period Britain was rather later than her main industrial rivals in the reallocation of resources from old industries to new. The degree of this has been exaggerated, but it is certain that the performance of many new industries was sluggish up to 1930.[1] This process of 'transformation' (Svennilson) was held back by the early start, which led to such a large proportion of the economy's resources being invested in the basic industries of the nineteenth century that by the time the new technology was introduced Britain's freedom to turn to new types of production was much more restricted than abroad; this condition will be called *over-commitment.* The nomenclature is not altogether a happy one, but is chosen to convey the impression that once resources are tied up in certain sectors ('committed') there are high costs involved in releasing them for other uses ('transition costs'); *ceteris paribus,* the greater the proportion of resources 'committed' the more inflexible the economy's structure. There is some kinship between the idea of over-commitment and Professor Lewis's 'theory of momentum'.[2] According to the doctrine of momentum, Britain was equipped in the first sixty or seventy years of the nineteenth century to sell textiles and railway materials, and got into a rut which made it difficult for her to realise the need to sell machinery at the end of the century. She became used to doing things in a certain way and found it difficult to change course, whereas countries like Germany developed an irresistible urge to invest in the newer industries which, according to the theory

[1] See H. W. Richardson, 'The New Industries Between the Wars', below, Section B, 8, and 'The Basis of Economic Recovery in the 1930s', below, Section B, 7.

[2] W. A. Lewis, 'International Competition in Manufactures', *American Economic Review,* Proceedings, XLVII (1957).

of momentum, led to a rapid adaptation of the economy as a whole to the new conditions. In this argument it is the cause of the 'irresistible urge' which is difficult to explain. The thesis of over-commitment obviates this problem by explaining the readiness of mature industrial economies other than Britain to turn to the newer industries in the fact that when the new technology was introduced a smaller proportion of their total resources was concentrated in the basic industries than in Britain's case.

Most commentators on the delays in the transformation process in Britain have emphasised the situation between the two world wars, when the lag is easily explained. Because of the high regional concentration of new industries in the south-east and midlands, occupational mobility also meant regional mobility; this aggravated the labour transfer problem, though extensive north–south migration did take place. The old industries were not allowed to decline but were artificially insulated from market forces; government intervention bolstered them up on the pretext of maintaining employment. In addition, there were obstacles to the mobility of capital. Lamfalussy has elaborated the concept of 'defensive investment' which occurs in stagnating markets; instead of inducing disinvestment, falling demand and declining profit rates give rise to a particular type of investment policy, reconstructing existing plant rather than extending capacity by introducing new production processes based on major innovations.[1] Such defensive investment was widespread in Britain between the wars, and old industries competed with new for available funds. Furthermore, the staple industries in the 1920s made little or no profits and the generally depressed situation was unfavourable for financing the new. But if, as seems probable, the obstacles to the growth of the newer industries had been more or less eliminated by 1930, it is evident that the readjustment problem plagued the economy long before the inter-war period. The sluggishness of 1918–30 was the backlog of delay in the development of the newer industries at the time of the original innovations. In other words, the trouble was not that Britain's new industries were less efficient than those abroad but simply that they were slow in getting under way. There were, of course, causes of this 'backwardness' not connected with Britain's previous extensive industrialisation. Market factors were very important: the advantage of a large standardised home market (a function of population size, higher levels of income, and a more equitable income distribution) helped forward some new industries in the United States to reach mass pro-

[1] A. Lamfalussy, *Investment and Growth in Mature Economies* (1961).

duction scales of output earlier than in the United Kingdom. Britain suffered from a limited resource base; hydroelectric power which was to prove cheaper than coal-produced electricity was not feasible except in the north of Scotland, and the country had very sparse supplies of petroleum and non-ferrous metals. But this was not a serious handicap; it merely resulted in a different pattern of new industries from that developed in economies more favourably endowed.

The argument here is that over-commitment was one of the more important factors explaining the slow growth of the new industries in the early decades. Up to 1914 the staple industries remained the main source of industrial expansion, though trends towards newer sections within broad industrial groups such as steel were apparent.[1] The 1907 Census of Production showed that coal mining, iron and steel, and textiles accounted for no less than 46 per cent of net industrial output, employed one-quarter of the occupied population, and supplied 70 per cent of all exports. The burst of major innovations in and around the 1890s (the internal combustion engine, the electric filament lamp, the turbine, viscose cellulose, electro-chemicals) laid the technical base for the growth of new industries. Beginnings were made in applying them, but more extensively abroad than in Britain. The burden of over-commitment was already there, but the dangers of relying on a narrow range of old-established industries were masked after 1905 by heavier demands than ever for Britain's staple exports due to development abroad and a capital export boom. The problem revealed itself after the collapse of the post-war boom

[1] The steel industry presents a difficulty for the over-commitment thesis. Steel can be regarded more as a new than a staple industry. Yet it was unlikely to be seriously affected by over-commitment, since on balance experience in the iron industry should have been an advantage for developing steel. The obstacles to the transfer of resources within an industry are much smaller than between industries. The steel industry is, nevertheless, regarded as a striking example of backwardness. How can this exception to the argument be explained? Steel, the major growth industry of the last quarter of the nineteenth century, should have proved the saviour of the mature economy faced with deceleration in its older basic industries. But it was an unfortunate historical accident that the industry was simultaneously developed in the newly industrialised countries which had resource structures favourable to exploiting the innovations in steel. Thus Britain, faced with strong international competition, was unable to achieve the growth rate in steel that might have been expected of her. Furthermore, backwardness in steel can be exaggerated. Performances varied greatly between firms, and the picture is not one of uniform bleakness. One firm studied by the author was very successful in making high profits even in depressed periods, and its managers were progressive (H. W. Richardson and J. M. Bass, 'The Profitability of Consett Iron Company before 1914', *Business History*, VII (1965)). This firm might have been the exception, but we need more studies of individual firms before we dogmatise about 'backwardness' in steel.

up to 1930. Heavy structural unemployment in the 1920s, the depressed fringe of the north of England, Scotland and Wales, the stagnation in exports were all signs of delays in readjustment. This is not to suggest that over-commitment was the sole or even the major cause of general unemployment between the wars; low levels of world effective demand which followed directly from low incomes prevailing in primary producing countries (squeezed between technical progress in agriculture and the slowing down of population growth in Western Europe) were more important.

The hindsight argument is that a more rapid transfer of resources to the new industries should have been achieved earlier. This does not mean that entrepreneurs and investors were irrational before 1914. From the point of view of the long-term future of the British economy the need for transformation was already there but the economic justification was not. Investors could obtain higher yields with security from investing abroad, while boom conditions (especially in exports) in the staple trades did not favour a shift of entrepreneurs from old industries to new. It paid the nation to continue to specialise in exporting the old-established goods and to leave the modest home demand for new products mainly to imports. Moreover, the high export dependence of the staple industries suggests that an earlier concentration on predominantly home market newer industries would have resulted in balance of payments difficulties. Thus a more intensive transfer of resources to new industries at this time would almost certainly have resulted in lower current real income than was in fact achieved. If contemporary entrepreneurs and investors can be faulted, it is because they weighted their expectations too heavily with past and current performances and gave too little attention to estimating future prospects. Businessmen were, on the whole, maximising income in the short run[1] and there was a divergence between these short-run interests and the long-term interests of the economy. The conclusion is that over-commitment was inevitable; nothing that those in charge of industry could have reasonably been expected to foresee before 1914 could have prevented the inter-industry structural lag in Britain. Given Britain's early start and the high proportion of her resources invested in the staple industries, and assuming that entrepreneurs and investors respond to the profit motive, only a planned economy could have pushed

[1] Kindleberger makes the same point: 'This is sometimes characterised as conservatism or timidity in the face of change. But it is perhaps more accurate as well as more charitable to regard it as maximising comfort in the short run' (*Oxford University Institute of Statistics*, XXIII 293).

forward the development of the new industries to the required level before 1914.

The analysis of over-commitment which follows rests on two main assumptions. First, that there are marked discontinuities in the flow of *major* innovations and the appearance of new industries. The Schumpeterian view that 'technological progress moves in fits and starts' is a necessary prop to the early start thesis, because if the path of technical progress is smooth and continuous the adjustment from one state of technology to another will be unlikely to give rise to serious difficulties such as 'transition costs' or problems of 'interrelatedness'.[1] Secondly, that there was some demand for the newer types of products in Britain before 1914. This assumption seems reasonable, for the imports of new products were sizeable[2] in addition to the outputs of the home industries. Thus, over-commitment refers primarily to the *supply* position and on the ability of capacity in the new industries to expand sufficiently to satisfy potential demand. To some extent, this dichotomy is artificial since strong stimuli to the growth of demand may come from the supply side (the setting up of new cost-reducing production functions), but it justifies leaving aside considerations of the size and character of the market for new goods.

Over-commitment interfered with the growth of the new industries in three main ways. In the first place, it led to a scarcity of production facilities for these industries. Secondly, the long and unchallenged predominance of Britain's staple industries affected entrepreneurial psychology and lulled businessmen into making decisions and judgements based too much on past experience, which led to a misplaced emphasis on short-run as against long-run benefits. Thirdly, the institutional framework against which decisions are made was so moulded by the lopsided industrial structure that the adoption of new industries was less economic in Britain than abroad.

[1] 'Interrelatedness' is a concept expounded by Frankel, in *American Economic Review*, XLVI, 645–56. As he puts it: 'Real capital, especially in the later stages of industrialisation, may be made up of a number of components such that they cannot be replaced separately, but only on all or nothing basis.' Renewal of one piece of capital equipment within an industrial plant may require replacement of other items not merely in the plant, but possibly in the whole industry or in the economy's infrastructure. For example, introduction of new chemicals may need not only new capital equipment within the firm but new types of rail or road containers for their transportation.

[2] In 1913 Britain imported chemicals to the value of £13·34 million, newer types of petroleum products £7·42 million, machinery £7·27 million, motor-cars (complete, chassis, and parts) £4·85 million, rubber tyres and tubes £2·78 million, and electrical goods and apparatus £1·59 million (*Statistical Abstract for the United Kingdom 1913–27*, Cmnd. 3253 (1929) pp. 322–4).

Whereas the early start thesis as such might be applicable to other advanced industrial economies, over-commitment was probably peculiar to Britain in the particular historical circumstances of the late nineteenth and early twentieth centuries. There is no other case where so high a proportion of an economy's resources was tied up in such a narrow range of industries, and where the effects of this condition were imprinted on the total environment in which economic change occurs.

## II

Did over-commitment limit the availability of factors of production to the new industries in the early stages of their growth? Apart from the competing demands of old and new industries for resources, there are two main considerations: the degree of elasticity in the supply of factors of production and the complementary question of the mobility of these factors under the influence of long-term growth trends in declining and expanding industries.

*Capital.* Although capital is not like land – and in the short-run labour – physically limited in the sense that it can be increased at any moment by saving, its growth is nevertheless restricted. For savings are in turn determined by other influences such as the level of income, available investment opportunities and changes in consumption habits. Moreover, the annual flow of savings made available has to be distributed in several ways apart from investment in industry; for example, part may be invested abroad and part is certain to be hoarded as idle balances. On the other hand, capital has a certain degree of mobility. Depreciation allowances give entrepreneurs the opportunity to change the forms in which their capital is embodied. Also, a sizeable proportion of an economy's capital is not in durable instruments but consists of stocks of basic industrial materials such as coal and steel which are unspecialised and can be used for old and new industries alike.[1] By obtaining part of the current output of the basic industries the new industries could in effect acquire the services of part of the capital equipment of the basic industries, and therefore in a real sense the capital of the latter was mobile.[2] The cost of materials used formed a substantial proportion of gross output in the newer industries even before 1914, varying

[1] Provisional estimates by C. H. Feinstein suggest that in the 1920s the proportion of stocks in trade and work in progress to total fixed assets (at depreciated value) varied within the range 15·5 per cent to 21·7 per cent. B. R. Mitchell and P. Deane, *Abstract of British Historical Statistics* (1962) p. 378.

[2] L. A. Seltzer, 'The Mobility of Capital', *Quarterly Journal of Economics*, XLVI (1932) 497–507.

between one-third and two-thirds.[1] How important this point is depends on just how 'basic' are the basic industries? An answer to the question requires knowledge of input–output patterns which are not available before 1914.[2] But the degree of mobility of capital can be exaggerated; whatever the proportion of bought-out cost the firms invariably required considerable capital for their own durable equipment.

Whether or not the extensive investment in staple industries made for a shortage of capital for new industries in the period between the late 1890s and 1914 depends partly on what happened to savings. Statistics of gross investment give a rough index of savings. The proportion that gross investment formed of gross income fluctuated only slightly in the period 1899–1913 between 17 per cent and 20 per cent, but because national income rose steeply the annual total of gross investment increased from £325 million in 1899 to £548 million in 1913 (at current prices).[3] In the inter-war period, on the other hand, savings fell off considerably by some £150–200 million (at 1927 prices) between 1913 and 1925,[4] and as aggregate profits were low it is possible that capital was scarce for the new industries.[5] Before 1914, however, there was no evidence of a general shortage of capital from the savings point of view, but how much of the supply was available for the new industries depended on the demand for

[1] Estimates compiled from the 1907 Census of Production show the following percentages (cost of materials used as a percentage of gross output) for the following new industries:

| | |
|---|---|
| Rubber | 66·6 |
| Drugs, dyestuffs | 60·2 |
| Cement | 47·6 |
| Motors and cycles | 47·4 |
| Engineering including electrical engineering | 47·1 |
| Paper, printing, etc | 43·4 |
| Scientific instruments and apparatus | 41·1 |
| Electricity undertakings | 37·3 |

[2] The year 1935 is the earliest for which an input–output investigation has been carried out in this country, T. Barna, 'The Interdependence of the British Economy', *Journal of the Royal Statistical Society*, A. 115 (1952) 29–77. To take two important new industries, electrical engineering and motors and cycles, the purchases of one basic group of materials, metal goods (comprising three categories: iron and steel manufactures, non-ferrous metals, and metals goods n.e.s.) amounted to £19·6 million (37·7 per cent) out of total purchases of the electrical engineering industry of £51·9 million and £23·3 million (23·8 per cent) out of a total of £98·0 million for motors and cycles (pp. 150–1).

[3] J. H. Lenfant, 'Great Britain's Capital Formation, 1865–1914', *Economica*, XVIII (1951) 160.

[4] *Committee on National Debt and Taxation*, Cmnd. 2880 (1927) pp. 16–22.

[5] This did not interfere very much with the expansion of *existing* firms in the newer industries. Courtaulds, for example, increased their capital from £2 million to £30 million in the 1920s.

alternative uses. In the first place, a high proportion of Britain's capital formation was invested abroad; annual foreign investment increased from £26 million in 1899 to £216 million in 1913, and this accounted for almost all the increase in gross investment in the same period. The relative growth of Britain's new industries is usually compared with the position in the United States and Germany, and since Britain invested far more abroad than the others before 1914 overseas investment made a heavier call on her capital resources. The British overseas investment portfolio was about four times larger than the German by 1913, while the United States was still a net debtor. Admittedly, Britain's capital exports grew to a large extent by means of reinvesting income from abroad, but there was no inherent necessity why these earnings had to be reinvested abroad rather than at home. The diversion of capital abroad in the great capital export boom before the First World War was undoubtedly associated with the marked decline in gross domestic fixed capital formation, from a peak of £212 million in 1902 (at 1900 prices) to £128 million in 1912,[1] at a time when structural readjustments in favour of new industries were going ahead rapidly abroad. Moreover, the export of capital usually took the form of exports of commodities and this fact intensified over-commitment, for it was the staple export categories such as railway materials and even cotton goods which gained most from the opening up of markets by overseas investment.[2]

Secondly, a proportion of gross industrial investment had to be set aside for depreciation and re-equipment purposes if the staple industries were not to be allowed to run down. Even if some running down might have been desirable in the long run, the boom in staple exports in the decade before the war assured that there would be no disinvestment in the basic industries.[3] Technical advances in the 1870s and 1880s called for re-equipment especially in iron and steel, but progress was so slow that re-equipment of old industries was making additional demands on limited domestic investment resources (particularly between 1904 and 1908) at the very time when Britain should have been developing the newer trades. Public com-

[1] C. H. Feinstein, 'Income and Investment in the United Kingdom, 1856–1914', *Economic Journal*, LXXI (1961) 374.

[2] Lewis, in *American Economic Review*, Proceedings, XLVII 584.

[3] Kindleberger argues that even the prospect of higher returns on investment in new industries would not lead to much outflow of resources from the old: 'To change out of textiles, coal and shipbuilding would have been impossible as long as these were marginally profitable, no matter how low the average profits compared with returns in other industries. The dogs were too old to learn new tricks except under stern necessity' (C. P. Kindleberger, *Economic Growth in France and Britain 1851–1950* (1964) p. 277).

panies were heavily concentrated in the staple industries, and the tradition for these companies to plough back a substantial proportion of their profits rather than to distribute them in dividends to shareholders (and possibly therefore to alternative uses) led to some inflexibility in the supply of capital funds. There were other demands on capital expenditure, housing, railways and local authorities, for example, but despite violent year-to-year fluctuations none of these categories took a secularly rising share of fixed capital formation in the two decades before 1914. In general, scarcity of capital may have hindered the development of new industries, especially as whenever capital was in short supply investors preferred the security offered by older industries or the high returns from foreign investment and shunned the greater risks involved in investment in new industries.

A possible objection to this conclusion is that in a world of unemployment how was it possible for the new industries to be deprived of capital? There are two answers to this. First, in conditions of dynamic equilibrium the rate of growth which fully utilises all available savings is not necessarily the rate of growth needed to secure full employment of the labour force. Secondly, even without overall capital shortage imperfections in the capital market may have made funds scarce for new enterprises in the newer fields of activity. It is a well known, though not undisputed,[1] fact that the London capital market was geared much more to foreign than to home investment. The argument is not, of course, universally valid. Saul has shown that in the motor industry firms found it relatively easy to obtain capital by public issue. He quotes examples which, as he puts it, 'surely give lie to the argument that the industry was held back in its growth by the inadequacy of the facilities provided by the stock exchange or because of public indifference'.[2] Paradoxically, however, most of the firms that resorted to the market for funds ended in disaster. One might suggest that the market seemed to favour the grandiose speculative projects but ignored the less spectacular, sounder, and probably smaller firms which were the potential sources of growth. Moreover, on Saul's own evidence there were firms such as Vauxhall and Standard which expanded very slowly because of the lack of external sources of capital and a slow rate of internal accumulation.[3] Although there are notable exceptions to

[1] A. R. Hall, 'A Note on the English Capital Market as a Source of Funds for Home Investment before 1914', *Economica*, XXIV (1957) 59–66; see also the comments by A. K. Cairncross and Hall's reply, *Economica*, XXV (1958).

[2] S. B. Saul, 'The Motor Industry in Britain before 1914', *Business History*, v (1962–3) 22–44.

[3] It is interesting that although Saul rejects capital shortage as a retarding factor in the growth of the motor industry, his main explanation is compatible with over-

the generalisation of a pre-1914 Macmillan gap, its existence has not been disproved to this writer's satisfaction.

*Labour.* The supply of labour may be increased in two main ways: by the growth of population and by an expansion in the proportion of the labour force to total population.[1] Demographic research has shown that in a mature (as opposed to a subsistence) economy population is unlikely to respond directly to an increased demand for labour—thus, even in the long run a shortage of labour is possible. As for mobility, the economic incentive to stay or move depends primarily on the level of employment and the size of inter-industry wage differentials, and readjustment will be held back if barriers prevent workers moving to higher paid occupations. Such barriers, including trade union restrictions and social resistances to change, are often important. If transfer is to be achieved from one skilled job to another the retraining problem may be serious; consequently, the occupational distribution of the labour force is a vital consideration in assessing the possibilities of mobility. Finally, if the age structure of the population is heavily biased towards young people there may be so many new entrants to industry that transfers are fully achieved by these entrants going into expanding industries, and a direct transfer problem will arise only if there are significant differences in the regional distribution of stagnating and growing industries.

Was there a labour shortage which might have hindered the growth of the new industries in the United Kingdom before 1914? Although the rate of population growth had slowed down to a moderate extent the absolute increase was sufficient to meet the demands of industry, mainly because the occupied force was becoming a larger proportion of the total population (36·5 per cent in 1881, 38·5 per cent in 1891 and 40·6 per cent in 1911). With the opening

---

commitment. He argues that the real cause of backwardness was the failure to shake off habits developed in the older established engineering industries, habits which made for overfussiness in building technically good machines and insufficient attention to the problems of catering for a mass market: 'The fact is that except for odd firms which were beginning to set the pace, the industry was quite unable to release itself from the traditional ways of engineering. . . . The industry remained the domain of the mechanic rather than the production engineer' (*Business History*, v (1962–3) 42).

[1] The latter is determined by a number of influences such as age composition, income levels, the degree of urbanisation, and the character of family organisation. Many of the relevant factors are non-economic: social attitudes to work by women, children, and minority groups; educational requirements, standards, and opportunities, government intervention and trade union organisation. M. Abramovitz, 'Economics of growth', *Survey of Contemporary Economics* (1952) American Economic Association (ed. B. F. Haley), vol. ii, p. 136.

up of new careers to women there was a relative transfer of women from overstaffed domestic service employment to manufacturing. Between 1891 and 1911 the female labour force in the metal, machinery and vehicle industries rose from 59,000 to 128,000, in paper and printing from 78,000 to 144,000, in chemicals 17,000 to 46,000 and in food, drink and tobacco from 163,000 to 308,000, while the increase in the domestic offices and personal services category was modest, 2,036,000 to 2,127,000. One of the greatest rates of expansion occurred in commerce where female employment rose from 26,000 in 1891 to 157,000; this helped to satisfy the demand for clerks and typists as administrative work in industry expanded along with the size of firms, and the replacement of men by women as general office workers released some men for employment elsewhere —possibly in industry (the ratio of male to female employees in commerce fell from 32:1 in 1881 to 4·6:1 in 1911). These factors were counterbalanced in part by a fall in the proportion of married women going out to work (occupied females fell from 34·5 per cent of total females in 1891 to 32·2 per cent in 1911) and by a reduction in the incidence of child labour. As for males, the occupied male labour force increased by 46 per cent between 1881 and 1911 and this permitted a rapid growth in employment in some of the newer fields: males employed in chemicals increased from 89,000 to 155,000 and in gas, water and electricity from 38,000 to 86,000 between 1891 and 1911. On the other hand, demands for labour by the staple industries were intensified; one industrial group alone, mining, doubled its labour force between 1881 and 1911 from 604,000 to 1,202,000 (14·7 per cent of the total increase in the occupied male labour force in this period).[1] Yet the evidence does not point to a labour shortage in the two decades before 1914, and the heavy emigration of the latter part of the period (net annual emigration of U.K. citizens to extra-European countries averaged 159,000 in the the period 1900–14) supports this conclusion.

It is probable that impediments to the mobility of labour were more important in delaying readjustment between old and new industries, and these were more in evidence between the wars than at the turn of the century. The annual flow of new entrants to industry between the wars was relatively small because of an unfavourable change in the age structure of the population and an extension of the school-leaving age. Mobility between old and new industries had to be achieved by real (usually regional) transfers of workers; difficulties in the way of retraining middle-aged skilled men, the

[1] All the statistics in this paragraph are based on the Census Reports 1881–1911 assembled in Mitchell and Deane, *Abstract*, pp. 59–60.

problem of finding employment for working wives, the housing question, all hindered the transfer process. By 1920 over-commitment had gone so far that Britain had less than 10 per cent of her labour force employed in agriculture. The low rural/urban labour ratio limited the scope for expanding the supply of labour to the new industries. Moreover, in recruiting workers from agriculture expanding home industries had to compete with the demand for labourers abroad. Some 20,000 to 30,000 emigrants each year in the decade before 1914 had worked in agriculture, and this exodus depleted even further the surplus available for transfer to manufacturing. It is much easier for industries to expand by recruiting agricultural labour than by attracting workers from other industries, for in the second case costs of retraining may be greater than initial training costs and higher wages will be required.[1] In countries abroad with large pools of agricultural labour and in a period of rapid technological change in agriculture surplus workers from agriculture could easily be absorbed for semi-skilled work in the newer industries; in Britain the agrarian labour force was so small that it could not be depleted much further. It might be suggested that because the staple industries employed only one-quarter of the total labour force that the above arguments overstate the dangers of over-commitment. But such a viewpoint would misunderstand the position, for the scope for transfer between non-industrial and industrial employment has been minimised by a rapid growth in numbers employed in the service and distribution trades, and this has intensified the competition for labour. Because this growth of service industries reflected rising income levels which were obviously associated with Britain's extensive industrialisation, it was not unrelated to the early start.

*Enterprise.* Whether we regard the entrepreneur as a dynamic innovator of the Schumpeterian type or merely as a passive decision-taker whose main function is to combine production factors, the supply of efficient entrepreneurs is very limited. Their availability is determined by several influences such as the structure of industry, the growth of technical education, the status of business compared with other professions, the degree of social mobility in society. As for the mobility of entrepreneurs, generalisation is difficult. Although there are isolated examples of a direct switch of entrepreneurs between industries, their mobility is usually dependent upon the rate of decline of individual industries. As industries never decline swiftly, mobility is likely to take the form of a redistribution of successive

[1] This is because assuming that the inducement to move requires a constant wage differential, earnings in the older industries were much higher than in agriculture.

generations; an entrepreneur in a declining industry will normally stay the pace until he retires or close down altogether rather than move from one industry to another. Consequently, it is a legitimate argument that if all the best entrepreneurs were engaged in the staple industries the new industries had to be satisfied with second-best in the critical early years. Such an argument, however, is based on the false assumption that the mechanism for recruiting entrepreneurs in the nineteenth century was efficient. After the years of early industrialisation the calibre of entrepreneurship may have declined (though the evidence is by no means conclusive): in an age of family businesses nepotism was rife and in many cases the business ethos was displaced by social ambitions. There was little scope for outsiders to become managers until the growth of the public company in the latter part of the century, but with this wider recruitment the new generation of entrepreneurs was as, if not more, efficient. Another factor broadening the base of manager selection was the spurt forward in technical education; from the 1880s engineers and technical managers were turned out in increasing numbers from technical colleges and similar institutions, and many of these entered newer industries such as electricity supply. Generalisation about the mobility of British entrepreneurs is impossible, but it is likely that this, too, depended on the development of the public company as this would lead to a wider spread of information about opportunities. The most important point is that the new industries required a different type of entrepreneur. Entrepreneurs in the old industries tended, as a result of their successful experience, to have a conservative attitude towards the possible benefits of new processes and products, and to be more concerned with the routine affairs of business. The need was for 'far-sighted, uneasy, venturesome individuals . . . who are ready to "cut loose from" a secure position and an assured income, and who have the gift of imparting their enthusiasm to other restless individuals (technicians, salesmen, labourers) and to still others, with private capital'.[1] Such men would be more likely to be recruited outside the ranks of established business. Over-commitment does not appear, therefore, to have interfered with the supply of entrepreneurs to new industries; the readiness of firms in these industries to adopt technical advances, their rates of productivity growth, and the extensiveness of their price reduction policies in the inter-war period gives some indication of the progressiveness of entrepreneurship in the newer trades. Finally, the new industries were structurally different from the old. In general, growth took

[1] Quoted from M. W. Watkins, 'The Aviation Industry', *Journal of Political Economy*, XXXIX (1931) 68.

the form of a few companies expanding in size rather than a rapid multiplication of the number of firms, whereas in some staple industries there were many small firms.[1] Consequently, in the new

[1] Concentration ratios (i.e. the percentage of the industry's net output produced by the three largest units) are the best available evidence to support this point. The following ratios are based on the 1935 Census of Production, and are tabulated in H. Leak and A. Maizels, 'The Structure of British Industry', *Journal of the Royal Statistical Society*, 108 (1945) 46–59. One would expect the degree of concentration to fall as the industry grows in size, and because some of the new industries were still at a fairly early stage of their growth the differences in concentration between old and new industries tend to be exaggerated in these figures. To give some indication of variations in the size of each industry the number of units of production employing more than 500 workpeople each is stated. Although caution should be used in making direct comparisons, the general validity of the statement in the text is confirmed.

| | *% of net output in 3 largest units* | *No. of units each employing 500+* |
|---|---|---|
| OLD INDUSTRIES | | |
| Railway carriages | 39 | 24 |
| Iron and steel (blast furnaces) | 34 | 28 |
| Shipbuilding | 27 | 36 |
| Cotton spinning | 26 | 96 |
| Iron and steel (smelting and rolling) | 21 | 71 |
| Coke and by-products | 18 | 71 |
| Brewing | 18 | 24 |
| Coal-mines | 9 | 287 |
| China and earthenware | 8 | 40 |
| Mechanical engineering | 7 | 237 |
| Woollen and worsted | 7 | 102 |
| Furniture | 7 | 45 |
| Leather | 7 | 7 |
| Clothing | 4 | 122 |
| Cotton weaving | 3 | 100 |
| Building and contracting | 3 | 96 |
| Timber | 3 | 23 |
| NEWER INDUSTRIES | | |
| Rayon manufactures | 84 | 7 |
| Dyes and dyestuffs | 84 | 6 |
| Telegraph and telephone apparatus | 80 | 8 |
| Photographic apparatus | 75 | 3 |
| Rubber tyres and tubes | 73 | 9 |
| Wireless valves and electric lamps | 66 | 5 |
| Electrical wires and cables | 53 | 15 |
| Aluminium | 53 | 6 |
| Electrical machinery | 48 | 27 |
| Motor-car manufacture | 45 | 17 |
| Chemicals | 40 | 58 |
| Wireless apparatus | 39 | 13 |
| Aircraft | 34 | 16 |
| Electrical engineering | 24 | 90 |

industries the required number of entrepreneurs was much smaller.[1]

What conclusions may be drawn from this general discussion? In some industries there was a trend towards developing new products within the original firm; for example, cable firms turned over to producing lighter types of electrical equipment. This growth in diversification of the activities of large firms allowed the production of new goods without the need to transfer resources between firms and to compete on the open market for factors of production. The supply of entrepreneurs was scarcely affected by over-commitment. There was no serious shortage of labour: up to 1914 continued population growth, a rise in the occupied to total population, and the opening up of new avenues of employment (especially to women) meant sufficient numbers and mobility; between the wars general unemployment on the one hand and higher profit rates in the new industries enabling them to offer higher wages on the other resulted in a fairly strong transfer inducement, though in certain industries periodic shortages of skilled labour were not unknown. The evidence suggests that if any factor was in short supply it was capital. This conflicts with the argument often advanced in recent years that capital accumulation has not proved a limiting factor in economic development.[2] While this may be true of the aggregate economy or for some individual firms, it does not alter the fact that capital supplies, in the short run at least, were insufficient for an efficient distribution between old industries and new during the critical period of structural change. Heavy overseas investment probably diverted resources away from the development of new domestic industries, and the London capital market was so preoccupied with foreign investment that it was not well placed for financing domestic industry. This, too, was a result of over-commitment, namely the survival of a narrow conception of banking functions[3] and the self-financing traditions of the staple industries which had proved successful in the early industrialisation period.

General evidence in support of the argument that deficiencies in capital supply were more important than labour shortages before 1914 may be found in the course of relative factor prices, for one would have expected that if adequate supplies were not available

[1] This assumes that with the expansion of individual firms in new industries there would be less than proportionate expansion in the number of entrepreneurs (that is, decision takers) as opposed to general executives. This assumption seems justified.

[2] For example, A. K. Cairncross, 'The Place of Capital in Economic Progress', in L. H. Dupriez (ed.), *Economic Progress* (Louvain, 1955) pp. 235–48.

[3] In Britain there was no organised co-operation between finance and industry as in Germany; see W. F. Bruck, *Social and Economic History of Germany from William II to Hitler, 1888–1938* (1938) ch. ii.

or were interfered with competition would have forced factor prices to rise. The price of labour, if average real wages are taken as a standard, at best stagnated, the most reliable index indicating a slight fall from 103 in 1900 to 100 in 1914, though there were modest fluctuations from year to year;[1] the price of capital, if interest rates are any guide, rose substantially. The average rate of interest on large issues (both home and foreign) issued on the London market rose from 3·35 per cent in 1900 to 4·98 per cent in 1913, while the yield on consols rose from 2·55 per cent to 3·40 per cent.[2] There were many reasons for this rise in interest rates but scarcity of capital was probably one of them. Finally, an *a priori* reason why capital was the factor in short supply for new industries is simply that these industries were, in general, more capital-intensive than the old.

## III

If scarcity of factors of production was not a major though a definite obstacle to the growth of the new industries, in what other ways did over-commitment slow down the rate of structural readjustment? This section is concerned with certain influences on entrepreneurial psychology, in particular with the manner in which over-commitment led entrepreneurs to make decisions on future prospects which were based too much on past experience.

Some of these influences were so pervasive as to affect the whole course of industrialisation. There are two main types of economic growth: *balanced growth* which is based on close economic interdependence between all industrial sectors, and *concentrated growth*, that is, growth in a few sectors more fitted for development with existing technological capacities in which rapid expansion enables the exploitation of economies of scale. In the sense that industrial growth in the nineteenth century was centred on the expansion of a few basic industries, Britain's development was a case of concentrated growth. Concentrated growth permits higher levels of output, but the divergence between output and consumption levels in the economy means an excess of production over home needs, and therefore foreign trade is necessary. Thus, in concentrated growth the problem is to weigh the balance between higher income on the one hand and the greater uncertainty involved in foreign trade on the other.[3] This

[1] A. L. Bowley, *Wages and Income in the United Kingdom since 1860* (1937) p. 60.

[2] R. A. Lehfeldt, 'The Rate of Interest on British and Foreign Investment', *Journal of the Royal Statistical Society*, LXXVI (1912–13) 205; LXXVII (1913–14) 433.

[3] For this analysis see T. Scitovsky, 'Growth—balanced or unbalanced?' in M. Abramowitz (ed.), *The Allocation of Economic Resources: Essays in Honor of B. F. Haley* (1959) pp. 207–12.

had an important impact on entrepreneurial judgements. First, entrepreneurs misunderstood the situation by regarding the benefits of concentrated growth as permanent rather than ephemeral, and were thus indifferent to the need for structural change. This showed itself in too much hesitation before the adoption of new techniques in certain of the basic industries,[1] and in the reluctance to apply innovations leading to completely new industries. Industrialists did not want to face the truth that the old tried methods which had made Britain great were inadequate to keep her great. Another instance of the same attitude was the tendency 'to underrate in highly technical industries the importance of scientific attainments in comparison with business ability',[2] vital in view of the increasingly close relationship between scientific research and the new technology. Secondly, while entrepreneurs appreciated some of the dangers in concentrated growth they almost certainly underestimated them. They were deceived into believing that the perils consisted only of periodic cyclical fluctuations in exports; what they failed to observe was that with the spread of industrialisation abroad the staple industries were bound ultimately to cease to expand, and in these circumstances a retention of the industrial structure of the nineteenth century would prove fatal.[3]

The policies adopted by British industry with regard to specialisation were a direct consequence of concentrated growth. Because she had industrialised first Britain had become the leading exporter of staple manufactured goods. The generally accepted free trade view was that the country's best interests were served by concentrating entirely on basic products and relying on industries abroad for specialities, the products of new industries and of newer sections of the old. The effects of this are particularly noticeable in the chemical and engineering fields. In synthetic dyestuffs, for example, Britain from the 1860s exported tar distillates to Germany in return for finished dyes, a policy which worked only until Germany started producing her own raw materials in the 1880s.[4] In the machinery trade, Germany received from Britain machines for long-mechanised industries such as agricultural and textile machinery, whereas Britain received from Germany machines for the newer branches of

[1] For classic examples in one of the most important industries see D. L. Burn, *Economic History of Steelmaking, 1867–1939* (1940) chs iv and x.

[2] S. J. Chapman, *Work and Wages*, pt I, *Foreign Competition* (1904) pp. 136–7.

[3] This implies no criticism of the policy of concentrated growth in itself. Britain had no choice, for balanced growth (as defined above) was impossible without the major innovations of the late nineteenth and early twentieth centuries.

[4] L. F. Haber, *The Chemical Industry during the Nineteenth Century* (1958) p. 163.

manufacture, electrical machinery for example.[1] The weakness in this policy was the inability to realise that other countries besides Germany and the United States (both mainly home market producers) would industrialise and in those branches of industry in which Britain was dominant.[2]

A similar lapse of judgement was the failure to realise that many new products were not necessities but luxuries, and consequently consumers abroad had to be convinced that they needed them; while others were standardised producers' goods in which competition was severe because alternative suppliers were available. This was again a legacy of the hey-day of British industrialism when her position had been semi-monopolistic, and exporting (except during slumps in overseas purchasing power) had not called for refined selling methods. The absence of sales aggression in export drives in many British firms revealed itself in many ways: an unwillingness to supply a cheaper class of goods even when demanded, to study consumers' wishes, or to take small orders; tardiness in granting acceptable credit facilities; poor methods of packing, high freight charges on British steamers, and the relatively small number of British commercial representatives abroad.[3] The merchant-house system of selling, characteristic of Britain's export trade and ideally suited to the sale of homogeneous bulk goods like cotton exports, was much less appropriate than direct selling (which facilitated the provision of detailed technical information by scientifically trained salesmen) for the newer types of capital goods such as electrical equipment and machinery.

Finally, marked prosperity phases of the trade cycle in which the staple industries shared led to over-optimistic expectations about the prospects of these industries, and masked the relative and in some cases absolute secular decline of these industries which became chronic in the 1920s. The most notable of these phases were the 1905–14 export boom (interrupted in 1908 and 1909) which took the form of a great expansion in the exports of capital goods to new

[1] E. Crammond, 'The Economic Relations of the British and German Empires', *Journal of the Royal Statistical Society*, LXXVII (1913–14) 794.

[2] In the shorter run, Britain was able to escape keener competition in the staple export trades by finding new markets for these goods in Empire countries. But this was no permanent solution, and merely delayed the need for the desired readjustments. See Kindleberger, *Economic Growth*, p. 287: 'But exports can expand when the economy has lost its capacity to grow in new directions. If these exports lead the economy to devote its energy to old played-out lines, with little entrepreneurial or technological energy, they may delay economic growth in the long run, while assisting it by sustaining incomes in the present.'

[3] *Opinions of H.M.'s Diplomatic and Consular Officers on British Trade Methods Abroad*, C. 9078 (1899) p. XCVI.

countries, and the post-war boom of 1919–20, the result of a temporary revival in demand for staple products caused by the trade stoppage of the war years. Both these upswings lulled British industrialists into imagining that the best days of the staple industries were still to come.

## IV

Over-commitment also made for external diseconomy effects and for a particular institutional environment which placed real obstacles in the way of inter-industry structural change in Britain as compared with overseas.

One of these obstacles was that, because the industrial structure of the United Kingdom had been closely moulded to the older industries and because the industrial development of overseas economies was of more recent origin, industrialists abroad were able to discern the pattern of modern industrialism more clearly and were consequently more fitted to apply the new techniques and to produce the new goods. How this was possible is most easily understood by appreciating the concept of 'development blocks'. A 'development block' is a concept emphasising the interdependence of industrial development. The point is that some inventions cannot become innovations before complementary progress has been made in another phase of the production process, which may require innovations in *other* industries. The result is that industries tend to grow in interrelated sectors with advance in one field being dependent on advance in another.[1] If 'development blocks' fail to be completed 'structural tensions' are said to exist. In Britain, for example, the

[1] E. Dahmen, 'Technology, innovation and international industrial transformation', *Economic Progress*, ed. Dupriez, pp. 297–8. For elaboration of a related theme see W. P. Strassman, 'Interrelated Industries and the Rate of Technological Change', *Review of Economic Studies*, XXVII (1959–60) 16–22. The idea of the 'development block' bears some relation to the Schumpeterian concept of a 'cluster' of innovations. According to Schumpeter, 'clusters' tend to appear because as soon as the various kinds of social resistance to something that is untried have been overcome, it is much easier not only to do the same thing again but to do *similar* things in different directions, so that a single success will always produce a 'cluster' (J. A. Schumpeter, 'The Analysis of Economic Change', in American Economic Association, *Readings in Business Cycle Theory* (1944) p. 10).

It is interesting to note that whatever its weaknesses the Schumpeterian long wave applied fairly well to the period 1896–1939 in the United Kingdom. In the first half of the period the new industries were trying to expand at any cost and to establish themselves in the economy (the high-cost phase characteristic of Kondratieff prosperity); whereas in the inter-war period the increasing emphasis in the new industries on cost and price reduction accords very well with the Schumpeterian analysis of the Kondratieff recession.

effects of the slowness in the extension of electricity supply in delaying advance in new industries could be described as a 'structural tension'. Similarly, the development of the motor-car in the early decades depended on complementary advances in other industries such as efficient ignition components and pneumatic tyres; until these innovations were put into practice 'structural tensions' delayed the motor industry's advance. Over-commitment meant that the British economy was still burdened by the 'development block' of coal, steam and iron which had been set up during early industrialisation. Abroad, on the other hand, since industrialisation came much later than in Britain, entrepreneurs although acting independently were able to construct the 'development blocks' of both the staple sectors and the new industrial sectors simultaneously, adopting the allocation of resources best fitted to both. For example, those industries which had been steam-driven in Britain could be powered by electricity and therefore in many cases run more efficiently.

Because the British economy had reached at an early stage a high level of industrialisation based on the staple industries it had been necessary at the time to construct extensive power and transport facilities to meet the needs of industrial expansion. Thus over-commitment resulted in a heavy dependence on coal, steam and gas and on railways, and this was an important factor in Britain's lag in adopting electricity and road transport. The burden was not confined to electricity and transport, for Britain's early development of a chemical industry impeded later advances in electro-chemicals.[1] The lag in the adoption of electric power was more serious, however, because of its repercussions on other industries. It was the main factor in the late development of the aluminium industry, and the scope for the turbine was limited by the slow progress of large-scale electricity generation; as late as 1907 not 6 per cent of the dynamo capacity privately owned in the engineering trades was

[1] As a contemporary put it: in Britain 'no revolution has been caused in the chemical industry by the introduction of electro-chemical methods. The open competition of old-established and well-developed methods makes the introduction of new processes a very slow matter, and even in the case of commodities which can only be prepared by electro-chemical means, it appears to be more economical to import these from countries like America where conditions are especially favourable for the development of new processes.

In America the electro-chemical industry has made very rapid strides. Untrammelled by the existence at home of chemical works on a sufficiently extensive scale to provide the rapidly growing demands, the newer processes have here found a very suitable locality for their development, and during their infancy enjoy the fostering influence of a protective tariff' (J. N. Pring, *Some Electro-Chemical Centres* (1908) p. xii).

activated by turbines. Refusal to turn over to electrictiy could initially be justified on cost grounds: 'Great Britain had undoubtedly attained great prosperity and technical efficiency in her use of steam plant, and there was therefore less inducement for her manufactures to adopt electrical driving. On the Continent, however, the introduction of the use of electricity coincided with the advance in manufacturing industries and there was every inducement to employ the new agent especially as it did not involve the scrapping of power plant still in good condition.'[1] Similarly with the railways, Britain's intricate but expensive network made the development of a motor industry and of road transport in general of less immediate importance.

Old capital equipment can often give strong resistance to new since, while it lasts, old machinery is able to continue to compete on a basis of prices which do not recover replacement costs. Nevertheless, had the resistance of old methods of production to new been a matter of pure economics, the incentive to retain the old would have been gradually whittled away as the production of newer types of capital goods became more efficient and cheaper. Unfortunately, social resistances to change were more intractable and entrenched interests combined to defend the old industries. Firms resisted change by drawing on accumulated reserves, while vested interests of central and local authorities found expression in subsidies and protection. The social resistance of these interests was all the more effective in that they acted as pressure groups to get legislation to back up their claims. Manufacturers of electrical plant were held back while Parliament and local authorities debated how the distribution and use of electricity ought to be prevented from infringing conventional conceptions of public privileges; local authority by-laws enabled strong gas-works where municipally owned to resist the rapid creation of rival lighting plant; Acts of 1882 and 1888 gave local authorities the opportunity to oppose any electricity project, and the obstacles to an efficient electricity supply were not removed until the Central Electricity Generating Board was established in 1926. The bolstering up of vested interests in old industries was intensified between the wars, and there were many examples of state assistance, subsidies and protection to strengthen their resistance. A well-known instance is in the road transport industry. Despite the fact that road hauliers charged lower rates than the railways, the government intervened with the 1933 Road and Rail Act to restrict the number of commercial licences for general carrying purposes, and the railway companies were given the power to oppose applications for licences

[1] *Report on Electrical Trades, Departmental Committee,* Cd. 9072 (1918) p. 7.

on the grounds that 'existing transport facilities were adequate', and that the granting of licences would lead to 'unnecessary duplication of services'.[1]

Where old and new products were strong substitutes for each other and were directly competitive on the open market, over-commitment once more acted as a brake on the rate of structural readjustment. For the fact that the old goods had been produced for so long and that output was so large meant that over the years substantial cost reductions had been made, and price competition was extremely fierce especially while the production of new goods remained in the high-cost stage. When electric lighting was introduced the British gas industry had attained a high degree of efficiency, and the relative prices of gas and electricity favoured gas in this country much longer than was the case abroad. In textiles, the sale of rayon made little headway in Britain before 1914, whereas expansion in Germany was rapid, partly because cotton textiles there were not developed to the same extent and partly because the state pursued a protectionist commercial policy which reduced the competitive effect of cheap imported cottons. In the 1920s Courtaulds, despite a monopoly position, had to follow a policy of repeated price cuts in order to expand output, and it was not until the mid-1930s that rayon yarn became as cheap as cotton.[2] On the other hand, despite its early restrictive effect, competition of this kind by the inter-war period was giving a great stimulus to technical efficiency in new industries.

That over-commitment had a strong impact on the institutional framework is shown in the survival of certain outdated policies which were anomalous in the critical period of structural readjustment. An instance is the retention of free trade in Britain before 1914 when all the new industries abroad were being built up behind high duties. Tariff protection may have been difficult to justify, but it is evident that the attitude towards it was governed less by objective analysis than by the belief that free trade had been of great benefit to Britain during her monopoly days, and this faith in free trade remained almost untarnished in spite of changes in external economic conditions. When the Fair Trade movement did get under way it concentrated entirely on protection for old industries; as for the new products the custom to rely on overseas sources prevailed. Tariff protection might have stimulated a more extensive development of

[1] For a detailed discussion of this see P. E. Hart, 'The Restriction of Road Haulage', *Scottish Journal of Political Economy*, VI (1959) 116–38.

[2] See the price statistics in D. C. Hague, *The Economics of Man-Made Fibres* (1957) pp. 36–7.

newer industries; a return to general protection would have been unnecessary, for a moderate scale of infant-industry tariffs would have served the purpose.[1]

Because of the persistence of traditional attitudes based on nineteenth-century industrial conditions the general environment was unfavourable for taking up innovations. The patent laws were unsatisfactory, the cost to a new firm of taking out a patent was very high, and foreigners were too easily allowed to work British patents[2] compared with more stringent patent laws in operation abroad. Both technical education and industrial research remained on a minute scale up to 1914. These circumstances were again the direct consequence of over-commitment. The anachronistic patent laws had been suited to the monopoly days of British industry and provision for technical education was unnecessary if one assumed no new advances in technology, on the grounds that existing knowledge could easily be acquired in the works. The trouble was that the great era when the staple industries had been producing and exporting at will had laid a dead hand on changes in policy; inertia could always be justified by reference to past conditions.

Finally, an important aspect of over-commitment and concentrated growth had been the adjustment of the British economy in the nineteenth century to a condition of large exports. For example, Britain had been willing to run down her agricultural sector and then rely on large food imports simply because the large export trade combined with 'invisible' earnings assured that the cost of these imports could easily be met. The nature of the new products, however, was such that they were (initially at least) primarily home-market goods.[3] Therefore, in so far as Britain succeeded in inter-industry structural readjustments she was faced with the problem of diverting a proportion of her resources from manufacture for export to manufacture for home use. The result of the dilemma was a weakening in the balance of payments position because Britain's limited resource base meant that falling exports could not be matched with a significant fall in raw material imports. The government was forced to adopt restrictive internal policies in an attempt to alleviate the

[1] In arguing that the advantages of protection to the new industries would have been outweighed by the dislocation of the pattern of multilateral settlements and by the slowing down of reorganisation in older industries, S. B. Saul (*Studies in British Overseas Trade* (1960) p. 41) falls into the trap of assuming that any return to protection would have had to be general.

[2] This latter defect was remedied by the new patent law of 1907. See G. Schuster, 'The Patents and Designs Act, 1907', *Economic Journal*, XIX (1909) 538–51.

[3] This is because consumers required high-income levels to afford them, and these levels were attained in only a few regions of the world until recently.

balance of payments problem, and this slowed down the growth rate and made readjustment more difficult. Germany, on the other hand, from the early days of industrialisation had depended more upon her home market than Britain. Consequently, it was easier for Germany than for Britain to adjust the structure of her international trade to the situation brought about by the growth of rival foreign industries and by the development of new industries at home.

## V

The argument of this article has been that the pattern and growth of the nineteenth-century British industrial structure, the level of output attained, and the time taken to reach it affected the economy's capacity for readjustment to new industries. Over-commitment added to the obstacles impeding resource mobility, gave rise to entrepreneurial and investment decisions which though not irrational suggested a rationality wedded to traditional attitudes, and altered the institutional environment in a way unfavourable to structural change. How important over-commitment was relative to other influences delaying the growth of the new industries is difficult to say. Other arguments, such as those stressing a deficiency of natural resources or a decline in the quality of entrepreneurs after early industrialisation, assume a progressive decline in Britain's capacity for change. They fail to explain the fact that by the 1930s the new industries in Britain were doing as well as, if not better than, those in other advanced industrial economies. The hypothesis of over-commitment avoids this dilemma, at least. For as the new industries gradually asserted themselves their weight in total output would increase and the direct effects of over-commitment, by definition, would be cumulatively reduced. This is what happened. After a delayed start and early falterings, the new industries began to reach mass production levels of output by the late 1920s and the 1930s and by 1939 had so firmly established themselves that their position in the post-war British economy was secured.

# APPENDIX

## Comments on E. Ames and N. Rosenberg, 'Changing Technological Leadership and Industrial Growth', *Economic Journal*, LXXIII (1963).

THIS appendix offers a few critical comments on the Ames–Rosenberg analysis of the early start thesis. Because their approach is analytical and theoretical and offers no empirical evidence either in support or against, it was felt inappropriate to deal with their article in the text. As the authors put it: 'Even if no late-comer thesis were a logical necessity (and we feel this is the case), some such thesis might well be true as historical fact' (p. 31). Yet their work is so important that anyone who holds that the early start thesis is valid in some set of circumstances cannot afford to neglect it. For this reason I wish to comment on a few of their arguments which bear upon the over-commitment hypothesis.

Their article is a courageous and in many ways impressive attempt to sort out the logical flaws of the early start thesis and to put forward the basic propositions of a difficult empirical and untouched theoretical problem. Those of us who have tended to make rash illogical statements in this field are less likely to do so again. But the value of their analysis is depreciated by virtue of concentrating their attack on the *general* validity of the thesis, whereas most supporters of the early start have applied the argument to *one* economy in *particular* historical circumstances (especially, the classical case, the penalty of the early start in Britain as compared with Germany and the United States in the late nineteenth and early twentieth centuries). By classifying all late-comers together (late industrialisers and non-industrial underdeveloped countries), and by assuming that the penalty of the early start is a phenomenon characteristic of all advanced industrial countries and which recurs in late-comers when they reach a high degree of development, are not the authors guilty of putting up their own Aunt Sally? Very few defenders of the early start would disagree with the authors' conclusion that 'industrial countries, even the "oldest and most advanced", possess, *on balance*, far greater versatility, flexibility, and capacity to accommodate to change than do predominantly agricultural, low-income economies' (p. 29).

Yet so much of their analysis is based on the twin assumptions (i) that the true basis for comparison is the old advanced industrial country (the early starter) and the poor agrarian economy (late-comer) and (ii) that the early start handicap is a recurrent phenomenon. Thus, for the major part of their analysis, they assume 'two countries, Eastland and Westland, identically endowed at the time of Noah with population and resources. Suppose that Eastland remains in an agrarian under-developed state until the year 1900; at that time it is in exactly the condition Westland was in 1700. Westland, however, began to industrialise in 1700, so that by 1900 it is an urban, factory society.' They state that they 'propose to discuss the thesis, developed by writers from Veblen through Kindleberger, that Eastland can develop more rapidly and/or to a higher level after 1900 than can Westland (pp. 13–14). Few economic historians would recognise here the early start thesis as they know it. A more appropriate comparison would be between the highly industrialised early starter and the partly industrialised late-comer with a social and economic environment favourable to further industrialisation and following within a matter of decades upon the early starter. Even here the handicap of the early start would probably only exist if the late-comer is building up its industries at a time when dramatic changes in technology are taking place.

The assumption that the early start penalty applies to all economies that reach a certain stage of development with a given technology leads the authors to make some shaky propositions. Take for example, what they describe as the 'leapfrog game'. This argues that late-comers, having overtaken the early starter by exploiting earlier and more fully a given set of innovations, will (assuming discontinuity in the rate of innovation) become early starters themselves in respect of the next set. There seems no justification for this view. Indeed it might be argued that the early start thesis is applicable only in the certain special conditions characteristic of the nineteenth century. In particular, the early start penalty need only arise in a capitalist free enterprise economy. In more recent times rapidly developing late-comers can avoid acquiring early start characteristics by intervention, such as the planned allocation of resources between industries or fostering an environment conducive to structural change. Also advanced countries today enjoy higher levels of income. Faced with the need to apply new future technology, the advanced late-comer may be so rich as to afford a diversion of resources for this purpose. In Britain in the late nineteenth century the burden on savings was heavier than the potential flow of savings available. The need to finance further growth in the staple industries, the requirements for extensive foreign investment, the upward pressure on wages following the growth of a more articulate trade union organisation; all these factors may have handicapped the capital financing of new industries.

The key passage as far as over-commitment is concerned is stated on p. 29: 'One measure of success in the operation of market forces is thus the responponsiveness of resources to the changes dictated by changes in the composition of aggregate demand. An economy which finds it increasingly difficult to accommodate itself to these changes will necessarily encounter increasing difficulties in sustaining its economic growth. It may be argued, then, that movement along any historical growth path involves the introduction of rigidities and resistances and thereby reduces an economy's capacity to accommodate itself to further change.' This argument is at the root of over-commitment. The authors criticise it on the grounds that: 'It presumes that the obstacles to resource mobility are an increasing function of an economy's maturity. But this extremely important proposition, when appropriately considered in a *comparative* sense, is not at all obvious' (p. 29) and go on to argue that it is not clear that immobilities in Britain were greater than in Brazil, or Bulgaria, or India. Once again we find the false comparison between the advanced industrialising early starter and the more or less underdeveloped late-comer. The presumption above should really state that obstacles to resource mobility are an increasing function of an economy's maturity *only above a certain level of development.* In other words, if we assume two industrialised economies, the older one more extensively industrialised in a few sectors and the second with a lower level of industrialisation in the same sectors, then inflexibility of resources will be greater in the former than the latter (but both will be more flexible than the underdeveloped agrarian economy).

There are several kinds of impediment to resource mobility in the early starter which have been discussed in the article above:

(i) The scope for expanding the labour force of new industries is limited by a low rural/urban labour ratio, for workers can be transferred more easily from agriculture than from old industries to new. This conflicts with the Ames–Rosenberg proposition that the more advanced the technology, the more the early comers will have the advantage that their labour force can be trained more easily (p. 22). The authors appear to have in mind here the contrast between the long-standing industrial worker of the advanced economy and the illiterate, untrained peasant of an underdeveloped economy. But if one compares the industrial worker of the early comer and the industrial worker of the late-comer following, say, between 30 and 70 years after the early comer, the costs of retraining are likely to be greater in the first case. Technical education facilities may be greater in the late-comer which may make for greater flexibility in the use of labour, whereas the early starter may have industrialised at a time when technology was relatively simple. But even for the late-comer the costs of retraining their industrial workers used to one type of technique may be greater than training an agricultural worker, literate but without industrial experience.

(ii) The institutional environment may become closely geared to the needs of an economy based on a given technology (see the attitudes towards commercial policy and patent laws in Britain discussed above).

(iii) 'Sociological' resistances. It is a reasonable hypothesis that the moulding of entrepreneurial attitudes into a fixed traditional pattern is likely to be more serious for a country relying on a set industrial structure for 70–100 years than for a latecomer where these industries may have been of significance for, say, only 20–30 years. 'Transition costs' may be, in the authors' words, 'an increasing function of time, as well as merely of output' (p. 24).

Ames and Rosenberg recognise, quite rightly, that the early start thesis depends on assumptions about sharp discontinuities in technological change. But the early start argument is much less plausible if 'as Usher has persuasively argued, technological change must be understood as a continuous process of cumulative synthesis emerging out of a perception of deficiencies in existing techniques and knowledge' (p. 20). Their preference for Usher's explanation is an important consideration leading them to cast doubt on the early start. But the conflict between Schumpeter's view of technology as being discrete change and Usher's continuity is only apparent. If one is looking at the process of invention as a whole continuity is likely to emerge, but if considering the effects of innovation on changes in the industrial structure one might be struck by discontinuity. Schumpeter himself accepted much of Usher's theory of invention and found no contradiction between it and his own. As he put it: 'What difference there is, is a difference of purpose and method only. This becomes evident if we reflect that any given industrial development, for instance the electrification of the household, may involve many discontinuities incident to the setting up of new production functions when looked at from the standpoint of individual firms and yet appears when looked at from other standpoints, as a continuous process proceeding steadily from roots centuries back. . . . We may characterise this as a difference between microscopic and macroscopic points of view: there is as little contradiction between them as there is between calling the contour of a forest discontinuous for some and smooth for other purposes. Not only have we no fault to find with the historic theory that stresses continuity, but on the contrary, we consider it one of the most promising features of modern historic analysis' (J. A. Schumpeter, *Business Cycles* (1939), i 226–7).

# 6 Economic Progress in Britain in the 1920s

## I

FOR many years now the 1920s have been regarded as a period of stagnation as far as the British economy is concerned. Contemporaries were in no doubt that these were bad years. Their anxious desire to return to normality or to what they considered to be the *belle époque* of the Edwardian era was an indication of the distress of the times. This impression is no doubt somewhat understandable since the period was notable for high unemployment, stagnating exports and declining basic industries. Many later scholars have continued to pass unfavourable judgement on these years. Arndt in 1944 for example, stated that Britain's economic progress was not commensurate with that of other advanced industrial countries.[1] By concentrating on Britain's poor export performance Lewis, in his *Economic Survey*, paints a very dismal picture of the 1920s and concludes that 'there was not even an interlude of prosperity'.[2]

Professor Youngson's comments are equally pessimistic: 'Times were dull, and the outlook was never particularly promising'.[3] Other writers have remarked upon the slowness with which the British economy recovered from the First World War and the failure to adapt the industrial structure to altered circumstances.[4] Some of the statistics presented give the impression that British indices of economic activity hardly increased at all in this decade. For instance, one would be compelled to conclude from the data used by Professor Ashworth and Dunning and Thomas that industrial production grew very slowly indeed throughout the period 1913 to 1929.[5] Finally the latest writer on the subject of Britain's economic growth has marked the decade down clearly as one of stagnation.[6]

Although most of the authors do make reference to some of the advances made in these years, especially to developments in the

[1] H. W. Arndt, *The Economic Lessons of the Nineteen-Thirties* (1944) pp. 20, 126.

[2] W. A. Lewis, *Economic Survey, 1919–1939* (1949) pp. 35, 41, 87.

[3] A. J. Youngson, *The British Economy, 1920–1957* (1957) p. 23.

[4] V. Paretti and G. Bloch, 'Industrial Production in Western Europe and the United States, 1901–1955', *Banca Nazionale del Lavoro Quarterly Review*, IX (1956) 195; E. Zupnik, *Britain's Postwar Dollar Problem* (1957) p. 23.

[5] W. Ashworth, *An Economic History of England, 1870–1939* (1960) p. 333; J. H. Dunning and C. J. Thomas, *British Industry* (1961) p. 19.

[6] C. P. Kindleberger, *Economic Growth in France and Britain, 1851–1950* (1964) p. 13.

newer industries, the general impression one gets from reading their work is that the 1920s were years of protracted economic progress. There is reason to doubt however, whether this judgement should be accepted as final. The note of dissent may be justified on the following grounds. For one thing, when discussing the 1920s too much attention has been devoted in the past to the basic sector of the economy and the twin problems of unemployment and exports; this, together with a failure to take account fully of the important qualitative changes then taking place, would inevitably result in a pessimistic view being recorded. As G. C. Allen remarked some years ago, it was the persistence of heavy unemployment that give the inter-war years a bad name, yet, in spite of this, substantial economic progress was made.[1] Secondly, a considerable amount of new statistical data has been made available in recent years and, as Lomax has pointed out, some of it suggests that 'the overall economic position . . . was by no means as black as has been painted'.[2] Finally, there has been a tendency to study the 1920s in isolation with insufficient reference to the progress of the British economy over time. A comparison of growth trends in the 1920s with those for the decades prior to 1914 produces some rather interesting findings.

The above reasons provide sufficient justification for presenting a reappraisal of the 1920s. The presence of heavy unemployment and stagnating exports cannot of course be denied, nor can the fact be hidden that Britain was still losing ground in the world economy, in percentage terms, during these years. On the other hand, there are no grounds for assuming that Britain's economic performance was disappointing. In quantitative terms, Britain's recovery to 1913 levels was comparable with that of Europe and progress in terms of growth was quite respectable, being considerably better than that recorded before 1914. Furthermore, this was by all accounts a period of fairly rapid technical progress and structural change which contrasts fairly sharply with the immediate decades before the First World War. Indeed, in many respects the 1920s formed a watershed between the old industrial regime of the pre-1914 era and the new industrial economy of the post-1945 period. For, as a result of the progress made in the 1920s, a viable base was created which ensured that steady growth would take place in the future. Taken all round, and considering the difficult circumstances prevailing in these years (e.g. unfavourable international factors and overvaluation of the £)

[1] G. C. Allen, 'Economic Progress, Retrospect and Prospect', *Economic Journal*, LX (1950) 464.

[2] K. S. Lomax, 'Growth and Productivity in the United Kingdom', *Productivity Measurement Review*, XXXVIII (1964) 9.

we might go so far as to suggest that this was a period of fairly rapid economic progress.

## II

Although in terms of manufacturing production and foreign trade Britain's relative importance in the world economy was declining in this period, this was simply the continuation of a trend which had been going on long before 1914 – in fact from the 1870s.[1] But it certainly does not follow from this that the British economy was stagnating in the 1920s or that recovery after the war was necessarily slower than that of Western Europe. In fact, data relating to gross domestic product and industrial production over the period 1913 to 1929 suggest that Britain's performance was fairly respectable compared with the main industrial countries taken as a group. Maddison's indices for G.D.P. per man-hour for twelve countries are presented in Table 1. These show that between 1913 and 1929 the increase in output per man-hour (adjusted for changes in unemployment) was 40·3 per cent, which was almost identical to the average increase of the twelve countries (40·9 per cent). The British increase was, in fact, considerably better than that of five other countries (Belgium, Denmark, Germany, Sweden and Canada) and almost the same as that of Italy. Furthermore, relative to other countries, British performance in the 1920s improved considerably on that of pre-war. Between 1900 and 1913, for example, the average increase in G.D.P. for ten countries was around 24·3 per cent compared with only 7·3 per cent for Britain. Prior to 1913 all the countries listed in Table 1 were growing faster than Britain.

Probably the most serious underestimation of Britain's progress in the 1920s has been in respect of industrial production. Most estimates of industrial production suggest that industrial recovery was very much slower than that of Europe. This is particularly true of the indices compiled by Hoffmann and O.E.E.C. On the basis of the latter estimates Paretti and Bloch presented material in 1956 which gave Britain a very poor rating indeed. According to their data, production had hardly exceeded the 1913 level in 1925 and at the end of the decade (1929) it was still only 16·2 per cent above the pre-war level compared with an increase of 24·6 per cent for Western Europe as a whole.[2] Even on this basis, however, Britain's performance was no worse relative to that of Western Europe than it had been in the

[1] See League of Nations, *Industrialisation and Foreign Trade* (1945) p. 13.

[2] 'Western Europe' comprises all the European countries which in 1955 were members of O.E.E.C. *Banca Nazionale del Lavoro Quarterly Review*, IX 195.

TABLE I

Output (Mainly G.D.P.) Per Man-hour (1913=100)

| | *Belgium* | *Denmark* | *France* | *Germany (F.R.)* | *Italy* | *Netherlands* | *Norway* | *Sweden* | *Switzer-land* | *U.K.* | *Canada* | *U.S.A.* |
|---|---|---|---|---|---|---|---|---|---|---|---|---|
| 1890 | — | 55·3 | 68·8 | 67·1 | 65·3 | — | — | 49·5 | 70·1 | 82·5 | 59·3 | 61·2 |
| 1900 | — | 70·4 | 85·4 | 81·2 | 73·4 | 86·9 | 76·8 | 66·6 | — | 93·2 | 70·9 | 75·8 |
| 1913 | 100 | 100 | 100 | 100 | 100 | 100 | 100 | 100 | 100 | 100 | 100 | 100 |
| 1929 | 137 | 132·5 | 154·6 | 113·2 | 143·7 | 150·2 | 160·4 | 115·7 | 166·3 | 140·3 | 121 | 155·5 |
| 1938 | 144·2 | 137·1 | 178·5 | 137·1 | 191·1 | 145·4 | 194·8 | 151·1 | 183·1 | 167·9 | 121·2 | 208·8 |

Percentage Change over Selected Periods

| | *U.K.* | *All countries* |
|---|---|---|
| 1890–1913 | 22·2 | 55·8 |
| 1900–13 | 7·3 | 24·3 |
| 1913–29 | 40·3 | 40·9 |
| 1929–38 | 19·2 | 15·9 |

Source: A. Maddison, *Economic Growth in the West* (1964) p. 232.

period 1901–13 when the increases in industrial production were 36 and 56·8 per cent respectively. A new index of industrial production constructed by Lomax indicates that earlier calculations have seriously underestimated the growth of British industry especially in the early 1920s (see Table 2).

TABLE 2

Index of Industrial Production in the U.K. (Excluding Building)

| | *Hoffmann* | *O.E.E.C.* | *Lomax* |
|---|---|---|---|
| 1913 | 110·3 | 97·1 | 92·6 |
| 1920 | 100·2 | 97·1 | 92·9 |
| 1924 | 100 | 100 | 100 |
| 1929 | 116·5 | 112·9 | 113·3 |
| 1935 | 125·8 | 128·6 | 127·9 |
| 1937 | 144·4 | 152·9 | 147·7 |

Sources: W. G. Hoffmann, *British Industry, 1700–1950* (1955) Table 54; O.E.E.C., *Industrial Statistics* (1955) and K. S. Lomax, 'Production and Productivity Movements in the United Kingdom since 1900', *Journal of the Royal Statistical Society*, A122 (1959) pt 2, 196.

If Lomax's revised index is compared with Bloch's for Western Europe the British performance appears much more respectable. As early as 1923 the British index had recovered to its pre-war level and in 1925 was well above it. In fact, industrially Britain's recovery from the effects of the First World War was far superior to that of Western Europe. After 1926 Europe's progress was more rapid; even so, by the end of the decade industrial production in the United Kingdom was nearly 22·5 per cent above the 1913 level, which was almost identical to the increase for Western Europe (see Table 3). This, in fact, was a much better performance than before 1914; between 1900 and 1913 the British increase in industrial production was just over half that of Western Europe's (30·7 as against 56·8 per cent). A further check was made by comparing the Lomax figures with those given by Svennilson for Europe and America.[1] By comparison with America the British performance looks very poor indeed but one must remember that America's achievement was exceptional by any standards. On the other hand, Britain's increase in manufacturing production fell only a little short of the average increase of Europe as a whole (see Table 4).

Although results may vary slightly depending on the coverage of the indices used it seems fairly safe to conclude that Britain's industrial performance in the 1920s matched that of Western Europe.

[1] I. Svennilson, *Growth and Stagnation in the European Economy* (Geneva, 1954) pp. 304–5.

TABLE 3

Total Industrial Production (Excluding Building)

| | U.K. (1924=100) | | | Total Western Europe (1938=100) |
|---|---|---|---|---|
| | *Bloch/O.E.E.C.* | *Hoffmann* | *Lomax* | *Bloch* |
| 1901 | 71·4 | 83·6 | 70·8 | 44 |
| 1913 | 97·1 | 110·3 | 92·6 | 69 |
| 1925 | 98·6 | 98·6 | 101·7 | 71 |
| 1929 | 112·9 | 116·5 | 113·3 | 86 |
| 1937 | 152·9 | 144·4 | 147·7 | 102 |
| PERCENTAGE INCREASES OVER SELECTED PERIODS | | | | |
| 1901–13 | 36 | 30·3 | 30·7 | 56·8 |
| 1913–25 | 1·5 | −9·4 | 9·8 | 2·9 |
| 1925–29 | 14·5 | 18·1 | 11·4 | 21·1 |
| 1913–29 | 16·2 | 5·6 | 22·4 | 24·6 |
| 1929–37 | 35·4 | 24·0 | 30·4 | 18·6 |

TABLE 4

Index Numbers of Manufacturing Production (1924–9=100)

| | *Total Europe (18 countries)* | *U.S.A.* | *U.K.* |
|---|---|---|---|
| 1913 | 86·6 | 62·3 | 92·2 |
| 1929 | 110·7 | 112·7 | 114·5 |
| Percentage increase 1913–29 | 27·6 | 80·6 | 24·2 |

Indeed, in the early 1920s it was considerably better, and although in the latter half of the decade Britain did not do as well, by 1929 she had managed to record an increase above 1913 comparable to that of Western Europe.

An alternative way of assessing the potential of the British economy in the 1920s is to judge it in terms of its performance over time. Here again the 1920s show up remarkably well. The annual rate of growth of national product per man-hour was considerably better than that before 1913 and compares favourably with the long-term trend. The growth of industrial production registers an even sharper break with past trends. Between 1920 and 1929 the annual rate of increase was 2·8 per cent compared with a long-term rate of 1·6 per cent before 1913 (see Table 5).

TABLE 5

Rates of Growth of National Product and Industrial Production

| | *Output per man-hour* | | *Industrial production* | |
|---|---|---|---|---|
| 1870–1913 | 1·5 | 1860–77 | 3·0 | |
| 1913–29 | 2·0 | 1877–83 | 0·5 | |
| 1929–38 | 1·9 | 1883–91 | 1·6 | 1·6 |
| 1938–51 | 0·4 | 1891–1902 | 2·4 | |
| 1950–60 | 2·0 | 1902–13 | 1·6 | |
| 1955–60 | 1·5 | 1920–9 | 2·8 | 3·1 |
| 1913–50 | 1·7 | 1929–38 | 3·2 | |
| | | 1948–60 | 3·7 | |

Sources: A. Maddison, *Economic Growth in the West* (1964) p. 37 and 'Economic Growth in Western Europe, 1870–1957', *Banca Nazionale del Lavoro Quarterly Review*, XII (1959) 68; K. S. Lomax, 'Growth and Productivity in the United Kingdom', *Productivity Measurement Review*, XXXVIII (1964) 6.

The same can also be said for industrial productivity. As Table 6 shows, the pace of productivity growth accelerated enormously in the 1920s and contrasts markedly with the very slow progress made between 1880 and 1914.

It is quite probable that the data on which these calculations are based tend to exaggerate the break in trend of productivity growth. The pre-1914 estimates of productivity are probably on the low side since they are based on the Hoffmann production index, the precise accuracy of which is open to question on grounds of weighting and

TABLE 6

Average Rate of Productivity* Increase in the U.K. Per cent per annum

| | |
|---|---|
| 1870–80 | 1·39 |
| 1880–90 | 0·59 |
| 1890–1900 | 0·18 |
| 1900–14 | –0·24 |
| 1920–30 | 3·6 |
| 1922–30 | 2·7 |
| 1924–35 | 2·2 |
| 1930–38 | 1·9 |
| 1950–60 | 2·2 |

*Per man-year

Sources: Based on the Hoffmann production index as calculated by E. H. Phelps Brown and S. J. Handfield-Jones, 'The Climacteric of the 1890s: A Study of the Expanding Economy', *Oxford Economic Papers*, IV (1952) 294–5, and London and Cambridge Economic Service, *Key Statistics of the British Economy, 1900–1962* (1963) p. 9.

coverage. Moreover these estimates have not been corrected for unemployment though a revision to take account of this would not make a great deal of difference to the long-term rate of growth.[1] On the other hand, the estimates for the post-war period are more comprehensive since they are based on the Lomax index. The rate of growth for the 1920s (1920–30) may be on the high side because of the inclusion of the immediate post-war years when productivity levels were fairly low. But the trend rate of growth is still 2·7 per cent for the years 1922 to 1930. Despite these reservations, therefore, it would still be safe to say that productivity growth was substantially higher than before 1914 and compared very favourably with the long-term trend after 1930. Even on the most generous estimation the rate of productivity growth was no more than 0·5 per cent in the three or four decades before 1914 and rarely rose (even in the short term) above 1 per cent, whereas during the 1920s it was well above 2 per cent per annum.

On the basis of the statistical evidence now available there would appear to be strong grounds for suggesting that there was a sharp break with past growth trends in the 1920s. The acceleration was most noticeable in industrial production and productivity, and to a lesser extent in national product, but most other indices of economic growth (e.g. real incomes and wages) show a distinct shift upwards in comparison with earlier periods.[2] Furthermore, the growth rates of the 1920s compare favourably with those achieved after 1930. In fact, there is every indication that this decade saw a return to the high growth rates which characterised the middle decades of the nineteenth century. In this respect, therefore, the 1920s can be seen as the beginning of a new period of relatively high growth rather than a period of economic decline.

## III

In the light of the above data it would appear that economic growth in Britain was quite respectable during the 1920s. But statistical evidence alone cannot convey fully the economic progress achieved in these years. Account must also be taken of the many important qualitative and structural changes which occurred and which taken together clearly suggest a distinct break with past trends. One of the

[1] See D. J. Coppock, 'The Climacteric of the 1890s: A Critical Note', *Manchester School*, XXIV (1956) 7, 8 and 12.

[2] Between 1899 and 1913 real income per head hardly rose at all whereas by 1929 it had exceeded the 1913 level by 16 per cent. Real wages rose even more rapidly compared with before the war. See B. R. Mitchell and P. Deane, *Abstract of British Historical Statistics* (1962) pp. 367–8.

most striking features was the way in which substantial productivity growth occurred without any significant increase in the capital stock. Between 1920 and 1930 total net investment (in real terms) in industry rose by less than £20 million[1] which is a marked contrast to the period 1895–1914 when physical equipment per head increased fairly rapidly yet productivity growth was very low indeed.[2] Moreover, there was no dramatic increase over pre-war in the rate of growth of power applied to industry. During the 1920s the average annual increase in horse-power per worker was around 3·4 per cent as against 3·1 per cent for the period 1870–1907.[3] This implies that capital resources devoted to industry were being used more productively than previously. This can be attributed to three main developments. There was a shift first of all in the pattern of investment resources towards the new high growth sectors of the economy. Secondly, important productivity gains were being realised as a result of technical improvements which necessitated little additional capital, e.g. the rationalisation of production methods, a type of technical progress which had been sadly neglected before 1914. And thirdly, gross investment or replacement investment was the main vehicle of new techniques. The last of these is particularly important since not only was capital replacement fairly rapid—gross investment rose by over £700 million in the period—but also there is evidence that it was being concentrated in more productive techniques than before 1914 when the chief tendency had been routine replacement in static techniques.[4] An obvious example of course is the rapid shift from steam to electrical power. Between 1912 and 1930 the proportion of power applied electrically to industrial operations rose from 25 to 66·2 per cent.[5] The change in the nature of replacement investment was not as rapid as it might have been nor did it affect every industry. Nevertheless it may well have been a crucial factor in productivity growth for, as Colin Clark observed in the 1930s, 'Without new investment the replacement of obsolete capital . . . appears to give all the necessary scope for the introduction of technical and organisational improvement and to bring about

[1] The investment figures used in this paper were kindly supplied by Dr C. H. Feinstein of Cambridge University.

[2] E. H. Phelps Brown and B. Weber, 'Accumulation, Productivity and Distribution in the British Economy, 1870–1938', *Economic Journal*, LXIII (1953) 27.

[3] P. S. Florence, *Investment, Location and Size of Plant* (1948) p. 126 and D. J. Coppock, 'Mr. Saville on the Great Depression: A Reply', *Manchester School*, XXXI (1963) 177.

[4] See D. H. Aldcroft, above, Section B, 4, and C. P. Kindleberger, *Economic Growth in France and Britain, 1851–1950* (1964) pp. 154–5.

[5] L. Rostas, *Comparative Productivity in British and American Industry* (1948) p. 55.

the rapid increase in productivity under which we are now living.'[1] If this process was still to mature it was in the 1920s that the seeds of change were sown and began to take root.

A few examples will suffice to illustrate more clearly some of the points made above. In part the productivity gains were brought about by a shift of resources away from the basic industries towards the newer ones. It is impossible to illustrate this precisely but it is almost certain that the old staple industries such as coal, shipbuilding and cotton accounted for a much smaller proportion of the total gross capital formation in industry in the 1920s than was the case in the period before 1914. On the other hand, five industries, rayon, electrical engineering, motor vehicles, chemicals, and paper and printing, all of which were growing rapidly, accounted for one-third (£251 million out of £750 million) of the gross capital formation in the eleven years 1920–30. Such industries witnessed a constant stream of innovations in the inter-war years and under the influence of rapid technical progress and economies of scale productivity increased rapidly and prices were reduced. The most remarkable transformation occurred in the motor-car industry. Not only were technical improvements being continually made to the finished product but during the 1920s production methods changed out of all recognition from those before 1913. Before the war and even for a short time after, the industry consisted of a large number of very small firms each producing its own individual products.[2] After 1922, however, the industry was rapidly rationalised. The number of producers fell by more than one-half between 1922 and 1929 and by the latter date three firms accounted for 75 per cent of the total output.[3] At that date all the larger firms without exception were reaping the benefits of mass production, mass markets and new manufacturing techniques. As a result of these dramatic changes the price of cars fell rapidly—by as much as 33 per cent between 1923 and 1929[4]—and the industry recorded one of the highest rates of growth in productivity. Furthermore, one must remember that the growth of the motor industry had important repercussions on other branches of industry. It stimulated or brought into being a whole range of industries including oil refining, rubber, electrical goods, glass, metallurgy and mechanical engineering.

[1] Colin Clark, *National Income and Outlay* (1937) p. 272.

[2] S. B. Saul, 'The Motor Industry in Britain to 1914', *Business History*, v (1962).

[3] P. L. Cook and R. Cohen, *Effects of Mergers* (1958) p. 366.

[4] C. Clark, *Investment in Fixed Capital in Great Britain*, Memo. 49 of the Royal Economic Society and London and Cambridge Economic Service (Oct 1934) 19.

Similar advances were made in many of the other new industries. Rayon became an industry of some importance in the 1920s. After a rather shaky start before 1914 a series of technical victories secured the industry's success. Between 1920 and 1929 production of rayon yarn increased from six million lb. to 52·7 million, and as a result of considerable improvements and economies in production prices fell rapidly.[1] The electrical manufacturing industry, like its counterpart on the supply side, put up a very impressive performance in this period. In 1929 output was practically double that of pre-war and the industry was far more efficient and competitive than it had been in 1913. A process of rationalisation and the adoption of more scientific methods of production brought significant gains in productivity together with a reduction in prices. It was estimated in 1929 that productivity was 20 per cent greater than in 1923 and almost 30 per cent more than 1913, while during the decade prices of many electrical products had fallen by about half. The success of the improvements can be seen from the fact that by the late 1920s imports supplied less than 10 per cent of home demand as against nearly 25 per cent pre-war and exports of electrical products accounted for nearly 22 per cent of the industry's output.[2]

Great as the achievements of the newer industries were, it would be misleading to attribute all the productivity growth to the shift in the pattern of resource allocation. There is evidence to suggest that in a number of the older industrial sectors productivity was growing fairly rapidly as a result of technical progress, increasing mechanisation and improved methods of production. One of the most notable achievements was in the coal industry which before 1914 had experienced an absolute drop in productivity, largely because of a failure to mechanise. In 1913 only 8½ per cent of the coal mined was cut mechanically and the proportion conveyed by mechanised means was even lower. Mechanisation proceeded quite rapidly after the war. By 1930 31 per cent of the coal produced was cut by machinery and 17 per cent was mechanically conveyed, resulting in an 18 per cent increase in productivity between 1924 and 1930.[3] Substantial improvements were also made in certain sections of the iron and steel industry. The labour productivity of blast furnaces, for example, increased by nearly 25 per cent between 1923 and 1930; this gain can largely be attributed to technical improvements such as the use of larger blast furnaces and the improvement in auxiliary

[1] The price of viscose yarn fell from 150 to 63 pence per lb. between 1921 and 1929. D. C. Hague, *The Economics of Man-Made Fibres* (1957) p. 36.

[2] *The Economist* (30 Nov 1929) 1010–11.

[3] J. H. Jones *et al.*, *The Coal-Mining Industry* (1939) p. 87; W. E. G. Salter, *Productivity and Technical Change* (1960) p. 177.

equipment, e.g. mechanical charging.[1] In cement the gains were even more spectacular. Productivity per operative rose by nearly 60 per cent in the 1920s. Here again the main factors were increasing mechanisation and the use of better equipment. By the beginning of the second decade of the twentieth century the cement industry had begun a vast programme of plant replacement which was completed in the twenties. This involved the adoption of the rotary kiln in place of the fixed kiln, together with the use of appreciably larger kilns. In addition, much greater use was made of labour-saving devices such as hydraulic drying and conveying the product mechanically for weighing and packing.[2] Significant productivity advances were also recorded in a number of smaller trades such as cutlery and boots and shoes due to the adoption of technical improvements,[3] while in machine tools and engineering the use of more efficient methods of production brought similar rewards.[4]

## IV

To appreciate fully the argument that the 1920s formed a sort of watershed between the old and new industrial regimes one must recognise the important role the war played in bringing about new developments. Although the war was detrimental in many respects to Britain's economic interests it did initiate or accelerate many changes, in both old and new industries, which began to mature in the 1920s. There can be no doubt that it opened the eyes of both industry and the government to the defects in our economy and to the fact that the efficiency of industry left much to be desired. As the Parliamentary Secretary to the Ministry of Munitions commented in 1918 '... the war has revealed with pitiless accuracy the defects in our industrial equipment'.

For one thing Britain was forced to manufacture many products which before 1914 she had imported from abroad, such as magnetos, optical and chemical glass, ball bearings, tungsten, ignition plugs, scientific instruments, dyestuffs and certain machine tools. Some of these trades were fostered by the government and after the war protected by a tariff. Hence pressure of war needs gave rise to important new industries such as dyestuffs, precision instruments, aircraft and radio communications—all of which continued to expand in the

[1] L. Rostas, *Productivity, Prices and Distribution in Selected British Industries* (1948) pp. 117–19.

[2] Ibid., pp. 80–4; Cook and Cohen, *Effects of Mergers*, p. 27.

[3] See S. Pollard, *A History of Labour in Sheffield* (1959) p. 284; and A. Fox, *A History of the National Union of Boot and Shoe Operatives, 1874–1957* (1958) pp. 418–24.

[4] See below for a discussion of these changes.

1920s. Apart from these virtually new creations many branches of industry received a direct stimulus from the war: some of the most notable advances occurred in food preservation, petroleum, new chemical solvents, artificial fibres and certain plastics. For example, it was the military need for a non-inflammable coating for aircraft that laid the foundation of the cellulose-acetate industry.[1] In addition, there was a wide range of new technical developments which were fostered during the period of hostilities; e.g. automatic welding, improved hull designs for ships which made construction profitable even in times of depression, fuel economy techniques and precision control in industrial operations. Many of these developments would no doubt have occurred in time anyway, but the fact is the war greatly accelerated the rate of progress and laid the basis on which further advances were made in the 1920s. To these must also be added the advances in new alloy metallurgy, new steels, the use of oil for deep sea propulsion duties, the beginnings of railway electrification and the spread of industrial electrification. The latter, rather surprisingly, has been the least publicised advance of these years despite the rapid strides made in the techniques of electricity generation at this time. Yet this was the period when electricity was applied extensively to industrial operations.

This spate of new technical developments was by no means the only highlight of these years. Perhaps even more important was the revolution which occurred in methods of production and in the attitudes of manufacturers to production problems in general. Perhaps for the first time businessmen were brought face to face with the grim reality that they had to adopt more scientific methods of production and reorganise their plant and equipment on more efficient lines, and generally pay much greater attention to securing economies in the use of factors of production. As Pollard rightly points out: 'Pressure of war needs, urgent appeals and direct aid by Government departments, and acute shortages of materials, fuel, machinery and labour created a new outlook and a more active approach which were not entirely lost even after the emergency had ended.'[2] The changes which occurred in production methods can be best illustrated by the machine tool industry. Before the war this industry had been noted for its backwardness in this respect. A large number of small firms produced a multiplicity of articles and, apart from one or two exceptions, standardised design and mass production techniques were almost unknown to British firms. As one

[1] R. S. Sayers, 'The Springs of Technical Progress in Britain, 1919–39', *Economic Journal*, LX (1950) 279.

[2] S. Pollard, *The Development of the British Economy, 1914–1950* (1962) p. 54.

official history remarked: 'The lack of organisation and the general conservatism which prevailed in the trade at the outbreak of war left room for much assistance in speeding up output and in the introduction of new processes and new methods of production.'[1] The pressure of war demands did much to wean the industry from its obsolete methods of production. Under government direction the industry was forced to streamline its operations so as to secure the largest possible output at the lowest cost. The number of different designs of tools was drastically reduced, and firms were ordered to specialise on particular types of machines and devise better and more accurate workshop methods and improve their plant layout. This process of rationalisation continued after hostilities, for as one committee noted the war had 'opened the eyes of manufacturers to the advantages of manufacturing in large numbers instead of ones and twos'.[2] The Associated British Machine Tool Makers, a body comprising eleven firms set up in 1916–17 to assist the government with its rationalisation plans, was continued, and by 1922 a further nine firms had joined it. Each member firm agreed to specialise on a narrow range of non-competing lines and to take steps to standardise the designs of their tools. As a result the production programmes of the constituent firms were considerably reduced and eventually each firm was restricted to producing only a few types of tools. The scheme proved to be a considerable success and great improvements in workshop organisation and efficiency resulted from it. Nor did the Association confine its activities solely to the production side. A joint sales organisation was formed with district offices in the main industrial centres of Britain and sales offices in some of the major foreign countries.[3]

Such changes were not confined to engineering and machine tools. The war had shaken many industries into the realisation that the old rule-of-thumb empirical methods were no longer appropriate. As one observer in Sheffield wrote in 1920, 'The war had done Sheffield industry good. It has shaken it up in a way that nothing else would have done, and with its modern shops, modern methods and resources of output almost double those of pre-war days, it is now well on its way to enjoy the fruits of the biggest boom that the world of steel has ever known.'[4] If the boom never materialised the benefits of

[1] *Official History of the Ministry of Munitions* (1924) vol. III, pt III, p. 66.

[2] *Report of the Departmental Committee on the Engineering Trades after the War*, Cd. 9073 (1918) p. 8.

[3] For further details and references, D. H. Aldcroft, 'The Performance of the British Machine Tool Industry in the Inter-War Years', *Business History Review*, XL (1966).

[4] S. Pollard, *A History of Labour in Sheffield* (1959) pp. 269–70.

war-time co-operation bore fruit in the 1920s. Throughout industry generally there was a far greater willingness than ever before to rationalise production methods, to economise in the use of factors of production and to replan factory lay-outs and improve management techniques. The rapid spread of electrically driven motive power was a reflection of such tendencies since its adoption not only saved resources but often necessitated or led to a revision of firms' production methods. Above all there was a greater awareness on the part of manufacturers of the benefits to be derived from scientific research and the employment of qualified technical experts. Before the war the application of science to industry had been seriously neglected in this country; few firms did much research and most manufacturers scorned the value of employing technically trained personnel. But the war soon altered these attitudes. Under the stimulus of the D.S.I.R. (established in 1916) a much greater interest began to be taken in scientific problems. After the war many new collective research associations were set up—between 1918 and 1923 the Board of Trade licensed no less than twenty-four—and some of these were subsidised by the government. In addition, many individual firms, especially in chemicals, engineering, steel and electrical manufacturing, established their own research units or increased the facilities which they already possessed. As early as 1925 it was said of the steel industry that 'all the great works have laboratories where problems incidental to their own branches of trade are dealt with. The Brown-Firth laboratories [where the early work on stainless steel was done] are good examples of individual initiative in this connection.'[1] This is in marked contrast to the steel industry's efforts in this respect before 1914. Of course Britain still remained a long way behind America and Germany in terms of research expenditure, as the Balfour Committee noted in 1927. But again what is significant is not that we failed to match up to our competitors but that at long last our manufacturers had come to realise the value of industrial research and that during the 1920s they were making a concerted effort to remedy past deficiencies.

One can argue, therefore, that during the 1920s technical progress was much more rapid than in the thirty years or so before 1914. Moreover, the changes which occurred were not limited simply to a few new industries; indeed there is evidence to suggest that qualitative improvements were taking place over a fairly wide sector of the economy.

It would be pointless, of course, to suggest that there was little scope for further improvements, since obviously this was not the

[1] Sayers, in *Economic Journal*, LX 281, quoting *The Times Trade Supplement*.

case. But neither should one underestimate the achievements which were made under conditions which at the time were not the most favourable. There is, of course, the reverse side of the balance sheet to consider—namely the twin problems of high unemployment and declining exports. Throughout the 1920s the number of registered unemployed rarely fell below the million mark for any length of time, while in real terms exports never regained their pre-war level; even in the best years 1927–9 the average volume of exports was no more than 80 per cent of the 1913 level. But a large part of the unemployment and export decline can be traced directly to the loss of markets for one or two commodities and the failure to develop substantial replacements for them. The problem was centred around a few contracting industries, such as cotton, coal and shipbuilding, which had featured so prominently in the pre-war export economy and it was these relatively labour intensive industries which accounted for the bulk of the unemployment and decline in exports after the war. In 1929 it was estimated that unemployment in the six leading staple export trades caused by a fall in exports since 1913 amounted to no less than 700–800,000 workers or practically the whole of the core of unemployment.[1] In fact, given the high level of unemployment and the disastrous decline in exports, what is really remarkable is the narrow range of industries affected and the small number of industries which actually failed to increase their output substantially over pre-war. Apart from textiles, shipbuilding and mining there were few industries which suffered an absolute check to production during the 1920s. And in any case, in terms of industrial output, the contraction of these industries was more than compensated for by the rapid growth which took place in the expanding sectors.

However serious the position was from a social point of view it should not cause us to overlook the fact that important structural changes were taking place at this time. In point of fact, the sharp contraction of some of the older industries was a positive long-term advantage since structural change would no doubt have been delayed even longer had these industries maintained the dominant position in the export economy which they had held formerly. Thus it is possible to see the contraction of the basic sectors and concomitant growth of the newer industries as an indication of the degree of success Britain achieved in adapting her economy to the basic forces which adversely affected her competitive power in the world economy. The process of structural adaptation was still far from complete by 1930 of course, but it was certainly more rapid than before 1913 and compared very favourably with that of Western Europe. For

[1] E. V. Francis, *Britain's Economic Strategy* (1939) pp. 55–6.

example, the share of the textiles sector in total manufacturing fell from 19 per cent in 1913 to 12 per cent in 1929 while the metal products group advanced its share from 19 to 25 per cent over the same period (see Table 7). Overall, the net output of the newer industries

TABLE 7

Share of Each Sector of Manufacturing Production

| | *1899/1901* | *1913* | *1929* | *1937* |
|---|---|---|---|---|
| Food, beverage and tobacco | | | | |
| O.E.E.C. | 27 | 19 | 15 | 15 |
| U.K. | 27 | 20 | 18 | 16 |
| U.S.A. | 24 | 20 | 14 | 15 |
| Basic metals | | | | |
| O.E.E.C. | 7 | 11 | 11 | 11 |
| U.K. | 7 | 7 | 7 | 8 |
| U.S.A. | 9 | 10 | 10 | 9 |
| Metal products | | | | |
| O.E.E.C. | 16 | 24 | 27 | 27 |
| U.K. | 16 | 19 | 25 | 29 |
| U.S.A. | 10 | 13 | 33 | 31 |
| Chemicals | | | | |
| O.E.E.C. | 5 | 6 | 11 | 12 |
| U.K. | 6 | 6 | 8 | 7 |
| U.S.A. | 5 | 6 | 8 | 10 |
| Textiles | | | | |
| O.E.E.C. | 23 | 18 | 14 | 13 |
| U.K. | 16 | 19 | 12 | 11 |
| U.S.A. | 20 | 19 | 11 | 12 |
| Other Manufactures | | | | |
| O.E.E.C. | 22 | 22 | 22 | 22 |
| U.K. | 28 | 29 | 30 | 29 |
| U.S.A. | 32 | 32 | 24 | 23 |

Source: A. Maizels, *Industrial Growth and World Trade* (1963) p. 46.

accounted for just over 16 per cent of total manufacturing production in 1930 compared with around 8 per cent in the immediate prewar years.[1] Employment figures show a similar pattern of adjustment. Between 1923 and 1929 employment in the expanding sector (largely composed of newer industries) increased by 22·3 per cent as against a fall of 10·7 per cent in the contracting industries, and during the same period the proportion of industrial workers employed in the former sector rose from 57·3 to almost 66 per cent.[2]

[1] The net output of the new industries included electrical goods (and electricity supply), motor-cars and cycles, aircraft, chemicals and allied goods, scientific instruments, and rayon and silk.

[2] *Ministry of Labour Gazette* (Nov 1929) 394–5.

Thus the rate of structural adjustment was by no means insignificant and though there was still much scope for improvement it is clear that by 1930 a considerable proportion of Britain's resources were already located in the dynamic sector of the economy.

The newer industries have frequently been criticised on the grounds that they failed to absorb the displaced resources (especially labour) from the old sectors and that they were unable to make up for the loss in exports. In some respects these criticisms are rather unfair. For one thing, this view tends to overlook the fact that because of the belated start some of these industries were still in their teething stages in the 1920s. Consequently they could hardly be expected to fill all the gaps left by the sudden and violent contraction of the basic industries, the causes of which were often outside this country's control. In an economy which had neglected adjustment in the past there was bound to be a period of dislocation while the necessary changes were taking place. But such difficulties as occurred merely reflected the rate at which this process of adjustment was progressing rather than an indication of the bankruptcy of Britain's industrial system. Indeed, it was the rapid progress made by the new industries during the 1920s which laid the foundations of a new growth sector for the future. What is important then is not the fact that the new industries failed to take the place of the old but that they were, as Richardson has observed, 'a potent force making for permanent structural change in British industry, and to place an arbitrary time limit . . . for the readjustment to be made is to ignore the difficulties involved'.[1]

A further point to bear in mind, of course, is that some of the maladjustments occurred as a result of basic differences in the structure of the old and new industries rather than because of a failure on the part of the latter to expand properly. Since many of the new goods were of a fairly sophisticated nature it was the home market rather than the export market that initially provided the main outlet for the products of such industries. This is particularly relevant in the case of Britain since her main export markets tended to be primary producers whose demand for new products was considerably less than that of the rich industrial countries. Moreover, because the techniques of production spread more rapidly than in the case of the old staples, many countries were able to satisfy their own demand for new products, while the fact that a number of industrialised countries had got off to an earlier start in this respect meant that they were in a better position than Britain to capture the most lucrative

[1] H. W. Richardson, 'The New Industries Between the Wars', below, Section B, 8.

export outlets. Alternatively, there may well have been a tendency for British producers to neglect the export market simply because their attention was devoted to satisfying the demands of a buoyant home market. There is evidence to suggest that the lag in British exports was due not so much to structural defects within the economy but rather to a loss in Britain's competitive position, and this might reflect in part the power of attraction of the home market for new products and hence a relative neglect of exports.[1] In any case, some of the newer industries did quite well in the export field. The electrical manufacturing industry exported one-fifth to one-fourth of its total production, while in the later 1920s nearly 40 per cent of the motor-cycles produced were sold in foreign markets. None of the new industries, of course, was able to match the export performance of the old staples, some of which had at one time exported over 50 per cent of their output. On the other hand it was not advisable that they should attempt to do so, for one of the basic weaknesses of the old staples was that they had been far too heavily committed to exporting, a fact which became all too apparent in the inter-war years when markets for their products collapsed.

Although this paper has only touched upon some of the more important aspects of economic progress during the 1920s it seems that a revision of the period is not entirely out of place. The evidence available suggests that both quantitatively and qualitatively Britain's economic performance was quite respectable. True, compared with America British growth rates show up rather badly; yet one is obliged to point out that economic recovery in this decade was far more rapid and substantial than is often supposed and compares favourably with that of Western Europe. Furthermore, as far as Britain alone is concerned, this decade (or 1913–29) ranks as one of the more buoyant periods in our recent history.

Whatever index of measurement is used there is no question that economic growth was more rapid and sustained than at any time in the thirty years prior to 1914. The notion that the 1920s is a watershed or turning point in Britain's economic history is confirmed by the important qualitative improvements which occurred in these years. Not only were vital structural adaptations being made to our industrial sector during this period but there is abundant evidence to suggest that many businessmen were making a concerted effort to modernise their methods and techniques. The most notable change was, of course, the shift towards a new growth sector. Had this

[1] H. Tyszynski, 'World Trade in Manufactured Commodities, 1899–1950', *Manchester School*, XIX (1951) 293.

transition not taken place in the 1920s the British economy would have been without the viable base which assisted its recovery from the Great Depression of the early 1930s.[1]

Of course, critics will argue that we have exaggerated the changes which took place and that it is impossible to speak of economic progress at a time when certain industries were contracting, exports stagnating and unemployment levels were unreasonably high. Certainly there were black spots in the economy but then the difficulties and problems involved in the process of adaptation were bound to be great in an economy which had delayed adjustment for so long. No doubt Britain's performance could have been better but given the difficult conditions it was remarkable that so much was achieved. One thing is certain, however: Britain did not suffer economic stagnation in the 1920s as Kindleberger would have us believe. Apparent stagnation there may well have been but underneath it was a period of real economic progress.

[1] See H. W. Richardson, 'The Basis of Economic Recovery in the 1930s . . .' below, Section B, 7.

# 7 The Basis of Economic Recovery in the 1930s: A Review and a New Interpretation

## I

THE main difference between Britain's economic experience in the 1930s and that of other countries was that her recovery from the world depression of 1929–33 not only started earlier but was more persistent. Signs of recovery began to show themselves in late 1932, the revival became noticeable in 1933 and gathered momentum until 1937. Towards the end of that year there was some falling off closely related to the recession in the United States. But in spite of contemporary fears this relapse did not reach the dimensions of a slump for industry, and trade revived under the stimulus of heavy government expenditure on armaments, and in 1939 production figures were higher than ever. The extent of recovery can best be illustrated by a few statistics. The production index (1925–9 annual average = 100) fell from 111 in 1929 to 92 in 1931, but then rose to 147 by 1937. Net capital formation took a larger share of national income, 7·7 per cent for the five years 1934–8 against 4·6 per cent in the preceding quinquennium and 6·6 per cent in the period 1924–8.[1] Other indicators of economic activity shot upwards too: the number of workers in employment rose from 10·2 millions in 1932 to 11·5 millions in 1937, profits rose by 10 per cent and wages by 7 per cent in the same period, while real national income went up from 103 in 1932 (1925–9 annual average = 100) to 125 by 1938. The improvement in the economic situation was real enough but unexpected, for in the twenties the British economy, seemingly paralysed by falling staple exports and rising general unemployment, had been lagging behind its rivals. This paradox has never yet been satisfactorily explained.

## II

In searching for factors which might have initiated the recovery, contemporaries attached much weight to government policy.

[1] J. B. Jefferys and D. Walters, 'National Income and Expenditure of the United Kingdom, 1870–1952', *Income and Wealth* (1955) and *National Institute of Economic and Social Research*, Reprint no. 6, p. 19.

Certainly this decade witnessed a new course in the government's role in economic life: in the field of foreign economic policy, the abandonment of the gold standard (and its corollary, devaluation of sterling), the introduction of general tariff protection, and controls on the export of long-term capital; in internal policy, legislation to promote rationalisation in staple industries, attempts to remedy defects in the structure of the capital market (especially the creation of new institutions to bridge the 'Macmillan Gap'), and cheap money. But there is little doubt that their importance was, in general, overestimated. The drawbacks of these policies are now well known: the effects of devaluation were transient; the new tariff's assistance to domestic industry was outweighed by its impetus to a world-wide 'self-sufficiency boom' which involved more import controls and higher tariffs, and hence lower exports; the extension of imperial preference only diverted British trade from its former channels without increasing its absolute total; and the marginal increases in exports gained from bilateral trade agreements were poor compensation for the loss of the pre-1930 multilateral trading system. Corroboration of the failure of external policies designed to encourage exports is given by the fact that the most noticeable characteristic of the recovery was that it was based on the home market; while both export and import indices stagnated comparing 1936–8 with 1928–9, production rose by almost 29 per cent. At home, the government's schemes for industrial reorganisation resulted in a dilution of the original aims and a fossilisation of unmodified industrial structures, and employment in the industries affected (apart from iron and steel) continued to fall. Similarly, the problem of the 'Macmillan Gap' remained unsolved before the Second World War.

British internal policy was conspicuous for the absence of Keynesian public investment policies which were adopted elsewhere; in fiscal policy the balanced budget was preferred to deficit financing. Moreover, British budgetary policy of the thirties was orthodox in its most extreme form. It is an axiom of theory that even a balanced budget may have employment-creating and investment-inducing effects by redistributing income from some sections of the population to others by means of taxation and government expenditure; if the size of the budget increases, a balanced budget could have an expansionary stimulus on income equal to that possible under deficit financing. But in the early thirties the 'balanced budget multiplier' was not allowed to work in a positive direction, for balancing took the form of deflationary action on both sides of the account—taxes were increased and expenditure slashed. Nevertheless, because this strictness was applied by the National government it was applauded by both businessmen and investors, and thereby increased confidence. Indeed, it may be argued that government policy in general, whatever its economic effects, had a favourable impact on the psychology of those concerned (directly or indirectly) with the management of industry, and thus helped recovery in this way. This impact was not confined to budget policy. Even protection, in this light, was a favourable stimulus: in the first place, it put agitators for protection such as the heavy sections of the iron and steel industry in a happier frame of mind; secondly, it increased profitability and reduced uncertainty about the future. Similarly, the influence of cheap money may have been mainly psychological via the impetus of lower interest rates in raising share prices as well as the prices of fixed-interest securities.

On the reasonable assumption that a home market recovery must be due to a revival of domestic investment, the two aspects of policy which might have been expected to exert a real influence were the capital export embargo and cheap money—for both may possibly increase the amount of capital available for investment at home.[1] Because Britain's resources were no longer adequate for financing the development of overseas economies (although her mechanism for doing so remained extremely efficient), the ban on foreign loans helped to accelerate required trends for Britain's readjustment to her new international economic position. It has been argued, however, that the embargo had a more immediate effect on the grounds that, by prohibiting excessive foreign lending, it increased the supply of capital available for domestic requirements.[2] This is not as obvious as it appears. There is, in fact, a strong possibility that if capital exports are controlled, capital which would have been sent abroad will not be invested at home but will merely shift to idle balances.[3] Some evidence for this in the thirties was that three channels of saving—the obligatory funds of local authorities, undistributed profits, and savings for security by the middle and working classes—provided enough in themselves to meet the whole of investment requirements;[4] in other words, 'the propensity to save was steadily tending to outrun willingness to invest'. It is very probable that the overseas investor who usually preferred high-yield securities suffered from a lack of suitable investment opportunities at home.

[1] Both these policies were interlinked, for the immediate purpose of the embargo on overseas capital issues was to facilitate the adoption of the cheap money policy. Thus, the significance of the ban on overseas loans as a factor in recovery depends in part upon an estimation of the importance of monetary policy.

[2] R. B. Stewart, 'Great Britain's Foreign Loan Policy', *Economica*, v (1938) 60.

[3] C. Iversen, *International Capital Movements* (1935) p. 189.

[4] C. Clark, *National Income and Outlay* (1937) p. 191.

Interest rates were reduced in the middle of 1932 in connection with the government War Loan conversion scheme, and Bank rate remained at 2 per cent throughout the period 1932–9 compared with 5 per cent between 1925 and 1929. The importance of cheap money as a factor in the recovery has been much disputed. If low interest rates are to subscribe to recovery it is by increasing the rate of investment, for this rate is the primary determinant of the overall level of incomes, but the fact that investment increased in the early thirties (industrial issues rising from £70·9 million for 1931–2 to £244·1 million in 1935–6) does not prove the effectiveness of interest rates as a cause; it is probable that a rise in the marginal efficiency of capital was a stronger influence. It is also doubtful if entrepreneurs allow their investment decisions to be affected by changes in the rate of interest.[1] Another point was that bank advances did not seem to respond to the reduction in interest rates; up to 1937 they remained well below the level of the late twenties. Indeed, it would seem that low interest rates were of more advantage to the governmen than to private industry. Quite recently, however, an acute observer has drawn attention to more favourable indirect effects of cheap money in the thirties. He suggests that monetary policy operated in the industrial sector by encouraging the widespread replacement of bank debt by issued capital, that heavy purchases of gilt-edged securities by the banks enabled firms to sell gilt-edged at a profit which provided them with working capital, and that cheap money drove certain institutional investors (insurance companies and investment trusts, for example) from the trustee and high-class debenture market into the industrial capital market in a quest for income.[2] These arguments demand a modification of the view that maintains that cheap money was unimportant. Nevertheless, there is a strong presumption why we can regard it as a lesser influence. Attempts to reduce interest rates in 1930 proved a complete failure.

[1] This was the conclusion of the oft-quoted *Oxford Studies in the Price Mechanism*, ed. T. Wilson and P. W. S. Andrews (1951) pp. 1–74. This was based on replies to questionnaires from businessmen in representative British industries, but since only 25 per cent of those asked replied the sample was probably too small. It was suggested (p. 68) that others did not reply because they regarded the inquiry as unimportant and were not convinced that interest rates made much difference to their decisions. This view has been challenged on the grounds that the dearth of replies implied exactly the opposite: that the rate of interest had a very strong influence on investment decisions, and businessmen refused to disclose this out of fear that the information might be used against them.

On the other hand, the cost to an entrepreneur of servicing his capital includes depreciation allowances and a premium for uncertainty, and these may be quantitatively more important than interest rates.

[2] E. Nevin, *The Mechanism of Cheap Money* (1955) pp. 250, 251, 266.

This was to be explained by the well-known theoretical point that 'when prices and demand are falling . . . the demand for investible funds may be at so low an ebb that there is no rate (short of a negative figure) which will lead to a revival of investment'.[1] If the effectiveness of a cheap money policy is dependent upon the existence of favourable conditions, it is evident that the factors bringing about these conditions are more fundamental causes of the revival in investment.[2]

Cheap money had a positive effect in the housing sector—and the housing boom of the thirties has been widely accepted as either the cause or, at least, the symbol of economic recovery.[3] Falls in the rate of interest affect the building industry early. Although mortgage rates did not fall to the same extent as other interest rates (from 6 per cent in 1931 only to 4½ per cent by 1935), this nevertheless represented a significant effect on the size of weekly repayments. But this was not the only influence of cheap money on building. The banks played a part complementary to the role of building societies by advancing to the builder part of the actual cost of building; in 1935 Barclays Bank alone advanced £11·6 million to builders, building material manufacturers and public works contractors.[4] These banking facilities were both extended and less expensive in consequence of cheap money. A third and even more important stimulus was caused by the relation between differential movements of rents and house prices on the one hand and changes in investment opportunities on the other. Rents remained high or even increased during the housing boom under the combined impetus of the great housing shortage and the rent decontrol policy of the National government, while houses were supplied at prices lower than ever before. At the same time, gilt-edged securities fell sharply because of cheap money and this meant that investment in a house became relatively advantageous compared with the low returns obtainable from these investments. Housing became increasingly attractive as an outlet for accumulated funds, and new houses assumed importance as an investment demand. Thus, of all houses built of less than £13 rateable value over the years 1934–9 about 40 per cent were built to let.

[1] G. Haberler, *Prosperity and Depression* (1946) p. 378.

[2] Of course, this conclusion does not alter the fact that cheap money was the right policy.

[3] This influence of cheap money on housing was extensively analysed by W. Stolper, 'British Monetary Policy and the Housing Boom', *Quarterly Journal of Economics*, Supplement (1941).

[4] A. T. K. Grant, *A Study of the Capital Market in Post-war Britain* (1937) pp. 241–2.

## III

In revulsion from the view that government policy was the vital factor in the recovery, economists appeared to find a satisfactory explanation in the housing boom for not only did this boom assume unprecedented dimensions but it seemed one obvious feature of the British economy in this period which was virtually absent elsewhere. Up to 1936, that is, until the stimulus was reinforced by the beginnings of rearmament, the boom was confined to residential building. Over the years 1930–9 inclusive about 2·7 million houses were built in Britain, the great majority by private enterprise. Most houses were built for sale to the middle classes and to the better paid wage-earners and most of them were financed through building societies (their mortgage loans more than doubled between 1929 and 1936, rising from £268 million to £587 million).

One noticeable characteristic of the boom was its early origins. Speculative builders were getting ready to increase output from the end of 1932 when the value of plans for dwelling houses increased by over 30 per cent. Even by 1935 – a year before the construction boom reached its peak – expenditure on new houses amounted to as much as 54 per cent of total net home investment in fixed capital as compared with 33 per cent in 1929. In the light of these statistics the conclusion appeared self-evident: 'The British housing boom was by far the most important single element contributing to the recovery of trade during the 1930 decade'.[1] Statistics of employment and investment seemed to substantiate this view. The building industry's index of employment (1931 = 100) rose to 130·4 in 1936 though the index for industry as a whole except building had risen only to 113·9; it was estimated that one-third of the increased employment in Britain in the thirties was due to direct effects of building. In 1933 housing was responsible for £117 million out of £168 million net home investment in fixed capital while at the same time investment in industrial and commercial capital was a negative quantity (£–30 million).[2]

[1] W. A. Morton, *British Finance, 1930–40* (1943), p. 318. For similar views see F. Benham, *Great Britain under Protection* (1941) pp. 220–5; A. P. Becker, 'Housing in England and Wales during the Business Depression of the 1930s', *Economic History Review*, III (1950) 321; T. Balogh, 'Economic Policy and Rearmament in Britain', *Manchester School*, VII (1936) 85.

[2] Clark, *National Income*, p. 193. These statistics on employment and investment are misleading if used for comparative purposes, for the figures for industry group all industries together. Thus significant growth in expanding industries was masked by disinvestment (involving scrapping) in the declining staple industries. This qualification is important for the development of our argument in the next section.

There were so many factors behind the housing boom that their relative causal weight is difficult to evaluate. Basic determinants of economic growth such as population movements, varying tastes and the changing distribution of the labour force formed one set of influences. For example, the continuous shift of labour into the service industries probably strengthened the demand for new houses, because the social standards of workers in these industries were such that they demanded, in general, a higher level of living accommodation than workers in manufacturing. Similarly, the growth in the number of families relative to total population (to be explained by the falling birth rate, the increasing marriage rate and the ageing population structure) contributed to the exceptional housing shortage, estimated at about one million houses. Secondly, because there is evidence for the existence of a regular building cycle of about twenty years in length[1] attempts have been made to explain the boom in these terms; it was argued that a boom had been due in the twenties but was delayed by the effects of rent control in keeping rents below costs, whereas after the fall in prices this factor ceased to operate (especially as rent decontrol was revived).[2] A third category comprised improvements in the conditions attached to house purchase; apart from the fall in the mortgage rate of interest, repayment periods were lengthened, minimum deposits strikingly cut down, and the security standards of building societies relaxed. Of these, the reduction in the mortgage rate was the predominant influence; a decline in this rate from 6 per cent to 5 per cent would result in a 9 per cent saving on a 20–25-year amortisation, and it was suggested that this saving could be decisive for marginal buyers. Moreover, it was argued that the fall in mortgage rates in September 1932 was followed, after a lag of six to seven months, by a sharp rise in building completions, resulting in a new half-yearly record of 80,000 for the number of houses built by unassisted private enterprise.[3] However, it is difficult to believe that this record figure was caused by the reduction in 1932 of the mortgage interest rate by a mere ½ per cent, from 6 to 5½ per cent.[4] Another stimulus was the fact that building costs fell by about 10 per cent between 1929 and 1935 as a result of

[1] For example, see B. Thomas, *Migration and Economic Growth* (1954); B. Weber, 'A New Index of Residential Construction, 1838–1950', *Scottish Journal of Political Economy*, II (1955); E. W. Cooney, 'Long Waves in Building in the British Economy of the Nineteenth Century', *Economic History Review*, 2nd ser. XIII (1960).

[2] W. A. Lewis, *Economic Survey 1919–39* (1949) p. 86. Because only two-fifths of new houses in the thirties were built to let, this argument may not be sound.

[3] R. M. MacIntosh, 'A Note on Cheap Money and the British Housing Boom, 1932–7', *Economic Journal*, LXI (1951) 167–73.

[4] M. Bowley, 'Fluctuations in Housebuilding and the Trade Cycle', *Review of Economic Studies*, IV (1936–7) 177.

the general fall in prices and a significant increase in labour productivity in the industry, and some of this fall was reflected in the price of houses. But this was a secondary stimulus rather than the basic cause, for it is inconceivable that the demand for houses should be so elastic that this 10 per cent fall in costs could be responsible for the 100 per cent increase in the number of houses built in this period.

A more plausible explanation of the boom than any mentioned above was the fact of rising real incomes for those in work. It is probable that 70 per cent of the population benefited from an increase in the standard of living during the depression years. This increase had two main aspects. In the first place, it proved impossible to reduce money wages sufficiently to keep pace with falling prices—a familiar depression phenomenon; in the five years 1929–33 while the cost of living fell by 25 per cent, wages fell by only 6 per cent. Thus real incomes rose, but simultaneously there was a shift away from purchases of necessities; expenditure on food, clothes, alcohol and tobacco fell from an annual average of £2,116 million in the period 1924–7 to £1,797 million in 1932.[1] Secondly, the terms of trade moved in Britain's favour in the thirties and this accounted for part of the rise in real purchasing power. Up to 1932 the terms of trade varied very little (with a slight tendency to improve), but in 1933 there was an increase of 10 per cent, and in 1934 and 1935 they continued to improve. Whereas the price index of food imports (1913 = 100) fell from 114 in 1929 to 71 in 1933 and only revived to 89 in 1937 and the raw material import index changed from 121 to 70 to 98 in the same period, the manufactured export price index fluctuated much less, from 105 to 81 to 93 respectively.[2] This gain in the terms of trade, because it was mainly a reflection of the lower prices of imported foodstuffs, released purchasing power for other forms of expenditure such as houses.

It is clear, however, that this rise in purchasing power was only effective because of the existence of a social force—'an almost revolutionary conception of what are tolerable housing standards among a vast section of the population'.[3] Thus, it is probable that this force coupled with rising real wages accounted for the housing boom in Britain, and that falling costs, lower mortgage rates and other factors merely reinforced the upward trend. There is one difficulty in this analysis. One of the characteristics of the trade cycle is that it is

[1] Benham, *Great Britain under Protection*, p. 227.

[2] K. Martin and F. G. Thackeray, 'The Terms of Trade of Selected Countries, 1870–1938', *Bull. of the Oxford University Institute of Statistics*, x (1948) 383.

[3] Sir H. Bellman, 'The Building Trades', in the British Association, *Britain in Recovery* (1938) p. 432.

responsible for short-period fluctuations in wages whereas it is obvious that it is long-period changes in income, or expectations of such, which govern the demand for houses. Moreover, in the trough of the depression one might expect the workers' propensity to save to increase due to insecurity about their jobs.[1] The only rational explanation why these obstacles were absent is that, for one reason or another, skilled workers in employment must have been optimistic concerning the future in the thirties.

Despite almost universal support in its favour, the housing boom *alone* is for several reasons an insufficient explanation of the recovery. First, detailed examination of housing figures reveals certain inconsistencies with the argument that housebuilding 'carried' general recovery. Although annual output in the period 1930–3 was 30 per cent above the average for 1919–30, the increase in production appears less startling in comparison with the years immediately preceding 1930 and following 1933. In fact, investment in new dwelling houses in 1932 and 1933 was lower than the average for 1926–9. Similarly, housing figures for the early thirties were low compared with output in the middle and late thirties. In 1932 and 1933 the number of houses built in either year was less than two-thirds of the total in each year up to the outbreak of war.[2] Was this output of 1932 and 1933 large enough to initiate a recovery when it is almost certain that in the absence of the additional stimulus of rearmament the far higher housing output of 1937 and 1938 would not have halted the recession?[3] To be able to answer this question in the affirmative it would be necessary to prove that the recession of 1937–8 was caused by the appearance of boom tensions at the upper turning point—a situation aggravated by the housing boom itself. In view of the fact that output recovered in 1939 this would be difficult, although the outbreak of war prevents an appreciation of the true nature of the cyclical pattern.

Secondly, in the decade before the war the fluctuations in building activity throughout Europe were closely connected with the general trade cycle: prolonged depression in France, deep depression in

[1] On the other hand, the propensity to consume of the wage-earning classes appears to show little variation in relation to the economic climate, remaining very high at all times.

[2] Output averaged 210,000 as against an annual average of 330,000 for the period 1934–9 (L. R. Connor's statistics, 'Urban Housing in England and Wales', *Journal of the Royal Statistical Society*, XCIX (1936), supplemented up to 1939 by *The Economist*, 'Housing Progress', CXXXIV (1939) 175).

[3] Of course, if one subscribes to those theories of the cycle which hold that the cessation of the downswing in itself is sufficient to cause a revival, this argument ceases to be decisive, for the importance of the housing boom as a force *strengthening* the recovery is not in question.

Germany (the number of houses built fell from 308,000 in 1930 to 131,000 in 1932) followed by a late revival (305,000 houses built in 1937) related to the preparations for war, and an early but persistent boom in the United Kingdom. Clearly, the correlation between housing and general activity in the thirties was no coincidence, but is it logical to maintain that general economic conditions in each case were following the trends in building rather than the reverse? The *reductio ad absurdum* of the argument that recovery in Britain was caused by the housing boom is that the severe depression in France was due to the absence of such a boom. Despite some attempts to explain the trade cycle in terms of causative changes in building, it seems more plausible to maintain that building was responsive to general economic conditions and to general cyclical influences.

Thirdly, although the livelihood of many industries is affected directly by building (for example, cement production rose from 4·39 million tons in 1932 to 8·34 million tons in 1939) it may be argued that in spite of this housing was too narrow a base to be responsible for general recovery. For it is a feature of the industries directly connected with housing (stone quarrying, brick-making, sandpits, saw-milling and woodwork, concrete, wallpaper-making and others) that they are mostly dependent on building alone, and therefore a housing boom is likely to have only limited repercussionary effects on investment in the economy as a whole. This is because most theories of the trade cycle stress as an important factor in the upswing the inflationary and investment-inducing effects of the buying and selling of materials and capital equipment between key industries.[1] On the other hand, there may be something in the argument that by creating employment in dependent industries the housing boom increased the total amount of purchasing power available for consumption spending, and thus revival may have spread in this way. Nevertheless, the above objections are considered strong enough to cast doubt on the building boom as a sufficient cause of the recovery, though it was obviously a very important cause.

## IV

There was no reason why the 'discretionary' purchasing power released by the growth in real incomes should have been limited to the buying of houses alone; there were many other outlets for consumer expenditure. In the thirties, however, there was no significant rise in retail sales; as a generalisation, people were buying fewer basic

[1] This factor seems to have been overlooked by those who argue that house-building has stronger 'accelerator' effects than other industries.

necessities and more of other things (both services and durable goods) which are not sold to the same extent in retail shops. Certainly, national statistics indicate a shift of expenditure towards durables in the thirties. From 7·5 per cent of national income in the period 1925–9, the flow of durable goods to consumers increased to 7·8 per cent in the next five years, 1930–4, and to 8·2 per cent in the years 1935–9.[1] Combined with the rise in incomes, real wages increasing from a plateau in 1927–9 of 118 (1914 = 100) to another plateau in 1933–5 of 131 (that is, by 14 per cent),[2] this meant a sizeable increase in total expenditure on durable goods. It was reasonable that this should be expended not only on houses but on goods such as motor-cars, wireless sets, household appliances, new fabrics, electrical equipment and electricity supply. Although observers have occasionally suggested that the increased consumption of the products of new industries may have assisted economic recovery,[3] it has never up to the present been argued that the expansion of these industries was a central and causal factor in the upswing. The remainder of this article will be concerned with elaborating this view.

In 1935 *The Economist* published a chart which showed a 'remarkable similarity' between residential building output and the registration of new cars. Both were fairly level though tending to decline slightly through 1930 and 1931, and both suddenly shot up well above their previous highest points in the last quarter of 1932; *The Economist* suggested that the close correlation between the two trends implied that the major cause was the same in both cases.[4] The explanation offered was that in the summer of 1932 a wave of favourable psychology swept the country, and the general confidence of the consumer released a large volume of spending power. This confidence coincided with the increase in real income, and therefore there was a large rise in the 'free margin' of purchasing power, that is, the share of income available for non-essentials.[5] It is to be

[1] Jefferys and Walters, in N.I.E.S.R. reprint no. 6, p. 21. Durable goods are defined as those lasting more than three years, and it is significant that this definition includes most products of the new twentieth-century industries.

[2] A. L. Bowley, *Wages and Income in the United Kingdom since 1860* (1937) p. 30.

[3] For example, Benham, *Great Britain under Protection*, p. 236; C. L. Mowat, *Britain between the Wars* (1956) pp. 457–61.

[4] *The Economist*, CXXI (1935) 796.

[5] Evidence of another influence having the same effect is supplied by population changes. In spite of the tendency for the number of marriages to increase steadily, the birth-rate was falling sharply at this time; the annual average number of births for the period 1931–6 was only 694,000 as against 800,000 for the period 1922–30 (*Report of the Royal Commission on Population* (1949) Cmd. 7695, pp. 45–6). Because in modern times the number of births is largely determined by individual decisions,

emphasised that consumer rather than business confidence revived; it was residential not factory building which boomed, and private cars not commercial vehicles. This analysis is not necessarily confined to houses and motors for it may easily be extended to include most products of the newer industries. The argument points, therefore, to the existence of great demands generated by expanding incomes and 'carrying' the general recovery by calling for increased production from housebuilding and new industries alike. Thus it may be suggested that the recovery was due to the growth of demands strong enough to override the cyclical influence of general depression. If this thesis is tenable both the expansion of the new industries and the housing boom may form part of the same explanation.

The links between the housing boom and the development of new industries were so firm, however, that it may be legitimately argued that the housing boom, both directly and indirectly, was dependent on the growth of these industries. In the first place, the attractiveness of a house was greatly improved by the development of certain new industries—the effects of electricity supply on lighting and power equipment in houses is the obvious example. An increased desirability of a product often has a similar effect on demand as if the product was a completely new innovation. Since the rapid extension of electricity supply was after the establishment of the Central Electricity Board in 1926 and coincident with the building of the Grid which was not completed until the middle thirties, this may have been a direct influence on the demand for houses during the boom. As the sums expended on advertising by building societies showed little change after 1930, it is arguable that it was this increased attractiveness of new houses which made publicity on their behalf effective. Even more significant was the tendency of the housing boom to be concentrated in the south, eastern and midland areas (in other words, the prosperous areas) of the country. Although this could be attributed to the higher incomes there, more fundamental was the fact that these were the areas in which the new industries

there was probably a general tendency, especially on the part of young married couples, to prefer to spend their incomes on houses and durable goods rather than on having and bringing up babies. By the thirties children, formerly regarded as essentials, had come to be looked upon by some people as dispensable luxuries costing money in the same way as houses, motors and domestic appliances. The position of children on the scale of preferences had fallen; in Dr Werner Stark's phrase 'people preferred baby Austins to baby boys'. This is a plausible explanation of the fall in the birth-rate. Its significance here is that the smaller number of births represented an additional shift in expenditure away from necessities (food and clothing for children) towards houses, motor-cars and other consumer durables.

were situated. The re-location of industry was calling for new dwellings to house the workers in these industries, and therefore, in a real sense, the housing boom was a response to the expansion of the newer industries.[1] Moreover, the possibilities of secular growth in housing output were extended by the increasing use of motor vehicles which facilitated and made practicable suburban building in areas where the towns and cities had no more suitable space for residential building. But there was another reason why the new industries' expansion was as satisfactory an explanation of recovery as the housing boom. It is more plausible that the increased real incomes would first be spent on cheaper durables such as radios and domestic electrical appliances rather than on houses, because the demand for houses (due to the long-term commitments that the purchase of a house entails) lags in time considerably behind changes in income.[2]

Yet there are a number of *a priori* objections to the argument that the new industries in Britain were the causal influence in recovery. Any interpretation of the upswing in the thirties must explain why recovery went much further in Britain than abroad. It is easy to suggest that because these new industries existed abroad (indeed, it is traditional to regard their expansion overseas as being more rapid than in this country) they could scarcely be the unique factor in Britain's recovery. But this view is invalid. New industries in Britain were handicapped from the start by an 'over-commitment' of the country's resources of labour and capital to the staple industries of the nineteenth century, and this made the transition to newer types of production more intractable. Thus, these industries did not share in the prosperity which was experienced by their counterparts in the American economy in the twenties. A feature of the business outlook in Britain in that decade was optimism in the capacity of the staple industries to revive and a false belief that the set-backs of the post-war slump were temporary, and this attitude delayed readjustment to the newer trades. By 1930, however, this burden of 'over-commitment' was being cast off. Connected with this was the fact that by 1930 the new industries, after two decades of gradual growth, were just beginning to reach the mass production stage of development, and this revealed new output potentialities. Thus, in the early thirties the new industries of Britain were subjected to certain stimuli

[1] Becker, a strong protagonist of the housing boom explanation, admits (*Economic History Review*, III 328) that along with the increase in purchasing power the development of new industries was the basic force behind the boom.

[2] Admittedly, this would be partly neutralised by the fact that houses probably stand higher on the average consumer's scale of preferences than new types of consumer durables.

which had already spent themselves in the United States in the previous decade.

Secondly, statistics given in the preceding section suggest that both in employment and investment manufacturing was less buoyant than building. But statistics of manufacturing as a whole disguise details of expansion and decline in individual industries. The apparent disinvestment in manufacturing in general at the floor of the depression is misleading, for it hides the fact that the new industries were very well placed to meet cyclical fluctuations. Profit rates were far higher in newer industries than old, and this enabled them to attract capital (to the extent that they needed to go to the market for funds); even in 1932 trading profits in the motor industry were only 11 per cent below the level of 1929, and by 1935 were already 50 per cent up on 1929.[1] It is also relevant that a high proportion of the new industries' earnings was saved in the period 1924–35 as opposed to the staple industries, and these resources enabled them to re-equip or invest in new processes at any time they chose independent of the state of the capital market. This proportion was over 60 per cent in the private car industry, 45 per cent for commercial vehicles and well over 30 per cent in other new industries such as electrical engineering. This contrasted with the basic industries (railways, cotton textiles and coal, for example) where firms in general disbursed more than they earned.[2] Similarly, from the employment aspect the rapid expansion in new industries was masked by the heavy fall in staple industries. Over the period 1929–39 the numbers engaged in coal-mining fell from 1,075,000 to 839,000 and in cotton from 555,000 to 378,000, while the vehicle industries increased their labour force from 245,000 to 459,000, the electrical cable, apparatus and lamp industries from 94,000 to 185,000, and electrical engineering from 84,000 to 123,000. By an extension of the same argument, it is legitimate to assume that when the index of industrial production began to rise part of the increase in output in new industries was cancelled out by a further fall in the old. The Board of Trade index began to revive in the late summer of 1932 (from 78) and reached the 1929 level of (100) in the autumn of 1934; there is no reason why this reversal in the fall in output, since it must have involved tremendous expansion in certain industries, should not have initiated the recovery rather than the housing boom. Indeed, Census of Production statistics show rapid expansion for all new industries between 1930 and 1935. Whereas the production index as a whole rose

[1] G. Maxcy and A. Silbertson, *The Motor Industry* (1959) p. 153.

[2] R. Hope, 'Profits in British Industry from 1924 to 1935', *Oxford Economic Papers*, 1 (1949) 176.

by only 19 per cent, electrical engineering went up by 133 per cent, motors and cycles by 56 per cent, aircraft by 35 per cent, rayon by 172 per cent, fancy articles by 111 per cent, chemicals by 31 per cent and electricity undertakings by 73 per cent.[1]

A final *a priori* argument against the possibility of the new industries being the main factor in recovery is that they formed too small a proportion of manufacturing output to bring about a revival. This does not appear justified. The new industries (according to A. E. Kahn's classification) were responsible for 16·3 per cent of net output in 1930 (as against 12·5 per cent in 1924) and for 19·0 per cent in 1935. Because productivity was higher in the new industries as compared with the old they were rather less important from the employment aspect: 12·7 per cent of total industrial employment in 1930 and 15·3 per cent in 1935.[2] But by 1935 they gave employment to 1,100,000 people, 50 per cent more than in the building industry. Later, we shall attempt to substantiate the argument that these new industries constituted an interdependent sector moving forward together rather than isolated industries going through unco-ordinated phases of spasmodic expansion. If this argument is valid it is evident that the base of this sector was wide enough to start the recovery.

Of course, even in these industries there was some fall in production in 1930 and 1931, but this was scarcely serious; for example, in one of the most unstable of the new industries, the motor industry, output dropped by only 5 per cent. Yet the fact that output did fall a little may provide another reason why the new industries were as strong a recovery stimulus as the building boom. The analysis is as follows: in the new industries output started to fall far later than in other industries, and consequently entrepreneurs were not subject to general depression influences to the same extent. It is probable that by the time the floor of the trade cycle was reached (which in any event is likely to be before net investment falls below zero) entrepreneurs in the new industries had hardly been contaminated by depression, and their expectations had remained optimistic. In view of this, it was quite logical for them to regard the fall in demand (and production) as temporary, and since, as we have shown, the financial resources of most firms in the new industries were ample it was equally logical for entrepreneurs to counteract this fall by new

[1] As given by G. L. Schwartz and E. C. Rhodes, 'Output, Employment and Wages in the United Kingdom, 1924, 1930 and 1935', *London and Cambridge Economic Service*, Memo. 75.

[2] Census of Production figures compiled by A. E. Kahn, *Great Britain in the World Economy* (1946) p. 106.

investment, especially in minor innovations and new processes. This stimulus of a moderate fall in demand may have been stronger (or at least more spontaneous) than if output had continued to rise slowly through the depression, for it is arguable that in this latter situation the inducement to invest would have been weaker. As the number of houses built scarcely declined at all it is unlikely that this stimulus was present in the building industry. Another important point is that the new industries received huge quantities of their raw materials from certain of the basic industries, especially iron and steel, so that an increase in demand (or expectations of such an increase) for the products of the new trades by inducing a growth in the production of basic materials was certain to have extensive reverberating effects on the economy as a whole. That the iron and steel industry shared in the prosperity of the thirties with home demand higher than ever (the value of production rising from £91·7 million in 1930 to £114·8 million in 1935) was mainly due to vastly expanded demands from such new industries as the motor industry and electrical engineering.

## V

To attempt to argue that the expansion of the new industries was an important cause of recovery simply on the evidence that this was mainly a response to increased real incomes in the depression would not be fully convincing. Consequently it is necessary to expand the argument. As a rise in real wages is a familiar occurrence in most depressions and because historical experience has shown that such a rise may have no recovery effects, it is evident that increased real incomes in themselves do not guarantee an automatic revival. It may be assumed that expanding real incomes will not aid recovery to any extent unless consumers are convinced of the desirability of certain goods, either not available or not appreciated before. In the trough of depression, in the absence of this conviction, it is possible that workers will prefer to save much of the margin in excess of essential consumption as security against bad times rather than to spend it indiscriminately. Part of the increased demand for durable consumer goods at this time was probably an 'initial demand', that is, one arising because the mass of consumers first realise the potentialities of a new product and its value to them; this was true in the early thirties of wireless sets, electricity, even of motor-cars. But this was not the only additional factor; it is also necessary to stress stimuli on the production side, for it is clear from the above arguments that rising real incomes (especially in times of depression) will not be transferred into increased consumption unless made effective – and the influence to induce such a transfer may come from the supply side. In fact, these influences were present in the form of new innovations, a rapidly improving technology, better production methods — all resulting in price reduction and improved products, and thus adding a further stimulus to demand. An examination of the new industries reveals that these technical advances were too ubiquitous to be ignored and were also, to a large extent, concentrated in the new industries to the exclusion of others. The fact that many of these advances were occurring simultaneously in so many of these industries around 1930 makes the trend too obvious to be merely coincidental. It is also evident that the early thirties witnessed in many of the new industries a major technical break-through with the advent of mass production methods. Indeed, it is argued here that it was the happy combination of favourable economic conditions for revival such as increased purchasing power and the mass production or rapid technical progress stage of development attained in Britain's new industries which, together with the housing boom, 'carried' economic recovery in the thirties.

Our claim for this hypothesis may be strengthened by some illustration. In the radio industry the main stimulus came from continuous rapid technical development. Up to 1929 it was still the hey-day of the home-constructed set; demand for manufactured sets was low and the price high. After 1929, however, the home constructor found it uneconomical to keep abreast of technical advances. By 1934 he was unable to compete successfully with the manufacturer who had meanwhile adopted modern machines (such as the press tool and the drilling jig) and quantity production methods.[1] The transition was aided by a number of subsidiary factors: investment in assembly lines and a consequent further reduction in the price of the product, more efficient and better styled radio sets (including portables), and the existence after 1930 of hire purchase facilities for radios. Technical progress thus had a cumulative stimulus on demand, and the number of radio licence holders swelled from 1·7 millions at the end of 1925 to 8 millions by 1936. In the motor industry, although there were gradual improvements in design, the main spur to demand was more fundamental involving a shift in production from the large specialist car typical of the twenties to the smaller mass-produced vehicle of the thirties which was not beyond the pocket of working- and lower-middle-class buyers. What was remarkable about this shift is the fact that it was achieved in a very short space of time; in 1928 only 25 per cent of cars sold were ten horse-power or less, yet by 1933 the

[1] S. G. Sturmey, *The Economic Development of Radio* (1958) p. 171.

proportion was 60 per cent. This expansion in production of small cars reduced prices in two main ways: the adoption of mass production methods led to a significant drop in costs of production and the change in the type of vehicle manufactured meant a drastic fall in the average selling price per unit. Thus the wider exploitation of the small car was the answer to the lower income levels prevailing in this country as compared with the United States, and this was equivalent in its effect on demand to a new innovation. The result was seen in a rapid growth in the number of registered motor vehicles on British roads, from 1,524,000 in 1930 to 2,043,000 in 1935 and to 2,422,000 in 1938.[1]

The prosperity of many firms in the electrical industries was maintained by the appearance on the market of new products. Some of these had only a limited specialist market, such as electric heating for public buildings and the application of large-scale electric cooking in hotels and restaurants, but others were of a far-reaching nature. In the early thirties the telephone was at last coming into its own; the campaign of the Telephone Development Association proved decisive, for with the issue of the Bridgeman Report in 1932 the authorities wholeheartedly gave their backing.[2] The consequence was that by 1934 new telephone exchanges and extensions were in demand all over Britain. One of the leading firms, Siemens, expanded their sales of telephone exchange equipment by about 80 per cent between 1933 and 1939.[3] In other branches of the electrical equipment industry the adoption of tariffs had an expansive effect on domestic production similar to the effect of a new product, and in certain cases was, in fact, responsible for the manufacture of goods new to this country. The result of this is seen most vividly in the case of domestic electrical appliances, on which 15 per cent duties were imposed under the Import Duties Act of 1932. Home production of vacuum cleaners expanded in number from 37,550 in 1930 to 409,345 in 1935, while imports were slashed by similar proportions. Under this stimulus the ex-works value of a vacuum cleaner fell from an average of £14 in 1930 to £8 in 1934. Similarly, the output of refrigerators more than doubled in value and the production of electric cookers more than trebled between 1930 and 1935.[4] There

[1] I. Svennilson, *Growth and Stagnation in the European Economy* (1954) p. 147.

[2] *Report of the Committee of Enquiry on the Post Offices* (1932) Cmd. 4149 pp. 10–15.

[3] J. D. Scott, *Siemens Bros. 1858–1958: An Essay in the History of Industry*, (1958) p. 211.

[4] Political and Economic Planning, *Report on the Market for Household Appliances* (1945) pp. 68, 211, 231. It is important to note that the demand for these appliances was to some extent dictated by certain trends in the building industry; for example, the construction of 50,000 all-electric flats between 1931 and 1937.

was also a striking spurt forward in the domestic manufacture of electric lamps from 55·6 millions in 1930 to 98·5 millions in 1935.[1]

Electricity supply was still engaged in its first main period of expansion with the construction of the Grid, costs were still declining and net revenue increasing, and the industry proved to be immune to the depression; the number of consumers soared from 4 millions in 1930–1 to 8·6 millions in 1936–7. There were a number of elements in the industry's immunity: electricity supply in this country had specialised mainly in the electrification of domestic premises and the fact that its development was aimed at the general consumer was a stabilising influence in the depression; on the other hand, industry was making increasing use of electricity (between 1920 and 1938 the supply of electricity to industry increased fourfold from 5,000 to 20,000 million kilowatt hours per annum[2]), and this trend intensified in the recovery years; finally, there was a significant reduction in price which provided a measure of security against cyclical fluctuations.[3] In consequence, annual *per capita* consumption of electricity outside industry and transport rose from 58 kilowatt hours in 1929 to 187 in 1938. In 1932, the peak year of the construction of the National Grid, the Central Electricity Board alone incurred a capital expenditure of £32½ million—it is significant that 1932 was the year which witnessed the start of recovery. As a final example, we may take the rayon industry. In 1934, as a result of continuous technical developments and economies of scale in production, viscose yarn became cheaper than worsted for the first time, while in the same year staple fibre became cheaper than wool fibre.[4] Again the chronology is convincing; this change in relative prices exerted an immense influence on the demand for rayon, and from 1934 the development and expansion of rayon staple output went on smoothly. Over the period 1926–8 to 1936–8 total production of rayon and staple fibre taken together increased from an annual average of 17,300 tons to 65,000 tons.

If technical developments in the new industries were as pervasive as these examples suggest, it is clear that the new processes and production methods involved would have necessitated heavy investment in fixed capital. Can our hypothesis, therefore, be reconciled with the facts? In the late twenties gross fixed capital formation in manufacturing (a fairly reliable index of the volume of industrial

[1] Monopolies and Restrictive Practices Commission, *Report on the Supply of Electric Lamps* (1951) p. 187.

[2] *The Statist* (17 Dec 1938).

[3] Between 1929 and 1938 the price of electricity for household use fell from 2·86 to 1·60 pence per kilowatt hour, for industrial use from 1·00 to 0·66 pence.

[4] D. C. Hague, *Economics of Man-Made Fibres* (1957) Tables, pp. 36–7.

investment) was about 500 million dollars (at 1950 prices) in both Germany and the United Kingdom. But at the bottom of the depression while the German total had slumped to 110 million dollars that of Britain fell only to 410 million dollars, and by 1937 although capital formation in Germany was still only 760 million dollars (despite the extensive rearmament influence), it had risen to 950 million dollars in Britain. Moreover, whereas in the late twenties gross fixed capital formation in the United States was eleven times larger than in the United Kingdom, in the boom year of 1937 the American total was only four times the British.[1] This reflects not only the mildness of the depression in the United Kingdom but also the more extensive recovery. However, the statistics have an added significance: because they refer only to industrial investment and thus exclude residential building, they imply that there was a close connection between investment in industry and recovery. We may assume that the importance of the new industries in this investment was out of proportion to their share in output, and not only because of the evidence presented above in favour of new processes in those industries. For since reconstruction policies dominated all the staple industries in the thirties, although such policies called for some new investment in fixed capital, it is clear that the amounts expended were limited. Electricity is a good example of the general trend. New capital issues on behalf of private electric light and power companies were responsible for £85 million in the period 1930–8, and new capital expenditure on behalf of the entire industry amounted to £272 million between 1930 and 1937. This was equal to as much as 5 per cent of national investment.[2]

We have suggested that in the early thirties there were a number of major technical advances in almost all the new industries, and that because these meant lower prices and more desirable products this trend coupled with increased real incomes initiated economic recovery in Britain. But if growth in one of these industries was independent of growth in another, in other words, if these technical developments were random coincidences and if technical advance in one field was cancelled out by a lag in another, our case will be weakened. On the other hand, if it is possible to demonstrate that, taken together, these industries formed a new industrial sector or 'development block',[3] by which we mean the growth of a number of

[1] T. Barna, 'Investment in Industry – Has Britain Lagged?', *National Institute of Economic and Social Research*, Reprint no. 10, p. 4.

[2] *Midland Bank Monthly Review* (May–Jun 1938).

[3] An important concept elaborated by E. Dahmen, 'Technology, Innovation and International Industrial Transformation', in L. H. Dupriez (ed.), *Economic Progress* (1955) pp. 297–9.

industries whose progress is interdependent (that is, expansion in one industry tending to accompany expansion in others), then the case for the new industries as a causal influence in the recovery will be considerably reinforced. In fact, the interdependence of the new industries was very close. The extension of electricity supply was responsible not only for increased efficiency of production in other industries but also for lower costs (since electric power became progressively cheaper than traditional fuels).[1] Aluminium, for example, could be produced much more cheaply on the basis of electric power and could therefore be substituted with advantage for steel and other metals. New end-products, motor-cars, radios and domestic appliances under the same impetus could attract demand even at modest levels of income. All this had a beneficial stimulus on the economy at large: 'the innovations in the production and use of energy formed an axis around which were centred many of the most important economic developments between the two world wars'.[2] The electrical equipment industry had a similar influence in that the progress of the motor-car was to some extent dependent on efficient lighting and ignition systems. Electrification and the growth of motor transport were also closely correlated in their effects: for example, both created new conditions for the location of industries. The motor industry had connections with other new industries; the growth of the rubber industry was dependent on the development of the motor-car, and the motor industry absorbed an increasing proportion of total rubber consumption, 62 per cent in the thirties as against 44 per cent in 1924 and 38 per cent in 1912.[3] Motor manufacture created large demands for new types of machine tools, while the expansion of the electronics industry called for the emergence of 'special purpose' machines for the production of radio parts. The early growth of the plastics industry was governed by the development of the radio, electrical and (to a lesser extent) motor industries. The rayon industry was allied to the chemical industry and in fact its growth owed everything to chemical research; for example, in the twenties the commercial development of acetate rayon had been a non-starter until the organic chemists discovered the 'Duranol' dyes effective for dyeing acetate. Rayon was also tied up with the rubber tyre industry, for it was a suitable material for tyre casings. Finally, there were the close links between the new industries and housebuilding mentioned above: the building of houses meant an

[1] The number of kilowatt hours which could be bought for the price of one ton of coal for industrial purposes increased from 194 in 1929 to 301 in 1938.

[2] Svennilson, *Growth and Stagnation*, p. 102.

[3] *The Economist*, CXXI (1935) 1142.

extension of electricity supply and wiring, and new demands for domestic appliances and rubber; on the other hand, the development of the motor-car as a commuter aid transformed existing conceptions of the position of housing sites. Altogether, the new industries' expansion (and the housing boom) formed a new dynamic sector in the economy, with output growing rapidly within each industry and being stimulated further by simultaneous advances in related industries. It is evident that such a base was wide enough to initiate the upswing.

## VI

One of the aims of this article has been to show that the existing interpretations of Britain's recovery from depression in the thirties are inadequate. The role of government policy if it was positive was minor. Recent attempts to revive cheap money as the causal factor are not convincing, for there remain strong theoretical and practical grounds why cheap money could not have initiated the recovery. The housing boom was clearly important, but reasons have been suggested why it was not *by itself* decisive. Of course, on any interpretation the housing boom was a vital stimulus especially from the point of view of employment creation, and our arguments are intended more to supplement than to supplant it. We have maintained that the real cause of Britain's economic recovery was a combination of factors on both the supply and demand sides creating a vast expansion in the output of durable consumer goods (and in the products of the new industries as a whole). On the supply side, a sector of closely ranked interdependent new industries introduced technical improvements, mass production methods and new innovations with a consequent appreciable reduction in selling price, and at the same time gained economies of scale by casting off the burdens which had handicapped them in previous decades; on the demand side, increased real incomes and new consumer demands combined to make the new levels of output effective. The result was rapid expansion in this sector which had a favourable influence on the economy as a whole, directly by promoting recovery of output in certain of the basic industries and by creating employment in industry thus making for a general revival in investment expectations and a secondary rise in consumption expenditure, and indirectly through its psychological effects.

A number of interesting implications may be drawn from this explanation. In so far as recovery was due to factors on the production side, it accounts for a revival from a cyclical depression by finding the cause at the heart of the economic process itself—that is, in innovation and technical progress. To the extent that recovery was caused by demand influences, however, our interpretation suggests an autonomous theory of the trade cycle. In a depression, on the one hand workers are thrown out of employment yet on the other, because money wages do not fall as fast as prices, the real incomes of those in work tend to increase. In other words, there is a redistribution of income from the unemployed to the employed, especially in the lower income groups. The income effect of this is that instead of most workers' incomes hovering some little way above subsistence level (that is, sufficient to cover necessities, a few luxuries and a little saving), the real incomes of a large sector of workers suddenly shoot upwards. This acts as a lever of purchasing power which (as a result of high propensities to consume) is translated at an early stage into increased demands for houses, consumer durables, and so forth, and this helps to push the economy out of the slump. Although this theory requires favourable conditions on the supply side — that businessmen are able and willing to respond to signs of a revival in demand — it is in many aspects more plausible than traditional interpretations of the cycle which explain the upswing in terms of an automatic psychological influence affecting entrepreneurial decisions to invest. For in these latter theories, consumer demand starts to recover only as a secondary effect as businessmen bring people into work, and incomes do not necessarily rise until recovery is well under way. In our interpretation the force making for revival is already there at the trough of the cycle, and the increased demands for consumer goods have cumulative expansionary effects by promoting new demands for factors of production.

Because, considered *in toto*, this explanation obviously combines both endogenous and exogenous elements, the former in the sense that the redistribution of real income is inherent in the mechanics of depression and the latter in the form of the effects of new industrial developments and cost-reducing innovations on production and investment,[1] it does not support the existence of a cycle of the self-regenerating type. In fact, it is arguable that many so-called trade cycles have not been due to true endogenous cyclical influences at all, but were instead (random?) fluctuations caused by the irregular pattern and tempo of inter-industry structural change. Certainly, there are historical parallels to be drawn with the argument that

[1] Exogenous theories of this kind have had a long list of adherents from A. Spiethoff, a summary of whose work is given in a translation by J. Kahane, 'Business Cycles', *International Economic Papers*, III (1953) 75–171, to J. S. Duesenberry, *Business Cycles and Economic Growth* (1958).

places emphasis on the spurt in the new industries' development as a factor in the recovery from the 1929–32 depression. The classic example is, of course, the role played by the building of and investment in railways in the 1840s, while less notable cases include the boom in electric utility companies of 1881–3 and the bicycle boom of 1895–6. However, the recovery of the 1930s was probably generically different from these earlier upswings. Whereas the nineteenth-century examples were characterised by speculative fever, the later recovery (to the extent that it was connected with technical advances in the new industries) displayed no speculative features. There were two main reasons for this: first there was less recourse to the capital market (and hence less contact with speculative investors) due to the fact that the oligopolistic structure of these industries enabled them in general to finance the new technical developments internally; secondly, these developments were much less speculative by nature simply because they had already been successfully absorbed into technology abroad (especially in the United States), and the element of risk involved was thus appreciably reduced. Moreover the recovery of the 1930s was more soundly based and stronger, for the advances were not limited to one field (that is, a single industry) but were applied simultaneously in a number of closely interdependent industries. Finally, the essential point about the nature of this revival is that it took the shape of an increased demand for certain types of 'high income' goods, and therefore was likely to operate only in mature stages of industrialisation.

This explanation of Britain's economic recovery in the thirties also calls for a reappraisal of the depression that preceded it. If recovery was primarily due to increased expenditure on the products of the new industries, partly induced by the arrival of these industries at their mass production stage of development, we may interpret this revival as a delayed response to the need of the British economy to make basic readjustments, a need stressed by the stagnation and relatively high unemployment of the twenties. Both production and national income fell only slightly and for a short period in the early thirties compared with the situation in countries overseas, and it is thus doubtful if a cyclical slump of the normal kind occurred at all in Britain. Depression was noticeable mainly because of the heavy unemployment, but it could be argued that this unemployment was primarily of a structural rather than a cyclical nature. Indeed, it may be possible to explain the whole inter-war period in Britain in the light of inter-industry structural deficiencies. Because the economy was burdened in the twenties by the 'over-commitment' of resources to the declining staple industries, this country never fully shared in the prosperity of that decade, and this assisted her recovery from the depression for much of the investment postponed after 1925 was undertaken after 1932. Recovery came early in the thirties because the sudden surge forward of the new industries made for a partial solution of the structural problems of British industry. This suggests that the early 1930s was another climacteric in the economic development of the United Kingdom. For before this period the expansion of the new industries was held back by limited demands, delay in the application of new forms of power, the stagnating influence of old traditions and the burden of the past; while from that time these industries have grown secularly and have emerged as new staples, thereby saving the British economy from the apparently inexorable fate to which it had been condemned by the growth of coal, textile, and iron and steel industries abroad.

# 8 The New Industries Between the Wars

FROM the vantage point of the sixties, the experience of the new industries[1] in the inter-war years would seem to suggest that in their progress could be discerned the basis of a new industrial future for Britain. Strangely enough, the orthodox view on the subject gives the opposite impression: it argues that the central fact about the new industries' development in this period was not that they were growing at a rapid rate, but rather that they were growing very slowly in relation to their position in other countries. More surprisingly, this judgement has been unanimous; scarcely anyone, overtly at least, has dissented from it. It is the purpose of this article to examine certain aspects in this judgement and to suggest that the expansion of the new industries between the wars was satisfactory, and consequently it is unnecessary to talk of Britain's declining entrepreneurship, her slowness to innovate, or failure to exploit export markets to the full to account for non-existent backwardness. It is believed that the attempt to decry the role of these industries is a misunderstanding to be explained partly by the fact that its protagonists have emphasised the wrong issues and made irrelevant comparisons, but largely because they have ignored (or did not have at their disposal) important evidence in recent books and articles which conflicts with their interpretation.

## I

In volume iii of his famous work *An Economic History of Modern Britain*, Sir John Clapham drew attention to the slow growth (aluminium, electrical engineering) or absence (dyestuffs, pharmaceutical products) of new industries in Britain in the period 1887–1914.[2] Possibly here lay the seeds of the orthodox judgement discussed above. What happened was probably this: economists and historians came from reading Clapham to look at the new industries in the twenties and thirties and found ample evidence for a similar trend;

[1] New industries include not only those industries which had their origins in this century such as the motor-car, radio and rayon industries, but also those which were in existence in the last century, but did not show any marked advance until this, such as the electrical, chemical and rubber industries.

[2] Section III.

without paying too much attention to the significance of the growth potential of the new industries revealed in their absolute increase in output, they merely extrapolated Clapham's argument referring to the period before 1914 into the inter-war years. Certainly, since the thirties economists have repeatedly put forward the view that the new industries' performance could have been better. The first expression of this judgement was probably A. Loveday in *Britain and World Trade* (1931): 'Today what is really important and significant in England is not the depression of the depressed industries, but the relatively small progress made by the relatively prosperous' (p. 160). In the standard work *British Industries and their Organization* (1933), G. C. Allen took a similar standpoint, reasonable in the period of world depression, but what is surprising is that the same argument remains unmodified in the fourth edition of the book published in 1959; for example (p. 24): 'What is significant about the British position is that this country shared in an exaggerated degree in the depression which existed in some trades and failed to advance as much as the rest of the world in the industries which grew most rapidly.' The same point is reiterated again and again; it reappears, for example, in that stimulating and well-known book *Great Britain in the World Economy* (1946) by A. E. Kahn (p. 74). The unanimity of opinion is accentuated by the fact that now that economic historians have begun to take an interest in the period they have followed suit without deviation. In his *An Economic History of England 1870–1939* (1960), W. Ashworth argues (p. 335): 'What seems probable however is that, in the 'thirties, though many promising and profitable types of production were begun, a large proportion of them were not carried nearly as far as they might have been, or as far as they were in competing countries.' The other recent work by an economic historian on the period, A. J. Youngson's *The British Economy, 1920–57* (1960), throws little light on the problem at issue, although it contains comments on the new industries in the twenties (pp. 46–9) and the thirties (pp. 107–11). However, one clue which suggests that Professor Youngson perhaps shares the view that the new industries were not doing as well as they might is given when he describes the new industries in the thirties as 'uncertain and struggling' (p. 211).

The above list of authorities is an impressive one and the arguments which they use to support their view are superficially strong. Upon closer inspection, however, these arguments contain weaknesses; at this stage only two will be discussed.

Professor Ashworth (op. cit., p. 344) stated that Britain imported more of the newer type of goods (or of manufactures for which there was a growing world demand; which he is referring to is ambiguous) than she exported. Admittedly, he adds the qualification 'probably', but nevertheless the effect of this statement on someone seeking to denigrate the new industries is that it gives them another nail for the coffin. Yet Professor Ashworth does not elaborate on the products to which he is referring, nor does he support his claim with statistics. The table given below seeks to remedy this: it gives details of imports and exports for some products of the new industries in the thirties. It is easy to see that these statistics contradict his argument; it would be interesting to know which goods he had in mind, for if his statement has any validity it can only be as the exception rather than the

TABLE I

Relation between Imports and Exports of the Products of some Newer Industries in the Thirties

| | | *Imports* (*annual average*) | | *Exports* (*annual average*) | |
|---|---|---|---|---|---|
| *Product* | *Period* | *Volume (nos.)* | *Value (£)* | *Volume (nos.)* | *Value (£)* |
| Motor vehicles | 1930–8 | 10,950 | 1,666,000 | 59,400 | 8,171,000 |
| Pneumatic tyres | 1930–8 | 88,060 | 112,000 | 1,333,740 | 2,712,000 |
| Electric lamps | 1930–9 | 50,511,000 | 224,000 | 14,028,000 | 519,000 |
| Insulated electric wires and cables | 1930–8 | .. | 479,000 | .. | 2,908,000 |
| Electronic valves | 1930–9 | 1,860,400 | 216,000 | 1,292,900 | 388,000 |
| Electrical machinery and plant | 1930–8 | .. | 383,000 | .. | 3,678,000 |
| Rayon piece-goods | 1933–8 | 25 million sq. yds | .. | 64 million sq. yds | .. |
| Rayon yarn | 1933–8 | 1·8 million lb. | .. | 9·5 million lb. | .. |
| Staple fibre and rayon waste | 1931–8 | negligible | .. | 8 million lb. | .. |

rule. It is evident from the table that the only products which are compatible with his statement are electronic valves and electric lamps—and those for volume only. If value is taken as the criterion the position is reversed, for the exports of both these products were far more valuable than imports. For other products conclusions are similar; for example, in the chemical fertilizer industry imports of superphosphates fell from 114,000 tons to 14,500 tons, 1931–8.[1] Of course there were a few speciality luxury goods to which Professor Ashworth's statement applies, such as watches. British production of watches was small before 1939, exports were negligible and most of the watches in use were imported from abroad. At best, however, the argument is misleading.

[1] Monopolies Commission, *Report on the Supply of Chemical Fertilizers* (1959) p. 21.

All the critics of the new industries stress their relative failure in exports. Moreover, they argue that in so far as they did export it was to a disproportionate extent confined to Commonwealth markets where trade received a stimulus from Imperial preference. The most extreme conclusion to be drawn from this is put forward by A. E. Kahn (op. cit., p. 107), who argues that there was 'no cause for this especially great dependence . . . upon relatively sheltered markets, except competitive weakness'.

The facts are not in doubt. In many cases the proportion of the new industries' exports going to the Commonwealth was three-quarters or more. But it is very naïve to postulate a causal relationship between this fact and the existence of Imperial preference. The argument that the orientation of the export markets for new products towards the Commonwealth was due to competitive weakness is completely unproven. There is indeed a far more feasible explanation. The new goods were in general expensive consumer and capital goods, such as motor-cars and electrical equipment, which are only of use to highly civilised and wealthy societies. Demand was consequently significant only in Western Europe and the United States where it could be satisfied by domestic industry and in the rich and rapidly developing primary-producing countries, pre-eminently in the British Dominions. Apart from these, there were no other countries with a level of income per head high enough to need these products in any quantity. Of the possible suppliers for the Dominions, moreover, Britain was the strongest candidate, for in return she constituted the greatest single market for primary products; it is a commonplace that factors favouring trade in one direction frequently favour trade in another. Thus it was quite logical that the British Dominions should provide the largest market for the exports of Britain's new industries.

Kahn's over-simplification of the question was probably due to an exaggeration of the importance of Imperial preference. His argument would only make sense if the new goods were subject to the ravages of competition in foreign markets but were immune from competition in the Commonwealth because of the security that Imperial preference gave them there. But this was by no means true, for Imperial preference sometimes proved of no avail when British exporters were faced with sales drives from their competitors in Commonwealth markets. Take the Australian market for motor vehicles, for example. During the world depression Britain was easily the largest supplier of motor-cars to Australia, but by the middle thirties the United States had taken over the lead; the result was that Britain's share of Australian car imports fell from 61 to 35 per cent 1932–6. The point was that competition in the products of the new industries was at least a potential danger in Empire, Commonwealth and foreign markets alike.

## II

Those who have stressed the inferior position of the new industries of Britain relative to those in other countries with respect to technical performance have relied upon two types of evidence: comparative productivity (especially Anglo-American) figures, and facts indicating a more impressive rate of technological innovation abroad than at home. The reliability of the two will be discussed in turn.

This is no place to pay disrespect to L. Rostas's pioneering work, *Comparative Productivity in British and American Industry* (1948), but it is necessary to point out the limitations of such a study. Changes in productivity over time within a country (particularly within an industry) are far more valuable than comparisons of the productivity of industries at one point of time between countries. If productivity figures are used for the former modest purpose (once the difficulties of measurement have been surmounted), the record is impressive. The rise in output per wage-earner in British manufacturing between 1924 and 1937 was considerable, amounting to 37 per cent. In the new industries the increase was even greater: in the motor industry output per man-year doubled 1924–35, while in the rayon industry output doubled in the short period 1930–5 as a result of an increase of only 18 per cent. in the labour force.

On the other hand, productivity was low in relation to the position in the United States; in the inter-war years the compound annual rate of growth in productivity per man-hour in manufacturing in Britain was only 2·5 per cent, while in the United States the rate was 3·5 per cent. As for the new industries, in 1935 productivity in their motor industry was three times that of the British and in the radio industry four-and-a-half times as large. But the question arises: are these comparisons meaningful? The dangers involved in the use of such statistics have been urged most cogently by W. E. G. Salter in his book, *Productivity and Technical Change* (1960).

His main point in this connection is that if technical progress, and consequently productivity, were greater in the United States than in Britain, this did not imply that Britain was 'inefficient' or that her management in industry was inferior. For technical progress was more widespread in the United States because of the nature of the economic environment there as reflected in standards of obsolescence.

In many industries the best plants in Britain compared well with those of the United States; the point was that there were more out-of-date plants in this country—and the explanation of this was not lack of entrepreneurial ability and foresight in Britain but the higher standard of obsolescence in the United States. Why was this standard higher in the United States? The answer is simple—the margin of obsolescence is determined by the level of real wages, that is, 'when labour is an expensive factor of production, an economy must adjust rapidly to new methods which require less labour' (p. 71). Thus the predominance of more efficient plants in the United States and the higher productivity may have been little more than an inevitable consequence of the fact that the level of real wages there was far above that in Britain.

If this argument is sound, in those industries where technical factors necessitated a high ratio of capital to labour American productivity should not have been much greater. There was some evidence for this: in the rayon industry which was particularly capital-intensive the ratio of American to British productivity was only 1·5. The fact that productivity was still higher in the United States was to be explained by another inherent advantage she possessed—her large and stable home market. This meant that American industries were able to take especial advantage, *at an early stage*, of large-scale mass production and distribution methods. This leads on to another point made by Salter. Productivity in the British new industries was relatively low because, being 'new' and therefore of limited size, they had scarcely begun in the inter-war years to explore the possibilities of large-scale production (p. 134). He cites the case of turbo-generators in the electricity supply industry; the capacity of the first was only 1,000 kilowatts but by 1950 units of 200,000 kilowatts were in use. This is an adequate riposte to those who criticise the new industries on the ground that they did not expand quickly enough to absorb the excess labour force from the old staple industries. The growth of the motor and the electronics industries since 1945 illustrates the tendency of the new industries, with the passage of time, to expand continuously to new levels of production. This trend was observable even before 1939, for the development of the new industries was far more rapid in the thirties than in the twenties, and was comparable with growth abroad. Indeed, it has been shown in an important article, 'Investment in Industry—Has Britain lagged?', *The Banker*, April 1957, by T. Barna, that in the thirties output per head in British industry was increasing faster than in Germany (31 per cent, 1929–38 as against 12 per cent) while in the United States output per head was stagnant. In view of the fact that the United

States, at least, had had a good start in the new industries, these statistics are significant, for they suggest that Britain was rapidly catching up. It is considered that general evidence of this kind is more meaningful than comparisons of productivity between countries at the level of the individual industry.

It is obvious that without the new industries — motor-cars, rayon, household appliances, radio and electrical engineering, for example — the increase in productivity and real income would only have been very small compared with what was actually achieved in the inter-war period. It is important, therefore, to understand how the new industries were able to assert themselves in the economy. Salter presents the following analysis (pp. 148–51). As technology in the new industries improves, and as the economies of scale are realised, their costs fall, and this makes for falling relative prices, rapidly expanding output, and increasing employment. This affects declining industries by means of both demand and cost pressures. The demand pressures operate via the price-reducing activities of the new industries; as the prices of new products fall declining industries are robbed of markets, for many of these products were adequate substitutes for old ones. The replacement of cotton fabrics by rayon and of gas and coal by electricity and oil are obvious examples. The cost pressures are most clearly visible in the case of labour costs, for as the new industries expand they require increasing numbers of workers to whom they are able to offer higher wages. This affects the general level of wages and the declining industries are also affected. The result of all this is to reinforce the decline of the old industries in total output.

It is only by understanding this—the nature of structural change in the economy—that the importance of the new industries in the inter-war years can be appreciated. The new industries are sometimes criticised because their increase in output and employment did not adequately compensate for the decline of the staple industries, but the criticism is hardly fair if it is based on the fact that the substitution of new industries for old was not completed in the inter-war period. This was not achieved by 1939 because of several factors: the old industries were predominantly export industries while the new tended to be home market industries, and thus Britain was faced with the difficult and laborious problem of diverting a large part of her resources from manufacture for export to manufacture for home use; the sharp contrast in geographical location between the old industries and the new (that is, the old being heavily localised in the north while the new tended to spring up in the Home Counties and the south) seriously aggravated the transfer problem, especially with regard to labour; the post-war boom of 1919–20 and certain external factors in the twenties masked the decline of the staple industries, and it was not generally realised until the next decade that the solution of Britain's difficulties did not lie in their recovery but in the reallocation of resources to the new. Those critics who point to the heavy unemployment of the thirties or to the small scale of the newer industries as an indication of their failure are drawing attention to irrelevancies. What is important is that the new industries were a potent force making for permanent structural change in British industry, and to place an arbitrary time-limit (such as 1939) for the readjustment to be made is to ignore the difficulties involved.

The admirable theoretical analysis of the relationship between productivity and technical change by Salter suggests that if one wishes to criticise the British industries' technical performance relative to those abroad one will have to find more reliable criteria of evidence than comparative productivity statistics. It is necessary, therefore, to use other sources of information to inquire whether or not the rate of technical innovation in British new industries was low in relation to other countries. This, of course, has been done, but critics of Britain's progress have tended to ignore the evidence in favour of Britain's performance, although a mitigating factor is that most of this evidence is of very recent origin.

A common argument is that research expenditure in British industry was at a low level compared with that of the United States. This fact was pointed out more than thirty years ago by the Committee on Industry and Trade, *Factors in Industrial and Commercial Efficiency* (1927). In the period 1920–6, the research associations of the motor industry spent only £25,000, the rubber industry £28,000 and the electrical industry £50,000; whereas in the United States, in 1924 alone, the General Electric Co. spent $3 million, du Pont $2 million and General Motors $1 million (p. 319; pp. 333–4). Of course, this did not necessarily imply a low rate of technical innovation. Although the correlation between research expenditure and technical progress was probably positive, there may be some truth in the argument that the more money an organisation has to spend the more it is likely to be squandered. It must also be remembered that the activities of the research associations of individual industries were not the only research under way. The government gave some direct encouragement through various channels: state-owned laboratories, development contracts given out to selected industries, its own manufacturing facilities. Most important of all was the private developmental research of the large firm.

The most quoted example of British failure and inadaptability in this century is the dyestuffs industry. Britain had failed to develop such an industry before the First World War, and although one was stimulated by government intervention in the inter-war period (that is, under the Dyestuffs (Import Regulation) Act of 1920) British backwardness persisted; even by 1937–8 Britain was a net importer of dyestuffs by value (though not by volume since we exported 97,000 cwt compared with an import of 45,000 cwt).[1] But in other industries there was a completely different picture. For the radio industry S. G. Sturmey's *The Economic Development of Radio* (1958) is a testimony to the constant stream of innovations introduced in Britain. The industry took up many technical improvements in the inter-war years such as automatic volume control, press-button tuning, multiple wave bands, static reducing devices, and better calibration of dials; portable radio sets and car radios were on the market from 1933 (pp. 178–9). As a separately housed unit, the Rice–Kellog moving coil loudspeaker was on the British market before it reached the American (p. 169). In an article in *Lloyds Bank Review*, October 1957, 'Science and Industry', T. Wilson points out the interesting fact that although the United States was ahead in the work on the television camera Britain had the first fully electronic television service in the world. Rapid technological change also showed itself in techniques of production: in the thirties most of the leading set makers adopted line production methods, in many cases with endless belt conveyors. On the debit side, Sturmey states that technical advance in receiving sets was faster in America before 1939, and that much of the progress recorded here was based on communicated American patents. This was also the case in several other related industries. For example, in the production of electric lamps although Britain was not responsible for any major development, leading British manufacturers were able to acquire United Kingdom patent rights under a series of agreements with the principal American and German companies; from 1912 British-Thomson-Houston, G.E.C. and Siemens had a patents pool. This method of taking up technical advances was not necessarily harmful, for the disadvantages of being the first with an innovation may in some cases outweigh the advantages. There was something to be said for letting other countries make the running and for us to follow, to profit from the mistakes of others and to avoid the risks of investment in research —in other words, to reverse our role of the Industrial Revolution and to allow other countries to pay the penalties of industrial pioneering. As Professor Ashworth reminds us, 'the adoption of techni-

[1] W. B. Reddaway, 'The Chemical Industry' in D. L. Burn (ed.), *The Structure of Industry*, I (1958) 247.

cal advances which originated abroad would nevertheless increase the efficiency of production at home' (op. cit., p. 415).

In other industries, too, Britain's performance seemed adequate. In the motor industry, the conclusion of the P.E.P.'s *Report on Motor Vehicles* (1950) is that technical development was largely confined to the post-1945 era (p. 55), but in fact there were continuous improvements in the inter-war period: better carburettors, more efficient brakes and combustion chambers, automatic voltage control in electrical equipment, thermostatic control of cooling systems, group lubrication, windscreen wipers, self-starters; besides the more obvious developments such as the diesel engine, pneumatic tyres, and generally better coachwork design. In the plastics branch of the chemical industry, as a short but interesting article by P. Morgan, 'The Plastics Industry, 1958', *National Provincial Bank Review*, February 1958, reveals, there were significant technical advances in spite of the fact that the output of plastics was less than 30,000 tons in 1939. The use of cellulose acetate as an injection-moulding material began in the late twenties for producing thimbles, golf tees and small radio components. Resin M (the forerunner of Perspex) was being produced in the United Kingdom from 1937. In 1933 Britain was responsible for one development which today seems of almost revolutionary importance, the discovery of polythene by I.C.I.—just one of the many results of the research on polyvinyl compounds in the thirties; by 1939 the first polythene unit had begun production. Finally, in electricity, Britain was the first with the idea of electrical heating for public buildings.

On this question of the tempo of technical innovation there is a danger in assuming that the conditions operating before 1914 continued in the inter-war period. There is little doubt that in the quarter-century before 1914, as a generalisation, the rate of technological change in Britain was slowing down—in some of the newer industries as well as in the old (although S. B. Saul in the article mentioned below warns against overestimating this). Take, for example, the following conclusion on the electric lamp industry: 'The British manufacturers of incandescent lamps had dropped far behind the Germans by 1900, as indeed had all the British electrical industries. . . . The obstacles . . . which largely persisted from 1897 to 1912 were apathy, limited ability and a lack of specialisation. . . . There was not a single lamp-research laboratory in Great Britain during all that time, and all important innovations were imported from Germany, Austria and the United States.'[1] It is very easy to extend this argu-

[1] A. A. Bright, *The Electric Lamp Industry: Technical Change and Economic Development from 1888 to 1947* (1949) pp. 161–2.

ment into the inter-war period, but it would be a false step of inquiry. In 1914 many countries of the world were enthusiastically expending the energies of industrial youth, while Britain appeared to be settling down to a restful and, perhaps, complacent middle age. Yet, did this necessarily mean that in the inter-war years she would announce her retirement?

To predict this from pre-1914 experience was to disregard the course of events. The First World War, of course, intervened and this proved a stimulus to rejuvenation. Whether the economic consequences of war are beneficial or not is still a matter for dispute, but it would be difficult to overlook the boost given by this war to the new industries. This is brought out in the famous article by R. S. Sayers, 'The Springs of Technical Progress, 1919–39', *Economic Journal*, June 1950. His view that the effect of the war was 'to accelerate rather than to innovate development' (p. 278) is probably substantially correct, but (as some of the following examples illustrate) is not applicable to every case. Moreover, the examples that Professor Sayers cites — the aircraft, the motor lorry, the rise of automatic welding and the development of certain plastics — are mainly the obvious ones. Large-scale production of valves grew up in response to the demands of the armed forces for large quantities for radio communication, and the commercial production of valves and radio sets was under way as early as 1919–20. The development of cellulose acetate rayon, which by 1930 accounted for 20 per cent of the world's rayon output, originated in research at a government factory during the war on the use of cellulose dopes for strengthening aircraft wings. It was the realisation that dye-making plant is rapidly adaptable to the requirements of chemical warfare which induced the government to give a grant of £2 million for the development of the industry in 1918, and to pass legislation regulating imports in 1920. Similarly, military demand factors were at work in aluminium and alloys research, in insulated cable production and in petroleum chemistry.

The trouble with evidence of this kind, however, is that it is too general and unsystematic. It is very easy to answer an accusation of technical backwardness with an example of technical progress in another industry or even in the same industry. What is required is a more detailed examination of the many factors governing the rate of innovation in each industry. In his article, 'The American Impact upon British Industry, 1895–1914', *Business History*, December 1960, S. B. Saul examines the effect of American competition in stimulating individual firms in certain sections of the engineering industry to adopt technical improvements and to introduce innovations during the two decades before the First World War. Until we get more articles of this type on the new industries in the interwar years, the problem of whether or not their rate of innovation was lower than it might have been is likely to receive no clear solution.

Another problem which deserves more attention is that posed by Salter (op. cit., p. 24) of how far the application of new techniques is due to the acquisition of new knowledge and how far it is attributable to changed factor prices. For if in certain industries Britain was behind in technical innovations in the inter-war period this was not necessarily a sign of lack of initiative, but could have been explained by the fact that it would have been uneconomical to introduce them. For example, because of the heavy unemployment on the one hand and the falling off in the rate of saving with a consequent scarcity of capital on the other, Britain's supplies of labour were plentiful relative to her supplies of investment and this militated against the rapid adoption of new techniques. Thus, *if* Britain was backward technically this may have been a reflection, not of the failure of applied science, but of the economic conditions of the time.

What we really need to know, of course, is how the many factors at issue affected the decisions of the individual entrepreneur. This can be observed not by referring to industries, but only by studying the individual firm—hence the importance of business histories. The following two examples are concerned with new industries: J. D. Scott, *Siemens Brothers, 1858–1958: An Essay in the History of Industry* (1958), and C. Wilson and W. Reader, *Men and Machines, A History of D. Napier and Sons, Engineers, Ltd., 1808–1958* (1958). Both shed light on how individual firms faced the problems of technological innovation.

Napier & Sons, by the first decade of this century, was a small specialist car firm. At the end of the First World War the firm realised that the future lay with moderately priced cars turned out by large manufacturers. The company therefore changed over to the production of aero engines; in 1919, 300 Lion engines were put into production in spite of the fact that there were no orders for them (pp. 110–11). This suggested that the outlook of the management (if foolhardy) was at least progressive. However, in the twenties the policy paid off; in the period 1924–35 seventy-three types of British aircraft had Napier engines, and in 1928 and 1929 world air-speeds records were set up with planes running on Napier engines. The firm did not figure prominently in the export trade, but there was a simple explanation for this—several of its engine designs were on the Secret List. On the other hand, the authors point out that although the firm was very progressive technically, it was not so commercially (p. 120).

This distinction is of general importance. For it may possibly be argued that Britain's failings were not due to tardiness in the application of new techniques or in scientific research, but to conservatism in the commercial field. British businessmen tended to be sceptical about the value of market forecasting, paid insufficient attention to the diversity of the demands of consumers (especially those abroad), and relied on rule-of-thumb and outmoded methods in sales policies.

Siemens was a much larger firm, originating as cable-makers but later branching out into other sections of the electrical industry. By the middle thirties it was possible to speak of a team or even of a research and development organisation consisting of a dozen or more workers at their branch in Preston (which specialised in lamp production). The firm represents an example of how a manufacturer can do well without making the basic innovations. In 1918 the British cable had a 'world-wide reputation' and was regarded as a sort of prize exhibit, yet all the important technical advances between the wars came from abroad. In spite of this, the methods adopted by Siemens, the leading firm, satisfied their customers. In the field of telephone cables, for example, the G.P.O. was satisfied with the 'minor improvements in the regularity of the product' (p. 139). In contrast with Napier, therefore, this firm was not very go-ahead in development, but the scale of the development undertaken reflected the commercial needs of the time in the sense that their customers were content with it. If this was 'backwardness' it did not prevent Siemens from expanding their exports in the late thirties, when the general trend was for international trade to decline. Just as Napier & Sons extended the range of their products by turning to aero engines, so Siemens in the years before the First World War began to manufacture electric locomotives, motors for rolling mills, batteries, telegraph and telephone line material, electrical machinery for use in ships, wireless telegraphy, 'fringe equipment' for the telephone industry, and lamps; the production of these was expanded considerably between the wars, especially in the case of automatic telephone exchanges and electric lamps (pp. 196–204). This willingness of firms to branch out into new lines was in fact typical of the new industries, and because it almost invariably involved new plant and sometimes new processes and techniques of production this characteristic indicates the progressive attitude of these industries towards technical change. In the twenties Dunlop experienced a similar widening of the scope of activities. In 1925 they turned to producing footwear, clothing, belting and rubber hose; in the next decade other products involving the use of latex were added to their range.

The evidence given in these two histories suggests that it is dangerous to generalise about the technological bankruptcy of British industry. But two swallows do not make a summer, and far more business histories of a reputable standard are required before any firm conclusion may be drawn. The need for them is important, for the individual firm has been responsible for many, perhaps the majority of, technical developments. For example, Courtaulds, the rayon firm, undertook an intensive development of staple fibre in the inter-war period. This culminated in the thirties in the establishment of two experimental and demonstration mills, the most important of which, the Arrow Mill at Rochdale, proved to Lancashire cotton manufacturers that staple fibre could be used extensively in Lancashire cotton mills. In the rubber industry, Dunlop's research was very successful: they were first in the field with aeroplane tyres (1910), bullet-proof tyres (1917) and giant pneumatic tyres (1921). They had been the first to use carbon black in the tyre tread, and in the inter-war years experimented in the use of rayon for casing.

## III

An important source of material on the new industries for this period is the reports of the Monopolies and Restrictive Practices Commission (now the Monopolies Commission). Extensively used, of course, for investigation into monopoly problems, it is not often realised that they are a mine of information on the new industries, containing not only details of amalgamations and trade associations, but also general histories of the industries concerned and statistics of prices, output, and imports and exports. A list of the reports concerned with newer industries is given below.[1] A large part of the information given in these reports is naturally about trade associations and amalgamation, and it is on these aspects that our attention will be concentrated.

In most cases the trade associations were formed in response to increasing foreign competition in the home market. The Tyre Manufacturers' Conference, set up in 1929, was an attempt to override the instability of trading conditions which had been a feature

[1] In the electrical industries, *Report on the Supply of Electric Lamps* (1951), *Report on the Supply of Insulated Electric Wires and Cables* (1952), *Report on the Supply of Electronic Valves and Cathode Ray Tubes* (1956) and *Report on the Supply and Export of Electrical and Allied Machinery and Plant* (1957); in the pharmaceutical industry, *Report on the Supply of Insulin* (1952); in the chemical industry, *Report on the Supply of Certain Industrial and Medical Gases* (1956) and *Report on the Supply of Chemical Fertilizers* (1959); and in other industries, *Report on the Supply and Export of Pneumatic Tyres* (1955) and *Report on the Supply of Standard Metal Windows and Doors* (1956).

of the twenties. Its main purpose was to maintain prices, but it did not always succeed; in times of depression severe competition again became the rule, and company losses were great. The initiative in the Electric Lamp Manufacturers' Association, a reconstitution in 1933 of the former body of 1919, was taken by G.E.C. and A.E.I.; the members sought to meet by higher quality and by exclusive agreements with distributors the price competition of both imported lamps, especially Japanese, and lamps produced by independent British manufacturers. The B.V.A. (British Radio Valve Manufacturers' Association), constituted in 1926, also had to struggle to maintain agreed list prices in the face of vigorous competition from abroad. The Cable Makers' Association had been formed as early as 1899 with the aim of reducing costs of production by maximum efficiency. By 1931, however, the industry was bedevilled by excess capacity; the Association tried to meet this by promoting rationalisation and amalgamation. The National Sulphuric Acid Association was established in 1919 to deal with surplus capacity of acid production, the result of enormous expansion during the First World War to cater for the needs of the explosives industry. Also in 1919 the Fertiliser Manufacturers' Association had been formed: its activities were extensive, including internal discussions on prices and attempts to counter the situation created by the sale of cheap foreign superphosphate in Britain. In 1921 the Association acquired a controlling interest in a Belgium company, Superphosphates Standaert, and agreements were made with foreign firms in Holland, Belgium and France between 1923 and 1930, under which these firms consented to restrict their exports to the United Kingdom to agreed quotas. There was a severe depression in the production of metal windows in the early thirties, and attempts to standardise the commodity broke down. Consequently, the Metal Window Association was set up in 1933 and by 1939 had restored the industry to full prosperity; in 1937, for example, sales increased by 36 per cent although the number of houses built increased by only 26 per cent.

The amalgamation movement was also widespread throughout the new industries. In the electrical industry (with particular reference to the valve section) Associated Electrical Industries was formed in 1928 and the company acquired all the ordinary shares of Edison, British-Thomson-Houston and Metropolitan Vickers. This was partly responsible for the great extension of British valve production from $5\frac{1}{2}$ million to 11 million, 1930–5. In the rubber tyre industry Dunlop expanded rapidly during and after the First World War, mainly as a result of internal development rather than of absorption. After 1927, however, the firm followed a policy of controlling distributive outlets; for example, a majority interest was obtained in the firm of C. H. Brittain of Stoke. In 1938 the company began retreading with the acquisition of the Regent Tyre and Rubber Co. In the chemical fertiliser industry in 1928 I.C.I. gained control of a number of Scottish companies and in 1929 three East Anglian producers amalgamated to form Fisons; in the next ten years Fisons acquired twenty-four fertiliser companies and formed five new ones which were registered as subsidiaries. The British Oxygen Company absorbed its greatest rival, the Allen-Liversidge interests, in 1930, and thereafter followed a policy of acquisition at any cost. For example, it attempted to move into south-west England and South Wales by driving out and taking over the Cornish firm of T. W. Ward Ltd, a manœuvre which was finally successful in 1944. Amalgamations and concentration were not, of course, limited to the new industries examined by the Monopolies Commission; other examples included Courtaulds in rayon, and Joseph Lucas and the Chloride Electrical Storage Company in the electrical equipment branch of the motor industry.

Although this trend towards monopoly and restrictive agreements could also be observed in the old staple industries, it was more prevalent in the new. The question arises whether the tendency to concentration in the new industries was due to the endogenous development of capitalism there or whether it was an exogenous effect of the prevailing economic situation during their period of growth, by which is meant the general depression of the inter-war years. While the depression undoubtedly presented a further incentive to cartelisation, it seems clear that this grew up in the new industries out of their normal course of development. This is substantiated by the fact that in the post-war era of prosperity the trend continued and was intensified, except where and until the Monopolies Commission and the Restrictive Practices Court intervened. But history, too, suggests reasons why this was so. Kahn (op. cit., p. 81) contrasts the situation in the old industries, where the psychology was defensive, with the new, where it was aggressive; in his view, the incentive to monopoly profits was strong simply because the new industries were not hampered by having developed into small, vigorously competing units. A. F. Lucas (in the standard work on industrial reorganisation between the wars, *Industrial Reconstruction and the Control of Competition* (1937), p. 40) argues that the tendency for the new industries to locate themselves in the newer industrial areas of the south and the Midlands struck a double blow at the competitive system. In the first place, it contributed to the general flux of industry which dislodged the British manufacturer from his old ways: secondly, it meant the rise of a group of new producers who were untarnished by the traditions of individualistic enterprise which had from the beginning characterised the staple industries. He concludes that it was this factor, above all, which led to the new industries' early denial of the philosophy of free competition. Both these arguments, while difficult to prove, seem plausible. Today, under the influence of the Restrictive Practices Act, it is too easy to condemn this trend towards monopoly and trade associations; but in the conditions of the inter-war period it was quite reasonable for one of the new industries' representatives to maintain: 'The day of the fixed price has come, and such a development must be considered as a real condition of social and economic progress.'[1]

The term 'fixed price' used in reference to the new industries between the wars may be misleading. Attempts to fix prices, whether by a monopolistic producer or a trade association, were made only at a given level of production—in other words, in the short run. In the longer run, the inter-war years witnessed a continuous reduction in price of all products of the new industries under the influence of technical progress and increasing economies of scale. The price index of motor-cars fell from 100 in 1913 to 51 in 1924 and 42 in 1936. In the electricity supply industry unit revenue derived by authorised undertakings from sales of energy to consumers was more than halved between 1921–2 and 1935–6. In the period 1923–38 the price of rayon viscose yarn fell from 9*s* to 2*s* 7½*d* per lb., and in the thirties the price of viscose staple fibre fell from 3*s* to 10*d* per lb. The retail prices of electric filament lamps set by E.L.M.A. fell by about a third, 1930–8. In the pharmaceutical industry the price of insulin fell from 25*s* to 1*s* 6*d* for a standard pack between 1923 and 1935. Finally, in spite of the criticisms of B.O.C.'s price policies, the average price of industrial oxygen by 1939 was less than half what it had been at the outset of the inter-war period. In many cases these price reductions were achieved only at the expense of the profits of large firms and the livelihood of smaller ones. The solution to the paradox of price-fixing agreements and constant price reduction is as follows: the growth of industry is always governed by demand conditions, but in the newer industries where many of the products were 'high-income' goods the influence of demand conditions was even stronger because demand for these goods was very elastic; without technical efficiency and its result in the market, a long-term and significant fall in price, therefore, the new industries simply would not have expanded at all; on the other hand, manufacturers were anxious to

[1] British Electrical and Allied Manufacturers' Association, *Combines and Trusts in the Electrical Industry* (1930) p. 22.

maintain prices in the short run. Thus, the extensive price reductions in the new industries were not the consequence of depression but a necessary condition of growth.

Attention was drawn above to Saul's article which shows how American competition in the period before 1914 stimulated British industries to introduce innovations and adopt new methods. The process was taken a step further, particularly in the inter-war years, when Americans actually began to invest in British manufacturing industry and to establish subsidiaries here of firms in the United States. The details of this are told in J. H. Dunning, *American Investment in British Manufacturing Industry* (1958). What is really noticeable about this investment was its concentration on the new industries. In the motor industry Ford and Vauxhall, in tyre production Goodyear and Firestone, in the electrical industry Associated Electrical Industries (in which the United States holding varied from 25 per cent to 40 per cent): these are obvious examples, but the range was wider. American investments in the United Kingdom were also in telephones, chemicals, gramophones, pharmaceutical products, machinery and musical instruments. In the thirties American firms established branches in those newer industries in the development of which Britain was possibly falling behind, such as the Hoover Company (1931) in domestic electrical appliances and the Remington Rand Company (1937) in office equipment. Indeed, the United States was responsible for introducing many new methods and innovations into this country. The effect of the establishment of subsidiaries of Bristol Instruments Company in industrial instruments and of Frigidaire and York Shipley in refrigeration was to stimulate British firms to expand in the same field (p. 46).

What was the significance of this development? The impetus was strengthened by tariff protection, and United States subsidiaries were often intended as a means of surmounting tariff barriers. But the causes of the development are not so important as its consequences. Opposition was raised to American investment by firms in the electrical and rubber industries, and this was manifested in stipulations limiting American holdings of shares and voting rights. Yet United States investment in British industry did not necessarily imply a condemnation of British industrial achievements and in fact had two important beneficial results. In the first place, American capital helped to utilise resources previously unemployed; 1919–39, 140 new enterprises were set up employing 60,000 workers (p. 298). Secondly, the fact that most of the American investment was in new industries and also contributed to the further expansion of British firms in these industries was a great advantage because it speeded up the adjustments in the structure of British industry necessary for highly industrialised countries, that is, the transition from old staple industries to the production of newer highly processed goods.

## IV

Those who decry the role of the new industries in the inter-war economy stress their export position. Their argument is: first, that the new industries exported a far smaller proportion of their output than the older staple industries, and that this was an unhealthy development in view of Britain's overall balance of payments difficulties; secondly, that most of their exports went to protected Commonwealth markets; thirdly, that the new industries of Britain fared less well in the export markets than those of her competitors. Superficially, the factual basis in support of these arguments is strong, but there is a great danger in interpreting the meaning of these facts.

In the thirties 17 per cent of the number of motor vehicles produced were exported; in rayon the proportion was smaller, 10 per cent of yarn being exported and little more than 6 per cent of piece-goods; sales abroad in the electronics industry amounted to less than 10 per cent of gross output. This formed a strong contrast with the staple industries, where in the most extreme case, cotton piece-goods, almost 90 per cent of output had been exported before 1913 and even in the thirties the percentage of production exported varied between 50 per cent and 60 per cent. The proportion of output exported by the other staple industries was rather less but the contrast was still noticeable. There were a number of sensible reasons to account for this. The new industries, with huge resources of capital and technical knowledge, adopted the latest methods of large-scale organisation and in fact spread round the world far more rapidly than had the old staple industries. This made for a more balanced distribution of new industrial production between countries, and consequently export markets were shared out more evenly. The prevalence of international agreements in these industries made direct inroads into exports, for a common feature in these agreements was the promise to 'reserve' to each member his home market. Moreover, as I. Svennilson points out in *Growth and Stagnation in the European Economy* (1954), the main developments of the period affecting manufacturing were domestic (p. 220). The development of electric power, the extension of the use of motor vehicles and increased town and surburban building were greater demand forces on the new industries than any operating abroad. Another point was that Britain shared in the common objective at this time—what

Svennilson calls a 'self-sufficiency boom': in face of falling exports, the accepted policy was to increase tariff protection and attempt to reduce the volume of imported manufactures. In such an international atmosphere the new industries were bound to look more to the home market, just as in the nineteenth century the staple industries, favoured by an insatiable world demand, had expanded mainly by catering for markets overseas. Indeed, it is possible to argue that the home market orientation of the new industries was a source of stability in a period of declining international trade. Finally, to blame the new industries for the balance of payments difficulties of the inter-war years is a distortion of the facts. The problem of the twenties was largely the result of Britain's attempt to retain her position as the world's leading creditor by lending abroad, and when the balance of payments again became negative after 1935 the main factor responsible was increased imports in response to rearmament demand.

The second point of issue, that of the concentration of the new industries' exports upon Commonwealth markets, has been discussed earlier in this article. One observation only will be made here. It is easy to exaggerate the extent of this concentration if certain industries alone are chosen for illustration. In the motor industry, for example, of sales abroad during the inter-war period (apart from during the depression when Empire purchasing power was severely reduced) about 85 per cent went to the Commonwealth. But taking the new industries as a whole (Kahn's classification) only 54·5 per cent of their exports in 1929 went to the Commonwealth, and it is likely that this was increased only slightly as a result of the Ottawa agreements. Moreover, it must be remembered that a high proportion (about 40 per cent in 1929) of staple exports went to the Commonwealth too.

The real attack on the export capabilities of Britain's new industries has been made in relation to their counterparts abroad and in the light of the changing structure of world trade. The best-known example of British deficiency in this respect is that illustrated by a German inquiry (*Der Deutsche Aussenhandel unter der Einwirkung weltwirtschaftlicher Strukturwandlungen* (1932), vol. ii, p. 156, quoted widely by E. Staley, *World Economic Development* (1944), A. J. Brown, *Applied Economics* (1947), W. A. Lewis, 'The Prospect before Us', *Manchester School*, May 1948, and G. C. Allen, op. cit.). This shows that, of a sample covering 80 per cent of British exports (by commodities), 42 per cent of our exports in 1929 were of goods which had increased less than 75 per cent, 1913–29, while only 4·3 per cent were of goods in which world trade had increased more than 150 per cent; in contrast, 28·6 per cent of United States exports were in the latter category. A. Loveday (op. cit.) draws similar conclusions from the new industries' performance in export markets in the twenties. In the period 1925–8 the Netherlands increased her exports of wireless apparatus by £1·75 million, whereas British exports declined; in gramophones and records, while British exports increased from £1·44 million to £2·78 million, United States exports soared from £830,000 to £2·26 million (pp. 168–70). These statistics are of doubtful value, for four years is too short a time for any trends to emerge. More important is the conclusion of the British Economic Mission to the Argentine (quoted by Loveday) that while Britain held on to her position in certain trades, in the newer categories — for example, aviation, road construction and motor transport — she had been completely outdistanced. It is probable, however, that all this evidence relating to the twenties has been given more attention than it deserves. If the new industries were still infant industries in the inter-war period, as is suggested here, it may be conceded that their development in the twenties was slow and argued instead that their achievements between the wars were centred in the thirties. That their export performance by 1929 was limited was only to be expected.

Of more relevance to this question are the statistics given by Svennilson and by H. Tyszynski, 'World Trade in Manufactured Commodities, 1899–1950', *Manchester School*, September 1951, especially as they cover a wider period. Tyszynski points out that Britain's share of world trade in manufactures fell from 29·9 per cent in 1913 to 22·4 per cent in 1937, and argues that because this fall would not have been as great if Britain had kept the same proportion of her exports in the old staple industries throughout this period the cause of the decline was not so much changes in the structure of world trade but in her capacity to compete. The indictment is not as well founded as appears on first sight, for in reference to the structure of trade the proportion of British trade in the expanding groups increased from 17·7 per cent to 31·2 per cent, 1899–1937, while world trade in this group increased from 13·4 per cent to 34·8 per cent (pp. 289–92). Thus, in spite of losses in her competitive position Britain did not lag behind the shifts in the structure of world trade to any great extent. This is supported by similar evidence in Svennilson (op. cit., Tables, pp. 294–5). He shows that the categories 'Machinery' and 'Transport Equipment' were the expanding ones in world trade. The share of these in British exports increased from 15·9 per cent in 1913 to 19·5 per cent in 1928 and 31·6 per cent in 1938 at the expense of textiles, which fell from 48·2 per cent to 44·9 per cent and 28·5 per cent of exports at the above respective dates—and this change signified a successful adjustment in the structure of Britain's export trade. A. J. Brown in *Industrialisation and Trade: The Changing World Pattern and the Position of Britain* (1943) presented statistics showing that the exports of machinery, electrical appliances, vehicles, and chemicals increased in relation to total exports from 14 per cent to 40 per cent, 1910–38 (p. 60). What are the implications of this? In the first place, the argument that Britain failed to compensate for the fall in staple exports by the expansion of exports of the newer industries is overstated. Secondly, the cause of Britain's decline in world trade and her *apparent* sluggishness in exporting new products in relation to her best competitors and her former predominant station is to be found in her competitive position; by this one means not an absolute deterioration in the power of individual industries to compete effectively in world markets, but a change in international economic relationships unfavourable to Britain consequent upon the the industrialisation of new countries and the appearance of new competitors. She was no longer a giant among pygmies, but one of many. This did not mean failure, only the inevitable adjustment of British industry to its proper place in the modern world.

In fact, in certain of the new industries Britain was keeping in advance of their importance in world trade. In transport equipment (including motor vehicles) British exports expanded from £7·6 million in 1913 to £29·6 million in 1937, while its share in world trade rose from 3·3 per cent to only 9·4 per cent in the same period; similarly for electrical goods Britain's exports rose from £7·7 million to £19·1 million in the same period while the share of electrical goods in world trade increased from 2·4 per cent to 4·7 per cent (Tyszynski, loc. cit., pp. 278–83).

The argument that Britain was falling further and further behind in the development of the new industries, particularly with regard to overseas trade, makes nonsense when one looks at their post-war position. For example, by 1956 50 per cent of the output of motor-cars were exported and the proportion of production sent abroad in electronics rose from 8 per cent to 15 per cent, 1938–56. Although it was probable that conditions after the Second World War were especially favourable for British exports of those products, nevertheless this dramatic transformation does not tally with usual interpretation of the new industries' experience between the wars.

If Britain appeared to be lagging slightly behind, a possible explanation is that the new industries were infant industries in the inter-war years, and that this lag was merely a symptom of growing pains. That the government regarded them as such is suggested by the fact that almost all the new industries had received some form of tariff protection before the fundamental change in British commercial policy. The adjustment was slow but, as the post-war record shows, successful. The reasons for the slow pace of development are easy to find. Britain had come to world supremacy as the producer of common consumer goods. The products of the new industries were of a different nature—usually either equipment for production and communications such as machinery, cars and communication devices or 'high-income' goods such as radios and gramophones. These were mainly capital goods industries, and it was more difficult for Britain to make the change. Britain also suffered from a lack of the increasingly important cheap hydroelectric power, petroleum and non-ferrous metals. The United States, on the other hand, was better equipped because of an environment which made for the smooth application of a rapidly progressing technology to industry and because of a highly developed home market which encouraged methods of quantity production at low unit cost. Svennilson makes an important point which throws light on Britain's slow adjustment when he suggests (p. 116) that the prevalence of industrial areas 'based on the direct use of coal, coke and gas' delayed the extension of electric power on which successful production in many of the new industries depended. Another factor of significance (Table, p. 241) is that Britain was the most industrialised country, 90 per cent of the occupied population in 1920 being employed outside agriculture, as against 58·3 per cent for Europe as a whole. This perhaps made the transition more difficult for Britain, for it is a reasonable hypothesis that the labour transfer problem between old industries and new is aggravated the higher the proportion of manpower already committed to the old manufacturing industries, and is alleviated when semi-skilled workers for the new may be recruited from agriculture.

One final point—was it necessarily a criticism of the new industries that their export position was not as strong as that of her best competitors abroad? It is too readily assumed that exports are the sole criterion of industrial achievement. Keynes once said that he saw no special virtue in exports for their own sake which were not required to pay for imports. As A. J. Brown points out (*Industrialisation and Trade*, p. 64) exports are not so important if imported goods, for which adequate substitutes can be produced at home at little more than the import prices, are replaced by home-produced goods, in such groups as iron and steel goods, cutlery, instruments, machinery, vehicles and electrical goods. In fact, in the inter-war period the imports of these goods tended to fall as home production of them increased. Moreover, as Professor Ashworth suggests (op. cit., p. 322), the new products were far more highly processed than the old and consequently the imports of raw materials were likely to grow less proportionately than the production of new goods, and there was thus possibly less need for expansion in exports. Indeed, the case that the new industries should have exported more than they did between the wars has never been proved.

## V

This article in its assessment of recent evidence on the new industries has been able to concentrate on only a few aspects of their development. The solutions offered to the problems raised have not been conclusive; what has been demonstrated, it is hoped, is that the traditional view has been too easily accepted. To take a poor view of the new industries' position was possible more than thirty years ago under the shadow of unemployment and general depression, but it is scarcely feasible now that these former 'new' industries have developed into the staple industries of modern Britain. Because a larger proportion of her resources was involved in the old basic industries of the nineteenth century, Britain's newer industries were later in maturing than those of, say, the United States. It is quite possible, therefore, that even in the inter-war period these industries were still fundamentally infant industries which had not yet benefited from full economies of scale, and on this view the difficulties they incurred can be passed off as inevitable teething troubles. This interpretation, simple though it may be, at least allows one to make sense of the inter-war and post-war experience taken together.

There are a number of unsolved questions hardly touched upon here which will have to be answered before a complete assessment of the new industries' place in the inter-war economy can be made. Did the protection of the new industries act as a deterrent (or perhaps as a stimulus) to technological advance? How great a handicap on the shift to new industries was the fact that Britain was more deeply involved in the fortunes of the old staple industries than her competitors? Was government intervention an obstacle or an aid to development; in other words, did the benefits of tariff protection and the extensive influence of public corporations on certain of the new industries outweigh the restrictions on road transport, the deadweight of the tax-licensing system for motor vehicles and the burden on small producers of the excise duty on rayon yarn? How far did the misplaced faith in the capacity of the old industries to revive in the twenties delay investment in the new? In view of the fact that the new industries generally had a high ratio of capital to labour, was the heavy unemployment of the inter-war years a factor limiting their expansion—because some of the older industries employed more workers per unit of capital invested? As there were obvious links between the new industries (motor-cars and rubber tyres, motor-cars and electrical equipment, plastics and radio parts, rayon and chemicals), how far was the fate of one industry bound up with that of another? Most important of all perhaps, what effect did the Second World War have on the new industries, and how many of the elements in their post-war expansion could be discerned before 1939? The answers to these questions may well be different for each industry. There is no *a priori* reason why all the new industries should have done well, or all done badly. Indeed, it is more likely that their fortunes were varied and their expansion was uneven. What is maintained here, however, is that if a generalisation must be made on the state of Britain's new industries between the wars, the judgement which maintains that they were doing as well as might be expected and were fighting to hold a respectable position in a competitive world is far more realistic and plausible than that which holds that they were falling behind.

# SECTION C

# Guide to Statistical Sources

OVER the past two decades a large amount of statistical data has been assembled on various aspects of the British economy over the past hundred years. In particular, there has been a steady stream of new information on income, capital formation, industrial production, employment and consumers' expenditure. These statistics should be used with caution, however. There are still significant gaps in the basic series and often two or more series are needed to span our period. Many of them are compiled from tentative estimates and extrapolations from benchmark years. Thus continuous time series compiled on the same basis do not exist for all components of the economy. This is particularly the case with industrial productivity, the capital stock and exports. For example, two series are available on productivity, one covering the period to 1914 based on the Hoffmann production index, and the other for the years 1920–38 which is derived from Lomax's new index of production. Since the coverage and weighting of these are different it is impossible to link them together satisfactorily. The further one goes back in time the less reliable the data become, though it should be noted that the estimates for the war and early post-war years (1914–21) are also unreliable. For the inter-war years estimates are more accurate since it was in this period that official statistical reporting improved both in quantity and quality.

It is important then that the student refers to the original publications in order to ascertain on what basis the calculations are made, exactly what they refer to, and what margins of error are involved. The tentative nature of many of the estimates should not preclude their use provided one is aware of their defects and limitations. Here it is not possible to outline the scope, methods of compilation and limitations of each individual series. Many of them have in fact been conveniently brought together and summarised in two recent publications: B. R. Mitchell and P. Deane, *Abstract of British Historical Statistics* (1962) and London and Cambridge Economic Service, *The British Economy: Key Statistics, 1900–1966* (1967). Both of these provide very useful statistical guides for the student of economic history. The comments below, therefore, are intended merely to draw the student's attention to the most recent work on a number of major economic indicators.

## National Income and Expenditure

The most recent series on national income, measured from the income and expenditure sides of the account, is that by C. H. Feinstein, 'National Income and Expenditure of the United Kingdom, 1870–1963', *London and Cambridge Economic Bulletin*, L (1964). This provides a continuous series for the period 1870 through to 1963 measured in current prices. Real income per head can easily be obtained by deflating the figures with a cost of living index and dividing through by total population. These estimates are an extension of work originally published in an earlier article, 'Income and Investment in the United Kingdom, 1856–1914', *Economic Journal*, LXXI (1961). The latter should be consulted for details about compilation and information on the way in which the estimates differ from those of A. R. Prest, 'National Income of the United Kingdom, 1870–1946', *Economic Journal*, LVIII (1948) and J. B. Jefferys and D. Walters, 'National Income and Expenditure of the United Kingdom, 1870–1952', *Income and Wealth*, V (1955). These estimates are now rarely used, while the early pioneering efforts in this field such as those of Colin Clark, *The National Income, 1924–31* (1932) and *National Income and Outlay* (1937) and A. L. Bowley, *Studies in the National Income, 1924–1938* (1942) are completely out of date. Similarly, most of the early studies on the distribution of national income have now been superseded by Feinstein's work. The latest and most useful analysis is his article, 'Changes in the Distribution of the National Income in the United Kingdom since 1860', published as chapter 4 in J. Marchal and B. Ducros (eds), *The Distribution of National Income* (1968).

## Consumption

The main components of national income are given in the articles of Feinstein listed above, but for the twentieth century more detailed estimates are available for consumers' expenditure in A. R. Prest and A. A. Adams, *Consumers' Expenditure in the United Kingdom, 1900–1919* (1954) and J. R. Stone and D. A. Rowe, *The Measurement of Consumers' Expenditure and Behaviour in the United Kingdom, 1920–1938*, vol. I (1954) and vol. II (1966). These provide a detailed breakdown of the main branches of consumption in both current and constant prices, together with a fairly extensive commentary on the methods of compilation. If a continuous series is required from 1870 the Feinstein figures in the *Bulletin* article of 1964 should be used. The above series exclude government expenditure, which covers both current and capital spending, and for this item students should refer to A. T. Peacock and J. Wiseman, *The Growth of Public Expenditure in the United Kingdom* (2nd ed. 1967) which contains a very elaborate breakdown of public expenditure by type of service. A useful summary is contained in J. Veverka, 'The Growth of Government Expenditure in the United Kingdom since 1790', *Scottish Journal of Political Economy*, x (1963).

### Investment

Continuous series of figures on gross and net domestic capital formation are given in Feinstein's 1961 and 1964 articles. Although these estimates are subject to a fairly wide margin of error they are a substantial improvement on previous ones, notably those of J. H. Lenfant, 'Investment in the United Kingdom, 1865–1914', *Economica*, XVIII (1951), Jefferys and Walters, *Income and Wealth*, v, and A. K. Cairncross, *Home and Foreign Investment, 1870–1913* (1953). The latter does contain some useful investment figures on individual industries, especially railways and shipbuilding, but it should be used with caution since revisions are being made by Feinstein. Some preliminary findings have already been published for the period 1856 to 1914 in Mitchell and Deane, *Abstract* (1962). For the inter-war years a detailed breakdown of gross and net investment in different industries is contained in C. H. Feinstein, *Domestic Capital Formation in the United Kingdom, 1920–1938* (1965). This is the first comprehensive study of capital formation for the period, though again it should be stressed that the figures, especially those for net investment, are subject to a wide margin of error. However, the main advantage is that the classification used is similar to that adopted by Chapman and Knight and Lomax for employment and industrial production (for which see below), so that it is possible to compare and relate changes in the growth of production, employment and capital for a number of separate industrial groups over the period 1920–38. The absence of satisfactory capital stock figures precludes a similar exercise being carried out for the pre-1914 period. The *Key Statistics* volume gives an aggregate capital stock figure from 1900 but there are no subdivisions. Annual capital stock figures extending back to the late 1860s are available in P. H. Douglas, 'An Estimate of the Growth of Capital in the United Kingdom, 1865–1909', *Journal of Economic and Business History*, II (1930) and E. H. Phelps Brown and

S. J. Handfield-Jones, 'The Climacteric of the 1890s: A Study of the Expanding Economy', *Oxford Economic Papers*, IV (1952). Use of these figures is not recommended since their reliability is doubtful. New estimates are currently being made by Feinstein though so far the results have not been published. There are no satisfactory figures for inventory investment. Foreign investment is included in the section on International Trade.

### Production and Productivity

Several attempts have been made to construct industrial production indices for Great Britain. One of the first series covering both industry and manufacturing was that made by Hoffmann in the 1930s and published in the English translation of his book *British Industry, 1700–1950* (1955). This provided a continuous index, together with separate indices for different industries, from the eighteenth century through to the 1930s. Various criticisms have been made about the Hoffmann data, particularly regarding the coverage and weighting used, though for the early part of the period it is still the only continuous index available. However, for the twentieth century a number of new indices have been compiled in recent years using Census of Production information as a benchmark. These include T. M. Ridley, 'Industrial Production in the United Kingdom, 1900–1953', *Economica*, XXII (1955) and A. Maddison, 'Output, Employment and Productivity in British Manufacturing in the Last Half Century', *Bulletin of the Oxford University Institute of Statistics*, XVII (1955). All these indices have now been superseded by the Lomax index, 'Production and Productivity Movements in the United Kingdom since 1900', *Journal of the Royal Statistical Society*, A122 (1959). This gives a continuous series for industry and manufacturing for the period 1900 to 1959 and it is broken down into over twenty industry groups. The data are not perfect by any means and it is worth comparing the results with those of Hoffmann, Ridley and Maddison. The overall index has been carried back to 1860 in K. S. Lomax, 'Growth and Productivity in the United Kingdom', *Productivity Measurement Review*, XXXVIII (1964) though the series is less reliable for the pre-1900 period, and unfortunately the detailed methods of construction are not given for the early part of the index.

There are no continuous series for productivity covering the whole period through from 1870, though if a suitable employment index were constructed (that is, one covering the same ground as the Lomax production index) it would be possible to obtain one from his new index. The two most commonly used series are the productivity index compiled by Phelps Brown and Handfield-Jones which covers the period 1860–1913 (published in *Oxford Economic Papers*, IV (1952)), and the one in *Key Statistics* from 1920. Unfortunately these two series cannot be linked because of differences in coverage and weighting, while the earlier index should be used with caution since it is derived from the Hoffmann production index. However, probably the most unreliable part of the latter is the estimate for building activity which is, in fact, excluded from the productivity index. Reliable productivity indices for individual industries are less easy to obtain. Phelps Brown and Handfield-Jones have a breakdown for a number of industries for the pre-1914 period but it is not advisable to place too much reliance on these, especially for short-run comparisons. For the twentieth century there is considerable information on individual industries in the following sources: L. Rostas, *Productivity, Prices and Distribution in Selected British Industries* (1948) and *Comparative Productivity in British and American Industry* (1948), and also in W. E. G. Salter, *Productivity and Technical Change* (1960). All these estimates are derived from Census of Production data. A more detailed classification based on the same source is given in G. L. Schwartz and E. C. Rhodes, 'Output, Employment and Wages in the United Kingdom, 1924, 1930, 1935', Memorandum no. 75 of the Royal Economic Society (1938).

The series discussed so far relate to either manufacturing or industrial production (i.e. manufacturing plus construction and certain utilities such as gas, electricity and water), but they exclude many segments of the economy (such as transport, agriculture and services) which go to make up gross domestic output. Output data for such groups is much more scanty. From 1920 onwards a breakdown is given by C. H. Feinstein, 'Production and Productivity, 1920–1962', *London and Cambridge Economic Bulletin*, XLVIII (1963). This includes separate series for a number of service sectors, such as the distributive trades, transport, finance, professional services and public administration, as well as indices for industrial production, mining and agriculture. It should be noted, however, that the quantity indicators used for many of the services trades are derived either from employment data or wage and salary bills making them less reliable than the series for industrial output. But since the trades classification is very similar the services indices can be used alongside the investment and employment data. For the pre-1914 period there is little information other than for industrial production, though a continuous series for gross domestic product can be obtained for the whole period from Feinstein's 1964 *London and Cambridge Economic Bulletin* article.

## Population and Employment

All population data are derived from the decennial Censuses of Population and brought conveniently together in Mitchell and Deane, *Abstract* (1962). Statistics on migration are also easily accessible. The most comprehensive survey of the geographical patterns of internal migration is provided by D. Friedlander and R. J. Roshier, 'A Study of Internal Migration in England and Wales: Part I', *Population Studies*, XIX (1965–6). There is a considerable number of sources for external migration but most of the figures are subject to wide margins of error, especially for earlier periods when the estimates are incomplete. Among the most important are L. Ferenczi and W. F. Willcox (eds), *International Migrations* (2 vols, 1929–31), B. Thomas, *Migration and Economic Growth* (1954) and N. H. Carrier and J. R. Jeffery, 'External Migration, 1815–1950: A Study of the Available Statistics', *Studies on Medical and Population Subjects*, VI (1953).

It is difficult to obtain a continuous and reliable series for employment for the period as a whole. The years 1920 to 1938 are well provided for by A. L. Chapman and R. Knight, *Wages and Salaries in the United Kingdom* (1953). This covers both salaried and wage earners (but excluding self-employed) with a detailed occupational breakdown. The figures have been adjusted to a full-time basis and so represent man-years in employment. For a more detailed coverage of government employment readers should consult M. Abramovitz and V. F. Eliasberg, *The Growth of Public Employment in Great Britain* (1957). The information in the *Ministry of Labour Gazette* is far less comprehensive since it refers only to insured persons in employment, and many workers were not included in the insurance schemes. A useful summary is contained in the issue for December 1938. On the other hand, the Ministry's data have certain advantages. The industrial subdivision is finer than that given by Chapman and Knight, information is available on a monthly basis and a useful regional breakdown is provided.

For the period prior to 1914 there is no comparable series to that of Chapman and Knight. The Censuses of Population contain details of the occupied labour force in various industries but no allowance is made for unemployment. It is generally assumed that employment grew at a similar rate to that of working population and an index constructed on this basis for selected years is given in A. Maddison, *Economic Growth in the West* (1964). Similar difficulties arise regarding unemployment data. Prior to the First World War the only figures are those returned by trade unions and these are summarised in

Mitchell and Deane, *Abstract* (1962). After 1922 a more comprehensive, though by no means complete, tally is available from the unemployment insurance returns and published monthly in the *Ministry of Labour Gazette*. These figures are broken down for occupations and for regions and summarised in *Statistical Abstract of the U.K., 1924–38*, Cmd. 6232 (1940). Useful articles drawing together much of the data on unemployment are those by W. Beveridge, 'An Analysis of Unemployment, I, II, III', *Economica*, III (1936), IV (1937), and D. G. Champernowne, 'The Uneven Distribution of Unemployment', *Review of Economic Studies*, V (1937–8), VI (1938–9).

## Wages, Prices and Cost of Living

There have been few recent studies in this field and most information on wages and retail prices is drawn from A. L. Bowley, *Wages and Income in the United Kingdom Since 1860* (1937), G. H. Wood, 'Real Wages and the Standard of Comfort Since 1850', *Journal of the Royal Statistical Society* (1909) and the Ministry of Labour. These provide fairly comprehensive series of wages for industrial workers and the cost of living for the latter half of the nineteenth century through to the 1930s. For the inter-war years there is a much more comprehensive analysis in Chapman and Knight, *Wages and Salaries* (1953), which provides data on average earnings for many occupational groups. The information from all these sources is conveniently brought together in Mitchell and Deane, *Abstract* (1962), while most of the official data are given in either the *Abstract of Labour Statistics* (1893–1936) or the *Statistical Abstract of the U.K.*

Though commonly used for measuring changes in the standard of living, these data have considerable limitations. Most of the wage series do not make allowance for unemployment or changes in hours of work and, apart from the Chapman and Knight estimates, the indices refer to wage rates rather than wage earnings. Moreover, and this applies especially to the period before 1914, the wage indices exclude certain occupational categories. Similarly, the cost of living data compiled by Bowley and the Ministry of Labour – the official cost of living index began in 1914 – are not entirely satisfactory. The use of fixed weights renders the indices somewhat out of date as expenditure patterns change. The Ministry of Labour's cost of living index for the inter-war years suffered badly in this respect since it was weighted on the basis of 1914 expenditure patterns. A further drawback is that the indices do not take account of changes in quality which are inadequately reflected in the prices of goods.

The most reliable series for wholesale prices is that provided by the Board of Trade. A continuous series is available for the whole period covering all categories of goods, though raw materials are weighted too heavily in the index. Two useful indices, one for consumer goods and the other for capital goods, are given in Jefferys and Walters, *Income and Wealth*, v. These cover the whole period through from 1870, though for capital goods prices in the later period students are advised to use the index in *Key Statistics*. A detailed breakdown of machinery prices from 1920 is given in H. J. D. Cole, 'Machinery Prices Between the Wars', *Bulletin of the Oxford University Institute of Statistics*, XIII (1951). It should be emphasised, however, that all price indices for capital goods are subject to wide margins of error. Export and import prices are dealt with below.

## International Trade

There is a considerable range of sources for statistics on Britain's overseas transactions. Indices for the total volume of imports and exports are to be found in A. H. Imlah, *Economic Elements in the Pax Britannica* (1958) for the years up to 1913. These can be linked with the series starting from 1900 in the *Key Statistics*. Volume indices of imports and exports for separate categories of goods are not readily available apart from the rather broad classification given in the *Key Statistics*. Information on foreign trade in current values is brought together from the official returns in Mitchell and Deane, *Abstract* (1962), with a commodity and geographical breakdown. An early work covering similar territory is W. Schlote's *British Overseas Trade from 1700 to the 1930s* (Eng. trans. 1952) and this contains a detailed breakdown by commodity in both current and constant prices. Some of these figures are inaccurate and should be checked before use.

Useful studies have been published on the commodity composition and structure of trade for Britain and other countries. Among those worth mentioning are: H. Tyszynski, 'World Trade in Manufactured Commodities, 1899–1950', *Manchester School*, XIX (1951); R. E. Baldwin, 'The Commodity Composition of Trade: Selected Industrial Countries, 1900–1954', *Review of Economics and Statistics*, XL (1958); A. Maizels, *Industrial Growth and World Trade* (1963). The League of Nations study on *Industrialisation and Foreign Trade* (1945) also contains data on shares in world trade for a number of countries. The student examining this aspect of the subject for the first time should consult Tyszynski's article which has a breakdown into seventeen commodity groups for eleven different countries including Britain. Changes in the shares of different groups are shown for each country for the years 1899, 1913, 1929, 1937 and 1950. Britain suffered losses in almost all commodity groups between 1899 and 1937 due largely to changes in her competitive position rather than to shifts in the structure of world trade. Later work, notably that by Maizels, arrives at similar conclusions with regard to Britain's performance in world trade.

For information on import and export prices and the terms of trade there is a variety of different sources which can be consulted. They include the works of Imlah and Cairncross already cited and A. G. Silverman, 'Monthly Index Numbers of British Export and Import Prices, 1880–1913', *Review of Economics and Statistics*, XII (1930) for the period up to 1913. Continuous series for the whole period are given in C. P. Kindleberger, 'Industrial Europe's Terms of Trade on Current Account, 1870–1953', *Economic Journal*, LXV (1955), *The Terms of Trade* (1956) and K. Martin and F. G. Thackeray, 'The Terms of Trade of Selected Countries, 1870–1938', *Bulletin of the Oxford University Institute of Statistics*, X (1948). These latter sources contain series for a number of countries other than Britain.

Foreign investment statistics before 1914 have recently been revised by M. Simon, 'The Pattern of New British Portfolio Foreign Investment, 1865–1914', in J. H. Adler (ed.), *Capital Movements and Economic Development* (1967). This source extends earlier work by H. H. Segal and M. Simon, 'British Foreign Capital Issues, 1865–1894', *Journal of Economic History*, XXI (1961). In the former study comprehensive estimates of Britain's portfolio investment are given, and these are broken down by area and by type. This new series is a considerable improvement on the figures prepared by C. K. Hobson, *The Export of Capital* (1914) and the residual estimates of Imlah, *Economic Elements*. For the inter-war years the main sources on foreign investment are Royal Institute of International Affairs, *The Problem of International Investment* (1937) and R. Kindersley's estimates in the *Economic Journal*, XL–XLIX (1930–9). Annual statistics on various items in the balance of payments are available in Imlah, *Economic Elements*, the R.I.I.A. volume and the study by T. C. Chang, 'The British Balance of Payments, 1924–1938', *Economic Journal*, LVII (1947), and republished with minor amendments in his *Cyclical Movements in the Balance of Payments* (1951). A valuable summary of the balance of trade figures on a quarterly basis is provided by I. Mintz, *Trade Balances during Business Cycles: U.S. and Britain since 1880* (1959). However, it cannot be stressed too strongly that much of the data relating to the balance of payments is subject to a wide margin of error. Information on the capital account, especially on short-term capital flows, is very unreliable, and inevitably there is a large unidentified balancing item. The estimates for the later period are probably no better than those for before 1914. Chang's work on the inter-war years, though not yet superseded, is not entirely reliable. His estimates for merchandise trade, for example, are on the high side, and it is worth while referring to *Key Statistics* for current account transactions. Readers are warned, therefore, to examine the data very carefully before drawing conclusions.

## International Comparisons

Comparisons between countries are not easy to make since reliable data for a number of countries are often unobtainable, or, where statistics do exist, the basis and methods of compilation vary to such an extent as to preclude effective comparisons. But in recent years considerable efforts have been made to standardise statistical procedures and for certain economic indicators there are now available continuous series extending back in time for a number of countries. The most convenient sources for long-run series on domestic output, exports and industrial production are as follows: A. Maddison, *Economic Growth in the West* (1964) which incorporates much of the information previously published in his articles, 'Economic Growth in Western Europe, 1870–1957', *Banca Nazionale del Lavoro Quarterly Review*, XII (1959) and 'Growth and Fluctuation in the World Economy, 1870–1960', ibid., XV (1962), and O.E.E.C., *Industrial Statistics, 1900–1959* (1960). Data on capital formation can be found in S. Kuznets, 'Quantitative Aspects of the Economic Growth of Nations: VI, Long-term Trends in Capital Formation Proportions', *Economic Development and Cultural Change*, IX (1961). This is one of a series of articles by Kuznets. Statistics on industry and trade are to be found in I. Svennilson, *Growth and Stagnation in the European Economy* (1954). Inevitably the series for any country are constantly under revision and an eye should be kept on the latest work published.

Finally, there is a number of important comparative studies on growth only a few of which can be mentioned here. Apart from the work of Maddison cited above readers are advised to consult the following: W. A. Cole and P. Deane, 'The Growth of National Incomes', ch. 1 in *The Cambridge Economic History of Europe*, vol. 6 (1965) edited by H. J. Habakkuk and M. Postan; J. Knapp and K. S. Lomax, 'Britain's Growth Performance: The Enigma of the 1950s', *Lloyds Bank Review*, LXXIV (1964); A. Maddison, 'The Postwar Business Cycle in Western Europe and the Role of Government

Policy', *Banca Nazionale del Lavoro Quarterly Review*, XIII (1960); V. Paretti and G. Bloch, 'Industrial Production in Western Europe and the United States, 1900–1955', *Banca Nazionale del Lavoro Quarterly Review*, IX (1956) and S. J. Patel, 'Rates of Industrial Growth in the Last Century, 1860–1958', *Economic Development and Cultural Change*, IX (1961).

# SECTION D

# Bibliographical Survey

THIS bibliography is not exhaustive; it concentrates on those books and articles likely to be of most use to students. Rather than present a long list, we have selected a number of key articles for summary and comment. This is not intended to be a substitute for reading the articles but to give some idea of their scope and to stimulate sufficient interest for the student to look at the originals. We have divided the bibliography into a number of broad subject headings for the reader's convenience, though in a few cases overlaps make the division arbitrary. The main statistical references have been dealt with separately in the previous section.

## 1. THE PERFORMANCE OF THE ECONOMY

W. ASHWORTH, 'The Late Victorian Economy', *Economica*, XXXIII (1966)

Suggestions on why the growth of the economy declined in the late nineteenth century. These include: a division of resources into building and suburban growth such as underutilised transport facilities (needed for the journey to work) and holiday resorts; completion of railway network in isolated areas contributing little to economic growth; scattered location of plants in many industries and the failure to exploit agglomeration economies; the allocation of more resources to expenditure on social services (e.g. education and sanitation). Not a comprehensive survey, but offers new lines of inquiry.

D. J. COPPOCK, 'The Climacteric of the 1890s: A Critical Note', *Manchester School*, XXIV (1956)

Challenges the Phelps Brown–Handfield-Jones thesis that there was a break in trend of industrial productivity and real income per head in the 1890s to be explained by completion of application of steam power and steel. Instead suggests that climacteric occurred in 1870s and is to be explained by a decline in rate of capital accumulation (which was in turn due to an exogenous fall in export growth), by changes in innovations (steam and iron), and possibly by a decline in entrepreneurial efficiency. Relies too much on the imperfect Douglas capital stock estimates and assumes too strong a link between capital accumulation and growth.

D. J. Coppock, 'The Causes of the Great Depression, 1873–96' *Manchester School*, XXIX (1961)

Examines secular price fall of the 1873–96 period on an international scale, and argues that price trends comprehensible only in terms of interrelationships of demand and supply factors, drawing upon the analyses of Lewis and Phelps Brown and Ozga. Rules out monetary explanation because of falling interest rates. Transport costs important but not crucial. Overproduction thesis unsatisfactory in view of deceleration in industrial growth, but the rate of growth in the potential supply of raw materials (but not of food) probably increased. He finds the key factor is the retardation in world industrial growth (due to falling trend of railway investment, capital-saving effects of application of iron and steam to shipbuilding and absence of wars which had helped to maintain demand in the 1850–73 period) and its effect on the demand for primary products. Argues that acceleration in world production from mid-nineties mainly due to transmission to world economy of the secular swing in U.S. production which was associated with the upswing of the transport–building cycle.

J. A. Dowie, 'Growth in the Inter-War Period: Some More Arithmetic', *Economic History Review*, XXI (1968)

Presents useful summaries of statistics based mainly on the Feinstein, Chapman and Knight and Lomax data. Confirms that inter-war period experienced growth as rapid as in any period since 1856. Suggests that aggregate growth as rapid between 1924 and 1929 as between 1929 and 1937. Points out danger of confusing the terms 'new' and 'expanding' and the difficulties of defining 'industry'. Also shows that there was considerable productivity growth in older industries.

M. Frankel, 'Obsolescence and Technical Change in a Maturing Economy', *American Economic Review*, XLV (1955)

D. F. Gordon, 'Obsolescence and Technical Change: Comment', *American Economic Review*, XLVI (1956)

M. Frankel, 'Reply', ibid.

A theoretical and empirical analysis of early start thesis, stressing importance of sunk costs and the problem of interrelatedness (i.e. interconnections among technological components of an industry or economy that make introduction of new, cost-saving changes into the system increasingly difficult) in mature economies. Examples include: railways where loading gauge decision early in the nineteenth century led to tunnels and stations restricting vehicles to 8 feet in width, steel industry where innovations had to be introduced simultaneously for maximum efficiency, cotton industry where introduction of automatic loom would have required redesigning of weaving sheds.

Gordon challenged this by arguing that existence of inefficient equipment is not a *current* handicap, and that mature economies are better placed because of experience and access to capital. Instead prefers to explain British 'stagnation' in terms of natural resource limitations and the position of the economy in overseas markets. Frankel's reply argues that comparison between a mature economy and a pre-industrial economy not very meaningful, and that Gordon's stress on environmental factors only a partial explanation.

F. R. J. JERVIS, 'The Handicap of Britain's Early Start', *Manchester School*, XV (1947)

A debunking of the early start thesis. Rather unsophisticated, and too many unsupported assertions, but there are some valuable points hidden among the rhetoric. For example, he argues that if plant has been fully depreciated production costs may be lower, and even hints at learning theory. Main weakness of the article is its neglect of transition costs.

C. P. KINDLEBERGER, 'Obsolescence and Technical Change', *Bulletin of the Oxford University Institute of Statistics*, XXIII (1961)

An excursion into the early start controversy supporting Frankel in his view that there is a penalty mainly concerned with interrelatedness, using examples from railways. Stresses importance of external economies, and asks whether a structure of small firms and the merchant system makes for a high propensity to innovate. Examples of slowness to innovate connected with external economies and inertia (institutional interrelatedness) include failure to change size of rolling stock to a more efficient size, failure to fit automatic brakes to freight wagons and failure to standardise gauges, braking systems, etc. Dismisses monopoly as a serious retarding factor, but suggests that non-economic behaviour prevalent.

J. KNAPP and K. S. LOMAX, 'Britain's Growth Performance: The Enigma of the 1950s', *Lloyds Bank Review*, LXXIV (October 1964)

Primarily a discussion of the British economy's post-war performance and the difficulties in deciding whether it was good or bad. Value of the article for the economic historian is that it presents data on the growth of the economy since 1870 with international comparisons in a palatable form (Tables I, V, VII, IX, X and in two graphs).

D. S. LANDES, 'Factor Costs and Demand: Determinants of Economic Growth', *Business History*, VII (1965)

A critique of the Habakkuk thesis that the differences in U.S. and U.K. growth in the nineteenth century can be explained by differences in demand conditions—that capital accumulation and managerial efficiency were functions of the rate of growth. Argues that Habakkuk understates the retardation and backwardness, and criticises the lack of empirical verification. A difficult article, but well worth study in conjunction with the book it attacks. The main weakness is that Landes offers nothing in place of the thesis he rejects.

W. A. LEWIS, 'World Production, Prices and Trade, 1870–1960', *Manchester School*, XX (1952)

Contains useful tables of world output, trade and prices for the period 1870–1950. Shows that world manufactures a relatively constant share of world trade over this period. Industrial economies imported about 75 per cent of primary products entering international trade, indicating a link between prosperity of industrial countries and quality of this trade. Signs of a Kondratieff recession in Great Depression period, but no clear support for theory of a long wave. Explains deterioration in terms of trade of primary producers in 1920s as a direct consequence of First World War which damaged effective demand through loss of 4½ years of manufacturing production.

W. A. LEWIS, 'International Competition in Manufactures', *American Economic Review*, Papers, 47 (1957)

A stimulating and suggestive article. Argues that slow growth in output after 1870s due to slow growth in exports, which acted as a constraint – 'If production had grown more rapidly, imports would have grown more rapidly, and balance of payments difficulties would have arisen unless exports had grown more rapidly.' Considers five explanations of Britain's lag: natural resource limitations, unfavourable location in relation to major markets, loss of technological leadership, 'doctrine of momentum', i.e. the inability to escape from a rut of selling cotton and railway materials, and lack of irresistible urge to invest and to develop new selling techniques. Prefers the last two as an explanation of deceleration in exports, the result being that deflationary pressure of imports checked investment drive and slowed down growth to pace which rate of growth of exports could support.

R. C. O. MATTHEWS, 'Some Aspects of Post-War Growth in the British Economy in Relation to Historical Experience', *Transactions of the Manchester Statistical Society* (1964)

Primarily an analysis of post-1945 growth in the context of the past hundred years. Presents Feinstein's estimates of output, employment and capital growth rates since 1856, and much more detailed estimates by industry and sector for the inter-war and post-war periods. Concludes that post-war performance compares favourably with previous experience, though in many sectors the inter-war growth rates were higher. Suggests that, apart from the period 1899–1913, the residual was a much more important source of growth than capital accumulation.

J. R. MEYER, 'An Input–Output Approach to Evaluating the Influence of Exports on British Industrial Production in the Late Nineteenth Century', *Explorations in Entrepreneurial History*, VIII (1955), reprinted in A. H. Conrad and J. R. Meyer, *Studies in Econometric History* (1965)

An important article, not least for its methodology. Meyer uses an input–output table to take account of the indirect as well as the direct effects of export decline, and finds that the decline in export growth was more than sufficient to account for the slower rate of industrial growth in the last quarter of the nineteenth century. Had the rate of expansion in exports not declined, industrial production would have increased at a rate of 4·1 per cent in the period 1872–1907 as against the 3·05 per cent growth rate attained in the period 1854–72. Internal explanations relying on supply inelasticities unconvincing. Suggests a number of possible reasons for the retardation in exports such as a decline in the rate of growth of world trade and shift in world demand away from commodities in which Britain had a comparative advantage.

A. E. MUSSON, 'The Great Depression in Britain, 1873–96: A Reappraisal', *Journal of Economic History*, XIX (1959)

A useful survey article, though it suffers from being too inconclusive. Shows that the term 'Great Depression' is a misnomer. Real wages and the standard of living increased, though offset by rather higher levels of unemployment. Output continued to expand, though productivity growth and capital accumulation were both checked. The decline in prices was the period's most obvious feature to be explained by several factors—monetary influences, a fall in freights and declining production costs. Profit margins and business confidence were damaged. Exports were subject to pressure as foreign competition intensified, but imports continued to grow. The situation was eased by favourable movements in the terms of trade. Agriculture was depressed (a view which has since 1959 been substantially modified). The article covers a lot of ground, though there is little attempt to assess the relative importance of each variable.

A. E. MUSSON, 'British Industrial Growth during the Great Depression (1873–96): Some Comments', *Economic History Review*, XV (1962–3)

D. J. COPPOCK, 'British Industrial Growth during the Great Depression (1873–96): a Pessimist's View', *Economic History Review*, XVII (1964–5)

A. E. MUSSON, 'British Industrial Growth, 1873–96: A Balanced View', *Economic History Review*, XVII (1964–5)

Musson argued that it is dangerous to draw pessimistic conclusions from post-1870 deceleration of growth rate, by stressing *absolute* expansion in late nineteenth century and the temporary nature of retardation because of rise in the growth rate after the First World War. Coppock's response argues that use of percentages facilitates intertemporal comparisons and shows that absolute increases in production *per capita* were lower after 1873 than before. He argues that international comparisons highlight U.K. deficiencies in exports and entrepreneurial efficiency, and suggests that unemployment levels were significantly higher.

A lively debate, but bears little fruit in terms of new evidence or interpretation.

E. H. PHELPS BROWN and S. J. HANDFIELD-JONES, 'The Climacteric of the 1890s: A Study of the Expanding Economy', *Oxford Economic Papers*, IV (1952)

States the case for a sharp check to productivity growth, income per head and real wages in the 1890s. Although managerial inefficiencies were a factor, main cause of climacteric was the 'working out . . . of the massive application and extension of the techniques of Steam and Steel', and the lack of development of new industries. A stimulating article, though its conclusions have been challenged. A useful statistical appendix though many of the indices have now been superseded.

E. H. PHELPS BROWN and B. WEBER, 'Accumulation, Productivity and Distribution in the British Economy, 1870–1938', *Economic Journal*, LXIII (1953)

Pioneering attempt to analyse the growth of the capital stock and its implications for economic growth. Capital/output ratio remained fairly stable; technical progress was neutral; the share of wages in national income remained stable between 1870 and 1913 and again between 1924 and 1938 though there was a marked upward shift during and after the First World War; the rate of return on capital also remained stable in each time span.

E. H. PHELPS BROWN and S. A. OZGA, 'Economic Growth and the Price Level', *Economic Journal*, LXV (1955)

Brilliant attempt to explain the secular price movements associated with Kuznets cycles. Rejects monetary explanation. Instead suggests that prices rise when industrial capacity grows faster than primary production and shortages of primary products are felt, and falls when raw material output grows faster than industrial capacity. Variations in rates of growth and hence changes in direction of prices are determined by exogenous factors, such as wars, exhaustion of resources, opening of new markets, technical advances and spurts in industrialisation. Offers valuable insights into interpretation of, say, the Great Depression of 1873–96.

E. A. G. ROBINSON, 'The Changing Structure of the British Economy', *Economic Journal*, LXIV (1954)

Descriptive article showing structural development of the British economy since eighteenth century. Some useful summaries of statistical data referring to imports, exports and the distribution of the labour force.

E. ROTHBARTH, 'Causes of the Superior Efficiency of U.S.A. Industry as Compared with British Industry', *Economic Journal*, LVI (1946)

A general article, not really historical, but very suggestive. Rejects 'size of economy' thesis since higher efficiency in U.S.A. already marked in 1870, when market smaller than in U.K. Sceptical about impact of early start. Argues that main elements in higher productivity of U.S. were stimulus to labour-saving investment of high wages which in turn reflected availability of land and the economies of mass production which could be exploited because consumers were willing to buy standardised goods.

J. SAVILLE, 'Some Retarding Factors in the British Economy before 1914', *Yorkshire Bulletin of Economic and Social Research*, XIII (1961)

Some reasons given for retardation in Britain's growth in the late nineteenth century: conservatism of managers; indifference towards raising educational level of the masses; obsolescence in the capital stock; plentiful supply of labour inhibiting labour-saving investment; lack of demand for standardised consumer goods; a lack of facilities in the London capital market for small-scale home firms; prosperity inhibited the need for change. Merely a list of factors with no attempt to assess their relative importance.

J. SAVILLE, 'Mr. Coppock on the Great Depression: A Critical Note', *Manchester School*, XXXI (1963)

D. J. COPPOCK, 'Mr. Saville on the Great Depression: A Reply', *Manchester School*, XXXI (1963)

Saville criticises the Coppock thesis that there was a world-wide deceleration in manufacturing production after 1873, by arguing that there is no evidence for this in the United States and Germany. Also takes issue with Coppock's denial of increase in primary production and falling transport costs as major factors in the price decline, and suggests there was evidence of a fall in primary product prices due to rising productivity even in the 1850s and 1860s. Argues that a retardation in Britain's industrial growth alone via its influence on the demand for primary products could have seriously affected world prices.

Coppock admits in his reply that his argument for world-wide deceleration in industrial growth is based on insufficient evidence but challenges Saville to present stronger evidence for the absence of deceleration.

A controversy which is concerned primarily with the use and abuse of time series.

R. S. SAYERS, 'The Springs of Technical Progress in Britain, 1919–39', *Economic Journal*, LX (1950)

A classic article which marks the origins of the modern interpretation of the inter-war economy. Argues that technical progress was 'spectacular' and widespread over many sectors of the economy. Shows the impact of the First World War as a stimulus to technical change and to organised research and development. Argument that innovation moderated slumps less convincing. Nevertheless, a must for the beginner student of inter-war economic history.

C. WILSON, 'Economy and Society in Late Victorian Britain', *Economic History Review*, XVIII (1965)

Criticises aggregate analysis of Great Depression period and argues for diversity of experience in industry as supported by qualitative historical impressions. In particular, attacks Hoffmann's indices for individual industries. Draws attention to growth in some minor industries, e.g. soap, mineral oil, clothing, service industries such as retail distribution. Argues that growth in incomes stimulated demand for new consumer goods, and that new industries not affected by entrepreneurial somnolence found in many of the old. Impressionistic, but a useful corrective against 'averages and aggregates'.

*Further Reading*

D. H. ALDCROFT, 'Economic Growth in Britain in the Inter-War Years: A Reassessment', *Economic History Review*, XX (1967).

E. AMES and N. ROSENBERG, 'Changing Technological Leadership and Industrial Growth', *Economic Journal*, LXXIII (1963). (Reviewed in Part B, the appendix to Essay 5.)

P. DEANE and W. A. COLE, *British Economic Growth, 1688–1959* (1962).

M. FRANKEL, *British and American Manufacturing Productivity* (Illinois, 1957).

H. J. HABAKKUK, *American and British Technology in the Nineteenth Century* (1962).

C. P. KINDLEBERGER, *Economic Growth in France and Britain, 1851–1950* (1964).

A. M. LEVINE, *Industrial Retardation in Britain, 1880–1914* (1967).

G. MAYNARD, *Economic Development and the Price Level* (1963).

D. C. PAIGE, F. T. BLACKABY and S. FREUND, 'Economic Growth: the Last Hundred Years', *National Institute Economic Review*, XVI (1961).

L. SOLTOW, 'Long-run Changes in British Income Inequality', *Economic History Review*, XXI (1968).

B. THOMAS, 'The Dimensions of British Economic Growth, 1688–1959', *Journal of the Royal Statistical Society*, A127 (1964).

## 2. INDUSTRY

W. ASHWORTH, 'Changes in Industrial Structure', *Yorkshire Bulletin of Economic and Social Research*, XVII (1965)

A careful use of Census of Population and 1907 Census of Production data to indicate main changes in industrial structure between

1870 and 1914. The chief gainers (metals, engineering, shipbuilding and coal-mining) were not characterised by very high efficiency. Structural changes boost income growth before 1890, but then fit in well with a check to income and productivity growth around 1900.

W. H. B. Court, 'Problems of the British Coal Industry between the Wars', *Economic History Review*, xv (1945)

A valuable survey of one of the most important industries and how it fared in the inter-war economy. Shows the marked contrast between pre-1914 and inter-war experience, how adjustment was retarded by the structure of the industry and its poor labour relations, and the irrelevance of the Sankey Commission diagnosis in 1919 because it saw the future in terms of the industry's successful past. In inter-war period demand stagnated, not least because of tremendous economies. Examines the Coal Mines Act of 1930 and demonstrates its relative ineffectiveness. Points to technical improvements and productivity growth, but not as fast as abroad.

T. W. Fletcher, 'The Great Depression of English Agriculture, 1873–96', *Economic History Review*, xiii (1960–1)

Refutes the former view that agriculture could be described as uniformly depressed, 1873–96. Shows that depression confined regionally to the south and east and to arable farms. Livestock farms of north and west fared much better and gained from lower feed prices. Shows that old view stems largely from biased membership of the Royal Commission of 1879–82 and from the confused conclusions of the rather more representative Royal Commission of 1894–7.

T. J. Orsagh, 'Progress in Iron and Steel: 1870–1913', *Comparative Studies in Society and History*, iii (1960–1)

Explores different definitions of 'lost leadership', and concludes that U.K. was well placed at the beginning of the 1870s but that she lost ground in subsequent decades. Why? Rules out market factors, capital shortage and resource availability as *major* factors. Suggests main cause of loss of leadership was technological backwardness and the associated phenomenon, lack of enterprise.

P. L. Payne, 'The Emergence of the Large-scale Company in Great Britain, 1870–1914', *Economic History Review*, xx (1967)

Explains why merger wave and growth of large scale firms in U.K. less extensive than in U.S.A. in terms of: (i) earlier industrialisation led to a smaller scale; (ii) specialisation of product; (iii) preference for family control and reluctance to raise capital from outside; (iv) ease of forming trade associations. Useful list of fifty-two largest British companies in 1905, and companion list of U.S. firms growing via mergers. Largest U.K. firms concentrated in drink, textiles and steel and engineering. Many new combines were hampered by top-heavy cumbersome directorates, a tendency for struggle for dominance to take place after rather than before the merger, and family nepotism.

Drawbacks are the failure to explain synchronisation of U.K. and U.S. merger wave in 1890s and 1900s and no attempt to measure the degree of industrial concentration (admittedly difficulty).

S. POLLARD, 'British and World Shipbuilding, 1890–1914: A Study in Comparative Costs', *Journal of Economic History*, XVII (1957)

Industry was successful between 1890 and 1914. A useful article explaining why British shipbuilding maintained 60 per cent share of world mercantile production, and exported on a substantial scale. Foreign shipyards uncompetitive. Home market (i.e. control of world shipping) large enough to permit substantial specialisation in yards and to maintain a high rate of capital utilisation. Some technical backwardness, but labour productivity high. Also benefited from access to cheap steel supplies, and a sound location (not only access to coal and iron but market orientation).

S. B. SAUL, 'The American Impact on British Industry, 1895–1914', *Business History*, III (1960)

A corrective against generalisations about backwardness in U.K. industry. Shows how many industries responded to U.S. competition, often by introducing American techniques. Argues that U.S. imports were often not competitive with those of the U.K., and the main competition was confined to industries using interchangeable methods such as machine tools, sewing machines, typewriters, agricultural and electrical machinery. Thus the growth in American competition did not justify pressure for tariff protection.

S. B. SAUL, 'The Motor Industry in Britain to 1914', *Business History*, V (1962)

A valuable analysis of the early growth of the most important of the inter-war new industries. Traces the origins of the early firms, and the background of entrepreneurs, and shows that the location of the industry depended largely on the bicycle industry. Examines how the firms obtained capital and suggests that the most efficient firms had no difficulties in this respect. Shows that the industry's backwardness was due to its slowness to abandon the traditional methods of the engineering industry, its stress on individuality of models and neglect of commercial considerations.

S. B. Saul, 'The Market and the Development of the Mechanical Engineering Industries in Britain, 1860–1914', *Economic History Review*, XX (1967)

An analysis of individual sectors of engineering industry which shows their diversity of experience—progressiveness in textile machinery, steam engines and sewing machinery, backwardness in some mass production industries such as watches and office machinery, while degree of success varied in others. Critical of generalised arguments such as sociological explanations of entrepreneurial backwardness. Argues that the nature of the market the crucial factor, but uses the term rather vaguely.

S. B. Saul, 'The Machine Tool Industry in Britain to 1914', *Business History*, X (1968)

A survey of the growth of this small but crucial industry. Shows that technical lead of heavy sector was continued by new firms, though lag behind United States in new production machine tools was not made up. Nevertheless, there was a sharp expansion from the 1890s pointing to an improvement in engineering practice in the older as well as the new sectors. However, gap between average and best practice was large. Surge forward handicapped by market factors, a general unwillingness to scrap and an irrational tendency for customers to understate benefits of new machines. Innovation spread largely by imitation of imported techniques from the United States.

W. A. Sinclair, 'The Growth of the British Steel Industry in the Late Nineteenth Century', *Scottish Journal of Political Economy*, VI (1959)

An attempt to remedy the view that U.K. steel industry backward in the period 1880–1900. Describes rise in open-hearth industry, and argues that Bessemer section has been given undue attention. Stresses the importance of rising home demand, especially by shipbuilding. Points to marked technical progress in open-hearth section. The main defect of the article is its failure to analyse what happened in the two decades before 1914.

A. J. Taylor, 'Labour Productivity and Technological Innovation in the British Coal Industry, 1850–1914', *Economic History Review*, XIV (1961–2)

A valuable analysis of an important industry aimed at explaining sharp check to productivity growth in 1880s. Suggests answers to be found in increased absenteeism, rising wages, reduction of working hours and dilution of skilled labour on the labour side, a slowing down in pace of technological innovation, the caution of colliery owners strengthened by a rising demand for coal and a ready supply of labour, and the difficulty of obtaining capital.

P. TEMIN, 'The Relative Decline of the British Steel Industry, 1880–1913', in H. Rosovsky (ed.), *Industrialisation in Two Systems: Essays in Honour of Alexander Gerschenkron* (1966)

Takes issue with views of steel decline based on retention of free trade, technological backwardness, structure of the capital market and declining entrepreneurship. Argues instead that falling U.K. share was the natural result of: rapid growth in domestic demand in U.S.A. and Germany, markets from which U.K. steel was barred by tariffs; and the equalisation of resource costs in the three major steel-making countries. U.K. industry grew more slowly because it had access to a less rapidly growing market, and the slow growth accounts for the older capital structure and smallness of technical change. Lower costs would not have enabled the industry to climb over the tariff walls.

*Further Reading*

D. H. ALDCROFT, 'The Performance of the British Machine Tool Industry in the Inter-War Years', *Business History Review*, XL (1966).

D. H. ALDCROFT, 'The Efficiency and Enterprise of British Railways 1870–1914', *Explorations in Entrepreneurial History*, V (1968).

D. H. ALDCROFT (ed.), *The Development of British Industry and Foreign Competition, 1875–1914* (1968).

D. H. ALDCROFT, *British Railways in Transition* (1968).

G. C. ALLEN, *British Industries and their Organisation* (1951 ed.).

P. W. S. ANDREWS and E. BRUNNER, *Capital Development in Steel* (1950).

BALFOUR COMMITTEE, *Reports of the Committee on Industry and Trade* (1926–1930, H.M.S.O.).

BARLOW COMMISSION, *Report of the Royal Commission on Distribution of Industrial Population*, Cmd. 6153 (1939–40).

T. BARNA, 'The Interdependence of the British Economy', *Journal of the Royal Statistical Society*, A115 (1952).

A. BEACHAM, 'Efficiency and Organisation of the British Coal Industry', *Economic Journal*, XXXV (1945).

M. BLAUG, 'The Productivity of Capital in the Lancashire Cotton Industry during the Nineteenth Century', *Economic History Review*, XIII (1960–1).

D. L. BURN, *The Economic History of Steelmaking, 1867–1939* (1943).

T. H. BURNHAM and G. O. HOSKINS, *Iron and Steel in Britain, 1870–1930* (1943).

T. J. Byres, 'Entrepreneurship in the Scottish Heavy Industries, 1870–1900', in P. L. Paynes (ed.), *Studies in Scottish Business History* (1967).

J. C. Carr and W. A. Taplin, *History of the British Steel Industry* (1962).

R. A. Church, 'The Effect of the American Export Invasion on the British Boot and Shoe Industry, 1885–1914', *Journal of Economic History*, xxviii (1968).

P. L. Cook and R. Cohen, *Effects of Mergers* (1958).

J. H. Dunning and W. A. Thomas, *British Industry* (1961).

C. Erickson, *British Industrialists: Steel and Hosiery, 1850–1950* (1959).

H. Feis, 'The Industrial Situation in Great Britain from the Armistice to the Beginning of 1921', *American Economic Review*, xi (1921).

M. P. Fogarty, *Prospects of the Industrial Areas of Great Britain* (1945).

L. F. Haber, *The Chemical Industry during the Nineteenth Century* (1958).

D. C. Hague, *The Economics of Man-Made Fibres* (1957).

R. H. Heindel, *The American Impact on Great Britain* (1940).

W. G. Hoffmann, *British Industry, 1700–1950* (1955).

J. B. Jefferys, *Retail Trading in Britain, 1850–1950* (1954).

J. Jewkes, D. Sawers and R. Stillerman, *The Sources of Invention* (1958).

G. T. Jones, *Increasing Return* (1933).

J. H. Jones, *et al.*, *The Coal-Mining Industry* (1939).

L. Jones, *Shipbuilding in Britain* (1957).

D. S. Landes, 'The Structure of Enterprise in the Nineteenth Century: the Case of Britain and Germany', *Extrait des Rapports du XIe Congrès International des Sciences Historiques*, v (Stockholm, 1960).

D. S. Landes, 'Technological Change and Development in Western Europe, 1750–1914', Ch. 5 in H. J. Habakkuk and M. Postan (eds), *The Cambridge Economic History of Europe*, vol. 6 (1965).

C. E. V. Leser, 'Scottish Industries during the Inter-War Period,' *Manchester School*, xviii (1950).

A. F. Lucas, *Industrial Reconstruction and the Control of Competition* (1937).

A. N. Neuman, *Economic Organisation of the British Coal Industry* (1934).

A. Plummer, *New British Industries in the Twentieth Century* (1937).

Political and Economic Planning, *Report on Location of Industry* (1939).

H. W. Richardson, 'The Development of the Synthetic Dyestuffs Industry before 1939', *Scottish Journal of Political Economy*, ix (1962).

L. Rostas, *Productivity, Prices and Distribution in Selected British Industries* (1948).

L. G. Sandberg, 'Movements in the Quality of British Cotton Textile Exports, 1815–1913', *Journal of Economic History*, xxviii (1968).

E. M. Sigsworth, 'Science and the Brewing Industry, 1850–1900', *Economic History Review*, xvii (1965).

H. A. Silverman, *Studies in Industrial Organisation* (1946).

S. G. Sturmey, *British Shipping and World Competition* (1962).

### 3. International Aspects

A. J. Brown, 'Britain and the World Economy, 1870–1914', *Yorkshire Bulletin of Economic and Social Research*, XVII (1965)

A useful discussion of Britain's role in the international economy. Suggests that pre-1914 world was not a golden age of growth in either incomes or international trade. Argues that U.K. competitive power in export markets declined. Foreign investment was associated with unemployment as a result of the transfer problem, and because it diverted capital from the domestic economy. Suggests that stabilising effects of banking policy were accidental due to main drains into and out of the Bank of England being internal rather than external. Gold reserves only 1½ per cent of G.N.P. yet gold standard worked.

A. K. Cairncross, 'Did Foreign Investment Pay?', *Review of Economic Studies*, III (1935–6)

Argues that foreign investment of late nineteenth century paid both for the private investor and for the economy as a whole. Rates of return obtained abroad were higher, and not offset by defaults. Economy gained from cheaper imports and higher exports.

A. G. Ford, 'The Transfer of British Foreign Lending, 1870–1913', *Economic History Review*, XI (1958–9)

Warns against assuming that interest and dividends from abroad were the direct source of capital exports, and argues that *ex ante* foreign lending created the current account surplus by expanding exports. Imports did not expand to same extent because of leakages into savings and fact that income-generating effect of increased exports was often offset by decline in home investment (home and foreign investment moved inversely in long run).

A. G. Ford, 'Bank Rate, the British Balance of Payments, and the Burdens of Adjustment, 1870–1914', *Oxford Economic Papers*, XVI (1964)

Puts forward the thesis that smooth working of pre-1914 gold standard exaggerated in that U.K. monetary policy passed on the burden of adjustment to the primary producers. However, this reverberated back on the U.K. by adversely affecting the export industries, tending to offset the immediate relief of a high Bank rate to the balance of payments by making new overseas issues more difficult. The balance of payments would have tended to worsen again but for the depressive effects of falling exports on incomes and hence on imports. This thesis is illustrated with a detailed analysis of the crisis of 1907.

A. G. FORD, 'Overseas Lending and Internal Fluctuations, 1870–1914', *Yorkshire Bulletin of Economic and Social Research*, XVII (1965)

Argues that British trade cycle before 1914 export-based, and that a major influence on variations in exports was the fluctuations in overseas investment. In the long run, there was a *trend* tendency for unemployment to rise in periods of foreign investment. On the other hand, another long-run effect of foreign investment was to raise productive capacity in the primary producing economies and to boost British exports.

C. P. KINDLEBERGER, 'Foreign Trade and Economic Growth: Lessons from Britain and France, 1850 to 1913', *Economic History Review*, XIV (1961–2)

Examines role of foreign trade as a leading or lagging sector, but concludes that this is less important than capacity for transformation in the domestic economy. Criticises J. R. Meyer and W. A. Lewis for their attempts to link retardation of exports directly with deceleration in growth rate. Argues that U.K. shifted to new export markets, a short-run solution which postponed the need for industrial transformation at home.

G. M. MEIER, 'Long Period Determinants of Britain's Terms of Trade, 1880–1913', *Review of Economic Studies*, XX (1952–3)

Compares different indices of U.K. terms of trade and shows that they all point to a broad improvement between 1880 and 1900 with some deterioration thereafter. Rejects view that commercial policies, changes in gold stock or classical theory of transfer mechanism (implying that net capital exports would lead to deterioration in terms of trade) had much of an influence because historical facts are against them. But overseas investment stimulated increase in supply of primary products and rate of growth in demand for these fell off, hence primary product prices declined. But for export products real costs increasing, and this was the main factor behind the export price index; the deterioration after 1900 was not due to a reversal in this trend but to a rise in import prices. Much of the increase in real income 1880–1900 could be ascribed to the improving terms of trade, and because there were no unfavourable repercussions on primary producers the gains were not offset by unemployment.

D. E. NOVACK and M. SIMON, 'Commercial Responses to the American Export Invasion, 1871–1914: An Essay in Attitudinal History', *Explorations in Entrepreneurial History*, 2nd ser., III (1966)

Traces the growth in U.S. exports after the 1870s, and their effect on Europe. Europe over-reacted because of large increase in U.S. imports and fact that it occurred in a period of depression. Argues that attitudes and responses can be very important, and puts forward the case for a 'behavioural economic history'.

R. NURKSE, 'International Investment To-day in the Light of Nineteenth Century Experience', *Economic Journal*, LXIV (1954)

Argues that conditions under which Britain invested abroad before 1914 quite exceptional. Shows that two-thirds of investment went to rich, sparsely populated 'regions of recent settlement' where opportunities for development very favourable. High proportion of investment went into infrastructure, especially railways. Rejects Marxist thesis that markets were conquered by capital exporting countries because (*a*) colonial territories avoided and (*b*) markets were created in new countries by European labour, capital and enterprise. Gives useful guidelines for post-1945 investment, but these, of course, have no historical interest.

S. B. SAUL, 'Britain and World Trade, 1870–1914', *Economic History Review*, VII (1954–5)

Argues the benefits of the pre-1914 multilateral payments system. 'Open-door' for imports from primary producers freed U.K. from competition of manufacturing countries in primary producing markets. Britain had an export surplus and European countries an import surplus with the primary producers. By exporting to latter, by supplying invisible exports and by interest receipts, Britain paid indirectly for her import surplus with industrial countries allowing these to finance their primary product imports. Thus, paradoxically, free trade protected U.K. from industrial competition in overseas markets. Suggests that protection would have destroyed this benefit, but would a limited system of infant-industry tariffs?

S. B. SAUL, 'The Export Economy, 1870–1914', *Yorkshire Bulletin of Economic and Social Research*, XVII (1965)

An analysis of Britain's export activities between 1870 and 1914. Useful tables, and data presented in more palatable fashion than in his earlier book. No central theme but a valuable survey with some useful suggestions: for example, the possibility that growth may react upon exports. Points out that decline in U.K. share of world trade marked until after 1890, and due far more to decline in competitive power than to commodity or area shifts.

W. M. SCAMMELL, 'The Working of the Gold Standard', *Yorkshire Bulletin of Economic and Social Research*, XVII (1965)

A clear analysis of a subject which students often find difficult. The gold standard worked before 1914 for several reasons: 'rules of game' applied, i.e. fixed currency values in terms of gold, free movement of gold, and domestic money supplies linked to gold movements; a high degree of wage and price flexibility; era of economic expansion enabled adjustments to be made without deflationary effects; sterling a world currency and in plentiful supply because of Britain's high import needs; strains cushioned by the international credit system; income effects reinforced gold standard adjustment mechanism: discretionary action by central banks minimised interference with domestic stability. Also shows how development of gold standard was associated with move towards more sophisticated monetary management, and indicates how reality differed from the classical gold standard adjustment model.

H. H. SEGAL and M. SIMON, 'British Foreign Capital Issues, 1865–1894', *Journal of Economic History*, XXI (1961)

Primarily a statistical article presenting disaggregated data (by area and type) of British overseas issues. Nevertheless points to interesting conclusions: there were two long swings in foreign investment (1867–77 and 1877–89) mainly due to fluctuations in North and South American series; some support found for Saul's thesis that changing direction of capital exports helped U.K. to insulate herself from external slumps; more intense fluctuations in American import of capital connected with private enterprise, while great stability in Empire countries connected with more government investment; no tendency for Empire share to rise, but heavy concentration on regions of recent settlement and neglect of tropics confirmed, as is preponderance of rail shares.

M. SIMON, 'The Pattern of New British Portfolio Foreign Investment, 1865–1914' in J. H. Adler (ed. for I.E.A.), *Capital Movements and Economic Development* (1967)

Continues the analysis of new overseas issues started in the previous article, and revises the 1961 series up to 1914. Analyses geographical distribution of new issues, and by type. Shows that there were 2½ long swings in new issues and that these were more intense in issues to North America and regions of recent settlement than elsewhere.

B. THOMAS, 'Migration and the Rhythm of Economic Growth, 1830–1913', *Manchester School*, XIX (1951)

A summary of the argument presented in his later book. Analyses role played by transatlantic migration in inverse Kuznets cycles of U.K. and U.S.A. Up to 1870s, turning points in U.S. immigration preceded those in railway construction; from mid-seventies this is reversed. Perhaps before 1870s pace of investment set by inflow of population, and afterwards rate of immigration determined by investment opportunities. U.K. foreign lending an important factor enabling immigrants to be absorbed in the United States. Long cycles in U.K. exports correspond to those in U.S. rail construction. Also gives evidence for inverse building cycles, and shows that U.K. national income, wages and employment move in opposite direction to emigration and foreign investment. A break in the Atlantic cycle pattern in 1890s, due to: south and eastern Europe becoming main source of U.S. immigrants; increasing importance of second generation Americans in labour market; shortage of land for settlers; end of phase when U.S. an importer of capital.

B. THOMAS, 'The Historical Record of International Capital Movement to 1913', in J. H. ADLER (ed. for I.E.A.), *Capital Movements and Economic Development* (1967)

This article places pre-1914 foreign investment in an international setting, and discusses some of the statistics. Argues that 'ebb and flow of international factor movements must concentrate on the process of interaction within the Atlantic economy'. In addition to earlier conclusions shows that there were long swings in population additions inverse to those in the United States, and argues that population could be a crucial variable. Argues (as did Meier) that movements in the terms of trade were a *consequence* of fundamental forces at work not a causal factor determining the distribution of the flow of capital between home and foreign investment. In the decade before 1914, however, pursuit of private returns overseas incompatible with social productivity of U.K. economy.

H. TYSZYNSKI, 'World Trade in Manufactured Commodities, 1899–1950', *Manchester School*, XIX (1951)

A statistical analysis of the structure of world trade in manufactures in the years 1899, 1913, 1929, 1937 and 1950. Analyses change in individual shares in terms of (i) changes in the structure of world trade and (ii) changes in competitiveness. Finds that only about 15 per cent of total decline in U.K. share in the period 1899–1937 due to shifts in the structure; the remaining 85 per cent is explained by

Britain's declining ability to compete within individual commodity groups. U.K. share fell in almost every group (expanding, stable and declining categories alike), but particularly in iron and steel and engineering products. These conclusions have never really been challenged, and indeed have been supported by subsequent research.

J. G. WILLIAMSON, 'The Long Swing: Comparisons and Interactions between British and American Balance of Payments, 1820–1913', *Journal of Economic History*, XXII (1962)

Another analysis of Kuznets cycles linking them to international flow of goods, capital and specie. Does not take extreme view of no long swing in U.K. output, but instead argues that this was damped by offsetting effects of net capital exports. There is evidence even of a mild long swing in *deflated* imports (but not in imports at current prices) which were positively related to home investment and (presumably) to income. Also argues that fluctuations in American demand a major cause of *long* cycles in rate of growth of U.K. exports, 1850–1900. In U.K. balance of payments flow of capital gives clearest evidence of Kuznets cycles. Concludes that British long swings triggered off by American long swings and possibly by long swings in the pace of growth in primary producing economies.

*Further Reading*

W. ASHWORTH, *A Short History of the International Economy, 1850–1950* (2nd ed. 1963).

R. E. BALDWIN, 'Britain's Foreign Balances and Terms of Trade in the Nineteenth Century', *Explorations in Entrepreneurial History*, V (1952–3).

F. BENHAM, *Great Britain under Protection* (1940).

A. I. BLOOMFIELD, *Monetary Policy Under the International Gold Standard, 1880–1914* (New York, 1959).

T. C. CHANG, *Cyclical Movements in the Balance of Payments* (1951).

A. G. FORD, *The Gold Standard 1880–1914: Britain and Argentine* (1962).

A. L. GINSBERG and R. M. STERN, 'The Determination of the Factors Affecting American and British Exports in the Inter-War and Post-War Periods', *Oxford Economic Papers*, XVII (1965).

R. J. S. HOFFMAN, *Great Britain and the German Trade Rivalry, 1875–1914* (1933).

A. H. IMLAH, 'The Terms of Trade of the United Kingdom, 1798–1913', *Journal of Economic History*, X (1950).

A. E. KAHN, *Great Britain in the World Economy* (1946).

C. P. KINDLEBERGER, 'Foreign Trade and Growth: Lessons from British Experience since 1913', *Lloyds Bank Review*, LXV (1962).

POLITICAL AND ECONOMIC PLANNING, *Britain and World Trade* (1937).

J. H. RICHARDSON, *British Economic Foreign Policy* (1936).

ROYAL INSTITUTE OF INTERNATIONAL AFFAIRS, *The Problem of International Investment* (1937).

S. B. SAUL, *Studies in British Overseas Trade, 1870–1914* (1960).

A. G. SILVERMAN, 'Some International Trade Factors for Great Britain, 1880–1913', *The Review of Economics and Statistics*, XIII (1931).

R. C. SNYDER, 'Commercial Policy, 1931–39', *American Economic Review*, XXX (1940).

B. THOMAS, *Migration and Economic Growth* (1954).

P. L. YATES, *Forty Years of Foreign Trade* (1959).

R. E. ZELDER, 'Estimates of Elasticities of Demand for Exports of the U.K. and the U.S., 1921–1938', *Manchester School*, XXVI (1958).

## 4. MONEY AND FINANCE

A. R. HALL, 'A Note on the English Capital Market as a Source of Funds for Home Investment before 1914', *Economica*, NS, XXIV (1957)

A. K. CAIRNCROSS, 'The English Capital Market Before 1914', *Economica*, NS, XXV (1958)

A. R. HALL, 'The English Capital Market Before 1914, A Reply', *Economica*, NS, XXV (1958)

Hall challenges the view that London new issue market unimportant as a source of funds for home investment with the aid of a detailed analysis of new issues for the period 1895–9. Also suggests that machinery for home new issues adequate. Cairncross shows that Hall's data misleading since he takes amount of capital offered rather than actual amount subscribed (and for period analysed the latter was only half the former), and points out that most of capital issued was for sale of existing concerns to new owners rather than for new investment. Most U.K. firms still relied on internal accumulation, and when new companies were floated on the market they were usually speculative concerns in consumer goods industries. Reaffirms existence of a Macmillan Gap for small firms before 1914.

In his reply, Hall suggests that data of apparent calls on new capital used by Cairncross were incomplete, and reasserts that 'it was possible for smallish *bona fide* firms to make new issues on reasonable terms'. No evidence given for this view, and the question is still unsettled.

J. R. T. HUGHES, 'Wicksell on the Facts: Prices and Interest Rates, 1844 to 1914', in J. N. Wolfe (ed.), *Value, Capital and Growth. Papers in Honour of Sir John Hicks* (1968)

This paper reassesses the role of monetary policy as an influence on the long-term growth performance of the British economy in the seven decades before 1914. It is, in fact, a test of the Wicksellian hypothesis that prices rise when the market rate of interest rises relatively to the natural rate, and fall when the market rate falls below the natural rate. Central bank policy from the early 1870s formed an environment which was unfavourable to investment borrowing. The deflation of this period encouraged emigration and foreign investment. It is argued that attention to monetary phenomena helps to explain other aspects of Britain's economic performance which are not satisfactorily accounted for by other factors. This article is a welcome reaction from recent investigations which have tended to dismiss monetary influences summarily. On the other hand, it is not fully convincing. It depends upon the rather abstract indefinable concept of a natural rate of interest, and it fails to specify clearly the links between price movements and investment behaviour.

D. WILLIAMS, 'Montagu Norman and Banking Policy in the 1920s', *Yorkshire Bulletin of Economic and Social Research*, XI (1959)

Argues that monetary difficulties of the 1920s stemmed from a short-run attitude to monetary policy (i.e. a response to changes in gold and foreign exchanges) whereas long-run effects were critical. Norman understated the domestic implications of monetary policy. Analyses return to gold standard in 1925, suggesting that operation of the standard in changed, unfavourable circumstances more important source of trouble than overvaluation itself. Shows clearly that banking policy was not a *cause* of unemployment.

D. WILLIAMS, 'London and the 1931 Financial Crisis', *Economic History Review*, XV (1962–3)

Contrasts the stability of the pre-1914 gold standard with the potential instability of the gold exchange standard of 1925–31, and shows how London's ability to supply the rest of the world with liquidity was weakened by the decline in Britain's long-term creditor position and the reduced flexibility of monetary policy. Long-run cause of financial crisis was the earlier slump in primary producing countries and the United States, but the key short-run factors were loss of confidence and London's inability to borrow enough funds from abroad.

D. WILLIAMS, 'The 1931 Financial Crisis', *Yorkshire Bulletin of Economic and Social Research*, XV (1963)

Similar in scope and interpretation to the previous article. However, contains a clearer description of the working of the gold exchange standard after 1925, more detail on the origins of the world depression, and a closer analysis of the final stages of the crisis, May–September 1931. Conclusion—that the crisis of 1931 was one of confidence—remains unchanged.

*Further Reading*

A. Boyle, *Montagu Norman* (1967).
S. V. O. Clarke, *Central Bank Co-operation, 1924–31* (New York, 1967).
A. E. Feaveryear, *The Pound Sterling* (rev. ed. 1963).
R. Frost, 'The Macmillan Gap, 1931–53', *Oxford Economic Papers*, VI (1954).
R. M. Goodwin, 'The Supply of Bank Money in England and Wales, 1920–38', *Oxford Economic Papers*, III (1941).
A. T. K. Grant, *A Study of the Capital Market in Post-War Britain* (1937).
T. Gregory, 'Lord Norman: A New Interpretation', *Lloyds Bank Review*, LXXXVIII (1968).
A. R. Hall, *The London Capital Market and Australia, 1870–1914* (Canberra, 1963).
U. K. Hicks, *The Finance of British Government, 1920–36* (1938).
J. K. Horsefield, 'Currency Devaluation and Public Finance, 1929–37', *Economica*, VI (1939).
H. L. Lutz, 'English Financial Policy and Experience, 1928–37', *Proceedings of the Academy of Political Science*, XVII (1937).
Macmillan Committee, *Report of the Committee on Finance and Industry*, Cmd. 3897 (1931).
E. V. Morgan and W. A. Thomas, *The Stock Exchange* (1962).
E. V. Morgan, *Studies in British Financial Policy, 1914–25* (1952).
E. Nevin, *The Mechanism of Cheap Money: A Study of British Monetary Policy 1931–1939* (1955).
W. F. Stolper, 'Purchasing Power Parity and the Pound Sterling, 1919–25', *Kyklos*, II (1948).

## 5. Fluctuations

D. J. Coppock, 'The Causes of Business Fluctuation', *Transactions of the Manchester Statistical Society* (1959)

Argues that 8–9 year Juglar cycle is a mythical concept for the U.S.A., the main cycle being that in transport and building. After 1870 we find a pseudo-Juglar in the U.K., but this was an accidental result of inverse cycles in building and exports to be explained, primarily, in terms of repercussions of U.S. transport–building cycle. Inverse pattern should have been broken by 1914–18 war and its consequences, but specific factors account for shorter U.S. building boom in the 1920s and for the delay in the British housing boom. A stimulating article, though the argument is not fully convincing.

D. C. CORNER, 'Exports and the British Trade Cycle, 1929', *Manchester School*, XXIV (1956)

Uses detailed analysis of U.K. exports by area and commodity for the period 1928–30 to discover the origins of the slump of 1929. There was an early weakening of demand in low income producing economies, reflecting an early fall in the prices of tropical commodities. Secondly, slump spread from United States in late 1929 mainly because of exhaustion of investment opportunities there. Rather a narrow investigation.

A. G. FORD, 'Notes on the Role of Exports in British Economic Fluctuations, 1870–1914', *Economic History Review*, XVI (1963–4)

Another paper to support Ford's thesis that international influence dominant in U.K. trade cycle. Fluctuations in exports the *proximate* cause of fluctuations in U.K. incomes, and export fluctuations were the indirect result of variations in overseas issues. Also stresses role of Europe as an export market, and its individual behaviour from 1890 explains why long wave in overseas investment less apparent in total merchandise exports.

A. G. FORD, 'British Economic Fluctuations, 1870–1914', *Warwick Economic Research Papers*, no. 3 (1968)

Mainly a statistical analysis. Examines role of exports, overseas investment and monetary factors in pre-1914 cycles. Shows that fluctuations in exports (particularly merchandise exports) the main cause of income fluctuations, and argues that variations in overseas lending had a key, if sometimes indirect, impact on the former especially up to 1893. Concludes that international influences crucial in U.K. cycles, and suggests that Europe's role has been underestimated. Monetary factors subordinate. Narrow treatment excluding influence of technical progress and other aspects of the trend.

W. A. LEWIS and P. J. O'LEARY, 'Secular Swings in Production and Trade, 1870–1913', *Manchester School*, XXIII (1955)

An analysis of Kuznets cycles in four countries—Britain, the United States, Germany and France. In the U.K., because exports and home investment moved in the opposite direction, this had a stabilising effect. There is no secular swing in British industrial production, but imports and building swing together while exports swing in the opposite direction. Argues that inverse cycles with United States unlikely to be explained by foreign investment since U.S. capital imports less than 0·5 per cent of G.N.P., 1874–95. Migration was an unlikely cause of inverse building cycles because differences in emigration rates made less than 0·25 per cent difference to the rate of population growth; suggests that alternation could have been accidental. Kuznets cycles in the other three economies different in the sense that they are found in industrial production. Secular swings also found in agricultural countries. Timing of U.K. foreign investment explained more by 'mob psychology' than by, say, terms of trade. To the extent that capital exports stabilised the U.K. they had a destabilising impact on the rest of the world.

F. V. MEYER and W. A. LEWIS, 'The Effects of an Overseas Slump on the British Economy', *Manchester School*, XVII (1949)

Concerned not with causes of depressions but their effects. Balance of payments deteriorated in almost every depression between 1870 and 1930s. Suggests that exports to American continent suffered most in slumps, while import decline concentrated on Asia and Africa. Also shows that export slumps hit different regions in varying degrees, but analysis of this related to post-war data rather than to any period before 1939.

J. S. PESMAZOGLU, 'Some International Aspects of British Cyclical Fluctuations, 1870–1913', *Review of Economic Studies*, XVI (1949–50)

A long statistical analysis of the British balance of payments position between 1870 and 1913. Concludes that outflow of long-term capital moved pro-cyclically and was possibly accompanied by opposite movements of short-term capital and gold. The findings suggest that improving activity in primary producing economies during the depression was the initial impulse to outflow of capital, which reacted quickly because of high sensitivity of London capital market. Balance of payments strains during booms were cushioned by the inflow of short-term capital. Deterioration of terms of trade in recessions offset the depressing effect of sharp cuts in overseas lending. Not an easy article, but interesting especially as it concentrates on the neglected trade cycle rather than on the Kuznets cycles which figure so largely in foreign investment investigations for this period.

J. S. PESMAZOGLU, 'A Note on the Cyclical Fluctuations of British Home Investment, 1870–1913', *Oxford Economic Papers*, III (1951)

An econometric analysis using data which have now been replaced. Concludes that variations in aggregate demand and long-term interest rates did not have an important influence on home investment fluctuations, and that changes in business conditions abroad were also unimportant except to the extent that they influenced business conditions in the U.K. But domestic investment nevertheless had a cyclical pattern.

E. M. SIGSWORTH and J. BLACKMAN, 'The Home Boom of the 1890s', *Yorkshire Bulletin of Economic and Social Research*, XVII (1965)

A very descriptive article emphasising the importance of building in the early stages of the upswing of the 1890s, reinforced by expansion in electrical and other kinds of engineering including the cycle trade after 1895. Also suggests that the boom was facilitated by cheap money.

*Further Reading*

R. F. BRETHERTON, F. A. BURCHARDT and R. S. G. RUTHERFORD, *Public Investment and the Trade Cycle in Great Britain* (1941).
H. V. HODSON, *Slump and Recovery 1929–1937* (1938).
I. MINTZ, *Trade Balances during Business Cycles: U.S. and Britain since 1880* (New York, 1959).
O. MORGENSTERN, *International Financial Transactions and Business Cycles* (Princeton, 1959).
H. W. RICHARDSON, *Economic Recovery in Britain 1932–39* (1967).
W. W. ROSTOW, *British Economy of the Nineteenth Century* (1948).
J. TINBERGEN, *Business Cycles in the United Kingdom, 1870–1914* (1951).

## 6. BUILDING

A. P. BECKER, 'Housing in England and Wales during the Business Depression of the 1930s', *Economic History Review*, III (1950–1)

An early survey of the building boom of the 1930s, and of the view that housing played a dominant role in the recovery. Divides analysis into treatment of demand and supply factors. In the former are included: the housing shortage; an increase in the number of families; slums and obsolete houses; the changing distribution of industry and population; rising real wages, and an increase in white-collar workers who were more likely to buy houses; publicity about home ownership; and transport improvements. Supply factors mentioned are: falling building costs; financial innovations, liberalisation of building society terms and more abundant investment funds; and government intervention, especially for slum clearance and overcrowding. No mention of the earlier work by Bowley and Stolper.

M. Bowley, 'Fluctuations in House-building and the Trade Cycle', *Review of Economic Studies*, IV (1936–7)

An analysis of fluctuations in housebuilding in the period 1924–36 stressing the importance of private house demand (particularly a change in tastes towards new houses) and the increase in the relative attractiveness of housing investment in a depression. Suggests that falling costs insufficient to explain the housing boom. There was little causal connection between housebuilding and trade cycle, but the article is rather inconclusive.

M. Bowley, 'Some Regional Aspects of the Building Boom, 1924–36', *Review of Economic Studies*, V (1937–8)

Looks at inter-war housebuilding from a regional point of view (using three subdivisions—the South, the Midlands and the North, and Wales). Shows that building industry was heavily concentrated in the South, due to demand of the metropolis and to greater extent of suburban living, but not to greater prosperity. Regional analysis shows preponderance of unsubsidised building in South, no relationship between population increases and the number of houses built, and a tendency for rate of building in the North and Midlands to increase relative to the South after 1930. Housing boom explained in terms of middle-class demand for new suburban houses, facilitated by transport improvements and social change.

E. W. Cooney, 'Capital Exports, and Investment in Building in Britain and the U.S.A. 1856–1914', *Economica*, XVI (1949)

An early investigation into a problem which has since received considerable attention. Presents data on London building industry (surveyors' fees for new buildings and houses built in Metropolitan Police District) which indicate long swings in building activity. Shows the inverse pattern of U.K. and U.S. building fluctuations and how they are linked through emigration and capital exports.

E. W. Cooney, 'Long Waves in Building in the British Economy of the Nineteenth Century', *Economic History Review*, XIII (1960–1)

An examination of inverse building cycles in U.K. and U.S.A. He suggests that these are not found in U.K. until 1870s. Stresses importance of migration and foreign investment waves, but suggests growing importance of foreign investment the most important single factor. However, recognises domestic influences. The article also contains a more detailed analysis of the first long building recession of 1868–73, and presents useful data on timber imports.

H. J. Habakkuk, 'Fluctuations in House-Building in Britain and the United States in the Nineteenth Century', *Journal of Economic History*, XXII (1962)

A masterly article. Suggests that residential building before 1860s in U.K. fluctuated with trade cycle rather than in twenty-year swings found in United States. Supports alternation of building cycles 1870–1914, but argues that domestic influences were important. These include: internal migration had a higher middle-class content, and was not closely connected with trade cycle, financial institutions more stable after 1866 and sources of finance available even in depressions. Long waves can be explained by lack of synchronisation between regional cycles and increased importance of suburban building which persisted for longer periods. Shows that for variations in emigration to be responsible for inverse building cycles they had to influence the rate of urbanisation in U.K. (i.e. emigration competed more effectively with rural–urban migration in upswings), and that overseas countries competed with U.K. building industry for funds. Also argues high U.S. building in 1880s and British in 1890s reflects different rates of application of electricity to traction (i.e. a random factor). Finally, emphasises local influences by showing how fluctuations in London building were influenced by changes in cheap transport facilities.

R. M. MacIntosh, 'A Note on Cheap Money and the British Housing Boom, 1932–37', *Economic Journal*, LXI (1951)

An attempt to show that cheap money the primary cause of the housing boom. Summarily dismisses other explanations: population movements, changing tastes, decline in building costs and rising real income. Argument based on falling mortgage rates, increased supply of funds for housing, and the coincidence of the coming of cheap money and the upswing in private building.

S. B. Saul, 'House Building in England, 1890–1914', *Economic History Review*, XV (1962–3)

A companion study to Habakkuk's in the sense that this article too questions the external origins of U.K. building cycles. Presents valuable statistical data showing considerable local variations in housebuilding. Also argues that the foreign investment–building cycle link assumes a rapid calculated response to changes in economic variables whereas housebuilding is characterised by speculative activity, slow market indicators and long reaction lags, e.g. evidence of a market lag between rise in empties and fall in building activity. Internal migration also important reinforcing the pressure on urban housing supply when emigration was low. No evidence of view that booms came to an end because capital was diverted elsewhere, e.g. into foreign investment.

W. F. STOLPER, 'British Monetary Policy and the Housing Boom', *Quarterly Journal of Economics*, Supplement, LVI (1962)

An exhaustive survey (170 pages) of the housing boom and its causes. Shows that boom was based on private unsubsidised house-building for the middle classes financed through building societies. Considers alternative explanations of boom but favours influence of cheap money not so much because of its influence on mortgage rates but because it stopped deflation, helped to shift the terms of trade in Britain's favour and brought about a shift of funds from export to domestic industries (especially building). It made investment in houses profitable, and increased the supply of funds for the finance of housebuilding.

*Further Reading*

M. BOWLEY, *Housing and the State, 1919–44* (1945).
J. PARRY LEWIS, *Building Cycles and Britain's Growth* (1965).
H. W. RICHARDSON and D. H. ALDCROFT, *Building in the British Economy Between the Wars* (1968).
H. W. ROBINSON, *The Economics of Building* (1939).

## 7. EMPLOYMENT AND LABOUR

A. K. CAIRNCROSS, 'Internal Migration in Victorian England', *Manchester School*, XVII (1949)

Contains useful data on migration in the period 1841–1911. Shows continued rural–urban migration up to 1880, checked in the 1880s, especially in the North, by heavy emigration and resumed in the following decade. After 1900 town-building slows down, and most of emigrants come from the towns. Shift in population distribution towards the South marked from the 1880s, but thanks to higher fertility growth in northern population greater in period as a whole, i.e. 1841–1911.

K. J. HANCOCK, 'Unemployment and the Economists in the 1920s', *Economica*, XXVII (1960)

Illustrates the failure of economists to get to grips with contemporary economic problems in the 1920s, and their disregard of the increasing availability of statistical data. For example, most of them recommended that the level of employment should be sacrificed to the requirements of monetary policy, and they tried to analyse what was primarily structural unemployment with trade cycle theory. A good reminder of now forgotten controversies.

K. J. HANCOCK, 'The Reduction of Unemployment as a Problem of Public Policy, 1920–29', *Economic History Review*, XV (1962–3)

An examination of the policies adopted to reduce unemployment in the 1920s and an explanation of the failure to employ more adequate measures. Shows that unemployment was regarded as transient up to 1927. No attempt to employ countercyclical budgeting measures because of the prevailing orthodox fiscal and monetary policies. Public works projects shown to be on a very small scale, and there is a brief analysis of the Industrial Transference Scheme under which unemployed in depressed areas were to be moved to other regions. Shows that Treasury View more subtle than is sometimes thought. Points out that unemployed were inadequately represented in Parliament, and this militated against adoption of stronger measures to cure unemployment.

S. POLLARD, 'Trade Unions and the Labour Market, 1870–1914', *Yorkshire Bulletin of Economic and Social Research*, XVII (1965)

Useful data on the growth of trade union membership and on real wages. Considers effectiveness of collective bargaining during this period. Concludes that there is some indication of ability to improve wage bargain, though this varied according to level of economic activity, type of industry, and stage of unionisation. However, shows that raising wages was an uphill struggle, and that trade unions did not succeed in raising the wages of their members alone but pushed the whole front forward, i.e. gains were made by non-union as well as union workers. Nevertheless, share of wages in national income remained constant; reason is that unions were fighting a defensive struggle to combat growing pressure of employers' associations and their attempts to keep down wages.

*Further Reading*

W. BEVERIDGE, 'An Analysis of Unemployment', *Economica*, III (1936); IV (1937).

W. BEVERIDGE, *Full Employment in a Free Society* (1944).

E. M. BURNS, *British Unemployment Programs, 1920–1938* (1941).

D. G. CHAMPERNOWNE, 'The Uneven Distribution of Unemployment in the United Kingdom, 1929–36', I and II, *Review of Economic Studies*, V (1937–8); VI (1938–9).

S. R. Dennison, *The Location of Industry and the Depressed Areas* (1939).
E. H. Phelps Brown and S. V. Hopkins, 'The Course of Wage Rates in Five Countries, 1860–1939', *Oxford Economic Papers*, II (1950).

8. General Texts

H. W. Arndt, *The Economic Lessons of the Nineteen-Thirties* (1944)
W. Ashworth, *An Economic History of England, 1870–1939* (1960)
British Association, *Britain in Depression* (1935)
British Association, *Britain in Recovery* (1938)
W. H. B. Court, *British Economic History, 1870–1914: Commentary and Documents* (1965)
W. A. Lewis, *Economic Survey, 1919–1939* (1949)
W. A. Morton, *British Finance 1930–1940* (1943)
A. C. Pigou, *Aspects of British Economic History, 1918–1925* (1948 ed.)
S. Pollard, *The Development of the British Economy, 1914–1950* (1962)
R. S. Sayers, *A History of Economic Change in England, 1880–1939* (1967)
I. Svennilson, *Growth and Stagnation in the European Economy* (1954)
A. J. Youngson, *The British Economy, 1920–1966* (1967)

## Bibliographical Postscript

Since the manuscript went to the press a number of useful books and articles have appeared the details of which are as follows:

A. R. Hall (ed.), *The Export of Capital from Britain, 1870–1914* (1968)
D. C. Coleman, *Courtaulds: An Economic and Social History* (2 vols, 1969)
J. Harrop, 'The Growth of the Rayon Industry in the Inter-War Years', *Yorkshire Bulletin of Economic and Social Research*, XX (1968)
D. S. Landes, *The Unbound Prometheus: Technological Change and Industrial Development in Western Europe since 1750* (1969)
P. J. Lund and K. Holden, 'Study of Private Sector Gross Fixed Capital Formation in the U.K., 1923–38', *Oxford Economic Papers*, XX (1968)
D. N. McCloskey, 'Productivity Change in British Pig Iron, 1870–1939', *Quarterly Journal of Economics*, LXXXII (1968)
P. Mathias, *The First Industrial Nation: An Economic History of Britain, 1700–1914* (1969)

E. H. Phelps Brown with Margaret H. Browne, *A Century of Pay: The Course of Pay and Production in France, Germany, Sweden, the United Kingdom, and the United States of America, 1860–1960* (1968)

S. B. Saul, *The Myth of the Great Depression, 1873–1896* (1969)

# Index of Names

# Subject Index